Foreign Policy in the Twenty-First Century

Also by Christopher Hill

NATIONAL FOREIGN POLICIES AND EUROPEAN POLITICAL COOPERATION (*edited*)

TERRORISM AND INTERNATIONAL ORDER (*with Lawrence Freedman, Adam Roberts, R. J. Vincent, Paul Wilkinson and Philip Windsor*)

CABINET DECISIONS ON FOREIGN POLICY: The British Experience October 1938–June 1941

TWO WORLDS OF INTERNATIONAL RELATIONS: Academics, Practitioners and the Trade in Ideas (*edited, with Pamela Beshoff*)

THE ACTORS IN EUROPE'S FOREIGN POLICY (*edited*)

DOMESTIC SOURCES OF FOREIGN POLICY: West European Reactions to the Falklands Conflict (*edited, with Stelios Stavridis*)

MARCHING TO CAPTIVITY: The War Diaries of a French Peasant 1939–1945 – Gustave Folcher (*translated and edited English version; first published in French, edited by Rémy Cazals*)

EUROPEAN FOREIGN POLICY: Key Documents (*edited, with Karen Smith*)

THE CHANGING POLITICS OF FOREIGN POLICY

INTERNATIONAL RELATIONS AND THE EUROPEAN UNION (*edited, with Michael Smith*)

INTERNATIONAL RELATIONS AND THE EUROPEAN UNION: Second Edition (*edited, with Michael Smith*)

NATIONAL AND EUROPEAN FOREIGN POLICIES: Towards Europeanization (*edited, with Reuben Wong*)

THE NATIONAL INTEREST IN QUESTION: Foreign Policy in Multicultural Societies

THE ART OF ATTRACTION: Soft Power and the UK's Role in the World (*with Sarah Beadle*)

Foreign Policy in the Twenty-First Century

Second Edition

Christopher Hill

First edition published under the title *The Changing Politics of Foreign Policy* in 2003
Second edition 2016

Published by
PALGRAVE

Palgrave in the UK is an imprint of Macmillan Publishers Limited, registered in England, company number 785998, of 4 Crinan Street, London N1 9XW.

Palgrave Macmillan in the US is a division of St Martin's Press LLC, 175 Fifth Avenue, New York, NY 10010.

Palgrave is a global imprint of the above companies and is represented throughout the world.

Palgrave® and Macmillan® are registered trademarks in the United States, the United Kingdom, Europe and other countries.

ISBN 978-0-230-22373-8

This book is printed on paper suitable for recycling and made from fully managed and sustained forest sources. Logging, pulping and manufacturing processes are expected to conform to the environmental regulations of the country of origin.

A catalogue record for this book is available from the British Library.

A catalog record for this book is available from the Library of Congress.

Typeset by Cambrian Typesetters, Camberley, Surrey

Contents

List of Tables

List of Figures

Preface to the Second Edition

The first edition of this book was written in an attempt to convince scholars, students and the interested public that foreign policy was still a subject of considerable political and intellectual importance. Whether or not it succeeded in that task, its work was effectively done by the event of September 2011. After the attacks of 9/11 few needed convincing that foreign and security policy, but also diplomacy and the strategies of non-state actors, were of vital importance. It is encouraging to see the revival of interest in foreign policy, with major new contributions from Hudson (2007), Mintz and DeRouen (2010) and Smith, Hadfield and Dunne (2012). While the literature is still dominated by the Anglophone countries, things are changing, in relation both to subject matter (Brighi, 2013; Hinnebusch and Ehteshami, 2014) and to the languages in which texts are written (Charillon, 2002; Wilhelm, 2006; Morin, 2013). Some concepts from this work, such as 'crisis management', 'misperception' and 'groupthink', have even entered general political vocabulary.

The first edition, entitled *The Changing Politics of Foreign Policy*, also attempted to convey the way in which foreign policy as a practice was changing under the impact of transnationalism, domestic politics and the economic and technological innovations summed up in the term 'globalization'. At the same time it strongly resisted the tendency of the globalization paradigm to play down the political role of states and to ignore foreign policy altogether. As that battle no longer needs to be fought, this new edition spends much less time on making the case for foreign policy and foreign policy analysis (FPA). It also has a new title. The original is still suitable, but invites the response that it should be revised to read 'the still-changing politics of foreign policy'! We have decided to go for *Foreign Policy in the Twenty-First Century*, which begs fewer questions.

The structure of the first edition has been retained. Nonetheless this edition has various significant changes, including the change of focus in relation to globalization. In particular the theoretical swing back towards both the state and the importance of domestic factors in international relations, epitomized by the emergence of neoclassical realism, is welcomed and incorporated. More attention has been given to the issue of soft power, which many states have taken an interest in. The sections on psychological approaches, on intelligence, on media 'spectacles' and on civil society have been rethought and developed. The European Union gets more attention throughout as a foreign policy actor, in which context new material is included from the author's research on multi-culturalism and its relationship with international politics. The security dimension of transnational relations, arising from the activities of Al Qaeda and Daesh (also known as ISIS), is also given more prominence.

In terms of detail, the examples used have been updated throughout – although not at the expense of abandoning a long-term perspective. Since an understanding of change presupposes a good knowledge of the past, the book still contains many references to key events in the twentieth century, and even beyond. The last century was, after all, a huge period of international upheaval, and of political as well as economic globalization – that is, of forging a single international system. Nonetheless, because it is important to relate theories to current concerns, policy dilemmas right up to Ukraine, the Syrian civil war and the crisis in the eurozone figure regularly. The intention is to help a new generation of readers, for whom not only the Cold War but also the hoped-for 'new world order' of the 1990s may seem remote, to engage with the issues. The nature of the existing literature means that examples are often drawn from Western Europe and North America, but a conscious effort has been made to do justice to the diversity of the international system.

The book was, and remains, an argument as well as a text, designed to engage my academic colleagues as well as those taking upper-level university courses. But in order to help students find their way around more easily we have moved from endnotes to the Harvard reference system. This means that many of the notes documenting the use of ex-amples, together with some of the older academic citations, have been cut. Readers interested in following up those things may wish to refer back to the first edition. Further reading has been provided at the end of each chapter, with the aim of bringing the classical sources on a subject together with newer, and sometimes provocative, treatments.

A perceptive reviewer of the first edition noted that a book of this kind could not help but be over-ambitious, through attempting to cover a wide historical and geographical range of empirical material, as well as the large corpus of theory produced by FPA and International Relations (IR) more generally. This is true, but I do not regret the attempt. The large number of examples used is not the sign of a naive belief in creating 'proof' by piling up detail. It is, rather, an attempt both to show that my interpretations are grounded in a familiarity with modern history in all its complexity, and also to stimulate readers to move beyond abstraction into the flesh-and-blood world of hard political choices. I value theory immensely, and reject unstructured empiricism, but believe that grand theory, of the realism vs. liberalism vs. constructivism kind so often employed in IR, only takes us so far in this context. (Note: The use of upper case for 'International Relations' (IR) always denotes the academic subject. The use of the lower case denotes actual relations in the world.) Much more useful are 'middle-range' theories, which focus on a specific aspect of behaviour and help us to identify patterns (if not iron laws) with respect, say, to the impact of public opinion, or to the role of personality. Even here some depth has had to be sacrificed in the interest of breadth. Yet any attempt to write about major social phenomena, whether foreign policy, war, modernization or poverty, has to make this choice.

Foreign policy is about how different societies interrelate, at times antagonistically but also managing to cooperate on a regular basis. This problem – which is also the defining issue of International Relations more generally – will be at the heart of the dramas, tragedies and achievements of the future. What is more, foreign relations are bound to impact on everyday life. It was true in the fifth century BC, when the Athenians put the population of defeated Melos to the sword, and it is true now, when a decision made in Beijing to invest in the car company MG creates jobs in Birmingham. In fact foreign policy in the broadest sense, meaning the bundle of activities which an entity (most often a state) pursues in order to cope with the outside world, and to help its people do so, touches on ever more aspects of what a polity is for. We have to be able to make sense of it.

CHRISTOPHER HILL

Acknowledgements

This second edition rests on the help provided for the first by a large number of people. I shall not repeat my thanks to them here. But I do wish to thank my publisher, Steven Kennedy, for his stalwart support and patience, as well as his successor, Stephen Wenham, for picking up the baton so smoothly. I thank my wife Maria, for the same virtues and many more. The members of my foreign policy research workshop in the Department of Politics and International Studies at Cambridge have been a consistent source of stimulation. I am grateful to the many able research students, in the UK and elsewhere, with whom I have had the pleasure to discuss foreign policy since the last edition, but Amnon Aran, Sarah Beadle, Elisabetta Brighi, Irena Caquet, Georgios Evangelopoulos and Reuben Wong have particularly engaged with my own work, to my great advantage. I have also benefited from fruitful exchanges with Dave Allen, Chris Brown, Fred Halliday, Stefan Halper, Ned Lebow, Margot Light, Alan Knight, Roger Morgan, Inderjeet Parmar, Aaron Rapport, Frank Rusciano, James Mayall, Hans Mouritzen, Joseph Nye, Brendan Simms, Karen Smith, Mike Smith, Anders Wivel, Michael Yahuda and Yaacov Vertzberger. Angela Pollentine and Suzy Adcock have provided indispensable professional and moral support from their roles as departmental administrators. Paul Fraioli has been a superb research assistant, with a keen eye and excellent judgement.

List of Abbreviations

ANC	African National Congress
AIDS	acquired immune deficiency syndrome
AIPAC	American Israel Public Affairs Committee
ANZUS	Australia, New Zealand, United States Security Treaty
ASEAN	Association of Southeast Asian Nations
BJP	Bharatiya Janata Party
BPM	bureaucratic politics model
BRICS	Brazil, Russia, India, China and South Africa
CDU	Christian Democratic Union of Germany
CERI	Centre des Études des Relations Internationales (Centre for International Relations)
CFC	chlorofluorocarbon
CIA	Central Intelligence Agency
CSU	Christian Social Union in Bavaria
DfID	Department for International Development
DGSE	Directorate-General for External Security
EC	European Community
ECOFIN	Economic and Financial Affairs Council
EEAS	European External Action Service
EEC	European Economic Community
EMU	Economic and Monetary Union
ENA	École Nationale d'Administration (National School of Administration)
ESDP	European Security and Defence Policy
EU	European Union
FAC	Foreign Affairs Committee
FCO	Foreign and Commonwealth Office
FDP	Free Democratic Party
FGM	female genital mutilation
FPA	foreign policy analysis
FRG	Federal Republic of Germany
G20	Group of Twenty
GATT	General Agreement on Tariffs and Trade
GDP	gross domestic product
ICC	International Criminal Court
ICJ	International Court of Justice
IGC	intergovernmental conference

IGO	intergovernmental organization
IMF	International Monetary Fund
INGO	international non-governmental organization
IPE	international political economy
IR	international relations
IRA	Irish Republican Army
ISAF	International Security Assistance Force
KGB	Komitet Gosudarstvennoĭ Bezopasnosti (Committee of State Security)
LDC	lesser-developed country
LDP	Japanese Liberal Democratic Party
LLDC	least-developed country
M5S	Movimento Cinque Stelle (Five Star Movement)
MITI	Ministry of International Trade and Industry
MFN	most-favoured nation
MNEs	multinational enterprises
MP	Members of Parliament
NATO	North Atlantic Treaty Organization
NCG	non-central government
NGO	non-governmental organisation
NPC	Chinese National People's Congress
NSAs	non-state actors
NSC	National Security Council
ODA	Overseas Development Assistance
OECD	Organisation for Economic Co-operation and Development
OIC	Organization of Islamic Cooperation
OSCE	Organization for Security and Co-operation in Europe
PLO	Palestine Liberation Organization
RAND	Research and Development Corporation
R2P	Responsibility to Protect
SALT	Strategic Arms Limitation Talks
SEA	Single European Act
SNP	Scottish National Party
SOPs	standard operating procedures
TNA	transnational actor
TNE	transnational enterprise
TTIP	Transatlantic Trade and Investment Partnership
UN	United Nations
UNCTAD	United Nations Conference on Trade and Development
UNSC	United Nations Security Council
USSR	Union of Soviet Socialist Republics
WTO	World Trade Organization

Chapter 1

Foreign Policy in International Relations

To the average citizen 'foreign policy' is a normal, if remote, part of the world of politics. Most people have little difficulty in accepting that foreign policy consists in what one state does to, or with, other states, involving a mix of conflict and cooperation. To many specialists, however, this conventional wisdom is deeply suspect. The concepts of state sovereignty and independence have been attacked for being both irrelevant in a changing world and undesirable from an ethical point of view. Accordingly, the idea that a government might have a discrete set of actions (let alone strategies) for dealing with the outside world has come to seem anachronistic, even naïve. The very divisions between home and abroad, domestic and foreign, inside and outside, have been questioned from a number of different viewpoints, conceptual and political. In consequence, a serious division has opened up, not for the first time, between the vocabulary of democratic politics and the professional discourse of academic commentators. Thus while the media are full of Putin's policies towards the Ukraine, or Egypt's relations with its neighbours, a senior political scientist of the author's acquaintance could ask the question 'do people still teach foreign policy?'. This book is an attempt to show that serious people do still study and teach foreign policy, and that there are compelling reasons for them to do so. What is more, students want to engage with the problems of foreign policy, whether in relation to dramas such as the war in Iraq, or the slower rhythms of negotiation on climate change.

Academic International Relations has tended to neglect the idea of foreign policy not only because of doubts about the independence of states, but also through a preoccupation with explaining the dynamics of the international system as a whole. This focus on structures – as with power balances for neorealists, international regimes for liberals and markets for the gurus of globalization – goes hand in hand with ignoring the question of agency, as if in embarrassment at having to grapple with actual politics. For many it seems more important to chart the move from bipolarity to multipolarity, or from the 'Westphalian' state system to 'interdependence', than to look through a close-up lens at decisions in national capitals, whether Berlin, Seoul or Cairo. While this is a natural reaction to the growing integration of world politics over the last century, its result is to obscure the differential actions which are taken to cope with the broad processes in which all states are immersed. The issue of where and by whom change might be effectively dealt with is too often just left hanging in the air by neorealists, globalization theorists and historical sociologists.

This is not to diminish the importance of all big-picture analysts. Michael Mann, for example, has produced a formidable and daring overview of 'the history of power' from ancient times to the present using a wealth of empirical detail in four volumes (2012a, 2012b, 2012c, 2013). This is indispensable both for our understanding of the development of human society as a whole, and because it shows how domestic and international trends are inextricably bound together. In particular his last volume (2013) treats 'globalizations' in the plural, showing how the current system is the product of separate but parallel integrative processes at the ideological, economic, military and political levels. Because Mann's focus is on power, discussions of particular actors, and of their foreign policies, occur regularly throughout the book. Not everyone can emulate Mann's *tour de force*, but there is every reason to follow his lead on relating agency to structure, and in particular in insisting on seeing the internal and the external as intimately connected.

Innovative work like this filters down only slowly to wider society. The gap between popular and specialist understandings of foreign policy is furthered by the professionalization of academic life, which in the social sciences has led to a proliferation of specialized, often theoretical, work which is both literally and linguistically inaccessible even to intelligent lay readers. The inability or unwillingness of many specialists to write plainly and lucidly has created a barrier between academic political science and the world which it studies and is supposed to serve. In some cases this invisible curtain is highly convenient, as it ensures that work is judged only by an ever-smaller circle of peers. Even within the profession this may lead to work being read only by those already disposed to agree with it. The huge proliferation of publications encouraged by value-for-money schemes like Britain's Research Excellence assessment exercise makes the situation worse – there is simply not the time to read and react to all the work produced even in one's own sub-area.

International Relations emerged as an academic subject area through a preoccupation with the practical problems of war and peace. Most of those working in it remain committed to improving the quality of world politics in one form or another, but the two phenomena outlined above – scepticism about states and their sovereignty, and the tendency to scholasticism – are making the conversation between specialists and citizens increasingly problematic. This is compounded by the fact that intellectual interest in international affairs is divided three ways: between the subject of International Relations, increasingly introverted in musings about its own evolution and philosophical underpinning; the specialists in a given country or area, who still tend to talk the language of normal diplomacy; and 'public intellectuals' from other disciplines who often feel a responsibility to intervene in the key ethical issues of foreign policy, but are not always well informed about the history and theory of international politics. These various divisions mean at best that debates are conducted at cross-purposes and at worst that in the area of external policy the democratic process is severely compromised.

It is my hope in this book to go some way towards redressing the imbalance caused by people talking past each other. I aim to provide a conceptualization of foreign policy that both encourages IR to refocus on problems of political choice and decision, and helps to create a more sophisticated public understanding of the interplay between the state and its external context. For both audiences the aim is basically the same: to break the association of foreign policy with the cruder versions of realism – that is, the assumption that behaviour can only be understood and/or guided by reference to a state's power – while showing that democracy and efficiency, as the twin totems of modern society, require a workable notion of foreign policy if they are not to be lost in a miasma of excessive generalization about 'global governance', the 'clash of civilizations' and the like.

Fortunately over the last decade or so foreign policy has begun to be liberated from the narrow and stereotyped views that are often held of it, usually associated with the tautological concept of the 'national interest'. International Relations as a subject has begun to reconstitute its notions of agency following increasingly tedious waves of attacks on realism in the 1990s, which established the weakness of state-centric accounts without putting much in their place. In particular a school has emerged known as 'neoclassical realism', discussed further later on, which allows at least that states are important as ways of filtering power realities (Lobell et al., 2009; Rose, 1998). Unfortunately it took the attacks on the United States of 9/11 to draw attention back to the importance of agency and of foreign policy. The pendulum then swung for a while too far back towards the view – especially in the US itself – that survival requires a national strategy geared to crude self-interest. The subsequent suspicion of multilateralism and of international institutions was just as unrealistic as the belief in a homogenising world which had preceded it.

The approach taken here is to rework the traditional idea of foreign policy, but not to defend a particular school of thought or appeal to a mythological past of paradigmatic unity. There are too many diverse views of the contemporary functions of foreign policy for the issue to be brushed aside. Equally, there is widespread public bewilderment as to where we can realistically expect meaningful actions to be taken in international relations, on issues from deadlock over Palestine through climate change to the quarantining of the Ebola virus in West Africa in 2014. The actual and appropriate roles of states, international organizations, pressure groups, businesses and private individuals are very often elided, and are far from being well understood. The very definition of international politics is at stake in the questions which a reconsideration of foreign policy naturally throws up, that is, 'who acts, for whom and with what effect?'.

An Initial Definition

The increased internationalization of much of daily life, especially in developed, commercially active, countries, causes problems when it comes to defining foreign policy and what should be studied under that heading. Is the focus to be reduced simply to what trained diplomats do and say, which would leave out many of the most interesting aspects of international politics, or should it be widened to include almost everything that emanates from the multiple actors on the world scene? These two end points of the spectrum invite a more nuanced definition of foreign policy, but also indicate a genuine dilemma: some assume that it is largely a ceremonial activity, with serious agency residing elsewhere. Others, particularly those concerned with the activities of the major powers, continue to assume that international relations resemble the 'great game' of Metternich and Palmerston. Both views screen out a crucial aspect of international politics with the potential for influencing the lives of millions – not least through fiascos and omissions. Foreign policy consists in a huge variety of activity, from Chinese–US trade tensions, through the Israeli attempt to prevent Iran from gaining nuclear weapons to the European Union's pressure on Croatia to hand over war criminals and Australia's stance on migration. It takes place in bilateral, multilateral and transnational fora, and is conducted by a wide range of state and para-state actors. It is certainly not a residual category to be associated only with embassy or foreign ministry business.

A brief definition of foreign policy can be given as a starting point: foreign policy is the sum of official external relations conducted by an independent actor (usually but not exclusively a state) in international relations. The phrase 'an *independent actor*' enables the inclusion of non-state entities such as the European Union, or Hezbollah; *external relations* are '*official*' to allow the inclusion of outputs from all parts of the governing mechanisms of the state or enterprise (that is, not just the foreign ministry) while also maintaining parsimony with respect to the vast number of international transactions now being conducted; *policy* (as opposed to *decisions*) is the *'sum'* of these official relations because actors usually seek some degree of coherence towards the outside world – and are assumed by others to be following a reasonably coherent and predictable line. Lastly, the policy is *'foreign'* because the world is still more separated into distinctive communities than it is a single, homogenising entity. These communities therefore need *strategies for coping with foreigners* (that is, those who are not part of their own polity) in their various aspects. This is in itself an alternative definition of foreign policy if one wishes to emphasize its purposive and cohesive dimensions (Hill, 1993a, 2001).

Definitions of political activities are notoriously difficult and foreign policy is no exception.[1] To some extent decision-makers themselves decide what foreign policy is through what they choose to do, but now that foreign offices do not monopolize external relations this only pushes the problem onto another level, that of deciding which personnel are to be counted as 'foreign policy-makers'. In a world where important international disputes can occur over the price of aircraft or school textbooks it would be absurd for foreign policy analysts to concentrate on relations between national diplomatic services. Although foreign ministries and their officials have tried to reinvent themselves by acting as gatekeepers and clearing-houses, in practice they have to accept a great deal of parallel diplomacy on the part of colleagues in 'domestic' ministries. It is for the same reason that the once popular distinction between 'high' and 'low' politics is no longer of much help (for example, Baldwin, 1985, p. 61; W. Wallace, 1975, pp. 11–15). High politics – in the sense of serious conflict touching on the state's most basic concerns – can be as much about monetary integration as about territory and the threat of armed attack. Conversely low politics – in the sense of routine exchanges contained within knowable limits and rarely reaching the public realm – can be observed in NATO (North Atlantic Treaty Organization) or OSCE (Organization for Security and Co-operation in Europe) multilateralism just as much as in discussions over fish or airport landing rights. This is because the *intrinsic content* of an issue is not a guide to its level of political salience or to the way it will be handled, except in the tautological sense that any issue which blows up into a high-level international conflict – and almost anything has the potential so to do – will lead decision-makers at the highest level suddenly to take over responsibility; their relations with the experts who had been managing the matter on a daily basis then become a critical matter. Thus low politics should refer only to those things, of whatever subject matter, which are routine and uncontentious at time *t*, and high politics to those things, of whatever subject matter, which have risen to the attention of high-level decision-makers because of their potential for conflict at time *t+1* and beyond.

The idea of foreign policy also implies both politics and coherence. Everything that a given actor does officially at the international level can generate foreign policy, but when we are asked to say what foreign policy consists of we usually refer to the more centrally political aspects of the activity, that is, actions, statements and values relating to how the actor wishes to advance its main objectives and to shape the external world – a version of David Easton's famous definition of politics as the 'interactions through which values are authoritatively allocated' – except that what connotes 'authority' is precisely what is at stake in international relations (Easton, 1965, p. 21). Foreign policy is a highly political activity, given the patchy nature of international order, but it is difficult to predict in advance what is likely to rise up the political agenda.

There is a similar issue with coherence. The very notion of a 'policy' in any field implies conscious intentions and coordination. It is the umbrella term under which huddle the myriad particular 'decisions' and standard procedures of an actor's behaviour. That very often the system of policy-making fails to live up to these aspirations is beside the point; the pursuit of a foreign (or health, or education) policy is about the effort to carry through some generally conceived strategy, usually on the basis of a degree of rationality, in the sense that objectives, time-frames and instruments are at least being thought about. Thus foreign policy must always be seen as a way of trying to make sense of and hold together over time the various international activities in which the state is engaged. To take things one step further, into the area of identity, it is one way in which a society defines itself, against the backcloth of the outside world.

Foreign policy is therefore both more and less than the 'external relations' which states generate continually on so many fronts and which some argue is the more useful term, especially in relation to the European Union, which for decades distinguished between its external relations and the Common Foreign and Security Policy (Nuttall, 2005). Foreign policy seeks to coordinate, and to establish priorities between competing interests with an external dimension. It may also attempt to project the values which the society in question thinks are universal, whether through the idea of an 'ethical foreign policy' or less directly, as with a commitment to overseas development aid. It is, in short, the focal point of an actor's various points of contact with the world.

Competing Approaches

Foreign policy may be approached in many different ways within International Relations. The subject has also been extensively studied by historians, at first via the detailed accounts of diplomatic historians and then through the lens of *'international history'*, which strove to relate diplomacy to its domestic roots, political, social, economic and cultural (Jervis, 2001; Lauren, Craig and George, 2007, pp. 137–51; Schroeder, 2001; Watt, 1965, 1983). Indeed, over recent decades diplomatic history has reinvented itself through some overlaps with foreign policy analysis. The tools of decision-making analysis are readily adaptable to detailed cases, and the opening up of many state archives has revealed the pathologies of such areas as bureaucratic politics or small-group dynamics. In the United States in particular there has been a deliberate encouragement of links between historians and political scientists, with much useful cross-fertilization (Lauren, 1979; May and Neustadt, 1986; Elman and Elman, 2001).

At a halfway house between history and political science lie *country studies*. There remain many scholars immune to the pull of intellectual fashion who develop over a lifetime their expertise on an individual state or region, almost always with the will and capacity to demonstrate the intimate links with domestic society. Area studies are strong in the United Kingdom and particularly so in France, as any reading of *Le Monde* will demonstrate.[2] United States foreign policy naturally generates most analysis, although from relatively few non-American IR academics (Aron, 1975; Coker, 1989; Dumbrell, 2010; Parmar, 2004, 2012). Journals like *Foreign Affairs* and *Foreign Policy* in the US, the *World Today* in the UK and *Limes* in Italy provide platforms for such expertise to reach an interested public. The other permanent members of the UN Security Council also continue to be studied in some depth, while there has been a notable upsurge of interest in the 'rising powers', or BRICS – Brazil, Russia, India, China and South Africa. Other states, especially Australia, Canada, Egypt, Indonesia, Israel, Japan and Nigeria figure quite prominently in the literature, while in Europe German and Italian foreign policies have had a higher profile than at any time since 1945. Other states tend to be dealt with in groups, as with 'African' or 'European' foreign policies, but this inevitably produces a degree of generality (Webber and Smith, 2002; Wong and Hill, 2011; S. Wright, 1999).

There is a need to break down some of the larger categories used, such as the highly problematical one of 'small states', and in particular to provide more detailed work on important cases such as Cuba, Iran, Pakistan, Poland, Singapore, Turkey and Vietnam.[3] Both IR and comparative politics have neglected country studies, with disastrous results in terms of our capital of expertise on the variety of states and their political cultures. A comparative perspective is indispensable, but that should mean a balance between generalization and particularity. Major theorists like Weber, Hans Morgenthau and even Kenneth Waltz always understood that ideas need to be complemented by a deep knowledge of individual societies and their problems (see, for example, Waltz 1967, his least-cited book, which compares UK and US foreign policy-making).

Realism is far and away the best-known approach in IR, and the most criticized. It is the traditional way in which practitioners have thought about international relations, emphasising the importance of power in a dangerous, unpredictable world. Realism became the orthodoxy in academic writing after the discrediting of the 'legalistic–moralistic' approach of the inter-war period, while during the Cold War it seemed self-evident that states, and military force, were the main features of the international system. Much realist thought was more subtle than this summary allows, as any encounter with the work of E. H. Carr (1939, 2001), Morgenthau (1948), Reinhold Niebuhr (1953), Martin Wight (1946, 1978) and Arnold Wolfers (1962) soon reveals. The humanistic aspects of this wave of writing – meaning a concern with personality, judgement, wisdom and history – have been rediscovered in recent years. This has produced the approach labelled 'neoclassical realism' – as opposed to the classical version associated with Thucydides, Hobbes, Rousseau and many others (Lobell et al., 2009; Rose, 1998; Toje and Kunz, 2012; Williams, 2005). It has also provided a welcome recognition that the domestic sources of international behaviour are as important as structural explanations, on the grounds that the power and capabilities alone cannot explain everything about the fate of countries. At the least, a state's nature and the quality of its decisions constitute intervening variables between the international system and outcomes.

Although FPA has been attacked for being itself realist – on the grounds that it is 'state-centric' – this is bizarre given that FPA emerged precisely as a reaction to the assumption too often made by commentators that the state was a single, coherent actor pursuing clear interests in a more or less rational manner, with success varying according to the talents of particular leaders and the constraints of circumstance. The work done in FPA invariably challenged the ideas of rationality, coherence, national interest and external orientation. As will be shown below, the subject is fundamentally pluralist in orientation. It is true that states remain central to FPA, but its methods may be used to study all types of actor in international relations (White, 2001). Indeed this book focuses on the broad concepts of 'actors' and 'agency' rather than limiting itself in principle to states. The only way that the label of realism can be justified is if those who believe that states are of continued significance in international relations are deemed to be realists by definition. Some writers have come close to this view (Vasquez, 1983, pp. 47–79, 205–15), but it is not a defensible proposition, as the large body of liberal thought about states and international society indicates.

Life was breathed back into realism, despite the attacks from foreign policy analysts, students of transnational relations and other liberal sceptics, by Kenneth Waltz's formulation of *neorealism* in the late 1970s (1979). Whereas realism, and indeed Waltz himself in his first classic book *Man, the State and War* (1959), had not been clear about where the drive for power originated – in human passions, in the state itself, or in a world which lacked rules – Waltz here was clear and systematic. His view was that the international system was dominant in certain key respects. It represented a balance of power with its own rules, so that if one wished to explain war or other major features of the international system as a whole the only resort was to a parsimonious theory addressing 'the logic of anarchy' (Buzan and Little, 1993). Neorealism captured the heights of IR in the United States through its scientific set of propositions and through the appeal to American observers of a theory based on power. By the same token it has had less appeal elsewhere.

To neorealists foreign policy analysis, with its interest in domestic politics and in decision-making, was simply not relevant, and indeed barely discussed. Waltz can be accused of inconsistency, given his previous book on US and UK foreign policy. Yet his theory does allow for a discussion of agency through foreign policy so long as it does not pretend to explain what inherently it is incapable of doing (Waltz, 1996). By reductionism Waltz means the tendency to understand the nature of a whole (that is, the international system) by reference to one of its parts (that is, the behaviour of an actor in the system). Another example would be an attempt to use FPA to explain war in general, as opposed to the origins of a particular war where it might have a great deal to contribute. For him, foreign policy is about strategy within the rules of the game, not changing its ineluctable nature. If that is done with skill, the outcome is more likely to be successful. If not, failure – in terms of achieving goals and protecting national security – will probably follow.

Neorealism deals in levels of analysis, with foreign policy analysis operating at the level of the explanation of particular units. This is not the place to debate the overall value of neorealism in IR, which has strengths at the level of the system itself. It is important, however, to show that it is highly limiting – and ultimately unusable – as an approach to foreign policy. Chapter 2 opens up the issues of structure and agency. For the moment it is worth stressing how few interesting political and intellectual problems are left for any actor in a system which operates in the top-down manner envisaged by Waltz and his followers (for example, Mearsheimer, 2001). Given the historical debates which have taken place on the role of German foreign policy in the origins of two world wars (with special reference to Prussian culture and Nazi leaders respectively), on the international impact of the differences between

Soviet and Chinese communism, or on the domestic politics of US policy in any of its major foreign policy ventures, it is self-limiting and self-defeating to assume the predominance of the 'pattern of power' in determining major developments in international relations. Neorealism has a deterministic quality which is at odds with the tendency of FPA to stress the open interplay of multiple factors, domestic and international – and thus also to allow for the creative use of counterfactuals (Tetlock, Lebow and Parker, 2006). Neorealism also assumes that states are primarily driven by the need to maximize their security, which in turn is to be achieved largely through the exercise of power and independence. Most students of foreign policy would see this as excessive generalization, doing less than justice to the variety of states' actual positions and goals, and with fluctuations over time.[4]

An approach which has so far had little particular impact on the study of foreign policy, although it is widely disseminated elsewhere in political science, is that of *public choice*, which derives from the rational choice assumptions of economics (Dunleavy, 2013; Kydd, 2010) but focuses on how collectivities make choices, developing their own conceptions of self-interest as well as reflecting those of the actors which make them up. In its stress on power as currency and on the drive towards equilibrium neorealism is closely linked to public choice. FPA, however, grew through attacking the assumption of rational action on the part of a unitary actor with given goals (usually power-maximization) which was associated with realism. It continues to be the case, while few IR scholars of any persuasion believe that the explanation of international relations can be reduced to the individual preferences of decision-makers seeking votes, political support, personal advantage or some other kind of measurable currency, even if those self-interested motives clearly count.

International relations and foreign policy present, above all, collective action problems which cannot be explained only by competition between individual preferences. As David Lake has pointed out, 'there is no necessary reason why the interests of self-seeking politicians should coincide with the national interest' (Lake, 2001, p. 716). This is hardly news to any foreign policy analyst, although there is certainly a real issue to deal with in relating the motives and behaviour of individual decision-makers to the collective ends of foreign policy, particularly since voters only tend to punish foreign policy mistakes when things go badly wrong, unlike domestic politics where politicians are afraid to raise taxes even by 1 per cent for fear of defeat at the next election.

Public choice theory could be a starting point to address this very problem of collective action, and the converse, that policies agreed jointly (often bipartisanly) may be remote from the actual preferences of individual politicians – let alone those of the voters. It will not be enough to see the state as a personified, unified, actor negotiating with other unified actors, but it does offer some possibilities, particularly in relation to foreign economic policy, to the environment, and to alliance politics, where pay-offs, free-riding and the like are more evident because deals are more quantifiable – usually in terms of money or troops. Yet even in these areas the assumption that states are unified actors is difficult to sustain empirically.

More generally, the economic formalism of both the rational choice and the public choice approaches and the contortions they must perform to cope with such matters as competing values, geopolitics, conceptions of international society and the complexities of political decision-making limit their ability to generate insights. Like game theory, public choice can be of considerable heuristic use, but to start from an assumption of self-interested preferences at all levels is too simplistic, because the influences and values which shape those preferences are bracketed out. It also limits the applicability to actual cases. International politics is about so much more than market success or failure.

After the end of the Cold War a wave of *post-positivism* brought a new perspective to bear on foreign policy. While members of a broad church, post-positivists unite in rejecting the fact–value distinction prominent among realists and behaviouralists, and consider that there is little point in attempting to work scientifically towards a 'truthful' picture of human behaviour. This is because politics is constituted by language, ideas and values. We cannot stand outside ourselves to make neutral judgements. That this view has provoked wide-ranging and often heated debate is not the issue here. More relevant is the extra dimension it has given to foreign policy studies – a competing approach to the pluralist and predominantly positivist orthodoxy, but one which (unlike globalization studies) confirms the importance of the state. Writers like David Campbell (1992, 1998), Roxanne Doty (1996), Henrik Larsen (1997), Iver Neumann (2002), Ole Waever (1998, 2002) and Lene Hansen (2012) (the last four representing the influential 'Copenhagen school') have examined the language of foreign policy and its dominant discourses. Indeed, foreign policy is seen as important precisely because it reinforces (undesirably, for the most part) national and statist culture. The emphasis is thus usually still on national discourses, even if they are generally viewed as being at odds with human needs. Language is seen as crucial to national identity, in the constitution of which the representation of outsiders ('the Other') through foreign policy will be a crucial element. Whatever the truth of this it is certainly true that language, whether official or private, rhetorical or observational, has a lot to tell us about mindsets and actions in foreign policy, and that it is a relatively untapped resource.

It is not surprising that this set of assumptions has led to attention turning to the European Union, whose foreign policy is very much in the process of being constituted, in part through interplay with the changing identities of its Member States' national foreign policies (Larsen, 2009; Waever, 2004; Wong and Hill, 2011), and largely through language. Constructivism, however, which has become the dominant strand of postpositivism, does not necessarily limit itself to language and discourse. In relation to the EU it has seized on the fact that the definition of interests (both national and European) is in flux, and that military force is not central to the European approach to international relations. In the case of the United States it can explain not only that country's strength but also its sense of exceptionalism.[5] It thus stresses the importance of seeing foreign policy through the lens of culture and ideas, as much as power and resources (Aggestam, 2004; Manners and Whitman, 2000; Sjursen, 2006; Tonra, 2001). The approach needs to be linked more effectively to the analysis of choice, and to confront the problem of the evidential base for its propositions. But it has rightly become an important part of foreign policy analysis.

All the approaches listed above have something to offer the student of foreign policy – they need not be seen as incompatible in every respect. For example, while history and country studies are an indispensable source of empirical knowledge it would be pig-headed to ignore the concepts generated by realism, public choice and constructivism. Still, there are limits to methodological eclecticism, and any book needs a standpoint. The present work is rooted in that tradition of FPA which starts with the dilemmas of decision-making and works outwards through the concentric circles which shape decisions, but without any prior assumption as to which set of influences – domestic or international, personal or bureaucratic, idiosyncratic or structural – might be most significant in a given case. More importantly, it sees foreign policy not as a technical exercise but as an important form of political argument. The rest of this chapter expands on what this means, beginning with an account of how FPA has developed.

The Evolution of Foreign Policy Analysis

FPA enquires into the motives and other sources of the behaviour of international actors, particularly states. It does this by giving a good deal of attention to decision-making, initially so as to probe behind the formal self-descriptions (and fictions) of government and public administration. In so doing it tests the hypothesis that the outputs of foreign policy are to some degree determined by the nature of the decision-making process.

Some in FPA were keen that the subject should earn the status of science, by using scientific method to generate 'if–then' statements about behaviour. The Comparative Foreign Policy school, which for a time was dominant in the United States, did not concern itself with the politics of foreign policy, internal or external. It was interested in finding correlations between the factors involved in foreign policy over as wide a range as possible, and eschewed contextual detail (Hermann and Peacock, 1987). Yet it became evident to many that this approach was a dead end, and the subject subsequently developed in a more open-ended and creative way, both inside and outside the United States.

Comparative Foreign Policy as a school was a world away from the kind of FPA which was developing in alliance with the more theoretically minded historians, and which is the basis of the present book. This approach employs 'middle-range theories' to examine particular areas of human activity such as perception or geopolitics, and is sceptical that an overarching single theory of foreign policy could ever be achieved without being bland and tautological (Light, 1994).[6] It also tacitly accepts Waltz's warning against reductionism. The Scandinavian attempt to promulgate 'weak (general) theory' to cope with the problem of integrating middle-range theories might succeed – but it is difficult to see what it would look like in practice (Waever, 1990, 1994). A great deal of high-quality scholarship has already come out of FPA's middle-range theories and the challenge is to build on them rather than to pursue a chimera. The theories are already integrated in the sense that foreign policy analysis is underpinned by systems theory, meaning that it conceives of the state as a system, which being embedded in a multi-layered international system is subject to a series of connections and feedback loops both up (internationally) and down to the various subsystems of national bureaucracy and society. This is probably as far as we can go with integrating them.

The approach taken here also celebrates the richness of available historical accounts, and archival material, and seeks to build on them. It is based on the assumption that foreign policy analysis can combine an appreciation of the circumstances of particular states and transnational actors with a comparative perspective, which should be open, conceptual and interdisciplinary. It should be analytical in the sense of detachment, of not being *parti pris*, but not positivist, in the sense of challenging the view that 'facts' are external and disconnected from actors' perceptions and self-understandings. FPA helps us to address the underlying questions of all political life, such as 'who benefits?' 'what is the right course of action?' and 'which institutions best serve our desired ends?'. In this it faces a number of distinct challenges.

Change is a perpetual challenge to social science, and foreign policy analysis is no exception. Changes in the fabric of international relations will always lead to the rise and fall of individual powers, but at times they also change the very nature of the main actors. That was the case with the collapse of the Ottoman and Austro-Hungarian multinational empires during the First World War, and it was the case with the dissolution of the European empires in the 1960s. The Westphalian state gradually reproduced itself over the three centuries after the symbolic date of 1648 but since the early 1970s it has faced significant difficulties in coping with new forms of transnational actor, notably terrorist groups and multinational enterprises. Some commentators were quick to foretell the death of the state, even if they have had to retreat a good deal since 9/11. Such developments intrinsically pose a challenge also to FPA, which has to adjust its framework to any change in the relationship between states and the alternative loci of decisions in the international system.

None of the changes in post-1945 international relations pose a threat to the purpose and existence of foreign policy as such. All of them, however, do impact on the language and currency of contemporary foreign policy, on its relationship with domestic society and on the means by which it is conducted. Foreign policy has certain fundamental and defining characteristics, but those who conduct it have to adapt to the specific demands of their own epochs. The nature of these demands for our own era – together with the elements of continuity – will become clear in the chapters which follow. Beneath the detail, however, lie certain key questions, theoretical and practical, which provide the rationale for the book as a whole.

In theoretical terms the main issue FPA faces is the extent to which foreign policy provides a site of agency in international relations. It can be argued both that its importance was exaggerated in the past and that it is far from being emptied of content now – leaving foreign policy with a role which is significant but hardly monopolistic. But such judgements in any case turn on more fundamental views about the nature of agency in world politics and its relationship to structures. Part of the answer may be given through theorising the state, evidently still a major source of political life, but not all of it. The state is one of a variety of different international actors, whose positions relative to each other and to structures need to be traced.

Another dimension of the problem is the extent to which actors, and the communities they embody, can still be said to have distinct 'foreign' and 'domestic' environments. If they do, then it follows that they will need some form of means of coping with the particularities of the foreign. But if the environments blur into each other so as to become functionally indistinguishable, do they not need to integrate policies and mechanisms accordingly? If one allows the more modest proposition that any entity with the capacity to make decisions has an 'inside' and an 'outside' (associated with the universal notion of 'minding our own business') does this mean, in the international context, that dealing with the outside is another way of describing foreign policy, or is it just an administrative boundary, with no qualitative shift entailed?

The third aspect of the theoretical challenge facing the study of foreign policy concerns the category of 'external relations'. If we conclude that there is a significant difference between 'inside' and 'outside', meaning that policy-makers do face two ways, and play two-level games, does this mean that everything which a system projects outwards falls under the heading of foreign policy? Conversely, how do those activities which are conventionally labelled 'foreign policy' relate to the multiple strands of a society's interactions with the world, private and public? Is it still possible to funnel a state's (let alone a society's) principal relations with the outside world through the practice of foreign policy, and its associated institutions? This issue is closely related to that of the very definition of foreign policy, on which a provisional answer has been given earlier in this chapter. Yet, as with other large political concepts such as democracy, definitions are in a constant dialectical relation with empirical analysis. This means that no position on the relationship of external relations to foreign policy will convince until the problem has been broken down into its component parts – as it will be in subsequent chapters through the discussions of bureaucratic politics, transnational relations and domestic society.

Finally, foreign policy analysis must also face the normative issues which its positivist origins obscured for too long. As an area of serious enquiry it must confront the possibility that it might contain built-in normative biases or, more prosaically, just not address certain value-based questions. It is certainly true that many of the interesting questions about foreign policy involve issues of value or principle. If FPA evades them, then it becomes less worthwhile. One such is how far foreign policy may be effectively harnessed to an ethical cause without damaging other legitimate goals. Another is the long-debated issue of how far foreign policy can or should be accountable to citizens who are probably ignorant of the issues but who will still have to pay some price for them – even perhaps to die in its name. The trade-offs between efficiency and democracy are particularly sharp here. The changing contemporary environment has given particular force to one enduring normative issue, namely how much responsibility to take for shaping the lives of others outside one's own society, including international order as a whole. Although states vary in what they can do, and must view the matter through the lens of self-interest, this is a perpetual ethical challenge for every foreign policy. The broadening of horizons enabled by technology and the pace of economic growth since 1945 have brought the issue of wider responsibilities to the forefront of policy-makers' concerns.

This brings us to the practical questions facing our subject. The first links theory to practice by asking what expectations is it reasonable for citizens to have of policy-makers, and for policy-makers to have of themselves? How much of what may be deemed desirable is also feasible? There are naturally limits to the extent to which a general answer can be given, but it must be the task of any analyst to relate the complexity of the environment to the needs and circumstances of particular actors. Capabilities can be the better brought into line with expectations if some sophisticated understanding exists of the degree to which choices are constrained, and of the margin there might be for initiative. Only by analysing actors and their milieux in conjunction can this be done.

How far can we generalize about foreign policy? The assumption of this book is that there are many common features and dilemmas which can be anatomized. Yet states clearly vary enormously in size, power and internal composition, to say nothing of non-state actors. In the twenty-first century it can still be argued that the world's only superpower is in a category of its own and has to be analysed as such. The United States shows few signs of angst about the importance of foreign policy, whereas the middle-range states are far more aware of the constraints on national action. It is revealing that in the American study of international relations, the state and its power is still a central theme, whether through the successful policy journals like *Foreign Affairs*, or through the still powerful academic school of neorealism. Globalization theory, which downplays the role of individual states, made far less ground than in Europe, or neighbouring Canada. The rising powers, however, tend to share US confidence in the possibilities of autonomous action. Where you sit, and who you are, really does influence what you see.

The changing politics of foreign policy is not, however, only about perception. The United States has to cope with substantive limitations on its freedom of action, despite its triumph at the end of the Cold War. It is also as subject to decision-making pathologies, and to ends–means problems, as any other actor. What is more, the interpenetration of foreign with domestic politics is universal, and varies only in degree and form. Domestic inputs into foreign policy, including conceptions of a desirable world and what can be done to improve it, vary according to political culture. For example whereas the United States has consistently believed that its own values should be exported, China felt much less need to proselytize, despite its own conviction of superiority, until its growing economic strength made its particular socioeconomic model, and stress on sovereignty – what has been called 'the Beijing consensus' (Halper, 2010) – attractive in developing countries. The nature of the variation and the possible links to foreign policy are issues to be mapped, whether as contrasts between democracies and autocracies, between rich states and poor or between ancient cultures and new states engaged in nation-building.

The principal practical challenge for a foreign policy analyst should be to make transparent to a wider public the often arcane processes of foreign policy-making. That means clarity over where key decisions are made and why fiascos happen. Both accountability and efficiency depend on a prior knowledge of how choices get formulated, who shapes them and how decisions are then implemented. As any specialist knows, the answers to these questions are by no means always close to those which might be inferred even by an intelligent reader of a good newspaper. Too often public discussion oscillates between fatalism about the impossibility of affecting international affairs, and the personalization of policy through the high expectations held of individual leaders. Foreign policy analysis, however, can dig deeper, helping us to understand the way in which the complexities of the decision-making process affect foreign policy, in terms of both the intrinsic quality of a decision and its eventual outcomes.

The Changing International Context

The politics of foreign policy are perpetually changing, depending on the country or the region, often unpredictably. This is why case and country studies are so important. There is no point in lofty generalizations if they do not convince those who know about – or live in – say, Brazil, Jordan or Cambodia. Yet as the result of imperial expansion, world war and economic integration we have become used, especially in the West, to viewing the world, and the international political system, as one. Any changes in the whole are seen as of great significance for the parts. Conversely, changes in a particularly important part can lead to upheaval in the system as a whole. We had a strong sense of this after the implosions of communism, the Cold War and the Soviet Union in the dramatic events of 1989–91. When the integrating phenomena summed up by the concept of globalization are added to the equation it is natural to conclude that we are living in a fully interdependent political network – an exaggeration, but something which goes well beyond the more limited conception of a 'society of states' (M. Wight, 1991).

There are four elements of the contemporary international context which can be taken to represent major change: the end of the Cold War; the process of globalization; the challenge to the Westphalian state system represented by the doctrine of humanitarian intervention; and the attack by Islamic fundamentalists on Western predominance epitomized by the claims in 2014 to have restored a 'Caliphate' in the Levant. Each of these great issues will be examined in turn in terms of their implications for the conduct of national foreign policy.

The end of the Cold War as marked by the implosion of the Warsaw Pact in 1989 was seen by some as a revolution in international affairs (Halliday, 2001). More plausibly, it can be viewed as involving 'only' the collapse of a particular state/empire, with large consequences for the balance of power but no different in kind from the end of Napoleonic France or Wilhelmine Germany, neither of which brought down the state system.

The end of an empire always alters the outlook and calculations of the other members of the system, and not only at the end of major wars. The dismantling of the French and British empires between 1945 and 1964 created many new states and weakened the two metropole powers. Yet adjustment soon took place. By 1973 it had become difficult to remember the world as it was before decolonization, while the position of France and Britain remained remarkably unchanged. Even to this day their permanent seats on the UN Security Council, while often criticized, are not in real danger. On the other hand, both decolonization and the end of the Cold War signalled the death of a set of particular ideas, and the arrival of new possibilities. The nature of a new order may not be immediately apparent, but it will be immanent. In the case of 1991 and after, what happened was not only the humiliation of a superpower, and the winding up of a particular set of international institutions, but also the destruction of a major transnational ideology.

The ideology of communist internationalism, coupled with the power of the Soviet Union, had been a straitjacket for the foreign policies of many different states, not just those in Eastern Europe. Poor states needing Soviet aid, or looking for reassurance against American power, found themselves defined by it. Opponents, likewise, either turned directly to the US and its allies for protection, or self-consciously adopted a strategy of non-alignment in the hope of escaping the bipolar trap. Some states found themselves the victims of various kinds of intervention. Large resources were consumed by those who saw themselves (rightly or wrongly) as threatened by Soviet imperialism.

All this disappeared very quickly. Russia is now attempting to recover its international status, but can only do so through interventions in its own near abroad, pursued by Vladimir Putin since the 2008 war with Georgia in what is almost certainly the vain hope of reconstituting a geopolitical entity on the model of the USSR. But the weakness of Russia's economy places limits on how far its hard or soft power can be developed. By the same token space has been created for the rise of India, Brazil and in particular China, with a corresponding US nervousness, although that could not have happened without the dramatic economic growth in these countries which gave their foreign policies a new confidence. Resources were released in all the ex-combatants of the Cold War (or should have been) for other purposes, domestic and international. In many cases internal politics were also reconfigured. France found it easier to move into a working relationship with NATO, and eventually rejoined its military structures, thus confounding those who had predicted the demise of the alliance. Italy began to develop a more confident national foreign policy. In both countries the domestic environment became more fluid as the result of the eclipse of what were previously strong communist parties. The central and east European countries made a beeline for EU and NATO membership, which in most cases they have achieved despite strenuous Russian objections.

The end of the Cold War thus introduced qualitative changes to international politics, and in some cases to the very relationship between foreign and domestic policy. But the changes did not threaten foreign policy as an activity. The emergence of *globalization*, by contrast, was thought by many to have rendered foreign policy redundant (Baylis et al., 2011; Held et al., 1999; Held and McGrew, 2003; Scholte, 2000). At least, the many works on the subject which proliferated gave this impression by the simple fact of ignoring it. In none of the major works written on globalization during the 1990s does the index contain a single reference to foreign policy. The authors tend to assume that foreign policy is diminished in line with the state's own reduced activity in an age of globalization, understood as the creation of an integrated world capitalist market which in turn fosters a global civil society through progress in information technology, travel and education. In its turn globalization was seen to have been boosted by political change, notably the emergence of the confident states of East Asia in the wake of the Vietnam War, and the collapse of the communist bloc in Europe.

In such a context, of political and economic optimism, it is hardly surprising that Francis Fukuyama inscribed the 'triumph of the West' and that politicians like Tony Blair took globalization as their mantra, making the simplifying assumption that the seven billion inhabitants of the planet were increasingly bound together in common concerns (Blair, 2001; Fukuyama, 1992). In so doing they bizarrely echoed the Marxists who had just fallen from grace, with their subordination of politics to economics and their exaggeration of the integrative effects of world capitalism. Only a few observers sounded a trumpet of alarm. Ian Clark's (1997, 1999) measured analyses of the simultaneous processes of integration and fragmentation provide an important sense of context to the heady sense of a transformed world evident in the new literature, but even he rarely touches on the implications for foreign policy. Even less interested in agency was the major critic of the globalization thesis, Justin

Rosenberg. His scathing analysis of the lack of historical and geo-economic substance in the writings of its main gurus has important implications for our understanding of the modern state and of its international context, but his is a demolition job designed to clear the ground theoretically, not an alternative account of how politics works (Rosenberg, 2000).

Thus the question of globalization, which began as an axiom difficult to challenge, gradually became the latest episode in the long-running argument about the relationships between economics and politics, and between the domestic and the external. This had begun with Adam Smith but was significantly boosted by Richard Cobden's linkage in the 1860s between peace and free trade, and was revived in modern times by the 1970s discussion of interdependence and détente. Just as Cobden did not win the argument in his time, so the hopes for interdependence were replaced by the 'second Cold War' in the early 1980s, and the post-Cold War forecasts of the death of foreign policy soon turned out to be premature (Richard Cooper, 1968; Hain, 2001; Keohane and Nye, 1973). For if foreign policy consists essentially in the political strategy conducted by independent units in relation to each other, then it could only atrophy through the *de facto* disappearance of independent units. Discounting the possibility of world government, this could conceivably come about by stealth, through the emergence of a cobweb of issue-based regimes in which units take up positions on the merits of a problem, without prioritising their national communities or sense of distinct identity. This would justify the description '*global governance*' which is today in common use, and not just by idealists. The slow emergence of such a cobweb was theorized as 'functionalism' by David Mitrany as early as the 1930s, and as 'world society' by John Burton in the 1970s (Burton, 1972; Paul Taylor, 1983). Yet it is an improbable account of where the world is moving to, for three reasons: (i) states would become empty shells and unviable as devices for satisfying their citizens, who expect their governments to protect priority goals through trade-offs with other states; (ii) there would be a significant danger of partial interests capturing the policy of any world state, thus subverting the notion of the 'common good'; (iii) the overall relationship between goals, resources, values and institutions – that is, the political process itself – could not be effectively managed on such a huge scale. Democracies, at least, consist of citizens who expect to hold decision-makers to account, and if accountability proves a mirage talk quickly turns to the condemnation of 'faceless bureaucrats' and 'unelected technocrats' – as we have seen with the growth of Euroscepticism inside the EU.

Much more significant in terms of the impact of globalization is the reshuffled relationship between foreign policy and foreign economic policy. The two things are too rarely considered in tandem, through the intellectual difficulty of keeping such a wide range of activity in focus at the same time. In times of peace it is natural to expect that economics will occupy a central place in foreign policy. Development heightens this expectation. Foreign policy for modern states is about promoting prosperity as much as security, and indeed about seeing the concepts as two sides of the same coin. In some areas of economic and social life the role of government has become limited through genuflections before the market principle, but this does not mean that it is nonexistent. Governments have to become more subtle and varied in their strategies for protecting the welfare of their citizens, sometimes working with other states, sometimes intervening indirectly (even clandestinely) to win contracts for national firms, but also using unrelated areas like defence expenditure for reasons of industrial and trade policy.

In any case, periods of calm and optimism do not last forever. Long before the dramatic financial crisis which began in 2007 the signs had been evident that the markets could not be left to their own devices without damaging consequences. The handling of instant financial transfers, multinationals' tax avoidance and rapid technological innovation meant that states had to adapt their external policy-making systems if regulation was to prove possible. The state reasserted itself, with bailouts and bank nationalizations taking place in various countries. Foreign ministries had no choice but to follow the leads of heads of government, finance ministries and central banks. But their subordination is immaterial. The fact is that states need some form of strategy and machinery for managing their external environment. That the latter now impinges persistently on domestic policy makes the conduct of their external policy more not less important, wherever it is formulated and whoever actually runs it.

The third major contemporary development in international relations could in the long run turn out to be the most significant. This is the pressure for a *law of humanitarian intervention*, or what Tony Blair called 'the doctrine of international community' (Blair, 1999; Vickers, 2000, pp. 41–2). The emergence of serious support for the idea that the right of a state to determine its own internal affairs should be qualified so as to prevent serious human rights abuses has the potential to transform the international system by setting common standards for both internal and external behaviour – in short, by moving towards a rudimentary international constitution (Evans, 2008; Hurrell, 2007, pp. 61–3; Weller, 2009, p. 283).

Up to this point foreign policy had been shaped by prudence, fear, practicality and internal value-systems, with international law as a form of opt-in constraint. Yet if what the French call *une loi d'ingérence*, or a right to interference, were to become established in the international community the very right of a state to sovereignty over its internal affairs, enshrined in Article 2 (7) of the UN Charter, would be called into question. The establishment of the International Criminal Court (ICC) at The Hague in 2002 was the first serious move in this direction.

Such a development heightens the importance of foreign policy among those countries asked to implement the law on behalf of the UN (or abrogating it to themselves), while for any state fearing intervention diplomacy becomes a vital means of avoiding or delaying hostile attentions. Thus all states have to take on board new considerations as they formulate foreign policy, but for those which have only achieved sovereign independence in the last half century or so it is disconcerting to see a new principle being introduced which cuts across it. That the ICC has been seen (somewhat unfairly) as being mainly concerned to put African leaders in the dock only increases the divisions. The risks facing states are twofold: interference in one's own affairs if attracting the hostile attention of the 'international community', and being drawn into new international commitments. In either case, domestic society would become more exposed to external developments, with potentially significant consequences.

Still, it is clear that any such challenge to the Westphalian system will be a long-drawn-out and difficult business. The United Nations Charter flagged the tension between human rights and sovereignty over 55 years ago, but left the issue hanging in the air. The Universal Declaration of Human Rights in 1948 was little more than a hopeful signpost, with no capacity for enforcement. The move after 1991 towards greater consensus at the UN on the value of human rights did indicate that the more powerful states were beginning to take the issue more seriously, but there is still a big gap between rhetoric and action (C. Brown, 2010, pp. 221–35; Wheeler, 2000). The unwillingness of Russia and China to criticize Bashar al-Assad's assault on his own people in Syria, the United States' support for the Egyptian military in its dismantling of the Arab Spring movement and the European Union's ritualized hand-wringing while its own members pursue trade deals with whatever regime suits their economic purpose, have meant that it is difficult to be optimistic that international legal obligations on human rights will become self-executing (K. Smith, 2010, 2013). The most that can be said is that we may have entered a long period of transition and contestation with respect to the foundational principles of international order. This makes foreign policy an even more critical site for political action, for all kinds of regime.

The final major change in the contemporary international environment is the *revival of religious conflict* – or rather, of conflict expressed in religious terms. Over the centuries we have often associated religious differences with violence, as during the Crusades, in sixteenth-century France or in the Balkans during the 1870s. But as the secularism of the twentieth century produced even greater devastation it seemed that religion was no longer a major factor in international affairs. For close observers this view had to be adjusted in the 1990s when Al Qaeda came into being, and ethnic cleansing in the Balkans had a clear religious dimension. This change was then forced into mass consciousness by the shocking images from New York in September 2001, with the literal collapse of two of the pillars of US capitalism at the hands of 19 young men armed only with unshakeable faith and a complete disregard for human life, their own included.

The phase of international politics thus initiated is about more than merely the West's struggle with a new enemy to replace the Soviet Union. It represents a new and critical combination of effective transnational terrorism on the one hand, and conflict in various occupied territories (some occupied in the 'war on terror', others of long-standing, as in Palestine or in Al Qaeda's perception of the Gulf kingdoms). This combination has produced four consequences which have changed the environment of foreign policy for many states.

The first is that the member states of NATO and the EU have shifted towards the view that they have other needs than territorial defence – although Russian behaviour in Ukraine has dented that belief, certainly in eastern Europe. The call has been for a shift of resources into special forces, low-intensity operations and conflict prevention – in other words, for an integrated approach between the diplomats, development specialists and the armed forces. This is to a degree because of the sense of the long-term failure of conventional combat in Iraq and Afghanistan. This brings us to the second major consequence of 9/11: certain states, whether denoted 'rogue', 'failing' or strategically vital, have become key sites of struggle: over the nature of a regime, over the groups they are allowed to host, and over the appropriate level of armaments (A. Roberts, 2015). Thus Israel blockades Gaza, and fears Iran obtaining the same nuclear status as itself, while the US displays anxiety about Somalia, Yemen, North Korea and Syria – and in 2014 Iraq again, with the rise of Daesh.

The third consequence is the increased confidence among the enemies of the West, among whom are both fanatical ideologues and those despairing of ever seeing justice for the Palestinians. These elements have concluded, not without reason, that they have discovered points of weakness in the defences of the developed West. The latter's previously overwhelming strength now seems to have a vulnerable domestic underbelly.

Fourth and last, the events of the first decade of the twenty-first century have focused more attention on foreign policy than was the case during the Cold War – except at times of high nuclear crisis – for the simple reason that the lives of ordinary citizens going about their daily business seem suddenly at risk. The bombs in Madrid, London, Bali, Ankara and elsewhere, together with acts of hostage-taking, have propelled foreign policy right to the front of TV news bulletins on a regular basis. While relatively small numbers are directly affected by terrorist incidents, their purpose of sowing widespread fear has partly succeeded. A dirty bomb or worse in a major capital would have even more dramatic effects, which is why strenuous counter-terrorism efforts have been made a priority. There is now a clear link between 'homeland security' (a revealing phrase, indicating the change in foreign and security policy's reach) and a state's external activity.

Argument and Structure

The study of foreign policy faces perpetual challenges of an intellectual but also a practical kind, given the difficulty over access to sources of information. Practitioners themselves have to cope with a confusing, mixed-actor international environment where obstacles and opportunities are by no means clearly delineated. For their part, mere citizens face a mass of events, information and competing interpretations which leave many confused. It is the task of FPA to try to resolve some of this confusion by clarifying basic concepts and by showing how foreign policy relates to the key question of agency in the modern world. This does not mean resorting to either extreme – of reasserting traditional notions of the primacy of foreign policy on the one hand, or accepting the tendency to downgrade states and their international relations on the other. The challenge is to delineate the changing contours of actions via foreign policy, and to put them in the context of other forms of agency in world affairs.

Accordingly this book has begun by examining where the idea of foreign policy stands, in the world and in the academy. The chapter which follows moves on to a more detailed discussion of the politics of foreign policy – meaning arguments over how best to act internationally, and how to balance the competing pressures and expectations which beset any foreign policy-maker. This touches on some difficult theoretical issues in terms of the relationship between foreign policy and the state, and of its meaning in the context of the 'agency–structure debate' so prominent across social science in recent decades.

The next group of chapters (3–6) deals with the inner circle of decision-making within the state, and with the problem of the ends–means relationship which is at the heart of foreign policy actions. Chapter 3 delves into the substance of agency by looking at the relatively restricted groups which are formally responsible for making decisions on external relations, and for exerting leadership. It examines how, for both political and psychological reasons, these actors often fail to realize their purposes. In principle the 'agents' of responsible decision-makers are civil servants and other hired guns, and their important discretionary powers are given separate attention in Chapter 4. Here the complexities of modern bureaucratic politics take centre stage, with their key tension between the need to break down problems into their various specialized areas, and the need to ensure coherence and consistency. The fifth chapter then tackles directly the serious obstacles to acting rationally given the multiple problems of decision-making and collective action. It focuses in particular on the question of how to think about the goals of foreign policy – for both analyst and operator – and how goals become adapted or distorted in practice, as with the familiar notion of 'mission creep'. The ineluctable process of 'learning from history' is central here.

Finally, agency has to be understood in the context of power, the central problem of political science. Chapter 6 investigates the meaning of power for states and transnational actors – its various forms and faces – and then applies the concept to the particular instruments at policy-makers' disposal, noting the difficulties of achieving stated goals even where resources are extensive and well organized. 'Implementation' is now accepted as a distinct and problematic dimension of foreign policy action. The ability of an international actor to use the capabilities theoretically at its disposal, hard or soft, and conversely to exploit its own weaknesses, is a key theme here.

Having given comprehensive coverage to the makers of foreign policy and their dilemmas the book then shifts its focus not so much from agency to structure – since actors and agents are also themselves structures – but to the international context in which action is played out. This is seen in classical terms as providing *opportunities* for initiating change and for promoting particular concerns, as well as *constraints* on what can be done. A crucial theme is the limits to determinism: that is, how any decision-generating entity has the capacity to fly in the face of pressures to be 'realistic', at least for a time. There is even what might be called the suicide option, of choosing to suffer extreme consequences rather than bow to historical forces. Thus while Czechoslovakia understandably surrendered to Hitler in 1939, Poland chose a heroic but doomed resistance. Politicians may take this option rarely, but its very existence helps to define what it is to be an actor. The right and the ability to make one's own mistakes is what makes us responsible human beings, and collective entities can also choose to defy the apparently inevitable, in the form of logic, history or the international community. If they lack even the capability to make their own decisions, as in the case of the chaos in Iraq during 2014, or in that of a purely intergovernmental organization like the Council of Europe, they do not possess the political or legal personality needed to be a true actor.

The international context is treated in two chapters which analyse the diverse forms of constraint and opportunity that actors experience. In Chapter 7 the growing variety of the international political system – Hedley Bull's 'anarchical society' – is examined with a view to identifying how far the development of international law, organizations and norms has borne down on states and other actors and to what extent their values have been internalized through a process of socialization (Bull, 1977). By contrast, geopolitics is treated as a more 'enduring framework' in the sense that the very existence of separate territorial units on the face of the earth creates issues of 'foreignness', of regionalism and of vulnerability to outside interference. Yet the uneven distribution of the world's resources among around 200 disparate societies, together with the changing values of resources created by technological advance, creates endless problems of choice over security, friendship and political economy – and a diversity of approaches. To talk the language of geopolitics here, therefore, is not to reintroduce a Waltzian focus on the balance of power. Geographical and historical specifics are taken to be more important than abstractions like bipolarity or multipolarity, while geopolitics is subject to great variation around the notions of threat and 'Otherness'. The world frames foreign policy choices, in part through physical constraint and in part through interpretation of its meanings.

The increasing variety of actors, and their ability to influence world politics, has created a multi level international environment where positions are far from predictable on any basis, let alone on that of a league table of military power. Small states like Singapore and Qatar can have more prominence than larger established units like Italy. Non-state actors like Daesh or Boko Haram can emerge from nowhere to take control of a swathe of territory. Even in conventional units the pursuit of a familiar national interest cannot be taken for granted. Modernity has produced a multi level process of foreign policy decision-making. This is most evident where states participate in institutions designed to increase their collective weight, such as the EU, but it is also the case for individual countries, where foreign ministries can no longer act as a gatekeepers. As a result many different ministries, and even some semi-official entities, end up speaking for the state on the international scene, with resulting confusions and turf battles. Heads of government then take centre stage as a single source of authority, but they do not always succeed in maintaining discipline. Thus the decision-making factors of Chapters 3–6 are integrated with those of the structures outlined in the second half of the book.

Chapter 8 moves from the complexity of the international environment to the impact of the accelerating economic and technological changes known as globalization. In so doing it looks both at the transnational actors which are key agents of this set of changes, and at how states cope with the new elements of their environment. The latter's choices have become complicated by forces which flow uncontrollably across borders, making geography *seem* less significant and undermining that sense of a distinctive community which is supposed to characterize a 'nation-state'. Liberal democracies, which encourage what the EU has called the 'four freedoms' – of people, capital, goods and services – have become more diverse in their demographic make-up as the result of mobility and migration. Their populations are also subject to a vast range of global influences through the internet, smart phones, Skype and personal mobility. As a result governments cannot be sure that their old assumption of a clear set of national interests, rooted in a domestic consensus, still holds. Any foreign policy is likely to come under scrutiny from unpredictable quarters both at home and abroad.

This does not mean that states are handing over agency and power to ad hoc coalitions of specialists working across borders. Although much external relations does indeed operate like this, there is always the possibility of an issue flaring up into controversy. Governments are then immediately reminded that they are accountable to their voters, not to some vague notion of international community, let alone the bureaucracy of a remote international organization.

For their part, many transnational actors now pursue 'private foreign policies', in the sense that they define their interests independently of any particular state, and have a wide range of activities operating across conventional boundaries. In the past it was generally thought that the big multinational firms which were the principal transnational actors during the Cold War generally preferred to stay out of politics. Even the notable exceptions, such as the undermining of left-leaning governments, only happened through alignment with the preferences of Britain (Iran) and the United States (Guatemala and Chile). Now, however, transnational actors are very often political, whether pressure groups on issues such as climate change or human rights, national diasporas seeking a realignment of borders, or revolutionary movements opposed to the current international order.

Chapters 9 and 10 pick up on one further possible consequence of transnationalism, namely its solvent effect on the distinctive communities which foreign policies are supposed to serve. Given the moral claims that can be made on behalf of 'duties beyond borders', decision-makers are faced with serving competing constituencies, while other states take an ever more direct interest in their internal politics (Hoffmann, 1981). Bearing this in mind, the theme here is that of 'responsibility', or the sense of beholdenness which decision-makers have to the community on whose behalf foreign policy is conducted, but to a lesser degree also to a perceived community with a much wider ambit.

The examination begins with the general issue of how domestic society relates to foreign policy, and which elements represent its most significant 'sources', in the sense that actions 'begin at home' even if they must be conducted abroad. Foreign policy is about mediating the two-way flow between internal and external dynamics. Part of the answer is sought in the comparative study of how far certain kinds of society produce distinctive kinds of foreign policy. The 'democratic peace' hypothesis, that democracies do not fight wars against each other, is the starting-point here, but there are other things to say about the impact of domestic structures on external behaviour – for example, the impact of revolution and turmoil, or levels of economic development, both of which can define an actor's external strategies as much as regime type, geopolitical position or material capabilities. The chapter ends by considering 'the second image reversed' argument (Gourevitch, 1978) as reworked by post-positivists to the effect that the kind of foreign policy pursued can help to constitute a particular set of values and social practices within the state concerned – a good example being Putin's combative international posture, which has heightened authoritarianism at home.

Chapter 10 follows on by looking at the particular problem of democratic communities in foreign policy-making: that is, how to reconcile the need to give leaders the freedom of manoeuvre they need in an intractable external environment, especially over security, with the requirements of popular consent and parliamentary scrutiny. This involves analysing the ever-increasing interest of public opinion in international relations, and the changing nature of patriotism in a more sceptical transnational age (Smith, 2000; Hockenos, 2003; Waller and Linklater, 2003; S. Huntington, 2004).

The book's final chapter takes stock of the revival of the state as a site of agency by looking at the problem of responsibility in a wider frame. It considers whether foreign policy in modern conditions can deliver what is expected of it, whether by citizens, decision-makers or academics. It argues that meaningful and intentional actions are still possible under the heading of foreign policy so long as they are based on a good understanding of not just external constraints and the limits of unilateralism but also the various kinds of interpenetration to be found between structures at home and abroad. These complications are both empirical and moral. Transnational relations and the proliferation of diasporas are changing the parameters of the constituencies with which foreign policy-makers have to deal and multiplying the criteria they use, making the term 'national interest' a wholly inadequate criterion for decisions (Hill, 2013).

*   *   *

The central argument of this book is that foreign policy is key to our understanding of international relations. It plays a major part in filling the hole in accounts of international relations with respect to 'agency', which is much discussed at the epistemological level but insufficiently operationalized. As Valerie Hudson has pointed out, 'IR requires a theory of human political choice. ... [The] one area within the study of IR that has begun to develop such a theoretical perspective is foreign policy analysis' (Hudson, 1995, p. 210).

This is because foreign policy is the official hinge between domestic politics and international relations. As Raymond Aron said ' "the problem of foreign policy" ... [is] the double problem of individual and collective survival' (Aron, 1966, p. 17). The word 'survival' is a product of the Cold War but it is still apposite given the environmental and other new challenges we now face. Citizens need the international system to work effectively for them just as much in times of peace as of war. Foreign policy has a crucial part to play both in protecting the interests of particular societies, vulnerable to a range of threats from rising sea levels to financial crisis to terrorist incursions, and in brokering agreements – bilateral, regional or universal – on the vast range of structural issues before them, from nuclear proliferation to mass migration. Since international cooperation is not self-executing, politics and diplomacy remain central to the human predicament.

The study of foreign policy thus represents a wealth of possibilities for those not blinded by prejudice against 'state-centric' approaches or dazzled by the hopes for 'global solutions to global problems' (Halliday, 1994b). Foreign policy is crucial, beyond the mere expression of statehood, as a means of brokering the perpetual two-way flow of demands, internal and external, on governments. As such, it has the capacity to shape the very environments in which it operates, although states vary greatly in their ability to do so.

Decision-makers now face a serious problem of *multiple responsibilities*. They are variously responsible to voters, special interests, diasporas, allies, regional partners, expatriates, humanity as a whole, future generations, international law, the United Nations, peoples requiring emergency assistance and those with historical claims. The list could be extended. Public policy in most of its aspects has somehow to be related to the outside world and at times (like that of the Ebola epidemic) raised to the higher level of international institutions. Foreign policy therefore faces a major challenge, needing to be purposeful but not deluded, democratic but not paralysed, ethical but still grounded in a particular society. If these gauntlets are not picked up by national decision-makers it is difficult to see where the initiatives and coordinating capacities which societies, separately and together, increasingly require are going to come from. What follows is an attempt to assess what may be feasibly expected of foreign policy, and what not.

Notes

1   Definitions of foreign policy have been offered surprisingly rarely. A reasonable alternative defines foreign policy as 'attempts by governments to influence or manage events outside the state's boundaries' (Manners and Whitman, 2000, p. 2).
2   See also the website of the Centre des Études des Relations Internationales (CERI), Paris: http://www.sciencespo.fr/ceri/en. CERI is one of the world's main centres for area studies.
3   Some of these gaps have been filled. Michael Leifer's *The Foreign Policy of Singapore: Coping with Vulnerability* (2000) is an authoritative treatment of an 'exceptional state' whose external impact is disproportionate to its size. But cumulative work is all too rare.
4   For a contrary view see Elman (1996).
5   Even Henry Kissinger, in his most recent book, qualifies realism by making significant concessions to the role of ideas (2014).
6   The concept of middle-range theory was introduced by Robert Merton (Reynolds, 1973).

Further Reading

There has been a welcome revival of writing about foreign policy and about foreign policy analysis in recent years, although some classic texts are still essential. The following are the best introductions to thinking about the subject:

Alden, Chris and Aran, Amnon, 2012. *Foreign Policy Analysis: New Approaches*. Alden and Aran break new ground in linking globalization theory to foreign policy.
Beach, Derek, 2012. *Analyzing Foreign Policy*. This is a comprehensive and thoughtful course text.
Carr, Edward H., 1939. *The Twenty Years' Crisis, 1919–1939: An Introduction to the Study of International Relations*. Carr's study is a classic of general IR, but also – in practice – of FPA.

Hudson, Valerie M., 2007. *Foreign Policy Analysis: Classic and Contemporary Theory*. Hudson's book is an excellent, systematic account of the range of foreign policy theories.

Stuart, Douglas T., 2008. Foreign-policy decision-making. In: Christian Reus-Smit and Duncan Snidal, eds, 2008, *The Oxford Handbook of International Relations*, pp. 576–93. This essay offers a sharp history of FPA from a US standpoint.

Wolfers, Arnold, 1962. *Discord and Collaboration: Essays on International Politics*. Wolfers provides a classic, almost timeless, set of essays.

Chapter 2

The Politics of Foreign Policy

All external relations are potentially political, but not all get politicized. The same is true of diplomacy, much of which is routine and non-controversial. But foreign policy is necessarily political. It is a macro-level activity whose fundamental purpose is to enable a community to cope with the outside world, and to manage the sum of the complex relationships which any actor will have with the other denizens of that challenging environment. It thus requires a strategic view of the balance between internally generated goals, values and interests, and external constraints. That view will vary enormously between actors, and over time, but the very striking of the balance, inside a given state or other actor, and at the level of the international system, has to be a matter of political judgement.

The politics of foreign policy, or who gets what out of foreign policy actions, and what happens when the needs and values of separate communities collide, is the central concern of this book. Its main themes have been chosen to illustrate the dilemmas faced by actors, and their consequences for the system as a whole. The three themes are: agency, the impact of the international environment and the nature of responsibility. To open up each requires some theoretical ground-clearing in relation to the nature of action and actors, the limits to choice and the varying hopes and strategies which attach themselves to the vehicle we call 'foreign policy'. Accordingly, this chapter provides the starting point of the analysis in relation to the fundamental issue of whom foreign policy serves in the age of popular sovereignty. It moves on to analyse the key relationships between sovereignty, the state and foreign policy, and then tackles the fundamental difficulty of how far the distinction between the domestic and the foreign is evaporating. Does the 'outside' still pose different problems from politics inside a state? At this point the nature of politics comes into question, and how it manifests itself at all levels of the foreign policy process from the leader's personal office right out to debates in the UN's General Assembly. Underlying all politics, however, is the issue of structure and agency, or which kinds of action are possible within the structures we observe in international politics. This problem is addressed by surveying the great diversity among the states which inhabit the international system, which inevitably places limits on generalization.

Foreign Policy for Whom?

States and foreign policies are close relations, but there are other actors which generate similar activities. Furthermore it is not always clear who represents whom in international relations. Some unrecognized states effectively conduct independent external strategies, even if their lack of normal representational facilities and their dependence on patrons set limits on them. Taiwan and Northern Cyprus are prominent cases, while there are many cases of dispossessed peoples pursuing international strategies, from the Armenians before 1991 through the inhabitants of East Timor and of Western Sahara to the Kurds and the Palestinians.

Hong Kong is a special, but notable, case. It has maintained extensive external relations in the sphere of political economy since becoming a special administrative region of the People's Republic of China in 1997, including accession to the World Trade Organization (WTO) before China itself. It does not risk seeking its own international profile, but its people's views on human rights and democratic governance are expressed through its relatively free access to the outside world, as in the persistent 'umbrella' protests of 2014. It thus has a de facto partial foreign policy even if it would never dare to use the term itself. Of this the main purpose, paradoxically, is to help mainland China itself to relax its domestic regime, thus easing the pressure on Hong Kong.

Most of these cases are relatively straightforward in the sense that they represent actors wanting to be states, or at least autonomous zones, with an emulation of state foreign policies. More problematic are the global strategies of transnational companies, now usually referred to as Multinational Enterprises (MNEs). Few would pretend that News Corp, Microsoft, BP and Gazprom do not involve themselves in politics. But whether their activities can be described as foreign policies is another matter. Big companies do have global strategies which go well beyond mere marketing or even production. Rupert Murdoch's activities with satellite television make him a major player in the international politics of Asia, just as his TV and newspaper interests have made it necessary for the last five British prime ministers to keep him onside. For years he proved a more significant rival for Silvio Berlusconi inside Italy than the opposition political parties. But businesses do not represent society and they have little ability to participate directly in the shaping of international order through institutions, law and security arrangements. Their interest in international politics is intensely narrow, focused on maintaining a small number of relevant variables within acceptable limits, and their impact is indirect. Despite the age-old controversies about arms sales and imperialism it is not even clear whether businesses have a clear interest in peace over war, or vice versa, either of which might lead them to political activity. The fact is that conflict brings profit to some, and bankruptcy to others.

On the other hand transnational companies are no different from most states, in their diversity and egoism. States and businesses also share the need to pay attention to both their internal and external environments – although MNEs by definition lack a single territorial base. Both have to compute the best ways to survive, and with luck prosper, in an intractable external environment which only a few actors seem to have the capacity to influence. They thus share a reliance on diplomacy. As Stopford and Strange (1991, p. 224) observe: 'World-class firms almost need a kind of foreign ministry and a cadre of corporate diplomats that combine local expertise and broad experience of dealing with governments in other countries'.

On the definition of foreign policy given in Chapter 1, there is no reason to restrict foreign policy analysis to states. Apart from liberation movements and MNEs, other actors such as regions, cities, churches and the more cosmopolitan interest-groups are increasingly taking a direct role in international relations. Yet do they truly qualify as independent actors? The Vatican clearly has a foreign policy – it is a micro-state as well as the possessor of formidable financial and ideological resources. Anglicanism also operates through a single organized network. Other religions, like Islam and Judaism, are either more diffused and divided, or dependent on states for assistance in the process of global projection (A. Dawisha, 1985). Still, even small sects like the Mormons, Hezbollah or Opus Dei have shown the capacity to pursue strategies across state lines, some more overtly political than others (Luttwak, 1994, pp. 8–19; Rubin, 1994, pp. 20–34). For their part regions, especially in federal systems, are capable of using the spaces created by democracy and free movement to take initiatives on the politics of trade and tourism, while the activities of Greenpeace, Amnesty International and Oxfam are inherently political, even if they have to assert the kind of neutral, humanitarian role associated with the International Red Cross and Red Crescent in order to gain access to the territory of suspicious states (Hocking, 1993a; Willetts, 1995). Thus, even where an actor is not wholly independent of states, lacks a clear constituency and has a narrowly defined range of concerns, it is still capable of a form of foreign policy action. The Al Qaeda terrorist network has demonstrated this with chilling consequences. Sovereignty may be lacking, but if the entity concerned is capable of autonomous decisions with discernible consequences for others then it has a degree of actorness. These transnational players represent a significant form of agency in international affairs, and should not only be discussed at the level of the system, in terms of interdependence or global civil society

(Risse-Kappen, 1995a). Their aims, policy-making processes and impact need serious analysis.

The transnational aspect, however, is marginal by comparison to the traditional meaning of the question as to whom foreign policy is for. This relates to the relationship between elite and mass which has preoccupied commentators since the First World War, when the pitiless sacrifice of millions led to the rise of the Union of Democratic Control in Britain and Woodrow Wilson's rejection of the old order from his position as President of the United States and then leader of his country's delegation at the Paris Peace Conference (Harris, 1996; Ceadel, 2000). The basic issue here, on which so far there has been little progress, can be put in the form of another question: if democracy and popular sovereignty are to be the hallmarks of modern statehood, is it acceptable for foreign and defence policies to be delegated almost wholly to a small elite, on the grounds that dealings with other states require secrecy, continuity, experience and personal contacts? Most people would reply in the negative, especially when they become aware of the sacrifices which foreign policy can require, directly of troops and indirectly of civilian populations. But striking the right balance between democracy and efficiency in this context has always been a major challenge. The 'open diplomacy' aspirations of Wilson soon proved unworkable, and even today few liberal democracies have procedures for accountability in foreign policy which come near those that apply in domestic areas. Leaders naturally claim that they are acting on behalf of their people, but it is highly revealing that the phrase 'in the national interest' has come to connote power politics more than democratic solidarity.

Foreign policy may be 'for the people' in a fundamental sense, but it is largely still made on their behalf by cognoscenti who complain about having their hands tied by public opinion yet evince little evidence of it in practice. Even in the United States, which has the most developed system of legislative participation in foreign affairs, the executive has found many ways to get around the Congress – being able to call attention to a 'clear and present danger' is a powerful weapon. What is more, in the West at least these experts form a transnational class underpinned by personal relations, intermarriage, subsidized conferences and multilingualism – all of which distance them from their own domestic constituencies. This is reminiscent of the aristocratic world of the eighteenth and early nineteenth centuries but it extends much further to include business, academics, interest groups, the media and the many forms of international organization. It is symbolized by the yearly meetings at the Swiss ski resort of Davos, where a global elite mixes easily despite (or more probably because of) their remoteness in style, discourse and location from the citizens of their home states.

The growth of an international middle class has, on the other hand, stimulated an impatience in many societies with the torpor of their leaders, while since the end of the Cold War there has been a steadily growing interest in international relations, especially among the younger and more educated, and in diaspora communities. The WikiLeaks revelations of US diplomatic documents, followed by those of Edward Snowden about the extent of the National Security Agency's surveillance, provide striking evidence of this point (Leigh and Harding, 2011; Harding, 2014). The number of pressure groups is rising and the notion that governments cannot be criticized on foreign policy without endangering national security has lost most of its credibility. The interconnections between domestic and foreign affairs are more widely understood, and the contrast between the ethical standards of the two realms is routinely challenged.

Given these trends, the need to work through the relationship between foreign policy and democratic politics, from both analytical and normative viewpoints, is pressing. The foreign policy of a state is a complex balance between: (i) concerns for the overall welfare of national society, as interpreted by governments in dialogue with various stakeholders, and at times with parliamentarians; (ii) concerns for general principles of international order and justice; and (iii) concerns for selected groups of foreigners designated as friends and/or as especially deserving of help. How these criteria are related to each other, and by whom, should be a key concern of contemporary foreign policy analysis. Clearly governments in such capitals as Washington, Moscow, London, Berlin and Beijing interpret the dilemma very differently – as each may also do over time. Some leaders run scared before what they view as a powerful public opinion, some are confident in their ability to lead, manage or educate, while yet others eagerly look to foreign adventures as a populist instrument for consolidating their domestic position.

The State, Sovereignty and Foreign Policy

No serious treatment of international politics can avoid taking a view on the state. Yet foreign policy analysis has rarely attempted to theorize it (Roy Jones, 1979). This is a triple failing given (i) that FPA has been broadly state-centric; (ii) that it seeks to bridge international relations and comparative politics; and (iii) that states have proved robust despite many predictions of their demise. A theory of what the state does, and what it is for, is needed so as to clarify the confusions which arise over terminology – notably between sovereignty, power and independence. More importantly, it will help us to examine how far the domestic and the international roles of the state gel. To the extent that they are at odds, what space does this create for other actors, and what limitations does it impose on foreign policy?

Sovereignty is the key issue here, for its symbolic and practical importance. It has a domestic meaning, as in 'the sovereign people', as well as the external conception of 'the sovereign state'. In the extensive but stalled debate on the subject, sovereignty and its meaning became a battleground between those who wish to see the state dethroned from its position as a central factor in international relations (C. Weber, 1995; R. B. J. Walker, 1995) and those who defended its primacy (James, 1986; Jackson, 2003). Although those who study foreign policy tend to identify with the latter position, there is no need for them to become trapped in a dichotomised argument. Sovereignty is a central legal concept in the current international system, and an attribute difficult both to acquire and to lose. Equally, a state's capacity to exercise the independent choices implied by sovereignty is often in practice curtailed, because power varies widely and is never absolute (Katzenstein, 1987; Krasner, 1999). All too often in the political world sovereignty is confused with power, leading many to believe that relative weakness renders sovereignty meaningless, and that sovereignty therefore depends on maximising power.[1]

Foreign policy exists in the space created by the separateness of states and by their very lack of omnipotence. Its purpose is to mediate the impact of the external on the domestic and to find ways of projecting a particular set of concerns in an intractable world. It depends on sovereignty not being extinguished where it already exists, but otherwise is more linked to the existence of a distinguishable set of domestic interests, which vary independently of the given fact of statehood. The formal possession of sovereignty creates the conditions for the conduct of a foreign policy. Conversely, where sovereignty is denied or the capacity to exercise it severely impeded, foreign policy becomes difficult – but not impossible. Ultimately foreign policy rests on the *effective actorness* of the state at home and abroad, which is more a matter of politics than of law.

In this context, how may the state be described, and how do the competing versions bear on foreign policy? The interpretations broadly divide into those which are *outside–in,* where the external role determines the state's internal character, and those which are *inside–out,* where the constitutional nature of the state is primordial and has distinctive effects on international relations (Dyson, 1980; Jackson and Sørensen, 2003). Into the first category falls the view that the state was formed through competitive politics in Renaissance Europe, and the growing operations of an international market (Hall, 1992). It became consolidated in what we describe as the Westphalian system, which gradually made possible territorial nation-states through external recognition and the principle of non-intervention in domestic affairs. A refinement would be the imperialist state whose myths and militarism condition the character of its domestic institutions (Tilly, 1975; Mann, 2012c, 2013). Into the second category falls the classical liberal view that the state is the product of a social contract to engage in common cause, but also the various views of the state as a prize to be fought over by competing classes or elites, most dramatically at times of revolutionary struggle (Kubálková and Cruickshank, 1985; Parry, 2004; Dryzek and Dunleavy, 2009, pp. 35–130). Each of these versions has its own particular consequences for the conduct of foreign affairs.

Yet no interpretation of the state which fails to bind the domestic and the international aspects together can be convincing. The history of the emergence of states shows that they developed slowly in the crucible of Europe-wide forces like the Reformation and specific internal conditions – such as the transformation of English government carried out by the Tudors, or the centralization of France under Louis XIV. Ascribing primacy to either internal or external factors across the board makes little sense. Thus it is important to conceive of the state in a way which does justice to the fact that it faces outwards and inwards simultaneously. What matters is whether the state works well for the people who live under its protection. Externally this means managing interdependence with other states and peoples, and being ready to provide security and defence against actual threats. Internally it means achieving social peace and the conditions in which a people can flourish, while not abusing the power entrusted to the agents of the state.

Before sketching an ideal-type of how this Janus-faced state operates, we need to make clear what the state is *not*. Despite the constant slippage in common usage, the state must be clearly distinguished from government, from civil society and from the nation. It is vital to recognize that a government is only a temporary holder of power, while a state represents the set of institutions, dispositions and territory which makes it possible for governments to exist – and indeed to change smoothly. A state also looks outwards, for recognition of its independence. Once achieved statehood is rarely extinguished completely – and then not without trauma. Equally, civil society exists separately from the state. If the latter becomes overbearing it erodes the liberties of the people; if it identifies society completely with itself it creates totalitarianism. Conversely, if it is too weak it produces insecurity through internal conflict and external vulnerability.

Lastly while the term 'nation' is just as elusive as that of 'state' the two things are very distinct – despite the revealing use of them as synonyms in the United States. A nation is a group of people that conceives itself to have a common identity, history and destiny. It seeks statehood, but may exist independently of it, just as the state does not need to be coterminous with any particular nation – although when working well it will usually breed a moderate sense of nationhood delineated by its own borders. The term 'nation-state' is an historic compromise which like most such does not create big problems until an excessive symmetry is pursued, whether by nationalists or by statists – Serbia under Milošević being an example of the former, Zimbabwe under Mugabe of the latter.[2]

What then is the modern state, seen in the round? A brief sketch follows of an ideal-type, in the sense that it identifies the core features of a state that exists simultaneously for its people and as a unit of the international system in the world. It contains normative elements in that the denial of popular sovereignty and aggressive international behaviour are both counted as deviant qualities. States are more than just pieces of real estate on the world map. They have certain essential features which provide a baseline against which to measure variance – for they can change types, as through democratization or rapid development. These features relate in an unbreakable interconnection to both the internal and external circumstances of a given society of people.

The first feature of a well-functioning state is the set of institutions representing the *res publica,* or the elements of legitimated power which a government runs in trust for the people. These include the machinery of justice, the police and armed forces, public administration and the institutions of political life. Their purpose is to ensure continuity, order and common purpose, and they are supposed not to be monopolized by any particular class, party or elite. This can never be guaranteed and at worst the state can become a private instrument – a 'prebendal state' – when the unit created by external recognition and territoriality becomes an empty shell to be filled by those possessing *force majeure.*[3] In that event, however, the sharp contrast between the external status of the state and its lack of public content creates not only domestic tensions but also pressure from the outside to bring things back in line. Less dramatically, states will vary in the extensiveness and dominance of their public institutions, especially in relation to economic life, to regional autonomy and to conscription into the armed services. Under the current rules of the international system this is a matter of legitimate diversity.

It might be argued that the above is a description of the 'constitutional state', while more common historically is the state as an agglomeration of power, pressing down upon the citizenry (Dyson, 1980, pp. 101–7). The response to this is that the latter is not a true state but the mere instrument of a dominant class or dynasty, even if functional in the international context. This is why we do not describe medieval kingdoms as 'states', for there was no machinery independent of the royal household being held in trust for society (which itself would have been an anachronistic concept).

Since the French Revolution, however, the claims and aspirations of most people have extended well beyond Hobbesian visions of order – except during war or other emergencies, when security is paramount. The very idea of the modern state requires institutions which are robust enough to remain separate from government and to keep the country functioning during periods of instability.[4] This has external as well as internal significance because without such institutions outside powers are drawn to intervene, as in Egypt and the Ottoman Empire in the nineteenth century, or frequently in Lebanon and Iraq during our own times.

Constitutionalism, indeed, is the second defining feature of modern statehood. To acquire legitimacy a state has to act as a guardian of civil society, ensuring (i) equity of treatment for all regardless of status, ethnicity or religion; (ii) the accountability of those in positions of power and (iii) the protection of public funds. The state should also, in a Hegelian sense, be the means through which freedom is enlarged as well as protected, the focal point of public discourse on the basic purposes of society and political organization. If it does not do this, but becomes instead the oppressor and controller of the people, presenting itself as the source of their legitimacy rather than vice versa, then it becomes by definition a special interest group exploiting the state. This is the danger with any one-party state. Where the state thus fails to provide the guarantees outlined above it falls into disrepute and other solutions are sought (in Italy, for example, this means either private 'protection' or, more respectably, 'Europe').

In the early twenty-first century the constitutional state does not exist in a vacuum. It is reinforced by external human rights regimes, by the UN system and by the power of the Western democracies – even if on occasions it is also undermined by their double standards and by the perceived exigencies of national security. It tends to reinforce its own legitimacy by noticing the fate of those in other states whose liberties are in danger. How far to go in that obligation is one of the central dilemmas of foreign policy. It is clear, however, that it is not possible to be insouciant about repression elsewhere without the state itself losing something in relation to its claim to be upholding the basic rights of its own citizens. The project of constitutionalism is now therefore in part a universal one, which is not to say that all states have to follow the same model, let alone that the United States and its allies have reached a satisfactory level of democratic practice. What it does say is that the notion of the state as the enemy of democracy inside and out, because it is indelibly associated with the values of *machtpolitik,* is not only outdated but fundamentally wrong. It is true that in practice many individual states have been misappropriated, by bad rulers or by external enemies. But statehood itself is a crucial aspect of modernity because it is tied to the secular concept of the public good. It needs reclaiming for liberalism, even if *on occasions* liberal states will need to follow the dictates of realism in order to ensure their own survival. But even non-liberals, as in the Communist Party of China, have to adapt their ideology to fit the state. Even a vanguard party cannot run a huge and complex society without the institutions of a state and some conception of the public good.

The last major definitional attribute of the state is the fact of its recognition by the international system – the key outside–in criterion. This is indispensable to statehood because if recognition of the right of the state to exist inside its territorial boundaries is not forthcoming, the way is opened for other states to contest its position, at best through isolation and sanctions but at worst through military intervention. What is more, the absence of diplomatic recognition and membership in international organizations deprives the state of standing in international law and of an effective personality in international political relations. It is a gross handicap, which is why the breakaway Yugoslav republics sought recognition in 1991 so keenly. Its very importance means that recognition is not awarded indiscriminately. Although states vary in their attitudes, which in itself causes conflict, the usual minimum conditions now are seen as: internal legitimacy, effective control over a given territory which does not derive from conquest in the recent past, and the capacity to enter into relations with other such entities (Brownlie, 1966, pp. 80–7; Roberts and Kingsbury, 1993, pp. 56–7). Where the 'international community' does confer recognition by admitting a new state to the UN, its acceptance is not of a particular government but of the fact that the state exists on equal terms with others and shares the same rights and duties in international law (Krasner, 1999, pp. 14–20).[5] It is also, seventy years on from Article 2 (7) of the UN Charter which enshrines the right to sovereign independence, not a *carte blanche* for statehood to develop in whatever way a dominant elite might wish. The growing presumption of some degree of a 'responsibility to protect' means that the worst excesses will draw external condemnation and quite probably sharper forms of pressure for change. That this tendency is inconsistently and often inadequately manifest is not a reason for discounting its arrival as an important new aspect of statehood.

Thus the essential features of modern statehood all involve both internal and external aspects and neither side can be privileged over the other (Sørensen, 2001). If the definition given here of the state is the liberal version, then liberalism is itself a divided house, between those who favour a minimalist state dedicated to facilitating free enterprise, and those who see the state as the guarantor of political and civil rights and the educator of public opinion. Furthermore there are no easy answers for the liberal state in its dealings with the outside world, which not only throw up dilemmas about obligations owed to foreigners, but also influence its own internal politics, possibly even to the point of upheaval.

It may well be that the state is a transient historical phenomenon – what is not? – but its demise as an institution cannot but be a slow and complex evolution in which conscious choice and agency will not figure prominently. The actions of millions of individuals over many generations inside multiple societies will decide what kind of successor institution the world ends up with, so that public policy in the here and now can only grope its way slowly towards new dispositions – as in the case of the European Union, where a single European state is still a remote possibility over half a century from its launch in that direction. Individual states will continue to rise and fall, but the role of the state as an institution of world politics can only be determined by system-level forces (Jackson and Sørensen, 2003).

To the practical issue of the main functions which states perform, there are two possible answers: one foreign policy-related and one domestic. The foreign policy answer has three parts, and amounts to the argument that welfare in a global system of patchy interdependence requires sociopolitical units which are both manageable and accessible to their citizens. This is because: (i) the world is not yet so secure that we can trust in international organization to ensure our physical and political survival – at some level each community needs a buffer against damaging external events; (ii) the international system, political and economic, is sufficiently large and complex that without some strategy to provide identity, direction and agency, states would wander aimlessly; (iii) any given society needs its 'defensible space', that is, the capacity to regulate social behaviour in a particular way, to manage admissions and to cherish particular traditions. To put the matter at its sharpest, in very many, perhaps most parts of the world it matters greatly to people on what side of a border they live on – Kosovo or Serbia, India or Pakistan, Mexico or the United States, Syria or Turkey.

The domestic answer is that the state is there to provide the conditions of peace, order and organization required for individuals to flourish. This goes beyond the Hobbesian concern over violence and anarchy to address the problem of how a modern society can so organize itself that collective goods are delivered – and in particular to ensure a safety net for the weak. Vital services like energy supply, air traffic control, policing and transport cannot be provided by the free market alone or by international regimes. They require an effective *intermediate* level of political organization to regulate, facilitate, lead and underwrite. What is more it needs to be responsive to citizens' views if it is not to risk revolt in this age of the masses. This vehicle we call the state and something like it would have to be invented if it did not exist.

If we combine the foreign and domestic policy answers it can be seen that the argument is really about three things: protection, democracy and the management of scale. These values cannot be provided without accepting both the need for a balance to be struck between domestic and international goals and the fact that there is no obvious substitute for the state on offer. The approach presented in this book is thus one of liberal realism, acknowledging the contingency and insecurity of world politics while being convinced that politics is always about choice, that human agency makes a difference and that the state does not have to be the defensive, paranoid fortress it is presented as in post-Hobbesian accounts. Liberal realism wants the democratic state to survive but also to grow and to promote constitutional values internationally, so that interstate, and intersocietal, relations can be conducted on a basis of secure and cooperative diversity (Herz, 1981, pp. 182–203; Hill, 1989). If this argument holds, then there are a number of important functions for foreign policy to perform, and the behaviour of those responsible for conducting it remains a matter of high importance.

Inside and Outside

The argument so far has stressed the interconnections between the domestic and the foreign. Foreign policy can never be abstracted from the domestic context out of which it springs. Without domestic society and the state there would be no foreign policy. This is not to dismiss the real-ist perception that the nature of international politics disciplines foreign policy and to reduce its degree of variation – in other words, that to play the game you have to stick to the rules. It is, rather, to argue that foreign policy cannot be reduced to a game like chess with set rules, a single dominant value and a unitary, optimising decision-maker. Robert Putnam has pointed out that foreign policy is a two-level game (at least), but in practice the many emanations from domestic society make inter-action much more than a game.

This is not to say that either the domestic or the foreign represents a hard and fast category. Writers like R. B. J. Walker (1993) and Cynthia Weber (1995, pp. 6, 10) have challenged the very distinction between 'inside' and 'outside' and there is certainly a grey area between the two. What is regarded as distinctively 'home affairs' is increasingly mixed up with the domestic environments of other states, and with international regimes. Ireland, with its large cultural overlap with the United Kingdom, widespread diaspora and heavy dependence on EU programmes, is a prominent example. Canada is another, being deeply interdependent with the United States. Yet the Canadian case also shows how palpable domestic communities still exist, given both Canadians' determination not to merge with the US, and the internal divisions between the (multicultural) Anglophone and (monocultural) Francophone communities. Yet a sense of distinctive community does not require nationalism. Rather, shared historical experiences, myths, culture in the widest sense, including food, language, architecture, jokes, music, sport and newspapers, all help to create the emotion of 'belonging' primarily to one society rather than another. This is true for all those except the international elite which dominates writing about international relations, and in so doing tends to project its own experiences onto the mass from which it is detached.

Thus domestic and foreign are two ends of a continuum rather than being sharply demarcated (Rosenau, 1997), while it is impossible to do without the idea of domestic society at both practical and theoretical levels (Hill, 2000). The world cannot be explained only in holistic terms, and even writers like Susan Strange (1994) who resist the conventional categories are forced to include states and security in their system of interpretation. In terms of policy, international institutions and summits are geared almost wholly to intergovernmental compromises, and the most powerful figures in world business have to acknowledge the difference made by a particular political context – as Rupert Murdoch has done assiduously in China, and energy companies have done in adapting to difficult regimes from Gaddafi to Putin.

The idea of the domestic is particularly indispensable when we confront the issues of democracy and accountability. Those propagating the idea of a 'cosmopolitan democracy', notably the globalization theorists David Held (1995) and Daniele Archibugi (2011, with Koenig-Archibugi and Marchetti), have not demonstrated how a world *demos* would express itself or how global democracy could work on equitable principles. How are popular concerns to be expressed and protected if not through the mechanisms of specific societies and polities? Does making an intergovernmental organization more 'democratic' make them more in touch with citizens, or accountable to parliamentarians? Is even a humanistic and transnational NGO like Oxfam or the Red Cross inherently a force for *democracy*?

At the international level the issue of democracy largely relates to the artificial issue of equal rights between states of differing sizes and power, as in relation to voting in the UN, which makes accountability to their citizens a very indirect business.[6] This is one of the key issues in the acknowledged 'democratic deficit' of the European Union, which at least has a directly elected European Parliament, but which has signally failed to create Europe-wide popular debates.[7] Even in established liberal states, democracy is often all too rudimentary and intermittent, but at least the structures and presuppositions exist for asserting the rights to representation, scrutiny and due process. This is not the case with such entities as pressure groups and social media. Their cacophony is an essential complement to formal processes but they cannot transcend their own special interests.

A focus on foreign policy is therefore for the present the most feasible way of addressing the question of how far democracy works in the global context. Through foreign policy one can assess whether the needs of a particular society are being protected or advanced in the context of the outside forces which affect them – and indeed this is the operational code by which leaders proceed, most obviously in the area of defence, but also in the wider categories of security and welfare (George, 2006, pp. 1–13). There may be limits to what governments can do to safeguard these values, and to live up to the expectations of their citizens, but they have no alternative but to try. Companies' obligations, in contrast, are to their shareholders, and international banks' (in principle) also to principles of good finance. Neither can be expected to serve society as a whole. That is why states turned out to be critical players in mediating the international financial crisis which broke out in 2008, while those in Europe locked into the common currency of the euro have seen much domestic turmoil from voters outraged at their countries' impotence.

Through foreign policy one can also raise questions of morality in international relations (C. Brown, 2010, pp. 208–20; Carr, 1939, 2001; Hoffmann, 1981; Walzer, 1977). To a certain extent this can be done by reference to individual responsibility and to the functions of the United Nations and its specialized agencies, but both of these levels are ineffectual without the commitment of national governments. It is as difficult at the practical as at the philosophical level to decide on the extent of one community's obligations to others, and to the principles of international order. Yet without reference to national foreign policy and its instruments, it becomes impossible to allocate responsibilities for a given problem, and for the best means of tackling it. To take one particular example: the practice of female genital mutilation (FGM) will only be ended when attitudes change within traditional societies, which will take generations. But the issue is only on the agenda through the activity of dedicated individuals and transnational pressure groups, which in turn are focusing on states to enact legislation. Law and power, sited in states, are needed to kick-start change, while the global nature of the issue inevitably makes it one of foreign relations. Asylum, for instance, has been granted to women on the grounds of their wish to escape from FGM (EIGE, 2013, p. 47).

Both the practitioner and the analyst of foreign policy must take notice of the two-way flows between the foreign and the domestic: foreign policy has its domestic sources (Rosenau, 1967), and domestic policy has its foreign influences (Gourevitch, 1978; Risse, Ropp and Sikkink, 1999).[8] Without a distinction between the two in the first place, however, tracing the flows would make no sense. Although there are some elements of domestication evident in the international system, with challenges to the rule of non-intervention, and some intergovernmental coordination of public policy, no serious observer would argue that this is anything but tentative and patchy. Conversely, although all states have to factor international considerations in their decision-making on issues from education to waste disposal, this is not the same as saying that their internal policies are determined by interdependence or globalization. Their own structures, paths of development and political cultures are crucial intervening variables between external trends and policy outcomes.

The domestic and the foreign are therefore distinguishable both in degree and in kind. What is more, every country fits the general model. The greatest powers may suffer internal dislocation by faraway events, as the United States found with the Vietnam War, while the smallest states may have their international position shaped by domestic inputs, as when Malta rejected the offer of a place in the queue for EU membership in 1998 after the result of a general election (Sedelmeier and Wallace, 2000). Every society has its particular cluster of traditions, groups, procedures and needs, just as it has a distinctive geopolitical position and ranking in the World Bank's league tables. All societies have practical as well as sentimental understandings of the distinction between home and the world.

The interplay between these two sets of characteristics shapes not just the country's foreign policy but also its general development. The first step towards an understanding of this process is to consider at a theoretical level the problem of what the capacity for action means in foreign policy, and which structures – inside and out – shape it.

Agency and Structure

One of the most interesting but inaccessible debates in social science during recent years has concerned the relationship between 'agency' and 'structure'. At the ground-floor level the debate has been about whether agents (those who are capable of action) are shaped by structures (whatever they may be) or vice versa (Hay, 1995; Wendt, 1999; Carlsnaes, 1992, 1994, 2002; Adler, 2002, pp. 104–6; C. Wight, 2006). This agency–structure debate has been good for foreign policy analysis. It has returned the perennial issues of causation, freedom and determinism to the agenda of international relations and it has led to a sharper examination of the rather unsophisticated conceptual basis of some foreign policy studies. On the other hand, it has produced a highly abstract literature, revolving around 'scientific realism', which has entailed a preoccupation with meta-ontology and epistemology (Evangelopoulos, 2013, pp. 152–252, 328–334).[9] It has also often been presented as the agency–structure 'problem', which by extension should admit of a 'solution'. This is not the approach taken here, where the mathematical analogy is seen as inappropriate to the immense political and historical complexities facing all those who wish to understand foreign policy. Rather it is assumed that causation always involves both structures and agents, and that – as a number of authors have pointed out, following Anthony Giddens – the two kinds of phenomena help to constitute each other in a perpetual process of interaction (Giddens, 1979, pp. 69–73).

Yet the consequence of the structurationist position is to dissolve the agents and structures into each other, which makes it impossible to attribute responsibility, or to distinguish between two very different kinds of causality: 'limitations and enablements' (structure), and the activation of an actor's powers (agency) (Mouzelis, 2008, pp. 225–60). It may be foolish to expect clear conclusions about the limits on agents' freedom of choice or their capacity for impact (two different things), but we may still analyse the parameters of choice and constraint on the one hand, and the capacity for what may be termed at a minimum the 'wiggle room' by which human beings persistently manage to remake at least some of their world (Cerny, 2000). Furthermore the relations between the multiple forms of actors which exist, and the variety of types of structure (many unobservable, and all dependent on our labelling them as such) cannot be reduced to any single pattern or assumption about causation.

Structures, broadly speaking, are the sets of factors which make up the multiple environments in which agents operate, and they shape the nature of choices, by setting limits to the possible but also, more profoundly, by determining the nature of the problems which occur there, by shaping our very life-worlds. Structures exist at all levels, from the family to the international system, and it is an error in foreign policy to suppose that 'structure' refers only to the external environment. The political, bureaucratic and social structures which condition foreign policy-making are of vital importance (Hollis and Smith, 1986). They are nested inside each other, like Russian dolls – leaving of course the problem of hierarchy between them, and how we would know.

Structures are as much conceptual as concrete entities because they often represent processes, or patterns of interaction. It is accordingly difficult to ascertain their existence and all too easy to imagine them into existence. Should we, for example, regard the state system as the baseline structure of international relations, or some deeper formation, such as world capitalism or the global ecosystem? Do indeed we need to ascribe precedence in relations between structures? Moreover, since structures are consistently influenced by agents, they are always in flux and should not be regarded as fixed entities like an engineering jig, with precise, limited and determining qualities. The nature of a structure will always be contested because even those at the less abstract end of the continuum, such as states, cannot be reduced to the sum of their visible parts, such as institutions.

If one follows this line of thought the principal intellectual problems which arise in relation to structures are first their identification, second their interrelations (possibly hierarchical) and lastly their relations with agents. *Agents* for their part are the entities capable of decisions and actions in any given context. They may be single individuals or collectives, and they may be characterized by conscious intentions or by patterns of behaviour which at least in part are not strategic – for example, the European Court of Justice's tendency over a long period to favour integrationism within the EU. However the term *actors* is, in my view, preferable to that of 'agents' given the latter's sense in English of subordination to a higher authority (an 'agent of X or Y') and its common use in the context of the 'principal–agent' problem (where we have to decide who is the puppet and who the puppet-master). Thus despite the usefulness of the noun 'agency' to describe action-ness, and the ubiquity of the 'agency–structure debate' in the academic literature, 'actor' will be the term preferred here for autonomous and purposive entities, with 'agents' used to refer to the bureaucratic entities at least nominally under the control of the primary political actors. This also fits with the common usage of 'states and other actors', in both the academic world and that of practical international politics.

Although the focus here is not on epistemology or ontology, the account given above of the agency–structure question needs some brief contextualising. In general, I follow the arguments made by both Barry Buzan (1995) and Walter Carlsnaes (1992, 1994, 2002) in their comments on structure and agency to the effect that a clear distinction must be made between units of analysis and modes of explanation (Hollis and Smith, 1992; Wendt, 1992). This the preceding 'levels of analysis' model did not do, as such (Waltz, 1959; Singer, 1961). Individuals, states and the international system are units of analysis, to be described in their own terms; yet they do not in themselves automatically represent explanations of outcomes. Conversely, it is unlikely that explanations of major political phenomena, including these units, will be found at one level alone. Rather, they should be looked for in sources such as structures, processes and interactions between units/actors. It is then important to bear in mind four fundamental distinctions, between:

- *Units and actors*. Units are useful ways in which we divide the world up conceptually, so as to calibrate space and time. They may include periods such as the 'short twentieth century', or the component parts of a system, such as the international economy. They will often be contestable. Actors, by contrast, are entities capable of the exercise of independent will and decision-making, and are relatively easy to identify. Actors can always be said to be units, but not all units are actors.
- *Actors and structures*, each of which may exist in many forms and with varying capacities for constituting the other.
- *Positivism and constructivism*, as epistemological starting-points for understanding foreign policy; the one seeing 'facts' as things that scientific observation can establish, the other stressing that accounts of the world are shaped by subjective preferences – and often power – so that if truth is possible at all it lies only in understanding how different versions of events have come to be produced and how they compete.
- *Voluntarism and determinism* – that is, the notion of free will for sentient beings on the one hand, and the idea that choice is illusory, or at best highly constrained, given the power of historical forces, on the other.

It is worth giving a basic statement of the assumptions which the present book makes on these important issues. As suggested above, the 'levels of analysis' approach will no longer do except in the basic sense of alerting newcomers to the different perspectives that may be obtained by looking at things from the viewpoints of the individual, the state and the international system as a whole. Ultimately it is not clear whether this 'analysis' can go further to deliver an explanation of causation or an understanding of meaning – let alone prescriptions for change. Accordingly it must be supplemented by the distinction between actors and structures, with some of the latter being simultaneously actors within a wider structure (such as a foreign ministry, which is an important structure to its employees but also with certain actor-like qualities of its own). Foreign policy-making is a complex process of interaction between many actors, differentially embedded in a wide range of different structures. Their interaction is a dynamic process, leading to the constant evolution of both actors and structures. This conceptualization is known as the 'strategic-relational approach' (Brighi, 2013, pp. 11–16).

In terms of how we might know anything about actors and structures, the approach here takes something from positivism, but it is not positivist. Neither, however, is it relativist, since it asserts that useful empirical knowledge is possible, on the basis of professional scholarship and a constantly critical attitude towards sources – certainly on subjects like behaviour in a major diplomatic confrontation, but even on more diffuse questions like national identity. It accepts that some of the painstaking work in foreign policy analysis which came out of the behavioural stable on crises, misperceptions and bureaucratic politics is both suggestive and systematic. On the other hand, the belief that political and social behaviour can be reduced to law-like statements, made on the basis of value-free observations of 'classes' of phenomena, is taken to be axiomatically mistaken. Human beings respond to any observation made about them and the complexity of their actions goes far beyond that which can be captured by the correlation of variables or a stimulus–response model. The greater the generalization, therefore, the blander it will be.

On the issue of freedom versus determinism I examine foreign policy and its dilemmas from a broadly pluralist position. Human beings are seen as always having choices, even if in many circumstances the dice are heavily loaded in one direction or another. Individuals make a difference because they are the original source of intentions. But they do not work in a vacuum; the pattern of their institutional and political environment inevitably shapes how they see the world. Moreover, at the level of the international system they are rarely prominent, and where they do count – as with the UN Secretary-General – they are constrained by their very visibility. Here agency is multiple and various, with states still enjoying a preponderant influence over the means of political mobilization. Pluralism exists in the sense that the system is not highly determined; spaces for action open up often and unpredictably. It is then a question of who is willing and able to occupy these spaces and on whose behalf decisions are taken. The most powerful states try to assert leadership, but even they find it difficult to shift the contours of the system, as was evident with the United States' 'war on terrorism' after the attacks of 11 September 2001 (Hurrell, 2007, pp. 280–3). Indeed, Al Qaeda has arguably done more to change the character of international politics over the last two decades than has the world's only superpower.

On epistemological and methodological issues, I do not accept the well-known position of Martin Hollis and Steve Smith (1990) not only that there are always 'two stories to tell in International Relations' – that is, *understanding* why actors take the positions they do, and *explaining* their outputs – but that these two accounts cannot be reconciled. If this were true, a great deal of illuminating historical scholarship would never have been possible. Technically, such work is not scientific explanation in the sense of establishing if–then propositions, but the past thirty years have shown that significant versions of the latter rarely turn out to be possible even using scientific methods. By contrast good history or traditional political science 'explains' in the sense of highlighting key factors and the nature of their interplay on the basis of evidence and analysis that a critical reader finds convincing – that is, they survive the test of the intellectual market.[10] Furthermore, 'understanding' is not just a matter of reconstructing the world view of actors themselves – one of the limitations of the first classics of foreign policy analysis (Snyder, Bruck and Sapin, 1962, 2002). It also involves placing their perceptions in the contexts of the myriad pressures on decision-making, internal and external, and of historical change.

As with agency and structure, both explaining and understanding are necessary in foreign policy analysis. We need to account for the complex sources of behaviour sufficiently well so as to ground generalizations, and normative positions, in empirical knowledge. Like most phenomena in social science, foreign policy is both general and context-dependent. It is not sensible to limit our chances of doing justice to the different dimensions by limiting the approaches employed more than we have to. Our ontology should be wide-ranging (foreign policy involves many actors), our epistemology open-ended (there are so many ways of deriving wisdom in this area) and our methodologies diverse (middle-range theories, weak theory, history, discourse analysis can all contribute). This is what pluralism means in the practice of foreign policy analysis.

Politics All the Way Down

Policy-making involves an inherent tension between democracy and efficiency. In foreign policy, citizens have implicitly ranked efficiency – in the sense of effectiveness in protecting their collective interests – higher than democracy, only taking a keen interest when crises loom or when their governments appear palpably incompetent. Yet political argument over foreign policy is now taking place with increasing frequency, and not just at times of crisis. It occurs in the public realm, involving interest-groups, occasional public demonstrations and the whole range of information media, as well as on the stage of formal parliamentary debate. But it also occurs inside government, between ministers at the highest level and between competing teams of ministers and officials in what we know as 'bureaucratic politics'. The impact of these various forms of domestic input is covered extensively in the remainder of this book, particularly Chapters 3, 4, 9 and 10.

Yet for the most part the politics of foreign policy takes place between the plethora of actors on the international stage. It occurs between partners within alliances, at the regional level among neighbours, and globally in many bilateral and multilateral contexts. While the issues which provoke domestic complications are unpredictable, rational analysis will generally give a state a good idea of how others will react to any given initiative. For in the short run at least most states are self-interested but cautious – when they are not, as with Argentina's assumption in 1982 that the United Kingdom would reluctantly accept an invasion of the Falkland Islands, the consequences are dramatic. The majority of issues do not entail a risk of war. But anything which is significant for country X is likely to be significant for at least some others, because foreign policy cannot take place in a vacuum. Expressing a preference then automatically gives leverage to any third party whose cooperation might be needed to realize that preference (March and Olsen, 1998). It is the existence of multiple points of such leverage which creates the endless contests and uncertainties of international politics.

The ensuing turbulence means that there will be varying expectations of what a successful foreign policy entails among both elites and publics. The concept of expectations can help us here by enabling us to distinguish the competing expectations of foreign policy which exist within societies, and indeed within governments themselves, despite the still common tendency to regard it as a technical area usually producing a cross-party consensus. What follows is a brief attempt to identify the principal expectations which exist in this key area of public policy, and how each generates competing views over values and priorities. They arise from the brokering functions of states in international politics, between the expressed wishes of the domestic constituency, the demands of the external milieu and the basic needs of the state *qua* state. Listing them enables us to see how thoroughly foreign policy is becoming politicized.

There are seven main expectations of foreign policy. While they vary in their detail over time and place, they are commonly held in all but the most unstable or inward-looking states. They are listed in ascending order, from the most particular to the most general. The political dimension is distinctively visible in each one.

- *The maintenance of territorial integrity and social peace against external aggression*: the possibility of aggression makes this in principle the most weighty of the expectations held of foreign policy, although the fear of war can repress debate on the key issues until it is too late, as with Chamberlain's and then Roosevelt's tip-toeing around the issue of Nazi Germany in the late 1930s. When crisis does arise foreign policy may then be more about mobilising national unity than ventilating the hard choices which need to be faced. By contrast, challenges to territorial integrity from inside, such as demands for regional autonomy, if connected to outside pressures, can become the most inflammatory issues of all, with decision-makers liable to see 'enemies' within as well as without. Russia's ruthless approach to Chechnya is a striking example.

- *Advancing prosperity*: despite the advance of monetarism and privatization most leaders accept that the promotion of their country's economic wellbeing requires action on their part and cooperation with other governments. Thus foreign economic policy is of critical importance even to those of a laissez-faire disposition. It is a highly political activity, including trade promotion, tariff negotiations and monetary diplomacy. Less visible are the benefits deriving from public–private cooperation over export credits, aid programmes and defence spending. In these contexts it is an important function of foreign policy to ensure that state resources are not exploited by vested interests, and that a clear sense of public good prevails.

- *Protecting citizens abroad*: foreign policy has both to work towards achieving the general conditions in which citizens can work or holiday securely abroad, and to help them when they get into trouble. This can range from prison sentences for the possession of drugs, through the exploitation of migrant labour to the taking of hostages by a hostile government or terrorist group. Much of this is a matter of routine diplomacy, but it can suddenly blow up into high politics, as in the famous Don Pacifico case of 1851, when the British government used the problems of one of its (Jewish) citizens in Greece to insist on its right to protect Britons abroad. Palmerston's dispatch of the fleet to Piraeus produced in the House of Commons 'a deeply felt and closely argued debate about the direction and ethics of [foreign] policy' (Hurd, 2010, p. 95).

- *Projecting identity abroad*: national identity is projected abroad in many ways, not just through government action. Nonetheless, countries cannot have good mutual relations without such things as state visits and subsidized exchanges, while intelligently run radio and television stations or cultural institutes can overcome the natural suspicion of propaganda – and even promote business. Yet this too can easily become political, as when governments tread on domestic sensibilities over historical memory by seeking to improve relations with former enemies. Korean and Chinese sensitivities over Japan are a case in point.

- *Making decisions on interventions abroad*: this is partly a matter of judgement on security needs – is the threat of military action necessary to protect energy supplies or to stop a distant state from acquiring nuclear weapons? – and partly a matter of the moral calculus required to decide whose suffering deserves a particular humanitarian commitment. On both counts the contemporary tendency is towards multilateral action legitimized by international law, but the bottom line has to be a national decision about entry into a coalition in the first place, or the possibilities of going it alone if one does not materialize. Either way the issue of public support is crucial, and the likelihood of domestic contestation high.

- *Fostering a stable international order*: extreme nationalists will not have this expectation, but otherwise most states accept that a high degree of predictability is in their interests. A more orderly, rules-based, global system means that threats will arrive less often, while goals which can only be achieved through cooperation (such as nuclear non-proliferation) become the subject of sustained diplomacy. Such 'milieu goals' are, of course, no less politicized than narrower national concerns pursued competitively (Wolfers, 1962).

- *Protecting the global commons*: this has become a central foreign policy issue for many states over the last three decades, whatever their position on global warming, or their geographical position. The importance of halting environmental degradation and of responding to climatic instability has been recognized formally in countless international fora (Giddens, 2011). Yet these goals can only be achieved by both universal agreement and national action, both of which have become intensely politicized. Only governments negotiating in multilateral fora can produce agreements on the things which go beyond the reach of individual states, such as CFC emissions or over-fishing. Treaties are painfully reached and may represent only lowest-common-denominator outcomes, but the alternative, of no agreement and trusting to the private decisions of citizens and businesses, is hardly more promising. While popular support for recycling or moving away from a carbon-fuel economy is indispensable, it will have no substantive effect until governments take the lead.

These seven issue areas make it clear that the practice of foreign policy is run through with competing political outlooks, interests and values. In democracies decision-makers face severe challenges in managing the interplay of domestic and international forces while keeping unrealistic expectations in check. They also have to accede to varying degrees to the requirements of constitutional process. Some of the debate that all this generates is about interpreting the particular interests of the country concerned, and some about joining practical outcomes to underlying principles. Even among apparently 'like-minded' states this can lead to considerable differences. Across the variety of the whole UN membership, the contrasts are even greater.

The Diversity of States

This chapter has tried to show that there is much more to foreign policy as an activity than meets the eye, by examining a number of different dimensions: its basic purposes and constituencies; the role of the state; the relationship of the domestic to the foreign; the theoretical problem of agency in relation to structures; and the way in which foreign policy raises political dilemmas at so many different levels. All this has involved a good deal of generalization. Yet the issue is less the fact of generalization than its extent. Each category that we use in social science inherently involves a general statement, whether macro as with types of international system, or micro as when sickness impacts on the performance of leaders. It is through the process of scrutinising such statements and testing them with evidence that we get as near to the 'truth' as we can.

When it comes to generalising about foreign policy the tendency is to break things down on the basis of states' different types, meaning particular constellations of internal and external characteristics: of position, size, borders and physical patrimony on the one hand, and political system, culture and level of development on the other. Such clusters are often used to generate statements about differentiated behaviour, for example on the foreign policies of small or micro states, of developing countries and of rising powers (Hey, 2003; Mohamed, 2002; East and Robertson, 2004; Narlikar, 2010). The 'democratic peace' debate is the most notable site of generalizations, with its much debated hypotheses about the peaceful nature of democratic foreign policy, but there has also been speculation about the external performance of interdependent 'postmodern states', and of the 'failing states' seen by many as the principal source of disorder in the international system (Cooper, 1996; Litwak, 2000; Foreign Policy, 2010; A. Roberts, 2015).[11]

These ways of breaking down the category of state foreign policies are suggestive. But as typologies focusing on a single major descriptor they are too reductionist and thus unable to probe into the nature of the interplay between inside and outside, between decision-making and its environments. This book aims to reveal the dialectical relationships between shared and distinctive experiences, between the common dilemma and the specific response. In order to do this we need an understanding of the concentric circles of foreign policy-making in action, beginning with those at the centre who hold formal responsibility for outcomes.

Notes

1   The classical origins of the modern doctrine of sovereignty are well traced
    in d'Entrèves (1967), while Hinsley (1967, pp. 158–235) explains its inter-
    national ramifications.
2   For an analysis of the genesis of nationalism in the context of international
    relations, see Anthony Smith (1998, pp. 70–96) and Mayall (1990).
3   The prebendal state is a notion coined by Richard Joseph, adapting the
    ideas of Max Weber (Jackson, 1993, pp. 13–31).
4   Max Weber is the founder of this conception of the state. See, for example,
    his 'Politics as a Vocation' (Gerth and Wright Mills, 1948, pp. 80–2, 95).
5   Articles 4 and 18 of the UN Charter provide for admission of a state by a
    two-thirds vote in the General Assembly, on the recommendation of the
    Security Council (where the veto would apply). Recognition of a new
    regime in any given state is a more piecemeal matter, and depends on bilat-
    eral relations as well as the UN.
6   The issues of the levels and nature of democracy in international politics
    have some similarities to the varying meanings of justice, explored by
    Hedley Bull (1977, pp. 74–94) in his discussion of 'order versus justice in
    world politics'.
7   Moravcsik (2005) argues that the current mechanisms through which
    national leaders meet in the European Councils to agree compromises
    represent a perfectly acceptable level of democratic accountability.
    Although he does not tend to term the strategies which states use in these
    sessions 'foreign policy', it amounts to the same thing.
8   Before IR writers like James Rosenau, historians such as Fritz Fischer and
    Pierre Renouvin were emphasising the domestic factor from the 1950s,
    following in the footsteps of Eckart Kehr's pioneering study (1930) of
    German naval policy before the First World War. Gordon Craig brought
    this back into prominence more than forty years later (Kehr, 1977).
9   'Meta-ontology' because the debate largely focused on philosophical issues
    such as the nature of 'free' agency without confronting 'the first-order'
    questions of what entities, actors and units to admit of in world politics.
    Wendt (1991, 1999) stresses the need to get down to substantive or first-
    order argument.
10 This is obviously close to the position of Karl Popper, who argued that
    theories should be falsified empirically, yet without denying the sociologi-
    cal factors which mean that the 'intellectual market' is coloured by its time
    – a view arising from the work of Thomas Kuhn. For the debate between
    the two see Lakatos and Musgrave (1970).
11 On the democratic peace debate see Chapter 9.

Further Reading

Campbell, David, 1998. *Writing Security: United States Foreign Policy and the*

Politics of Identity. Revised edition. Campbell's monograph is a pioneering and influential theory of the importance of foreign policy to identity, and vice versa.

Charillon, Frédéric, ed., 2002. *Politique Étrangère: Nouveaux Regards*. The literature of FPA is predominantly Anglophone; these reflections from a mix of French and international scholars are a useful reminder of the insights to be found elsewhere.

George, Alexander, 2006. *On Foreign Policy*. This extended essay comprises the all-too-brief last thoughts from one of the United States' leading thinkers about foreign policy.

Lobell, Steven E., Ripsman, Norrin M. and Taliaferro, Jeffrey W., eds, 2009. *Neoclassical Realism, the State, and Foreign Policy*. This is a good collection of essays, theoretical and empirical, bringing realism and foreign policy back together after the neorealist dead end.

Snyder, Richard, Bruck, H. W. and Sapin, Burton, 2002. *Foreign Policy Decision-Making (Revisited)*. One of the first books to address the problem of decision-making in foreign policy (in 1962) is re-issued with two useful new chapters, one by Valerie M. Hudson and one by Derek H. Chollet and James M. Goldgeier.

Sørensen, Georg, 2001. *Changes in Statehood: The Transformation of International Relations*. Although this text is not explicitly about foreign policy, it directly addresses the interconnections between domestic and international politics.

Chapter 3

The Actors: Taking Responsibility

Decision-making is the starting point if we wish to understand the dilemmas of acting in the international system. Agency means individual human beings taking decisions and implementing them on behalf of entities which possess varying degrees of coherence, organization and power. Any analysis of this activity needs to focus first on the political dimension, then on the associated bureaucracies, which provide so much of the continuity and expertise which make action meaningful, and third on the problem of rationality – or the capacity to pursue objectives in a logical manner in the particularly inchoate environment of international relations. Finally, foreign policy actions cannot be understood without an appreciation of the phase of implementation, given that outcomes are so often markedly different from original intentions. This chapter and the three which follow tackle these aspects of agency in sequence, beginning with the most visible level, that of political leadership.

At the level of the international system, states or other entities can perfectly well be treated as unified actors. Although shorthand, it still makes sense to say that 'Iraq invaded Kuwait', or 'Germany will not relax its policy on inflation'. That is, after the processes of decision-making appropriate to the country concerned, the state took up a position which was acknowledged as a move by other states, which then reacted in their turn. Tracing these various moves gives us the 'events' of international politics.

Realists believe that the information thus generated about patterns of manoeuvring can explain a good deal of international relations, including the behaviour of individual states. That is not the position of foreign policy analysis, which is premised on the belief that we can only fully understand what states do by looking at two further interactions: between their international position and their domestic context, and between the problem being faced and the nature of the decision-making process employed to handle it. What is more states now share the international stage with other significant actors, most of which seek to sidestep governments and sometimes to undermine them. It soon becomes necessary when focusing on an event or a particular actor's behaviour to break down the action into its various levels and components. Was Iraq's decision to invade Iran in 1980 Saddam Hussein's alone? If it was, did he nonetheless have the broad support of his people? What was the thinking behind the calculations that must have gone on inside the Iraqi military establishment? Similarly, in the case of Germany, how far is policy on the euro the product of cross-party consensus and how far is it the product of Chancellor Angela Merkel's strong leadership? What are the positions of the various ministries concerned with economic policy and relations with EU partners? The answers to such questions need country specialists to provide their expertise, but their formulation in the first place derives from the body of theory and analysis which has been built up through the study of decision-making, and a determination to look behind formal role-descriptions and official rhetoric.

It is politicians who carry the can at home and abroad for decisions in foreign policy although their precise titles and locations in the political structure vary a great deal according to the type of state or other actor they represent. The heads of multinational corporations, or financiers such as George Soros, may resemble more the strategic players of game theory, monitoring a limited number of variables, in contrast to politicians who have to juggle a vast range of concerns. But they share the high profile and vulnerability when things go badly wrong, unlike the armies of bureaucrats behind the scenes. Thus Tony Hayward, the CEO of British Petroleum found himself conducting difficult negotiations with the federal government in Washington after the Deepwater Horizon oil spill in the Gulf of Mexico in 2010, and soon had to resign. When things go wrong for states the consequences for them can be even more severe, so it is important to understand how roles and responsibilities are delineated at the highest levels. We start with individuals, move on to the inner group designated here 'the foreign policy executive', and end with an analysis of the workings of cabinets and their equivalents.

Power at the Top

In most states the formal office-holders dealing with foreign policy questions are limited in number, although the growing scope of external policy is bringing more people into play. The nominal chief of foreign policy operations in most states is the foreign minister, whatever his or her precise title (for example, 'secretary of state' in Washington, DC). Foreign ministers are still of considerable importance by virtue of being the main reference point for outsiders to deal with but they struggle to keep control of their vast portfolio, increasingly invaded as it is by other ministries, while they are always vulnerable to interference from their head of government. This relationship is discussed in the next section; for the moment it is enough to stress that heads of government, whether or not they initially intend it, are invariably drawn into spending a large proportion of their time on foreign affairs. Conversely, outsiders rarely assume that a foreign minister has full powers, and often try to open a direct channel to the head of government. A further potential confusion is created by the fact that some heads of government are also heads of state (as in France, the United States and South Africa), and therefore have ceremonial as well as executive functions which place them on a higher level of protocol, with more weight but less accessibility than a simple head of government.[1]

In most states the functions are separated between two individuals. The separate head of state, whether dynastic monarch or elected personality, has some function in foreign relations, but is much less of a figure than the chief executive. Most informed outsiders, for example, would know that in 2015 Matteo Renzi was the prime minister of Italy. Only a small proportion would also be able to identify Sergio Mattarella as the Italian president. Matterella is new to the job, but his predecessor Giorgio Napoletano, through symbolising the state and being above factional politics, had real influence in unblocking internal crises and in improving relations with partner countries. Richard von Weizsäcker was similarly successful in this role for the Federal Republic of Germany between 1984 and 1994, embodying its democratic and pacific values and making it clear that his compatriots accepted responsibility for their past (Mény, 1993; Zelikow and Rice, 1997). In Britain Queen Elizabeth II has been a critical and subtle player in preserving good relations with the Commonwealth in the post-colonial period.

The other members of the political foreign policy elite vary more widely from country to country. Where there is some form of cabinet government the foreign minister will have to keep all colleagues informed on the main lines of policy and get their active support on an issue of high significance. Some will be continually involved in aspects of external relations by virtue of their own responsibilities (such as agriculture ministers inside the EU) and their actions will need coordinating, both with each other and with the foreign ministry. In general more and more departmental ministers are discovering an external dimension to their job, but it would be wrong to suggest that many of them make it their priority or indeed that they have an international conception of public policy. Special knowledge still counts. The key colleagues for a foreign minister will normally be those responsible for defence, economics and trade, in that order.

A few other key individuals should be included in any description of the top office-holders in the area of foreign policy. The chief of the foreign intelligence service might be a visible figure but is more likely to operate in the shadows. Either way he (only exceptionally she) will be answerable to the head of government and/or the foreign minister, and will be a central figure in any high-level discussions on policy. Similarly the chairman of the chiefs of staff of the armed services, on one definition strictly a bureaucrat, is likely to have permanent and direct access to the highest circles of foreign policy-making, particularly where war is a possible outcome. In a completely different vein, the chair of the parliamentary foreign affairs committee, where one exists, may be drawn into top-level consultations if the need for a wider political consensus is particularly strong. Such a figure can also be used as a public mouthpiece, with a useful ambiguity as to authenticity built in. Where there is actually a formal division of power on foreign policy as in the United States, the key chairs and senators are at times parallel foreign policy-makers to the president, and have to be courted assiduously by the White House so as to avoid embarrassing divisions in relations with other states – which learn quickly how to exploit any mixed messages.

In the case of transnational enterprises the responsibility for international strategy is less clear. Normally the chief executive of a multinational company will be party to any decisions with political implications – that is, those involving deals with governments. He or she may have a higher international profile than most politicians, even if few attain the fame of Steve Jobs or Bill Gates. There may also be a director or vice president with special responsibility for an international division, only loosely responsible to shareholders (I. Clarke, 2013, pp. 38–60). As Stopford (1996) says, these people need to be 'diplomats' in protecting their interests globally. Globalization has involved much integration of transnational production and communication networks, although 'the emergence of the truly "placeless" global corporations is still a long way off' (Howells and Wood, 1993, p. 153). For an international pressure group or political party the situation is different. The former run on tight budgets and cannot afford to have many executive officers flying the world on diplomatic business, even if the need for negotiations with governments is more pressing than it is for companies. In any case they tend to prize the collective nature of their decision-making. Nonetheless, the two or three individuals at the top of organizations like Amnesty International become well-known and engage in much para-diplomacy (Power, 2001).

Political entities are usually more directly imitative of state structures, because they wish ultimately to acquire them. Thus Oliver Tambo was the foreign secretary in exile of the African National Congress (ANC) for all the time that its president, Nelson Mandela, was in prison, and he ran an extremely effective international policy – albeit reliant on the political and logistical support of sympathetic governments (Mandela, 1995, pp. 347, 731). Similarly the Palestine Liberation Organization (PLO) ran a foreign policy in all but name for many years under the leadership of

Yasser Arafat. His successor, Mahmoud Abbas, has sought and received more international recognition as a legitimate head of government, but having less charisma, as well as a chronically divided political base, he has been less effective in international diplomacy. Liberation movements do not survive, however, by relying on one man for their strategy. They rest on tight-knit cells operating in a disciplined and collective way – as in Gaza where Hamas could not otherwise have survived Israel's various assaults on its personnel. In contrast Osama bin Laden's Al Qaeda network skilfully exploited its leader's wealth and charisma while remaining diffuse and horizontal in structure. Since bin Laden's death in 2011, Al Qaeda has lost ground to other jihadist movements such as Daesh, but it remains an icon for those determined to use terrorism against Western targets.

The issue of who holds formal office is not the trivial question that it might seem to those searching for 'the powers behind the throne'. Although it is crucial to distinguish between formal and real power, and never to assume that decisions are made as the official flow charts have it, those who occupy positions of responsibility have a great deal of potential influence. In foreign policy they dispose of the resources of the state, and – because external policy requires relatively little legislation – they operate within a fairly unstructured institutional environment. This enables a relatively small group to exert leadership in foreign policy and to personify the state in their actions. At this level individuals have considerable scope to influence events. How they do so depends, as we shall see, on a mix of factors: the personal and political qualities of the personalities involved, the nature of the issue being decided and the political structures of the state in question.

The Foreign Policy Executive

In most political systems any important area of policy will be supervized by a combination of the head of government, by definition free of any particular portfolio, and the departmental minister, the specialist. This is particularly the case with foreign policy, where the international expectations of head-of-government involvement are high and where it is difficult for others to develop an equivalent level of expertise. On the other hand, some of what goes to make up foreign policy in a developed state is handled by economic ministers who themselves participate directly in international meetings on finance or trade and therefore possess a knowledge which the foreign ministry generalist will struggle to match. In so far as foreign policy, therefore, seeks to integrate the various strands of external relations, it will be conducted by what can be termed a 'foreign policy executive', consisting in the first instance of the head of government and the foreign minister, but often widened according to the issue-area to include defence, finance, economics, trade and development ministers. Those responsible for internal security, and for legal matters, are also increasingly involved. There may well be others, close to the head of government, whose job is to help on matters of overall strategy. In one-party states the party secretary and/or chief ideologist will have central roles (Hill, 1991, pp. xviii, 224–47).

The reason why foreign policy, even on a wide definition, is particularly susceptible to being made by an inner executive, is twofold: on the one hand most politicians spend much time looking over their shoulders to their domestic base, and do not wish to 'waste' time on cultivating foreign contacts from which there might be little return. On the other hand, the international environment still presents a long and steep learning-curve for any politician wishing to participate. Consequently, when that curve has been surmounted, ministers are usually on the circuit for life, since their hard-won expertise is valued both at home and in the various intergovernmental organizations (IGOs) and international non-governmental organizations (INGOs) where openings can be found – witness the careers of Mikhail Gorbachev, Javier Solana, Gareth Evans and Helen Clark.[2] Moreover, in foreign policy the number of unforeseen issues which arises is disproportionately high, giving the advantage in policy-making to those who hold the power of initiative and response. Foreign policy problems are also often relatively unstructured, in the sense that there is no obvious framework or timetable to govern them in contrast to domestic issues, often based on a manifesto commitment, expert report or parliamentary legislation. Once again this means that responsibility falls onto the shoulders of the small number of politicians with the special knowledge and flexibility to respond.

There is a degree of overlap between the kinds of issues I have described and the nature of crisis. But the argument is not that foreign policy is dominated by crises, or that crises tend to be run by a few individuals at the top. Foreign policy has a large proportion of humdrum business, so that for any given state crises are comparatively rare. Furthermore, even crisis does not automatically produce a highly personalized decision-making system – fear of catastrophe often leads to deliberate attempts to build consensus and to spread responsibility around a wider group than usual, even if purely operational matters have a restricted circulation list. John Kennedy's careful consultations during the Cuban Missile Crisis of 1962 and the Soviet vacillation over the Czech problem in the summer of 1968 are well-documented examples (Allison and Zelikow, 1999, pp. 113–14; K. Dawisha, 1984; Roberts and Windsor, 1969, pp. 62–78).

The point is, rather, that because even foreign policy issues tend to be fluid and unstructured they represent a blank canvas on which it is inherently difficult for a committee to work. Thus the foreign policy executive tends to take the initiative by default, through outlining proposals and then inviting responses from colleagues more on implementation than on fundamental directions. An autocratic political system exacerbates this tendency, but even in democracies the political structure usually makes foreign policy a special area, with maximum freedom for the inner elite.

On a minority of occasions a foreign policy issue will turn out to be highly structured, with a clear issue, documents on the table and a reasonably long time period for consideration. In these circumstances the foreign policy executive will either choose, or be forced, to allow wider participation from cabinet colleagues, or whatever the relevant political group might be. Examples of the kind of issue in question are treaty negotiations, such as the Anglo-Soviet negotiations over an alliance in the spring of 1939, when Prime Minister Neville Chamberlain was forced to make concession after concession to Cabinet members more eager to see an agreement than he was. This could happen because concrete proposals were being taken line by line by a Cabinet committee, and the full Cabinet was able to monitor progress with some precision. It was also perceived by most ministers to be an issue of the highest importance (Hill, 1991, pp. 48–84).

A similar issue would be the application of any state to join the EU. This is not something that can be rushed through. The ten states which entered in 2004 had a huge range of legislative issues to consider in detail, because the question of accession penetrates deep into domestic society. No foreign policy executive could manage all this alone, or would be allowed to. Yet, on the EU side, enlargement policy was a classic case of a fluid, general and creative process in which leaders holding the initiative set the strategic direction (for a range of motives among the member state, some contradictory) and developed the policy rhetorically, with only the technical aspects of implementation given much thought (Cameron, 2012, pp. 87–94; Schimmelfennig, 2003; Schimmelfennig and Siedelmeier, 2005; W. Wallace, 1996, pp. 1–29). The broad-brush approach meant that some of the policy ramifications, such as the free movement of labour between rich and poor states) were not fully thought through. Even when the issues are clear from the start, some detailed negotiations, like those in the framework of the General Agreement on Tariffs and Trade (GATT) and the World Trade Organization are usually so intricate and long-drawn-out as to require specialized and continuous involvement – as with the diplomacy between Iran and the P5+1 over nuclear technology.[3] This creates a powerful tendency to delegate matters to the two or three individuals who have the confidence of the head of government.

Thus an individual personality, particularly in the two positions of head of government and foreign minister, but also in enlarged versions of the foreign policy executive, can have a significant influence on policy. The psychological dimension of such influence is considered later in this chapter, but first the need is to show how and to what extent such impact takes place.

The foreign policy executive gathers around it an inner coterie of trusted colleagues, security advisers and *éminences grises*, but unless strong personalities are at the helm little may happen. Prior knowledge of foreign affairs is not even necessary. Motivated leaders learn on the job, as with Margaret Thatcher as prime minister of Britain. For most of her first term of office (1979 to 1983) she was dependent on the expertise of her foreign secretary, Lord Carrington. After his departure over the Falklands invasion the prime minister quickly became one of the most active and notable figures in world diplomacy. Thatcher made her mark on Britain's foreign policy, most obviously in relations with the European Community (EC), but less predictably in reviving policy towards eastern Europe and in creating a special relationship with Mikhail Gorbachev. Leaders often hanker after a place in history, which today usually means world history.

For better or for worse, therefore, many heads of government end up by having a distinct impact on their country's foreign relations. This is true for both big and small states, as a list which includes Zhou Enlai, Mikhail Gorbachev, Lee Kuan Yew, Vaclav Havel and Hugo Chavez immediately demonstrates. It follows that changes in government can have a disruptive effect on foreign policy depending on whether a major personality is leaving or entering office. When François Mitterrand became president of France in May 1981 he arrived as a shop-soiled character who had been twice defeated – by de Gaulle and Giscard d'Estaing – and seemed desperate for power at any cost. By the time he left office in 1995 he and Helmut Kohl were the acknowledged architects of the new European Union. Likewise Harry Truman in 1945 seemed a provincial figure in comparison to his predecessor Franklin D. Roosevelt. Yet by 1949 Truman was the dominant influence over the West's role in the emerging Cold War.

The ability to lead is dependent on circumstances being ripe (Greenstein, 1987, pp. 40–62; 2000, p. 193). Conversely, some apparently influential figures are more significant for their ability to embody either the Zeitgeist or the wishes of a particular political movement than for a sharp personal contribution. Ronald Reagan epitomized this quality. His interest in detail was notoriously low, but he brilliantly articulated 'a cultural narrative of American myths' in the interest of restoring confidence and assertiveness to the foreign policy of the United States, particularly in relation to dealings with the Soviet Union (Gold, 1988). As the leader of Russia for most of the period since 2000 Vladimir Putin has seemed to outsiders to be an historical throwback with his brutally assertive realism, but in his own country he has approval ratings which have touched 80 per cent, notably over his forward foreign policy in Ukraine. For mass opinion he has come to symbolize his country's resistance to the forces which had seemed bent on humiliating Russia in the 1990s. And as such he has started to attract followers among admirers of populist nationalism in the West.

If heads of government have a natural tendency to get drawn into foreign policy and to become their own foreign minister, there is no iron law to say that they will end up in a dominant position. This is not just because the summits at which leaders are most visible are relatively infrequent or because not all possess the personal capacity for statesmanship. As important is the fact that some political cultures are more resistant to the cult of personality than others (the Scandinavian states have generally produced neither dramatic foreign policies nor charismatic leaders), and that many governments simply do not last long enough for an individual leader to make a major impact. Even if there is some continuity, and the will to be assertive, over-work, illness or political distractions can prove serious impediments. Georges Pompidou struggled as French president with the illness that was to kill him in 1974. The Soviet Union had sick or otherwise incapacitated leaders for perhaps 18 of its 67 years of history before Gorbachev (L'Etang, 1995). The arrival of Yeltsin in 1991 simply meant nine years more of the same given his problem with alcohol. In terms of mental strain, Richard Nixon, generally thought of as a foreign affairs expert and highly innovative in diplomacy, was reduced to virtual hysteria by the Watergate crisis. On one night at its height, he made 51 phone calls between 9 p.m. and 4 a.m. His image, and his position, thus soon became irretrievable. As for foreign ministers, they suffer notoriously from an excess of work and travel. Hillary Clinton boasted of having circled the globe eighteen times during her term of office as Secretary of State between 2009 and 2013, while at the time of writing the French foreign minister Laurent Fabius is attempting to beat this record. But as long as fifty years ago the British Cabinet was aware of the problem. It commissioned a report on the subject from former Prime Minister Lord Attlee, who concluded that the foreign secretary and the chancellor of the exchequer were over-burdened in comparison to all other ministers, including the premier.[4]

The Nixon-Kissinger period demonstrated the vital importance of the relationship between chief executive and foreign minister. Kissinger had been national security adviser in the first Nixon administration from 1969 to 1973, but this had undercut the State Department and he was more than willing to take on the position of secretary of state himself the second time round. The trust which he and Nixon shared was of vital importance in allowing these two assertive foreign affairs specialists to work together, and permitted Kissinger to run US foreign policy more or less effectively during Nixon's final crisis. The famous move towards China, from 1969 to 1971, was in the first instance Nixon's doing, but it only went forward so successfully because Kissinger worked with it, respecting the limits of his own position. While his diplomatic skills were indispensable he did not engage in the kind of competitive leaking that often damages US diplomacy.

We can identify three possible models of the relationship between head of government and foreign minister, each with its strengths and weaknesses depending on how the personalities involved behave and how they interact with events. Table 3.1 sets out the possibilities.

Politicians show surprisingly little self-awareness about this crucial relationship. Pairings arise more out of the need for political balance, or from the whim of the head of government (who possesses the crucial power to hire and fire) than from any attempt to meet the demands of the situation. In the first Blair administration in Britain, for example, Robin Cook agreed to become foreign secretary, but did so unwillingly, since this was the only post available at a suitable level of seniority. As a result he and the Prime Minister did not make as good a team as that between (initially) Blair and Gordon Brown, the chancellor of the exchequer, on economic affairs. In this case, the bases of agreement and a division of labour had been established in advance (Riddell, 2001, p. 37; Hennessy, 2000, pp. 476–523). Two strong personalities inside the foreign policy executive can cause serious problems. Anthony Eden regarded himself as more expert than the ageing Winston Churchill by the time the latter formed his second administration in 1951, and his reluctance to accept interference with his duties as foreign secretary caused personal tensions and errors of policy (Shlaim, Jones and Salisbury, 1977, pp. 20–2; Shuckburgh, 1986, pp. 28, 41, 74–8). Where personal differences reinforce political divisions, the clashes can be savage and burst into the public realm. This was the case with the relationship between Prime Minister Felipe González of Spain and his foreign minister, Fernando Morán (who eventually resigned). On one occasion Morán was so upset by a pro-NATO speech made by González in Germany that he left the official entourage and returned home (Preston and Smyth, 1984, pp. 76–8). Another significant example of a relationship brought near to breaking point came in the weeks following the 11 September 2001 terrorist attacks, when Israel's Prime Minister Ariel Sharon vetoed the

Table 3.1   Head of government–foreign minister relations: three models

1   **Equality:** trust, ability and matching reputations can create a strong team and continuity. The weakness is the danger of becoming detached from other colleagues and of appearing too dominant. Examples of effective partnerships: Truman and Marshall (US, 1947–9); Truman and Acheson (US, 1949–53); Nixon and Kissinger (US, 1973–4); Geisel and Azereido da Silveira (Brazil, 1974–9); Gorbachev and Shevardnadze (USSR, 1985–90); Howard and Downer (Australia, 1996–2007); Merkel and Steinmeier (Germany, 2005–9, and from 2013). Alternatively equal strength can lead to antagonism, as with Churchill and Eden (see above), Mitterrand and Cheysson in France (1981–3) or Kohl and Genscher (Federal Republic of Germany (FRG), 1982–92), where their different political parties exacerbated personal tensions (unlike the Merkel-Steinmeier couple in a Grand Coalition), or miscommunication, as with Galtieri and Costa Mendez (Argentina, 1981–2).[5]

2   **Subordinate foreign minister:** where a weak individual is appointed, often deliberately, it gives the head of government a free hand and turns the minister into a functionary. The weakness is the danger of an excessive concentration of power and an increasing arrogance of judgement. Examples: Eden and Selwyn Lloyd (UK, 1955–6); Khrushchev and Gromyko (USSR, 1957–64); Saddam Hussein and Tariq Aziz (Iraq, 1983–91); Blair and Beckett (UK, 2006–7), Putin and Lavrov (Russia, since 2004). Various heads of government have decided indeed to do the two jobs themselves, as with Nehru (India, 1947–64), Adenauer (Germany, 1951–5) and Berlusconi (Italy, for most of 2002). It used to be very common in new states, where resources were scarce (Boyce, 1977, p. 60).

3   **Assertive foreign minister:** this can work surprisingly well where there is a clear division of labour and excellent communications. It works badly where there is less a willingness to delegate on the part of the head of government than a lack of competence, and/or where political rivalry develops between the two figures. Examples of the former: Attlee and Bevin (UK, 1945–51); Reagan and Schultz (US, 1981–5). Of the latter: Eisenhower and Dulles (US, 1953–8); Chernenko and Gromyko (USSR, 1984–5); Kohl and Genscher (FRG, in the early part of Kohl's chancellorship, when his main concerns were domestic); Clinton and Warren Christopher (US, 1993–7); Julia Gillard and Kevin Rudd (Australia, 2010–12). In the US Barack Obama and Hillary Clinton began as rivals inside the Democratic Party, to the point where Clinton was dubious about becoming his secretary of state, but in the course of their work together (2009–13) they became a strong team, probably worth moving into the category of 'equality'.

meeting which Foreign Minister Shimon Peres had arranged with Yasser Arafat.

Foreign ministers are vulnerable to removal in the early phases of their tenure, in particular being made scapegoats for failure, as with Michèle Alliot-Marie who resigned in February 2011, when the events of the Arab Spring subjected her and the French government to ever greater embarrassment through their ties to the dictator Ben Ali in Tunisia. Maxim Litvinov was sacrificed readily by Stalin to his change of policy towards Germany in 1939; Alexander Haig paid the price in 1983 for pressing too hard and too quickly to run US foreign policy by himself. Antonio Samaras of Greece was dismissed by Prime Minister Mitsotakis for being excessively nationalist over the 'Macedonian' problem, only to respond by setting up his own political party to prolong the dispute (Tziampiris, 2000, pp. 109–35).

But the longer they survive the more vital their experience and contacts become. Litvinov's successor, Vyacheslav Molotov, survived for ten years (and returned for three more after Stalin's death), Gromyko for twenty-eight, and Hans-Dietrich Genscher for seventeen, becoming steadily more indispensable. Sheikh Yamani, as the oil minister of King Fahd of Saudi Arabia, performed much the same vital function of continuity for nearly two decades. The position of these individuals was strengthened by the fact that they had become important not just to their own state but to wider international networks. So long as they are not perceived at home as having 'gone native' (as Sir Geoffrey Howe was by Mrs Thatcher and her circle) then their embeddedness in international diplomatic networks makes them difficult to sack. If they resign on a point of principle, as Anthony Eden did from Chamberlain's government in 1938, as Cyrus Vance did over President Carter's approval of the hostage rescue mission in his absence in 1980 and as Ismail Fahmi did in protest against Egyptian President Sadat's personal decision to go to Jerusalem in 1977, the consequences can ultimately be very damaging (Middlemas, 1972, pp. 151–4; Rubin, 1985, pp. 194–6; Calvert, 1986, p. 96). Even Howe had his revenge: Thatcher was brought down by an undeclared and subtle coalition of opponents from her own Cabinet and other European leaders, all of whom saw her humiliating treatment of a respected foreign secretary as the last straw (Howe, 1994, pp. 581–676; Thatcher, 1993).

The Psychological Factor

Because personalities are central to top-level decision-making it follows that we need to pay attention to the psychological dimension. This has been explored extensively in the context of foreign policy at the level of both the individual leader and the group (Boulding, 1956; De Rivera, 1968; Jervis, 1976). Most of the attention has been directed towards the *cognitive* aspects of the human mind, that is the intellectual functions, as opposed to the *affective*, emotional, roots of behaviour. In part this has been a scientific reaction against the overwhelming influence of Freud and the (unprovable) notion of the dominant unconscious in the first half of the twentieth century. The work which Simon (1955), Braybrooke and Lindblom (1963), and Steinbruner (1974) drew on dealt largely with the less dramatic, but arguably more important for political behaviour, subject of information processing.

The wheel has now turned again, so that the emotional aspects of group solidarity and social identity are well to the fore (T. Hall, 2011). The strength of the psychological approach to foreign policy-making should be its ability fruitfully to combine insights into both cognitive and affective processes. This means going beyond the traditional but artificial separation between the rational and the emotional (Brecher, 1999; Bueno de Mesquita and McDermott, 2004). Emotion inevitably plays an important part in shaping attitudes and therefore decisions (Bleiker and Hutchison, 2008). Studying feelings and their interaction with thinking is the raison d'être of political psychology, which fed into IR through FPA and which has now progressed to study the interface between the neurological and the psychological. This in turn entails links to the natural sciences and to medicine (Stein, 2012). Multifaceted cognitive approaches, which look not only at how information is processed but also where choices come from, promise a more holistic approach but still risk a reductionist, physiological, approach to human emotion (Mintz, James and Walker, 2007).

Historians were aware of the psychological factor before FPA through an interest in mass behaviour and in particular in the spectre of totalitarianism. The first is of only indirect relevance here, dealing as it does with the psychology of crowd behaviour and of the hysteria evinced in *la grande peur* (the fear of a counter-revolution in rural France) in 1789 (Cobban, 1963, p. 157). Given some of the scenes in post-revolutionary Iran, or in the genocide and refugee crises of the African Great Lakes zone in the 1990s, to say nothing of the Nuremberg rallies, it would be imprudent to neglect this dimension of international relations.

More directly relevant to foreign policy action is Adorno's theory of the authoritarian personality (Adorno et al., 1950). This idea has generated considerable controversy, but some central propositions remain, namely that certain personalities display symptoms of personal and intellectual rigidity which get them to positions of political power but also damage their performance in office. They tend to be hierarchical (that is, dominant, but also uncritical of those above them), ethnocentric and unable to cope with ambiguity or nonconformity (Vertzberger, 1990, pp. 172–3). At its extreme this produces the paranoia of Stalin and Saddam, both of whom kept their colleagues in a state of physical fear, but even in more muted form it is likely to distort the decision-making process, as with Erdogan's increasing impatience with dissent in Turkey or Castro's determination to hold on to all the levers of power in Cuba even beyond the point at which illness had rendered him feeble.

A good many 'psychobiographies' have been produced on the lives of key statesmen and women, especially those of US presidents, but relatively few have attempted the task of trying to place personality in the context of the process of political causation, weighing up the respective impact of individual and contextual factors (J. D. Barber, 1972; Etheredge, 1978). One successful attempt was that by Alexander and Juliette George on the life of Woodrow Wilson, whose particular form of self-righteousness was rooted in his experiences with a caustic father and, later, as professor and then president at Princeton University. Wilson's character and idealism turned out to be of particular significance given the 'window' for change represented by the allied victory of 1918 and the subsequent peace (George and George, 1965; Kahler, 1999, pp. 285–6). Other attempts – of variable success – have been made to explain the lives of Martin Luther (Erikson, 1958), Adolf Hitler (Waite, 1998), Lyndon Johnson (Kearns, 1976), Richard Nixon (Volkan, Itzkowitz and Dod, 1997), Mao Zedong (Chang and Halliday, 2005) and Margaret Thatcher (Abse, 1989). The CIA has tried endlessly to make sense of foreign leaders in psychological terms, so as to have some chance of predicting the behaviour of enigmas like North Korea's Kim Jong-il (Carey, 2011; Post, 2008). Yet the key issue is less the peculiarities of a leader's personality than the political space which might or might not exist to allow these qualities to impact on events. In this respect Fred Greenstein provided an indispensable analysis of how an individual personality has more scope for impact on events in less stable regimes, and/or in more fluid circumstances than normal (Greenstein, 1967, 1975; Hermann, 1980).

Personality and context can sometimes be usefully connected by using the concept of charisma, formulated by Max Weber to refer to the magical, semi-religious appeal that some leaders can have, in the first place to their own followers, but sometimes, as with Nelson Mandela, much more widely. The leader requires first of all qualities of strength and emotional insight, and then needs to be right for the circumstances – in which there is usually a political and emotional vacuum to be filled. Henry Kissinger rather disparagingly referred to charisma as an instrument of primitive, Third World polities (perhaps because he did not possess it himself), while at times it is difficult to distinguish it from the characteristics of a mere icon, like Che Guevara. Margaret Thatcher, like Gorbachev, was charismatic internationally but not domestically, while John Kennedy's charisma was immeasurably enhanced by his violent death. Nasser and the Ayatollah Khomeini were compelling figures to their own people but somewhat perplexing elsewhere.

It is not necessary to have charisma to be an effective leader, let alone in foreign policy, but equally its possession will bestow advantages. De Gaulle, Sadat, Tony Blair and Hugo Chavez would all have been far less influential if they had come across in public like their greyer colleagues, or if circumstances had not helped them become versions of Hegel's 'world historical individuals'. Of course the use of charisma also risks high costs. When politicians let loose the power of mass emotion, they risk believing their own propaganda, subordinating rationality and alarming outsiders. Ahmadinejad and Netanyahu are examples from our own time. Peace, security and prosperity usually require less glamorous and more concrete methods, as the career of Angela Merkel perfectly illustrates. The natural product of her peaceful, staid society, she has used competence and ordinariness to project a kind of inverse charisma (Packer, 2014). It is often thought that coalition governments of the German type predispose to such behaviour, but this is not always true (Kaarbo, 2008, 2012). The behaviour of the parties and personalities which make them up is equally critical.

One of the richest areas of scholarship of foreign policy decision-making has been that relating to perception and misperception. There is not the space here to do justice to all the subtleties of the extensive literature, but certain key points must be made in order to clarify further the limits on rationality and to understand how leaders' understandings of foreign policy affect outcomes.

Any discussion of perception entails a set of contentious philosophical issues relating to the way we apprehend the world and the extent to which our subjective understandings of it vary. There is a common view, attributable to R. G. Collingwood, which holds that it is not possible to make legitimate statements about human behaviour except through a reconstruction of the views of the relevant individuals themselves: that is, through some form of historical enquiry (Dray, 1994, pp. 59–75; Reynolds, 1973). This is not incompatible with foreign policy analysis in principle, but it does rule out the kind of positivist approach taken by much of the American literature, which seeks to test 'if–then' hypotheses. Most commentators compromise by falling back on the notion of misperception, which does imply a 'reality' that an actor might not perceive 'correctly', but largely as a lever to open up particular historical problems, accepting that the concept is essentially contested and that generalization must be cautious. This is the approach taken here, on the assumption that there is a difference, however uncertain, between decision-makers' *psychological environment* (how they perceive the world) and their *operational environment* (events as they happen independent of any one person's perception) (Sprout and Sprout, 1962, pp. 122–35; 1965). I also follow Vertzberger (1990) when he concludes that 'a certain level of misperception is inevitable in every decision-making system'.

Decision-makers cannot avoid having *images* of others which will be as affected by their own cultural and political baggage as much as by the objective evidence. Images are clusters of perceptions which help us make sense of the world. Once established, they change relatively slowly, as with the two superpowers' images of each other during the Cold War. If an actor has no choice but to change an image overnight, it can be personally and politically catastrophic. After Neville Chamberlain was forced to acknowledge in September 1939 that his image of Hitler had been too benign, his self-assurance disintegrated. He fell from office a broken man within nine months, and died within the year.

All too often, images harden into *stereotypes*, losing the capacity to evolve and becoming ever more remote from the evidence. Lyndon Johnson held quasi-racist views of the North Vietnamese for which he and his soldiers were to pay dearly. The images held of continental Europeans by some British politicians have verged on the comic over the years, but they continue to have serious consequences. Any bilateral conflict is likely to produce symmetrical prejudices that are very difficult to dislodge. Stereotypes are brittle, inflexible simplifications, and any decision-making system of the slightest sophistication will have built-in mechanisms to challenge them. But if the politics of a country is built on 'Othering', or finding its own identity in contradistinction to feared and hated outsiders, then stereotypes will persist and compound the existing problems. The hysterically defensive policies of North Korea are evidence of both political and psychological insecurities in the top party cadres.

Misperceptions are the most common psychopathology affecting decision-making. Common as garden weeds, they can either be trivial or of devastating significance, depending on the context and the system's capacity for auto-correction. Even judgements about success and failure, on which turn key decisions, are highly subjective notions (Johnson and Tierney, 2006). Not all misperceptions are put properly to the test, given changing conditions and structural biases. However, those which involve explicit predictions – like the domino theory predicting the fall of all Southeast Asia to communism should South Vietnam go down – can be falsified by events.

The statement that 'decisions are taken in the psychological environment but implemented in the operational environment' is a simple but central insight. Decision-makers have no choice but to take continual bets on how other actors will behave and events unfold. By committing themselves to 'actions' in the external environment, they find out the accuracy of their assessments and the fate of their bets. The operational environment provides relentless feedback. Misperceptions are discovered to have been of various kinds: of *intentions*, where it is easy to exaggerate both enmity and friendship, and of *capabilities*, where an adversary tends to be excessively feared in peacetime and underestimated in time of war; *of both friends and enemies*; and *of those either too familiar or insufficiently known*. Action always teeters on the edge of incompetence because of the uncertain nature of the underlying perceptions. For example, the favourable judgements which the West made in the 1990s about Boris Yeltsin and, most crucially about his impact on the new Russian state, led eventually to severe consequences for both his country and for international order. The same was true of the overlong faith shown in Iraqi premier al-Maliki between 2006 and 2014, which encouraged the rise of Daesh and risked the collapse of the whole Iraqi state apparatus.

Misperceptions can arise from various sorts of problem, affective, cognitive and organizational, and often a combination of all three (Vertzberger, 1990, pp. 7–50; Jervis, 1976). A small number of cases will be cited here by way of illustration. At the affective level, decision-makers display the human tendency to bias, whether for or against another actor or country, to some degree. Personal relationships develop – 'sentimental alliances' – that while initially advantageous, can prove obstacles if policy tensions arise. Blair and George W. Bush, Berlusconi and Putin, have been recent cases in point. Conversely, some negative views prove almost impossible to shift, as with a whole generation of Israeli leaders against Yasser Arafat.

Another primarily emotional predisposition is the common tendency to over-emphasize self, so that understanding an adversary proves difficult. This can fall well short of full-blooded narcissism and still do damage. As Robert Kennedy pointed out in the aftermath of the Cuban missile crisis, the failure to put oneself in the other side's shoes (that is, empathize) is potentially the most fatal of errors. It will prove difficult to predict or understand their responses, and ultimately will prevent you from allowing them to save face in the event of a climb-down (R. Kennedy, 1969). It is natural, but lazy, to assume that others operate on the same assumptions as oneself – or if not, that they are people with whom one cannot do business. Realism has traditionally assumed that foreign policy-makers everywhere are on the same page, and those influenced by economics think that we are all 'pretty rational' (Little, 1988, pp. 53–4). But such views overlook cultural, geographical and historical differences, producing oversimplication. They can come spectacularly unstuck.

One source of misperception with both affective and cognitive elements is tracked thinking, or tunnel vision, meaning the difficulty human beings often have in relinquishing a view, or an assumption, once adopted. This is partly because we become emotionally attached to 'our' way of seeing things, which is in turn linked to our sense of identity, but also because when a pattern appears in information flows or the behaviour of other people, the human mind grasps at it as a way of reducing uncertainty. This may be reinforced by organizational SOPs. Thus, when the British diplomatic and intelligence services received warnings about an Argentine attack on the Falkland Islands in March 1982, they did not at first take them seriously because so many similar warnings had proved barren in the past (Freedman, 2005, pp. 158–62). Tracked thinking not only misses critical data; it also prevents creative initiatives. For example if the Indonesian elite could have relaxed their assumptions about East Timor being crucial to the security of their state they would have been able to move forward more rapidly on finding a solution to the insurgency in the ex-Portuguese colony.

A similar syndrome is the search for consistency that we all engage in. People feel uncomfortable with contradictions in their outlook and generally try to resolve them – often at the expense of understanding subtlety and complexity. When new information arrives which is at odds with existing views, it causes stress, famously labelled by Leon Festinger (1957) as 'cognitive dissonance'. This is a normal part of information-processing, to which there are three possible responses: (i) ignore the new data and continue with existing beliefs; (ii) rationalize the data so that it is incorporated into existing beliefs; or (iii) adapt the beliefs to take the new data into account. The path taken will depend on the individual and the extent to which the decision-making system is open or closed with regard to new developments. Robert Axelrod (1976) showed that decision-makers operate on the basis of 'cognitive maps' which are not easy to change, while Janis and Mann (1977, pp. 212–18) have stressed the way in which both individuals and systems are 'vigilant' in heading off uncomfortable insights. There is an affective component as well in that decision-makers also display what might be termed a 'peace of mind imperative', because the possibility of an upheaval in their overall belief system is simply too alarming to be allowed. This may be why so many politicians still resist the overwhelming scientific evidence of significant climate change.

A final source of misperception is the drive for cognitive economy, or simplicity. This is what Steinbruner (1974) has called the 'universal tendency to generalize'. Intellectually the desire for manageability is in conflict with the drive to understand complexity, but in a political environment the former is powerfully reinforced at the expense of the latter. Too much detail, or expertise, kills understanding in an overburdened decision-maker and leads to a hostility to academic 'hair-splitting' – which is possibly the opposite kind of mistake. Thus Churchill demanded, even of his high-powered scientific adviser Lord Cherwell, 'action this day' and conclusions only on one side of a sheet of paper. There is also a tendency, which can be seen at work in some of the other sources of misperception cited, towards an economy of values, that is, avoiding having to reconcile too many criteria at once, which would entail unmanageable trade-offs both in one's own mind and across the decisional system. This is probably the origin of the persistent preference for presidential 'doctrines' in US foreign policy from the Truman Doctrine up to Clinton and George W. Bush, although since the same tendency is not evident in most other countries one would have to say that a cultural factor and/or an imitative process is at work here (Kegley and Wittkopf, 2005, pp. 8–12).

When we come to the collective psychology of foreign policy decision-making, we arrive first at the theory of *groupthink*. This concept, introduced by Irving Janis in 1972, represents a major qualification of the theory of rational decision (1972; 1982; 1989). Lindblom suggests that whatever consensus a decision-making group can reach is in and of itself rational, but Janis analyses a series of 'fiascos' which he attributes to suboptimal small-group behaviour. He shows how consensus is often reached, not by the free discussion of a range of options but by a mix of fear, hierarchy, conformism and ignorance. Groupthink essentially consists in the tendency of groups to seek rapid internal agreement even at the expense of the merits of a problem, and then to stick to their consensus in the face of contradictory evidence. Criticisms of the orthodoxy, especially when that is associated with the group's leader, become exceptionally difficult, sometimes because there are actually some members ('mindguards') whose function, like party whips in the British House of Commons, is to discipline dissent.

Janis's theory of groupthink, with its accessible case-studies of some of the worst foul-ups in US foreign policy, attracted much attention and criticism ('t Hart, Stern and Sundelius, 1997). Accordingly it is a term which has passed into general usage, especially after the invasion of Iraq in 2003 when George Bush, Tony Blair and their advisers seemed bunkered down and impervious to debate. Yet there are a number of significant qualifications to the theory which need taking into account, namely: (i) not all groupthink causes serious problems; (ii) there are other causes of concurrence-seeking than groupthink; (iii) countervailing pressures such as bureaucratic politics exist to unsettle any comfortable consensus; (iv) small groups do not always display symptoms of groupthink and (v) small groups cannot be understood except in a wider institutional and political context.

Despite these caveats there is an important core of truthfulness to the approach. In particular, it is clear that if decision-makers wish to avoid *irrationality* they would be well advised to avoid an atmosphere of clubby back-scratching, or worse servility, in their top-level groups. A certain amount of built-in political and intellectual tension (too much will cause the opposite problems) is a necessary but not sufficient condition of effective policy-making. The siege mentality of Lyndon Johnson's 'Tuesday lunch' group made changes of direction difficult, just as the British Cabinet in March 1939 did not like to challenge the authority of the prime minister and foreign secretary, despite the executive's sudden and bizarre change of policy on Germany (Janis, 1972, pp. 102–6; Hill, 1991, pp. 19–46). Anyone who has sat in a committee or political group will recognize the groupthink insights.

This evidence from political psychology shows that foreign policy decision-making is subject to a wide range of psychological pressures at both individual and group levels. In the face of this it is simply not possible to maintain that decisions are made on the basis of classical rationality. Even bounded rationality presents severe problems, some of them normative. To act effectively means juggling a vast array of factors. Still, leaders do manage. They take decisions which do not always rebound on them, and they often give the impression of managing to take a serious, reflective approach to foreign policy. How is this possible?

Sometimes the answer is luck. The British diplomat Sir Robert Vansittart suffered from a visceral distrust of Germans which made him constantly demand action against Hitler. Despite being promoted out of harm's way he was eventually proved right in his policy prescription, but for the wrong reason (Dilks, 1971, pp. 27–9). On the other hand, even this might have been less luck than hunch, or intuition. It would be foolish to disregard the importance of this ability – which is essentially a mixture of judgement, experience, imagination and the capacity to empathize – in foreign policy, where no amount of efficiency is going to render everything knowable. Decision-makers at times have no choice but to accept the limits on rationality and to bring other qualities into play, some of them using the emotional rather than the calculating side of the brain.

Miriam Steiner (1983, p. 413) was one of the first to see that 'in a world with important nonrationalistic elements, true rationality requires that nonrationalistic capabilities and skills be appreciated and developed side by side with the rationalistic ones'. More recently prospect theory has focused on risk-taking, showing us how people take bigger risks when they think they are losing, than if they are facing the possibility of increasing their gains. In gambling terms, we chase our losses and preserve our gains. On the face of things this looks like something to be analysed rationally, using game theory, but in practice the definition of what might be a loss or a gain, and what matters to us in the first place, will depend on subjective judgements and other emotional factors – as every gambler knows (Kahneman, 2011, pp. 278–288).

Feeling and intuition are just as vital attributes of decision-makers as thinking and sense-based observation. Thus the impediments to rationality are not quite the obstacles they seem; some issues indeed cry out for lateral thinking, while concepts like judgement, leadership, empathy and charisma combine the intellectual and emotional sides of personality. Ultimately we need a combination of cognitive psychology with an understanding of creativity and intuition if we are to understand how foreign-policy decisions are – and should be – made (Ripley, 1993; Smith and May, 1980, p. 121).

Cabinets and Other Forms of Collective Leadership

Although it is sometimes easy to get the impression that the foreign policy executive, and key personalities, monopolize key decisions – an impression the individuals themselves often do little to discourage – the government as a whole rarely becomes completely detached from foreign affairs. In times of war and crisis the issues cannot be avoided; in times of peace the external dimension of economic policy broadens ministers' perspective.

Most leaders use what is conventionally called a 'cabinet', even if it sometimes bears little resemblance to the British original. In the Soviet bloc, and still in China, the key part of the hierarchy was the Communist Party, not the formal government, and the top decision-making unit was the Party's Politburo, not the state's Council of Ministers. Elsewhere other designations have been used – in Gaddafi's Libya it was the Revolutionary Command Council, and in Taliban Afghanistan it was the Interim Council of Ministers. The fact remains that all but the most tyrannical leaders need some forum in which to bring together senior colleagues, so as to share ideas and coordinate strategy. These may be generically referred to as cabinets.

On various occasions leaders will convene ad hoc inner cabinets to deal with particularly difficult problems, especially in war-time. Prime Minister Blair, famous for his preference for 'sofa government' was persuaded of the value of a war cabinet four weeks after the attacks on New York and Washington in 2001. In more routine times it can happen that an informal inner cabinet congeals around the foreign policy executive, dealing with what is perceived as the highest matters of state. This relates to what R. A. W. Rhodes has called the 'core executive' in a state – the 'final arbiters of conflict between different parts of the government machine' – key political figures and their advisers (Rhodes, 1995, pp. 11–37) But such arrangements are rarely fixed; formal arrangements always create problems as to who is in and who excluded from any given special committee. It is much better for the leadership, although not for cabinet accountability, to encourage a certain amount of uncertainty as to the extent of informal consultations in those private meetings which in any political system have the capacity to decide the outcome in the larger forum (Hennessy, 1986, 2007; Blondel and Müller-Rommel, 1997, p. 275).

The increasing complexity of external policy, and in particular the need to promote joined-up thinking between foreign policy and homeland security, has led to an increasing interest in the concept of a National Security Council (NSC), pioneered by the US in 1947 during the early days of Cold War nervousness (Stevens, 1989, pp. 55–62). The two European members of the UN Security Council, Britain and France, have both created NSCs during the last decade. These amount to more specialized gatherings than the cabinet, or council of ministers, and wider ones than the foreign policy executive, which retains the power of initiative in daily business.

To some extent the membership of such groupings is self-selecting. There is a relatively small number of senior politicians who can be trusted with intelligence information and who are familiar with international affairs. These people monopolize the key roles, a process which tends to be self-perpetuating. This was particularly evident in Italy between 1960 and 1992 when the same names appeared and reappeared as either prime minister or foreign minister. In the thirty-three governments formed during that period, Aldo Moro was prime minister five times and foreign minister nine. Mariano Rumor was prime minister five times and foreign secretary three; Giulio Andreotti was prime minister seven times and foreign minister five (Ferraris, 1996, pp. 517–21). In Britain the circulation of elites has been less sluggish, but the restriction on access to matters of state is formalized in the title of 'privy councillor', which is conferred for life on current and former ministers of the Crown and other 'distinguished subjects', including the leader of the Opposition. Councillors have to swear an oath of secrecy, which allows consultation on a highly confidential basis in 'the national interest'.[6] Michael Foot, leader of the Opposition in 1982, famously refused confidential information on these terms so that he would remain free to criticize the government over the Falklands War (Hastings and Jenkins, 1983, pp. 378–9). In France, because of the pre-eminence of the Elysée Palace in the Fifth Republic, it is even easier to draw certain key figures into decision-making informally. By the same token systematic coordination on important matters can be very hit-and-miss, with the prime minister and his party colleagues often out of the loop (Porch, 1996, pp. 465–7, 494–5). This failing eventually led to President Sarkozy creating the Defence and National Security Council in 2009, supported by a permanent secretariat.

Full cabinets remain in the background on routine foreign policy matters. They can easily become pro forma institutions, with the real work being left to a small number of relatively expert politicians, usually in a standing subcommittee. This is more due to the weight of documentation to be digested in a short time than to manipulation on the part of the foreign policy executive; most ministers are more concerned with not dropping the ball in their own area than with trespassing on those of others. Moreover, given that trade and monetary questions are even more arcane than security problems, it is an illusion to suppose that the changing nature of diplomacy has broadened the base of cabinet discussions on international questions. Instead, it has created a new problem of coordination, between different kinds of externally oriented responsibilities – for defence, finance, trade and development, and for those which cross the foreign/domestic divide such as security and migration. Foreign ministers, and heads of government, naturally assume this coordination role, but the atomization of the process is difficult to resist.

Despite the weight of specialization the cabinet, politburo or security council can never be taken for granted. It can come to life unexpectedly, and when united can threaten the political survival of the head of government. This was the case in Britain on 2 September 1939, when a rumbling Cabinet rebellion headed off Chamberlain and Halifax from further appeasement after Hitler's invasion of Poland, and over the Suez crisis of 1956, when the behaviour of Prime Minister Anthony Eden and Foreign Secretary Selwyn Lloyd in committing the United Kingdom to a disastrous invasion of Egypt without full consultation led to a quiet revolt that ousted Eden within six months and destroyed Lloyd's reputation. The fact that this can happen makes the foreign policy executive more cautious about overlooking colleagues than they might otherwise be. In the case of P. W. Botha, last president of apartheid South Africa, the reverse was true. The failure of Foreign Minister Pik Botha and heir-apparent F. W. de Klerk (the education minister!) to consult Botha over their decision to visit Kenneth Kuanda in Zambia forced him into open protest and resignation in August 1989.

This uncertainty does not amount to a real system of checks and balances. Two ministers resigned from the British Cabinet in August 1914, but it was not enough to stop the war proceeding. Stalin was in shock for three days after the German invasion of 22 June 1941, but no one dared replace him, and when he recovered his control became even more absolute (Braithwaite, 2006, pp. 58–92; Hosking, 1992, pp. 270–3). More important is the political culture in which the institution exists. By 1964 the Soviet system had become allergic to the personalized leadership it had endured since 1917. Thus General Secretary Khrushchev was replaced in a bloodless coup by Kosygin and Brezhnev, in large part because of his handling of the Cuban missile crisis and other foreign policy problems (Haslam, 2011, pp. 175–6). Collective Politburo decision-making was gradually established, becoming a powerful norm in the Brezhnev years. In any system this has major advantages through restraining the ambitions of strong personalities (A. Brown, 2014). In Japan, the norm is that no nail ever sticks up from the floorboards for too long, and foreign-policy decisions, like cabinet government in general, tend to be by consensus. In 1986 then-prime minister Yasuhiro Nakasone was criticized for departing from this tradition, partly through a minor cult of personality (he established the 'Ron–Yasu' relationship with Ronald Reagan) and partly for daring to sack – under foreign pressure – the education minister who had publicly denied that Japan had committed war-time atrocities against China. Nakasone did not, subsequently, have the prominent career he expected (Edström, 1999, pp. 119–30; Hirano, 2009).

Thus, if we consider together the foreign policy executive and the 'cabinets' to which it is answerable, rarely more than twenty people in total, we can see that the foreign policy executive holds the powers of initiative, information, convening meetings and (in the case of the head of government) also the appointment of colleagues. This means that much foreign-policy business is overseen by a small number of specialists, some of it now institutionalized in the form of security councils. Only when a problem is both of high priority and structured in such a way as to make it possible for a committee to engage with the issues in detail does the balance of advantage swing to the larger group. This is sometimes the case in crises, where there are high stakes, but more often crisis simply exacerbates the tendency to rely on the foreign policy executive for rapid and creative responses. It is, therefore, not wholly surprising if the executive is seen from outside as personifying the state. Individual leaders have a range of opportunities to be real foreign policy actors.

Leading Responsibly

Most scholars agree that leaders make a difference in foreign policy. Had Rabin and Peres rather than Begin and Sharon been leading Israel in 1982, says Shlomo Gazit (1989, p. 262), there would probably have been no invasion of the Lebanon. It is true that Begin and the Likud Party had been elected by the Israeli people precisely because they were more hawk-ish on security questions, but that still left the prime minister and his colleagues a lot of scope for taking their own decisions. Since Israel is a democracy, they were supposed to lead responsibly, that is, bearing in the mind the wishes of their party and the electorate but still using their own judgement and values to assess what the circumstances required. For 'responsible' is an ambiguous word, referring on the one hand to a person's answerability to specified others, and on the other to behaviour which is generally sober and sensitive to context, that is, to values which go beyond personal interests and relate to the wider systems of which they are a part. Thus it goes even beyond the notion of 'smart power', which is mainly about choosing the right instruments to get what you want (Nye, 2008). In relation to foreign policy, this means accepting some responsibility for a country's region, and even for the international system as a whole. It thus starts with the Weberian ideal-type of legal-bureaucratic leadership but extends to a notion of mutual responsibilities for a shared environment.

Political leadership in every area of policy involves high visibility. In foreign policy this tendency is accentuated because of the world stage on which leaders perform. This drives them to engage, positively or nega-tively, with their equivalents in other states, with whom they sometimes have closer relations than with their own colleagues, producing a trans-governmental elite of personal connections. This makes it possible for the foreign policy of the state to be 'captured' by a recirculating coterie of individuals with a particular dominant perspective or even set of private interests. This is what critics said, not wholly without justice, about the transatlantic elites who ran NATO and other Western institutions after 1947. It is more obviously true in the Arabian peninsula, where the revolt of Osama bin Laden against the US presence, and the rumbling discon-tents in Bahrain and Yemen, have all focused on the domestic conse-quences of apparently unshakeable foreign policy alignments.

Even when a small elite monopolizes foreign policy, it does not follow that they are exploiting the state in the narrow sense of venality. More likely is that they come to identify themselves with the state, holding strongly to a particular image of what foreign policy should be doing and seeing their own line of policy as so much more 'responsible' than the alternatives. For it is all too easy both for insiders and outsiders to assume that the key personalities running foreign policy – the visible executive – are by definition articulating the national interest. The same mistake may occur with non-state actors (NSAs), most obviously through the Roman Catholic Church's embodiment in the character of the current pontiff. It happens even in the 'faceless' corporate environ-ment, as when the problems of a multinational company get reduced to the dynastic politics of an Agnelli or a Murdoch, but it is in the world of states, where units of all sizes enjoy formal equality that personification becomes inevitable. Sometimes this is consciously exploited; more often, it leads to confusions on all sides as to who is really speaking for whom, and for which interests. Gorbachev, for instance, revolutionized Soviet foreign policy, but turned out to be less representative of his people than most outsiders had assumed. Like Churchill in 1945, Gorbachev was summarily expelled from office at the hour of his greatest fame.

As an area of public policy foreign policy still has its peculiarities. Whereas health, education and transport are always close to the centre of popular concerns, but only rarely bring forth great dramas, foreign policy can run in its own channels unseen by all except the specialists, only to break into the collective consciousness at moments of high drama, with the potential to do serious damage to the very fabric of the state and to its citizens' lives. Indeed the upsurge of international terrorism after 2001 has led to diplomats and intelligence agents becoming themselves the subjects of dramatic entertainment, as with the hugely popular US and Israeli TV series *Homeland*, whose title is revealing given that its subject is the dangers of international relations. Given this, responsible leadership consists on the one hand in not being lulled into complacency by the lack of daily domestic interest, and on the other in not over-dramatising potential threats. It has to take the long view, trying to manage affairs so to prevent the emergence of dangerous crises (military, political or economic) which can overturn everything. It is *crisis-* (not conflict-) prevention which should be the touchstone of foreign policy, given that conflict in some form is inevitable and crisis is not. At the same time, an excessive belief in the ability to influence the outside world, with a corresponding over-insurance in costly defence policies against only notional risks, reduces resources for domestic needs and may pervert the values of the state. Both superpowers suffered from this to some degree during the Cold War, and the Soviet Union collapsed as a result (Kennedy, 1988).

While the responsibilities of foreign policy should weigh heavily on decision-makers' shoulders, they do not always do so. Some insist on their own, overconfident, strategies which are little more than a costly bet with history. Either way, there is a good deal of scope for actorness for the individuals and small groups who find themselves deciding on behalf of peoples in international relations. Top leaders have quite a margin in which to err or to show wisdom, even allowing for the constraints of the structures in which they are operating. Their role is to *interpret* a society's needs for security, prosperity and independence in a long perspective. Yet in so doing, they do not act alone. In the modern era foreign relations cannot be conducted by gifted amateurs with a small number of personal assistants. Thus a formidable bureaucracy geared to international policy has grown up, and it is to the question of how far these seemingly non-political officials behave as genuine 'civil *servants*', and how far they are themselves shapers, or actors, that we now turn.

Notes

1   For example, General Geisel, head of state and government in Brazil between 1974 and 1979, led the whole foreign policy process, even if Itamaraty, the foreign ministry, usually initiated the process (Pinheiro, 2013).
2   Since dictators often last decades in office experienced outsiders can acquire privileged access to them. This was the case with Yevgeny Primakov of Russia, who got to know Saddam Hussein well in various posts over thirty years.
3   The P5+1 is the term used to describe the five permanent members of the UN Security Council, plus Germany, when acting in concert.
4   The Attlee Report is available in the UK National Archives in File PREM 11/2351. It was brought to public attention by Peter (now Lord) Hennessy in the *Independent* (1989).
5   For an interesting discussion of whether policy is affected by the splitting of the foreign policy executive between different parties in a coalition government, see Oppermann and Brummer (2014).
6   The Privy Council itself is a formalistic body. On 4 August 1914 it met to declare war on Germany in the presence of the King, one minister and two court officials (A. J. P. Taylor, 1965, p. 2).

Further Reading

Brown, Archie, 2014. *The Myth of the Strong Leader: Political Leadership in the Modern Age.* Brown's book makes a major contribution to the literature on leadership, with a special chapter on 'The foreign policy illusions of strong leaders'.

Hill, Christopher, 1991. *Cabinet Decisions in Foreign Policy: The British Experience, September 1938–June 1941.* This is one of the few empirically detailed analyses of top-level foreign policy-making.

Johnson, Dominic D. P. and Tierney, Dominic, 2006. *Failing to Win: Perceptions of Victory and Defeat in International Politics.* The innovative case studies contained here illustrate the subjective dimension of success and failure.

Kaarbo, Juliet, 2012. *Coalition Politics and Cabinet Decision Making: A Comparative Study of Foreign Policy Choices.* Kaarbo's monograph is an empirically rich study of whether coalitions really are more cautious in their foreign policies.

Nye, Joseph, 2008. *The Powers to Lead*. The inventor of 'smart power' shows here how this concept might be employed in international relations.

Mintz, Alex and DeRouen, Karl, 2010. *Understanding Foreign Policy Decision Making*. This is a comprehensive and up-to-date survey of the various models of decision-making, while remaining fully aware of the importance of context.

Stein, Janice G., 2012. Foreign policy decision making: Rational, psychological and neurological models. In: Steve Smith, Amelia Hadfield and Tim Dunne, eds, 2012, *Foreign Policy: Theories, Actors, Cases*. 2nd edition, pp. 130–46. This concise analysis from one of the leading authorities on decision-making includes recent research in neuroscience.

Chapter 4

Agents: Bureaucracy and the Proliferation of External Relations

All modern leaders are heavily dependent on their professional staff, whether the *éminences grises* who participate in summits, or the desk officers who follow day-to-day events from subjects which vary from Burma to the World Health Organization. This is true even of autocrats like Bashar al-Assad; they may ensure obedience by fear more than by legitimacy, but they cannot run a complex set of external relations and social control solely through the clan members of their power base. Every system requires both water-carriers and able senior staff who know how to run embassies, manage the armed forces, gather and assess the mountains of information now available and assist in the many technical negotiations which constitute contemporary international relations. Many of them are thus policy makers, sharing the responsibilities of politicians on the basis of trust, continuity and personal dedication (Page and Wright, 1999).

The importance of these cadres in foreign policy-making has long been recognized by scholars, and much literature now exists on the political impact of bureaucrats and the extent to which foreign policy is really in their hands. This chapter examines the hypothesis of bureaucratic control by comparing the Weberian ideal type to practice across different systems of society and government, with the help of the theories of 'bureaucratic politics' developed by political scientists. It will also discuss the way in which the foreign policy bureaucracy is no longer confined to ministries of foreign affairs, but extends horizontally across most governmental departments, provoking new problems of coordination and control.

Agents not Agency

The arrival of industrialization and a complex division of labour in nineteenth-century Europe fostered existing developments towards modern systems of government and administration. In particular the twin doctrines of democracy and meritocracy began to shape the expanding apparatus of the state. So far as foreign policy-making was concerned the impact of the new meritocratic thinking preceded that of democratic accountability. Both had been present in the great symbol of modern upheaval, the French Revolution. Napoleon's revolution in French administration, with its key notion of *la carrière ouverte aux talents* (i.e. careers open to all on merit) had been made possible by the sweeping away of feudal privileges between 1789 and 1793, and the unleashing on the world of the great idea of popular sovereignty. Democracy was soon to stall in the Paris of the Jacobins, Bonapartists and then the restored Bourbons, while the mere idea of a democratic foreign policy had to await the campaigns of Richard Cobden and John Bright half a century later. But Napoleon's will to rationalize and mobilize meant that the need for a more professional official class began to be acknowledged across Europe as the nineteenth century proceeded.

In Britain the Northcote–Trevelyan report of 1854 led eventually to the civil service reforms of 1871 whereby formal grades of administrative and executive service were introduced as part of the move against corruption and incompetence. The army and navy reforms begun in the 1870s were designed to the same general end, so that positions could no longer so easily be gained on the basis of birth and connections. This was partly the result of glaring incompetence during the Crimean War of 1854–6. Similarly in France, the devastating defeats of 1871 led to a reconsideration of many aspects of state policy, including education and the armed forces. The subsequent reforms meant that the country was to provide a far more formidable adversary for Germany in 1914. For its part, the newly unified Germany, with Prussia at its core, was proving a model of new administrative practice for other countries, even if the element of promotion on merit was still circumscribed by the powerful presence of the Junkers' elite in both army and government.

The ideas of rational conduct and a clear chain of command/authority were important to the new German model of administration, but they were by no means unproblematic, as the foremost theorist of modern bureaucracy, Max Weber, was subsequently to make clear (1917a, pp. 145–6, 161, 196–209). A modern system had to go beyond the notion of unqualified obedience to the next rung in the hierarchy; this was, after all, the motif of absolutist forms of government. The ethos of democracy increasingly demanded a system in which obedience was owed only to legitimate government, and where legitimacy derived from the popular will. Moreover, obedience had to go hand in hand at all levels with both standards of efficiency and with accountability: politicians were to become ever more accountable to parliaments, and to the press, while their subordinates were accountable both to their immediate superiors and to a growing corpus of written rules, necessary to systematize an ever more complex administration of interlinked parts. Finally, it was becoming clear that both bureaucrats and their masters needed to be technically competent. Status would no longer be enough; in an era of industrial and military competition, they were increasingly being judged by results.

In premodern days, the clerks and secretaries who were the forerunners of today's 'secretaries of state' were judged by a particular form of efficiency – their ability to perform the prince's will, or rather their ability to convince him that they were advising him well. Until the age of mercantilism, there were no abstract indicators, whether economic or relating to 'power', against which performance could be measured. With the arrival of meritocratic thinking, however, in the wake of the enlightenment, came a sense of loyalty to the *res publica*, independent in the last analysis of the orders of any politician. This was a reworking of the classical distinction between the private and the public spheres in the light of notions of popular sovereignty (Arendt, 1958, pp. 28–37, 50–8).

By the late nineteenth century it was becoming accepted that an official should serve legitimate political authority but also some higher notion of the national interest in the event that the former proved corrupt or particularly inept – the view taken by in those officials in the 1930s who leaked information on Britain's weak defences to an out-of-office Winston Churchill. It was, of course, to be hoped that such a fundamental conflict of loyalties would arise only rarely. For the most part the new breed of civil servant was to be loyal, professional, clear-sighted and non-political. The ideal type of the modern official as articulated (but not invented) by Weber was that of someone who had been trained to implement policy decided upon at the political level, without themselves becoming politicized (M. Weber, 1919a, p. 332). The human temptation to play politics was to be neutralized by the provision of proper job security and salaries, as well as by an ethos of responsibility and *esprit de corps*. More negatively the incentives to use office in the traditional way for the pursuit of personal wealth and advancement were supposedly diminished by supervision and by the fear of denied promotion or even dismissal. This new class was to consist of reliable *agents*, in the sense of acting on behalf of others. But in today's terms they were not themselves a site of *agency*, or independent actors.

This was the ideal type. Certain states implemented it earlier or better than others, and it is in any case a task which requires perpetual vigilance. Arguably some states, even developed ones, have still not made much progress on it today. But wherever one looks, foreign policy was almost the last area to be reformed. The association of diplomacy with international elite networks meant that the impact of democratic and meritocratic thought fed through slowly.

Bureaucracy and Foreign Policy

The coming of the 'age of the masses' affected diplomacy in only piece-meal fashion, even if the two world wars caused major upheavals. Woodrow Wilson articulated the principles of 'open covenants, openly arrived at' in 1917, with its assumption that the old 'freemasonry' of international diplomacy had been responsible for the disastrous errors leading to the First World War. Efficiency, merit and democracy were conjoined in a new philosophy of foreign policy as a form of public service. As it happens, the values of professionalism had already begun to creep into the British, French, Japanese and American foreign ministries by 1914, with a gradual acceptance that intellectual ability was as impor-tant as social connections. After 1918 further changes were seen in Soviet Russia (where, however, one caste soon replaced another in the diplo-matic corps), and Germany, although the highly turbulent and ideologi-cal 30 years which followed made this a period in which the advancing role of civil servants was inevitably stalled (Allison and Szanton, 1976, pp. ix–xiv, 24–43; Bacchus, 1983, pp. 3–6; Z. Steiner, 1982).

Diplomatic dynasties continued to survive in the twentieth century – but the era of the gentleman diplomat was steadily giving way to an order in which officials were seen as both indispensable and wholly subordi-nate. This was as true of the United States, where state service enjoyed only moderate prestige and where each presidential election produced a new raft of political appointees to control the higher echelons of the State Department, as it was of the Soviet Union, where the organs of the state were infiltrated and controlled by the Communist Party. As late as 1956 Khrushchev could boast that 'Gromyko only says what we tell him to' (Ulricks, 1982, p. 531). In Britain, the ideological hostilities of the 1920s, when the Foreign Office barely concealed its lack of trust in the first Labour government's ability to defend the national interest, were put to rest during Labour's first full term (1945–50) when the prime minister and foreign secretary worked closely (and cautiously) with senior offi-cials to construct a new order in Europe. With France finally settling down under the Fifth Republic to an era in which respected presidents were served by able functionaries from the *grandes écoles*, the second half of the twentieth century seemed to have established bureaucracy as the neutral buffer in the political process, vital for technical expertise, implementation and advice, but always subject to the decisions of the people's elected representatives.

It was just at this time, the 1950s and 1960s, that academics were beginning to question the truth of such a neat model, and to see bureau-crats themselves as powerful players in the policy process. Individual officials had already drawn attention to themselves, like Sir Eyre Crowe and his famous memorandum on British foreign policy of 1907, or André François-Poncet, the influential French ambassador in Berlin from 1931 to 1938 (Adamthwaite, 1977, pp. 152–3). More common was the tendency of ad hoc personal advisers, such as Woodrow Wilson's Colonel House, or Tsar Nicholas's Rasputin, to come to public attention as Svengali figures. During the Cold War, after the first sensational impact of George Kennan's 'long telegram', ideological discipline tended to depersonalize diplomacy. But the steady growth in size of bureaucratic apparatuses, as in the number of states, embassies and international organizations, plus the remarkable economic expansion of the post-war years, all served to highlight a changing balance of power, in terms of numbers, resources and expertise, between politicians and officials.[1]

To outside observers the existence of a readily identifiable foreign ministry and diplomatic service at the service of each state meant that foreign policy administrators constituted at the least a compact body of high competence, and at the most a self-serving elite with a strong sense of *esprit de corps* and its own status. Either view made them obvious candidates for study as the real authors of foreign policy.

The Ministry of Foreign Affairs and the Diplomatic Service

The past fifty years have seen the emergence of many rivals to conventional diplomats from within the bureaucracy. Nonetheless, the foreign ministry and those serving abroad (who have increasingly come under central control, after long enjoying autonomy) represent a formidable engine in the making of policy. The ministry and its staff perform three vital functions:

- *Information gathering*: no state can manage without the means to collect and analyse information on the range of issues in which it has interests. Although journalists now have better and quicker sources on developments in wider society, there is no substitute for the inside knowledge of their host administrations which good diplomats possess. In conjunction with the intelligence services they can also monitor policy implementation in detail, when journalists have long ago moved on to other stories. This is why one of the first steps of the British government after the fall of Kabul in the war of October 2001 was to re-establish the embassy and to send the head of the South Asia Department of the Foreign and Commonwealth Office (FCO) to run it (Cowper-Coles, 2012). Iver Neumann (2012, pp. 31–3) has said that diplomats still gather a particular kind of information which amounts to 'knowledge production', or the critical interpretation of facts which are readily available and of encounters with local policy-makers which are not.

- *Policy-making*: politicians formulate their foreign policies in opposition and have the assistance of their party machines in government. But they still rely heavily on their expert officials to sift the vast quantities of incoming information (in many languages), to interpret and predict the actions of other states and to formulate policy options on the thousand-and-one detailed questions which never come to public attention. Only in one-party states can the party machine represent an alternative to this concentration of specialized advice, as in China, where the Politburo and its 'Foreign Affairs Leading Group' stands above even the specialist bureaucracies of the foreign ministry and the People's Liberation Army (Collins, 2002, pp. 306–8; Hamrin, 1995; Lu, 2001, pp. 45–60).

- *Memory*: every system needs continuity in its external relations, and career diplomats institutionalize it by serving as the system's collective memory, with the help of their record-keeping system. Without the capacity to relate myriad past commitments and treaties to the present, and to each other, decision-makers would be left floundering in chaos, given the complexity of the contemporary international system. Alternatively they would turn inwards, as with countries like North Korea which are too paranoid to permit the development of independent expertise. Conversely, the possession of institutional memory produces pressures for conservatism in foreign affairs. If the working assumption of diplomats and their legal advisers is the classic rule of international law, *pacta sunt servanda* (agreements are for keeping), then it is difficult to strike out in new directions, with the result that domestic radicals (of all persuasions) become frustrated with what they see as the inertia and obstructionism of their own foreign ministry. This is particularly evident in the case of European Union law, whose supremacy over domestic legislation foreign ministry officials have to assert.

Although in some cases foreign ministries become demoralized and/or are deliberately subverted, they still have major institutional strengths. In the first instance they still attract high-quality personnel, selected by competitive examinations. The social and intellectual sources of recruitment may be narrow – history and law graduates from comfortable backgrounds for the most part – but the diplomatic service now represents an elite of ability as well as ethos. In 1984, 28 per cent of all French ambassadors had been educated at the top-ranking École nationale d'administration (ENA), while 75 to 80 per cent of ENA's own recruits came from Paris's Institut des Études Politiques ('Sciences Po'). These institutions and their equivalents elsewhere are funnels for students of high calibre. Even in small countries like Ireland and Portugal the quality of their diplomats is perceived abroad as being high. In the two cases cited the task of running the six-month revolving presidency of the EU has never proved a technical problem, even if at times the volume of work has been excessive (Keatinge, 1996; Lorenz, 1996).

Secondly, although now at times bypassed by heads of government and subject to competition from other ministries, foreign offices have a considerable degree of autonomy, virtually constituting a sub-elite within the machinery of government. Their control over external representations, their privileged contacts with foreigners and the continued mystique of international affairs means it is difficult for other parts of the administration actually to interfere in their business. This can attract resentment and hostility, as with Truman's often-expressed view of foreign-service officers as 'the striped pants boys', or the Nazi Party's determination to control its too-reasonable diplomats by compelling them to become members of the Party (Doss, 1982, pp. 244–6). Still, for countries as diverse as Argentina, India, Norway and South Africa the foreign ministry and its diplomats constitute a distinctive and high-status profession without which the state would be significantly disadvantaged in the international system.

Lastly, foreign ministries adapted during the twentieth century to the vastly greater range of business confronting states by accepting the need to organize themselves on both geographical and functional lines, not oscillating between the two models as used to be common. At various times each has been in fashion; for example, the European Commission, which until the arrival of the European External Action Service (EEAS) was a proto-European foreign ministry, had three reorganizations in less than a decade, swinging back and forth between the geographical and functional principle (Nuttall, 1997, pp. 303–19). The Dutch foreign ministry dealt with the problem by consolidating its regional directorates: political, economic and aid-related (Everts, 2001, pp. 172–4). In general, it is now recognized that a foreign ministry needs both area specialists and experts in functional questions like energy and the environment, themselves reflecting the emergence of ever more specialized international organizations (Barston, 1997, pp. 11–31). Foreign ministries may be stretched thin in the attempt to cater for this range of knowledge, but only they possess the *combination* of the different skills required.

These continuing strengths are only part of the story. Increasingly foreign ministries and their employees are seen as dinosaurs being supplanted by home-based experts and non-governmental para-diplomats. There are various reasons why diplomatic services are under challenge, in the very era when they have finally become modern, meritocratic organizations:

- *Lack of technical expertise*: diplomats are seen as over-generalist and over-stretched, incapable of discussion on equal terms with economists, scientists and businessmen. Even the 'specialism in abroad' counts for less now that travel is so easy and so common. Ministers make day trips and use video conferences. In Britain Foreign Secretary Robin Cook had to introduce a secure electronic mail system in the late 1990s since his officials were receiving hot information later than the foreign editors of most newspapers. Twenty years later foreign ministries have caught up on the technology front and use it to their advantage.
- *The spread of mini foreign offices*: most domestic departments now engage directly in international relations by sending their own experts out to meet their equivalents in another state or to participate in a specialized international organization. This is particularly the case in the European Union, where the Economic and Financial Affairs Council (ECOFIN) is a serious rival to the Council of (Foreign) Ministers as the working 'Cabinet' of the EU. In Japan the Ministry of International Trade and Industry (MITI) used to have more prestige than the foreign ministry, together with its own network of external contacts. In the 1980s it caused problems by encouraging Toshiba to break the rules of the CoCom (the Coordinating Committee associated with NATO from 1949–93 to control the export of strategic goods to hostile countries) by selling computers to the USSR. This was obviously within the purview of classical foreign policy, and it gradually led to a fight back which ended in MITI's own substitution in 2001, by a Ministry of Economy, Trade and Industry, with less emphasis on an assertive national trade policy. In Mexico 'almost every Ministry has a *Dirección General de Asuntos Internacionales*' (Rozental, 1999, p. 154, note 24).

In consequence hardly any government department anywhere can be regarded as wholly 'home' in its remit. Between 1960 and 1980, for example, the number of domestic ministries with their own international units in Finland and Sweden rose from two in each case to six and ten respectively (Karvonen and Sundelius, 1987, pp. 30–1). Similarly, as early as 1975 the US's Murphy Commission investigating 'the Organization of the Government for the Conduct of Foreign Policy' found that of more than 20,000 civilian employees working full-time on foreign affairs (excluding the many in support agencies and in intelligence) only about 4,000 worked in the

Department of State. In 2014 there were 89,204 federal employees working abroad in over 140 countries of which only 22,291 were employed by the State Department. (The Department of Defense was the largest employer with 47,229.)[2]

- *Poverty of resources*: foreign ministries use up small amounts of public expenditure – in general less than 1 per cent of the total. The State Department's budget is rather less than the Pentagon's jet fuel bill. Yet far from strengthening their position, not being a burden turns out to be a political disadvantage. It is one of the paradoxes of modern government that those departments which use most resources, and cause most headaches, such as education, health and social security, seem most able to protect their budgets, while the foreign ministry, whose outputs are less tangible but far less expensive, is constantly vulnerable to cut-backs and bad publicity.[3] What is more, cuts here mean the loss of trained manpower, the effects of which cannot quickly be reversed.

- *Lack of domestic constituency*: following on from the above, foreign ministries have few natural supporters within their own societies. Foreign policy requires little domestic legislation and in consequence few members of parliament have the potential to become allies of the department. Few, indeed, have a deep knowledge of international affairs – as opposed to the superficial knowledge gained from junkets and world news. Whereas defence ministries can look to those manning bases or employed in the arms industry, and finance ministries find allies in those hostile to the tax burden, the foreign ministry is easily labelled as – by Margaret Thatcher in Britain, and Jessie Helms in the United States – 'the department for foreigners'. Indeed diplomats can easily get out of touch with their domestic base. Even when they return home for periods, they only serve in the nation's capital. Moreover, diplomacy generally has a stuffy image, the opposite of street and business credibility, especially as relative salaries in the public sector have declined, with the result that many of the best and the brightest go elsewhere. Even French 'enarques' began in the 1990s to be attracted away into private industry. This trend has begun to be reversed, as awareness has grown of the limits of a business vision of the world.

These foreign-service weaknesses are real. It has seemed to many in recent decades that the distinctive diplomatic apparatus as we know it might disappear to be replaced by what Britain's Berrill Report envisaged in 1977 as 'a foreign service group' within the wider bureaucracy – in other words, a system in which service overseas at some point becomes normal for most staff, and where 'external' policy is simply one aspect of policy in general. The bigger embassies in Washington and other major capitals these days do tend to have more staff from domestic ministries than qualified diplomats. On the other hand, a terminal prognosis misses some vital signs. On the issue of technical competence, for instance, the more effective foreign ministries have adapted by increasing training in economics, and by allowing some staff to specialize. Furthermore, the greater diversification of external relations has created new needs for coordination and synthesis that foreign ministries, if they can escape the traditional mindset, are well placed to meet.

It is by no means obvious in any case that specialized economic issues are best left to economists, as the crisis of 2008 dramatically demonstrated. In 2014 the French Foreign Minister Laurent Fabius was given added responsibilities for trade and external business activity on the grounds that, in the words of a senior official, 'the foreign ministry is the crisis ministry' (Irish, 2014). Similarly the controversies over first Iraq's weapons of mass destruction and then Iran's pursuit of nuclear technology and Syria's chemical weapons, showed that the policy issues at stake were ultimately political, even if technical knowledge was an essential prerequisite. The ability to understand political and historical context is essential, together with the ability to keep experts 'on tap and not on top'.

To the extent that a foreign service can do this without falling back on the spurious justification that only diplomats understand foreigners or the processes of negotiation, then they will maintain the high status that even today attaches to their profession. Despite their domestic vulnerabilities diplomats continue to be valued by the politicians and journalists who lean on their skills in daily life, and who have seen at close hand how the profession has become more stressful and demanding. The G20 summits may take all the headlines, with political advisers, 'sherpas' and flown-out domestic officials to the fore, but behind all the fanfare is the indispensable daily grind in which foreign ministries have a prime role. Few presidential or prime ministerial offices, even in the major capitals like Washington, Bonn and Paris, can do without the diplomatic machinery at their disposal. Even Henry Kissinger, perhaps with some sense of regret for having been hard on his officials, dedicated a book to 'the men and women of the Foreign Service of the United States of America, whose professionalism and dedication sustain American diplomacy' (Kissinger, 1994, p. 9). It is also noteworthy that while the creation of the EEAS in 2009 was supposed to take in all the functional 'external relations' of the EU, it has in practice concentrated on classical issues of diplomacy such as stability in the Balkans and the Middle East (Juncos and Pomorska, 2014).

Proliferating Rivals

Outsiders dealing with a particular state are thrown into a quandary when they have to deal with a range of different departments or agencies. Is the adversary playing a strategic game by speaking with competing voices, or is there a genuine problem of fragmented decision-making? There is clearly a great deal of room for misunderstanding when so many states seem incapable of speaking with one voice.

This happens increasingly because foreign ministries now find themselves in a situation of structural rivalry with domestic competitors and because they do not always succeed in rising to the new challenge of coordination. Whether it is because of 'complex interdependence' or because of endogenous changes in the state (and the two processes are difficult to separate out) many states are now facing a horizontal decentralization of their foreign relations, meaning the foreign ministry's loss of control over many external issues to other parts of the state bureaucracy. From the wider perspective of the interests of state and society the problem of unitary action means that opportunities for linkage may be missed in international negotiation, that outsiders will be able to play on internal divisions or confusions and that long-term strategic planning becomes almost impossible.

The rivals to foreign ministries may be listed in four categories, three with substantive concerns and one with a procedural mission. First is *the military*, which in principle should work with the foreign ministry, but which has its own sizeable vested interests and direct links with equivalents overseas. Its actions can, not always intentionally, constitute a parallel foreign policy with serious political consequences – as with the Anglo-French military conversations of 1905–14, which gradually created a de facto alliance between the two countries (Williamson, 1969, pp. 59–88). Since the military possesses considerable physical resources, a domestic constituency and its own network of attachés and intelligence sources it has the capacity to embarrass conventional diplomacy. This is to say nothing of the numerous countries where at one time or another the military has played a disproportionate part in government, and thus been able to invert the normal principal–agent relationship between foreign policy and defence. This can happen even in democracies, especially in war-time, as with General MacArthur's attempt to subvert President Truman's policy during the Korean War. Ironically another general, Dwight D. Eisenhower, then took over as president for eight years, at the time of the increasing militarization of foreign policy during the early Cold War – a fact to which he was sensitive, coining the term 'military–industrial complex' as a warning to his successors. In the Soviet Union the military remained cowed by the memory of Stalin's purges of

1937–8, but after the dictator's death became a force for over-insurance in the arms race which eventually brought their state to its knees in 1989. The Third World continues to produce examples of military regimes which are often cautious in their foreign policies but also lacking in the finesse and coalition-building capacity which experienced diplomats bring to bear. Greece in the 1970s, Turkey in the 1980s, and Myanmar and Egypt in recent years are all good examples.[4]

The second category of rival to the foreign ministry is that of the *economic ministries*. These will vary in number and title according to the state, which might possess one or more departments dealing with foreign trade/commerce, finance, development/foreign aid, industry, agriculture, fisheries and shipping – to say nothing of central banks, an increasing number of which are constitutionally independent of political control, although by the same token conservative and predictable. These entities are the basis of the hypothesis that interdependence is dissolving foreign policy and replacing it with a mosaic of functional, transgovernmental networks (Slaughter, 2004). The important roles of finance officials in the International Monetary Fund (IMF) and Economic and Monetary Union (EMU) meetings and of trade officials in GATT/WTO negotiations seem to bear out the argument. In rich countries development ministries dispose of more money than foreign ministries and become protective of their prerogative. An ex-ambassador to South Africa complained in 2014 that despite its reputation for effective coordination the British system was failing to get departments to work together. In particular the Department for International Development (DfID) was subject to 'the silo mentality'. It 'is extremely reluctant to spend money through the agency of other departments' (Boateng, 2014).

Karvonen and Sundelius (1987) made a detailed empirical study of this question, largely in relation to Finland and Sweden but also carefully located in a comparative frame of analysis. They conclude that although the picture is inevitably variegated, given the variety of state cultures and the genuine uncertainties about the best way to proceed, foreign ministries have often reasserted their central role in the 'management of interdependence'. Indeed, in 1983 the Swedish Commerce Ministry was dismantled and its international trade functions transferred to the foreign ministry. Canada, another country not sure about which functions a foreign ministry should cover, went in the opposite direction. In 1992 the Department of External Affairs shed its responsibilities for foreign aid and for immigration, only to take on international trade, acquiring its current name, the Department of Foreign Affairs and International Trade. Either way, as the 'domestic' parts of the machinery of government have grown, so too has the need to relate them to international issues and machinery. The problems of coordination and control have consequently increased (East, 1981; Karvonen and Sundelius, 1987, pp. 153–7; Neumann, 1999, pp. 152–69).

Intelligence: A Special Case?

The third form of rival to foreign ministries deserves lengthier treatment. The intelligence services are at once indispensable and difficult to integrate into public policy-making. They are capable of murky behaviour, sometimes at the behest of politicians along the lines of King Henry II's hint to his knights ('who will rid me of this accursed priest'?) which led to the murder of Archbishop Thomas Becket in his own cathedral. During the Cold War the Bulgarian regime was responsible for the murder of a journalist in London, and the Chilean dictatorship killed ex-Minister Letelier on Embassy Row in Washington. Syrian military intelligence was thought to be behind the Hindawi plot to bomb an El Al plane flying out of London in 1986, and Libya eventually accepted responsibility for the downing in 1988 of PanAm 103 with the loss of 270 lives. In the same decade the United States engaged in the shady 'Iran–Contra' deal as a way of sabotaging the left-wing Ortega government in Nicaragua during the 1980s. Since the Cold War such cases have become less frequent – or perhaps just less obvious. Israeli agents still hunt down those deemed responsible for attacks on their citizens wherever there were to be found, while the British government has demanded the extradition of a Russian security service official on the charge of murdering Alexander Litvinenko in a London hotel.

Yet most of the work of security and intelligence services, at least in systems with some sense of decency, does not sink this low. One of the key elements in foreign policy-making is the routine use of intelligence material, gained from both foreign operations and domestic counter-intelligence (Hibbert, 1990). Much is not even 'spying', but the systematic use of material in the public domain, even if in the electronic age the issue of what exactly is or should be in the public domain is a fiercely contested debate.

There are two important elements to the expansion of mass surveillance via texts, phone calls and social media. The first is the general growth in state power which it represents, driven for the most part by foreign and security policy concerns. Although the huge mass of data to be sieved relies heavily on ever more sophisticated algorithms and super-fast computers attempting to identify the very small proportion of traffic which might suggest illegal activity, there is little doubt that it also enables intrusion into everyday life on an unparalleled scale, while governments tend to give their own concerns the benefit of the doubt over the liberty of an individual. Thus the United States has taken a hard line with whistle-blowers like Bradley Manning and Edward Snowden.

The second important implication of the expansion of mass surveillance is the issue of whether it encourages the intelligence services, as the guardians and interpreters of key data, to run an alternative policy to their political superiors, under the cover of official foreign policy (Verrier, 1983; P. Wright, 1987). It is hardly unknown, after all, for members of what has been called 'the permanent government', to regard politicians as not sufficiently knowledgeable or even trustworthy to make critical security decisions. However this may be, the relationship between intelligence and politics is of crucial importance to the success of foreign policy, and although much information-gathering is a low-level business, ultimately the issues are played out at the highest level. Intelligence also sits right in the middle of the civil–military relationship, which can be crucial, as when the inexperienced President Kennedy was persuaded to approve the abortive invasion of the Bay of Pigs by a mixture of CIA, Cuban exiles and military advisors, or when General de Gaulle put a decisive end to the Fourth French Republic in 1958. In such crises good intelligence and security service support can decide who is able to act effectively, and who not. Both the military and the security services can claim a special expertise which puts the generalist politician on the back foot. Given this, one of the most remarkable phenomena of recent times is the ability of Erdogan in Turkey to break the structural power of the military, and thus the secular legacy of Kemal Ataturk. It is difficult to imagine that he could have done this without significant help from the intelligence services.

Because both the successes and the failures of intelligence are spectacular, the foreign policy executive has to pay the closest attention to the advice of intelligence chiefs. Political leaders can be raised high or brought right down by their judgements about the use of intelligence. Jimmy Carter, for example, never recovered from gambling in 1980 on the attempt to liberate the American hostages in Teheran by military means. He was ill-advised by his special forces, and paid the price at the presidential election the following November (Beckwith and Knox, 1984; Brzezinski, 1983, pp. 491–500). Winston Churchill, by contrast, attained his mythical status as a great war-leader in part because of his astute use of intelligence, such as his insistence on prioritising the work of the Bletchley codebreakers. In the 1930s he had exploited past experience and personal networks to second guess successfully the official British data on German rearmament (Andrew, 1989, pp. 181–93; Handel, 1989, pp. 6–8).

The key variables in the successful use of intelligence are fourfold: the quality of the intelligence; its ability to reach political leaders; leaders' judgements; and the independent actions of the intelligence community. It is the last two which concern us here. A secure executive has wide discretion whether or not to take notice of intelligence. De Gaulle was sceptical of it and preferred to pursue his own previously thought out *'grandes lignes'* (Porch, 1996, pp. 473–4). Moreover, if the official intelligence services cannot or will not follow instructions, it is always possible to set up informal, parallel systems, as President Reagan did with Colonel Oliver North and his operatives in the Iran–Contra scandal, or François Mitterrand with the 'Elysée cell' he set up in dissatisfaction with the state counter-terrorism operation (A. Armstrong, 1989, pp. 28–9; Porch, 1996, pp. 450–1; Tower et al., 1987, pp. 102–48). There is barely any public scrutiny to check these actions except after the fact, when things go wrong and/or illegalities get exposed, as with the Franks Report (1983) after the Falklands War (generally judged to be an over-speedy whitewash) and the Chilcot Inquiry after the Iraq War of 2003 (endlessly delayed). Then mud sticks to everyone, especially those ultimately responsible, even if they have had little knowledge of the details. The fact that most intelligence services are fragmented between home security, foreign operations and military intelligence (with each of the armed services often having its own branch of intelligence) makes it often difficult to decide on the most useful information amidst all the 'noise', but it also makes it possible for politicians to divide and rule. The CIA's failures over Al Qaeda, for instance, have given the White House some leverage over this otherwise formidable foreign policy player, while the rival Defense Intelligence Agency is institutionally limited from straying too far into non-military subjects.

The intelligence services naturally have an interest, through the carefully selected information they let out, in playing down their role vis-à-vis their political masters. This should not lead us to underestimate the degree of autonomy they often enjoy in foreign policy matters. This is partly operational, with potentially embarrassing results, as with Edward Snowden's revelations about the US National Security Agency and its hacking of Angela Merkel's mobile phone, and partly strategic, in that they are able to place their people inside the head of government's entourage, and into rival sources of analysis such as research institutes and universities. Most important, their information is fundamentally uncheckable by anyone outside their own circle, unlike that of the academic, journalist or even career diplomat. Few leaders have the time or inclination to look at raw data, and those, like Churchill or Margaret Thatcher, who do have a tendency to be their own intelligence officer have no basis, other than intuition, and a limited capacity for cross-checking, for evaluating it. They all have to rely on human filters (Gazit, 1989, pp. 271–2; Handel, 1989, pp. 27–8; Luvaas, 1989).

It is clear that a state's foreign policy can at times be splintered by powerful internal elements running their own line – or it can appear to be so, when it suits various parties not to assume a single locus of responsibility within the acting state. This has been the case for many years in Pakistan, where the various branches of the civil and military intelligence services have undermined official policy – notably in their support for the Taliban – in ways which go well beyond normal bureaucratic politics.

Again, a great deal depends on the political culture of the particular country. In Soviet Russia the secret police methods of Stalin, combined with the state's sense of being under perpetual siege by hostile foreign powers, led to the KGB becoming institutionalized as a major force in all aspects of top decision-making. If the Communist Party was the parallel power structure to the state, then the KGB was the parallel structure to the party. Often the most able people would gravitate towards the intelligence services because of the relative freedom, personal and intellectual, which they could enjoy compared to the ideologically top-heavy party cadres. These were the people with the clearest sense of what life was like in the West and of how far the Soviet Union was slipping behind under Leonid Brezhnev (Kissinger, 1994, p. 797). It was not therefore wholly surprising that their candidates, first Yuri Andropov and then Mikhail Gorbachev, should have found themselves in the position of supreme power in the USSR (Bialer and Mandelbaum, 1988, pp. 277–8). After more than two decades of apparent democracy its dominant leader, Vladimir Putin, is from the same stable.

This kind of power is less likely to be found in countries with a wider range of effective institutions, although this is not to say that the intelligence services cannot veto the advance of key individuals they distrust. In general, intelligence is a factor which must be reckoned with in the analysis of foreign policy, as in any serious historical study of international politics (Watt, 2001). It is all too easy to skim over the surface of events without asking about the advice top leaders are getting, or about the covert operations – with or without explicit authorization – that do not always square with declaratory policy. Clear answers to such questions can rarely be found, but at least intelligence is now an established area of academic enquiry, thanks to the efforts of scholars like Christopher Andrew (2009; Aldrich, Andrew and Wark, 2008) and Robert Jervis (2010).[5]

The historical record shows that intelligence services are inherently semi-independent, and can sometimes be decisive, in the conduct of a state's foreign relations. By the same token their own internal divisions, relatively limited resources and relatively narrow range of concerns mean that the security services should not be seen as the perpetual string-pullers of political marionettes. Political leaders usually manage to set their own broad foreign policy parameters, and where there is consensus and continuity they are determined by deeper forces than the influence of Mossad or France's Directorate-General for External Security (DGSE). Indeed, despite its prestige Mossad has had much difficulty in toning down the increasingly strident nationalism of the Netanyahu government in recent years. Intelligence can become crucial when it is least expected, but most politicians have plenty of other things to worry about, at home and abroad, than the machinations of their own secret services. What is more, spectacular failures such as the inability to predict the attacks of 11 September 2001, or the misrepresentations of Saddam Hussein's weapons of mass destruction, do damage to institutional reputations which can take decades to repair (Delahunt, 2008; Kean, Hamilton et al., 2004).

Bureaucratic Politics and the Problem of Coordination

The consequences of proliferating external relations lead us to the last set of rivals facing the modern foreign ministry – those who think they can pull the threads of complexity together rather more effectively than can the diplomatic generalists. These people have no departmental base but rather reside in the central institutions of the state. They are in the prime minister's office and/or cabinet secretariat (in a parliamentary system), the president's personal 'cabinet' (in a presidential system) or the party machine in a one-party state. They exploit their closeness to the head of government and their capacity to take an overview of the whole system. They often also control high-level appointments across the bureaucracy. All this makes for formidable rivals to the foreign ministry as it seeks to reconcile the many different strands of external relations. Yet while a prime ministerial or presidential office can set the main outlines of policy, it easily gets out of touch with detail, expertise and implementation. Its concern with public policy as a whole can lead to the external dimension being unjustly neglected, manipulated for purely political reasons or distorted by ideological preoccupations, with unpleasant surprises the eventual result. The challenge for foreign policy-makers today, therefore, is to build on the foreign service's unique role in assessing how a state's activities look from the outside, and judging how much of a united front is actually desirable, while ensuring that no gap arises between classical foreign policy and the various international dimensions of domestic policy. Striking the balance, and keeping the major departments of state in harmony with each other along the way, is one of the great tests of modern government.

This is where theory needs to re-enter the discussion. If we are fully to understand the simultaneously fragmented and unitary character of foreign policy-making, we need theories which address the roles of bureaucracy, of choice and of government. Fortunately a rich literature exists of precisely this kind under the general heading of 'bureaucratic politics'.

The theory of bureaucratic politics was introduced by Graham Allison (1969, 1971), building on previous work done by Charles Lindblom, Richard Neustadt, Herbert Simon and others. It was subsequently developed by Allison himself (Allison and Zelikow, 1999), Morton Halperin (1974), Robert Gallucci (1975) and others, and applied in numerous case studies. Although it has also been subject to healthy criticism it has become an accepted lens for understanding policy-making. Outside academe, however, things are rather different. Although practitioners would not quarrel with the model, and often live up to its predictions, they are barely aware of its propositions, let alone its implications for the wider issues of choice, democracy and responsibility. For their part most citizens have little sense of the complex realities of foreign policy-making. They have a healthy understanding of politicians' capacity for self-interest, but not unreasonably expect the major departments of their country's bureaucracy to pull broadly in the same direction.

Yet this is precisely what does not happen, according to the theory. Allison's two models, soon collapsed into a single theory entitled 'governmental politics', are well enough known not to need recounting in detail (Hudson, 2007, pp. 89–101). Put baldly, the hypothesis, worked out in a case study of superpower behaviour during the Cuban missile crisis of 1962, was that ministries and other bureaucratic units pursue at best their own versions of the national interest and at worst their own parochial concerns, so that foreign policy-making becomes a market place in which decisions are produced by horse-trading more than logic. But the fundamental assumptions of the argument should be examined, first because they have been sharply criticized and second because they have implications for the problem of action in foreign policy. If we wish to know where agency lies in modern international relations, we must consider the proposition that the state tends to decompose into its various separate parts, as well as the degree to which the fissiparous tendencies of bureaucracy might be countered through intelligent leadership or constitutional provisions.

The bureaucratic politics approach has two major implications for the study of foreign policy: it reinforces the whole domestic politics approach, against the scepticism of neorealism and geopolitics, and it presents a picture of decision-making in which 'foul-ups', as opposed to either rationality or inevitability, are very prominent. In both these respects it is thus central to the subject of foreign policy analysis, which developed precisely as a means of forcing the domestic environment onto the agenda of international relations and through subverting the claims of decision-makers to be acting intelligently and/or in the public interest.

The bureaucratic politics model (BPM) complicates the question of agency in foreign policy for one self-evident reason and two more subtle ones. The basic reason is that bureaucratic politics insists that clear, rational decisions on the merits of a problem tend to be supplanted by the mere 'resultants' of an internal process of bargaining and manoeuvring, in which the outcome will probably not correspond to the initial preference orderings of any particular actor (Lamborn and Mummie, 1988, pp. 24, 32). In other words, internal dynamics shape policy to produce compromises that are unsatisfactory in terms of their external efficacy. Some see this as another version of the view that democracies are at a disadvantage in their dealings with autocratic states, but there is no reason to believe that the latter are immune from competing bureaucratic interests or coalitions – rather, the reverse.

The agency problem is more tangentially affected by a second aspect of the bureaucratic politics theory, namely its assumptions about the place of rationality in the calculations of what Allison calls 'the players ... men in jobs' (Allison, 1971, p. 164). When they act according to their particular bureaucratic positions are they acting irrationally, or just suboptimally? Or are they, conversely, acting just as the 'rational actor model' suggests, but at the level of individuals and departments rather than unitary states? Either way, what difference does it make to foreign policy outcomes, and to the location of responsibility for decisions? These questions hit on the biggest weakness of the theory: that the springs of choice are left unclear. If policy-makers prefer to pursue the interests of their own ministry, department or office, instead of liaising to construct an effective national position, why should this be so? How do they profit if the state as a whole is served less well than their parochial departmental interest? If career advancement is their criterion they might be better served by displaying an awareness of strategic national needs. To turn Allison on his head, they are more likely to make the effort in the service of a collectivity like the state, whose very survival might be thought to rest on their ability to relate ends systematically to means. It would be almost bizarre to deploy the same resources in the interests of a sub-unit. Indeed, it is not obvious that separate administrative units have competing interests, beyond the trivial level of finance and survival. One can further argue that the problem of rational actorness applies at both levels, the unitary state of Model I and the bureaucratic entity of Model III: that is, the assumption in both is that human beings are fundamentally calculating machines who optimize concrete preferences without much regard for political beliefs, moral values, personal loyalties or sense of identity, is flawed.

The bureaucratic politics model does, however, have much empirical evidence to support it. To the extent that it is correct it has profound implications for our notions of foreign policy action, making it difficult to rely on a notion of state-as-actor in international relations. States as such become less important because the state apparatus becomes less a motive force than an arena in which competing fiefdoms fight out their self-regarding games. Foreign policy in this perspective either gets made by accident, or is captured unpredictably by different elements at different times. This was the line taken, for example, in Halperin's book on the US Anti-Ballistic Missile System decision of 1967 (1974, pp. 1–10, 99–115). Here he showed that a system originally designed to protect against the USSR was described as being deployed against China, with all the obvious consequences for relations with Beijing, largely because of the battles which had been fought within government, particularly between Secretary McNamara and the Joint Chiefs of Staff.

If this is a true description and one of general applicability, then we have to live with the fact. As Jerel Rosati once pointed out, it does make the idea of responsible, democratic decision-making difficult to sustain (1981). Yet it is a category error to presume that because bureaucratic politics undercuts the constitution and presidency of the United States the theory must be mistaken. It may describe something which is undesirable, but that does not make it fanciful. More relevant is the conclusion that if policy-making is plagued by intertwined bureaucratic conflicts, then the formal responsibility of office-holders for final decisions is more nominal than real. Moreover, if the culture legitimizes this kind of behaviour then it must signify that a sense of duty to the government of the day, and to the public behind them, has not been widely disseminated.

Bureaucratic politics and agency are mutually entangled for one final reason. A key idea underpinning the theory is that of role-socialization, meaning the presumed ability of an organizational context to socialize its staff into its own particular values, over and above apparently superordinate concerns such as official policy, and the national interest. Thus foreign-service personnel will pursue very different concerns from those of the military, which is itself riven by inter-service rivalry – given that the navy is never going to agree that ships should be mothballed so that more tanks can be bought, and so on.

This is an all too plausible picture of how individual politicians can go native – it is often forgotten that in her first ministerial post, as secretary of state for education, Margaret Thatcher was a high-spending minister in favour of state schools, just as Enoch Powell, later a prophet of doom on immigration, had welcomed a labour force from the Caribbean when he was minister of health. Yet the argument has two weaknesses. Firstly, it is by no means clear what the 'unit' is that has such determining effects on a person's behaviour. Is it, for example, in the case of a high-ranking defence official, the department as a whole, the minister's inner group or the particular armed service/functional division for which he or she happens to have responsibility? And do lower-level functionaries only identify themselves with their immediate unit, or with all the divisions which are on top and around them? Secondly, even if we can identify stable units for given 'players', what is the 'line' which they are supposed to be pushing, and how do they know? Such suppositions as 'the military are hawkish' or 'diplomats promote appeasement' do not withstand a moment's serious scrutiny. There are too many divisions within groups, and variations according to the issues at stake.

If there is a relationship between organizational context and substantive policy preference, then it is a more subtle affair than this. Martin Hollis and Steve Smith (1986), as the most effective critics of this part of the bureaucratic politics model, have made amendments which make it more useable. Instead of a mechanical model which either reproduces the problems of rational action or depicts decision-makers as robots programmed by their position in the administrative order, they suggest that the roles individuals take on when they become part of an organization should be regarded as both constraining and enabling. Bureaucrats are constrained by their terms of reference, their superiors and the culture (or 'expectations') of their group, but they also have opportunities to interpret their given roles in new ways on the basis of their own personalities and particular circumstances. This description acknowledges that we are all shaped by the goals and values of the work we do, while allowing for change and human volition.

A key question in social science is 'where do preferences (or values, or ideas) come from?' – a question which pinches sharply on the theory of bureaucratic politics, given the assumption that roles are the source of key preferences. In practice, there is no substitute for empirical flexibility: that is, accepting that outcomes may well have been strongly influenced by bureaucratic competition, without falling into the trap of imposing the model rigidly on particular cases or countries. There are, after all, many key variables involved in the making of foreign policy, and the theory of bureaucratic politics deserves the status of single-factor explanation no more than any other.

Assuming that bureaucratic roles condition preferences to a degree there remains the question of how far competition between agencies undermines an effective foreign policy. The theory has problems here too, through taking an overly narrow view of what constitutes 'politics' within the policy-making system (Freedman, 1976). The resource–competition view does less than justice to the differences of formal responsibility and modes of understanding the world that exist between, say, career diplomats and those working in a finance ministry. These different groups will engage in politics, but usually at a more serious and elevated level than that of mere pork-barrelling. Their official responsibilities – here for relations with foreign governments versus sound finances – are simply different. Equally, they may be prepared to favour goals which cut across their particular departmental perspective. For example, in countries like Brazil, India and Japan it would be no surprise to find that foreign ministry officials favoured the prospect of permanent membership of the UN Security Council. Yet there will also be plenty of officials in other departments who will favour the move for broader reasons to do with their country's prestige and influence, even if a more active foreign policy would take resources away from domestic needs.

This means that the bureaucratic politics theory must be used in conjunction with both wider conceptions of politics and the roles of the formal *political* actors. Through their power of hiring and firing, but also through the manifesto commitments which they embody, the agreements they reach with foreign leaders and the sheer capacity for grand gestures which all powerful leaders enjoy, a head of government can change the rules of the bureaucratic game and start the whole dance off again to different music. This happens in the United States with every change of president but the same applies in other states, as we saw in Chapter 3. The theory must also take account of the variability of contexts in which bureaucratic politics are played out, meaning different levels of development, power and stability – as well as varying periods and political cultures. Halperin was myopic when he wrote that 'as we believe, all Governments are similar to the US government as we have described it here' (1974, p. 311). The US system is massive, inherently competitive and designed to serve the world's only remaining superpower. To understand its components alone is a major undertaking (Rosati and Scott, 2013, pp. 97–338). Most observers have concluded that while the model may be well-suited to describe the United States, the degree and nature of the problem are not reproduced in many other places (Karvonen and Sundelius, 1987; K. Dawisha, 1980; Hill, 1978; W. Wallace, 1978). Some cultures, indeed, display some of the opposite pathologies, as in Japan, where there is an obsessive concern with consensus ('*ringi-sei*'), and to a lesser degree in the centralized states of France and the United Kingdom, where the structure favours the forces of coordination over those of fragmentation. Moreover, most systems have informal networks which cut across the nominal interdepartmental divisions and produce elites with a strong sense of overall direction and/or common interest.

It is also important not to exaggerate the importance of officials. Some foreign policy disasters have less to do with decision-making fiascos –

whether bureaucratic or otherwise – than with more 'structural' forces such as geopolitics, ideological conflict or the configuration of classes. For example, had there been dozens of wise Persian-speaking CIA and State Department officials, or had the Shah not been admitted to the United States in October 1979, US–Iranian relations would still have taken a dive as the result of the revolution (Halliday, 1994a). Officials themselves, in memoirs and interviews, naturally highlight problems of resources and coordination, but a different vantage-point, and in particular a longer historical perspective, tends to make their concerns seem ephemeral (Donovan, 1997, pp. 143–63).

This raft of qualifications about the BPM is only worth making because at its core it is a powerful asset, with a set of insights which is strong and parsimonious. Allison argued that if governmental politics occurred even in conditions of extreme crisis, then it must be endemic. There have been various pertinent criticisms of the historical basis of his case study made – many dealt with in the second edition of 1999 – but more than enough remain valid. On the Soviet side, recent documents have suggested that there was confusion between Moscow and its military in the field as to who was supposed to be in control of the anti-aircraft batteries on Cuba which shot down an American U2 (Allison and Zelikow, 1999, pp. 353–4). As for the United States, the navy was certainly reluctant to pull back the blockade line so as to create more time for diplomacy, and some air force chiefs (notably Curtis LeMay) pushed so hard for air strikes, even after a deal had been done, that President Kennedy had to exert maximum authority to ensure control over events.

In more normal times, budget allocations produce interdepartmental rivalries of an intensity that can leave foreign policy the victim. This was the case with the Navy vs Air Force dispute of the early 1960s which led to the cancellation of the Skybolt missile programme despite the fact that the system had already been offered to the UK (Neustadt, 1970). The issue of the Guantánamo camp also produced major turf problems after 2001 (Hudson, 2007, pp. 95–101). Outside the US there are also many examples of bureaucratic politics being at the very least an intermittent problem. In the Soviet Union after 1978 the newly created Department of International Information provided another rival to the Foreign Ministry run by Andrei Gromyko, leading to him complaining strenuously about the existence of parallel systems (Shevchenko, 1985, pp. 189–90). The Israeli secret services are known to have put agents into their own prime minister's office, while the coalition's war in Afghanistan in late 2001 saw the Italian foreign ministry at odds with the more cautious officials of the defence ministry (Gazit, 1989, p. 266; Luzi, 2001). Just as important have been the tensions inside the German state (often arising from coalition politics) between the chancellor's office, the foreign ministry and the economics ministry – to say nothing of the fiercely independent Bundesbank in its heyday. At times the German position on a future European monetary union oscillated wildly according to which institution was briefing the press (Andreae and Kaiser, 2001).

Thus any system which is big enough to have a normal division of labour between ministries is likely to have a tendency to bureaucratic politics, however much the culture encourages solidarity. In complex systems, decisions are almost always the result of inter-agency compromises, and therefore in strict terms sub-optimal. But as we shall see in the next chapter the checks and balances involved can turn out to be valuable (Jervis, 1997). Given that decision-making is about formulating options and weighing costs versus benefits, the politics which occurs between departments is always potentially critical. Just as important, however, are the purely organizational characteristics of bureaucracy, which the BPM first alerted us to and then mistakenly subsumed under 'politics'.

The Heart of the Matter: Organizational Process

There is a great tradition of writing about bureaucracy long pre-dating the BPM. From Weber, Michels and Ostrogorski through to Herbert Simon and Chester Barnard a body of thought emerged from which the pathologies of modern organizational life have become clear. These theories of organization focus on procedural routines and on the handling of information. What they have to say about the problem of rationality is of great interest, and this will be dealt with in the next chapter. The main point of interest here is the way in which officials shape policy through their functional behaviour and their ubiquitous presence. As Richard Betts noted in relation to the power of the military, 'the real problem ... is indirect influence and the extent to which it may condition the decision-makers' frame of reference' (1977, p. 209). There are at least five ways in which this happens, independent of any bureaucratic politics:

- Firstly, administrative systems tend to 'factor' problems so as to be able to deal with them more efficiently. That is, everything is broken down into its component parts and classified into headings and systems that suit the pre-existing organizational structures but may not suit the problem itself. This is partly a rational and partly an historical process, but either way it makes it difficult to see the problem in the round. Where competence exists, the problem will be dealt with well, but the converse is also true. Thus, US diplomacy on the law of the sea in the late 1970s and early 1980s was hampered by the fact that the State Department's 'Bureau of Oceans and International

Environment and Scientific Affairs' was evidently inadequate (Bacchus, 1983, p. 50). If it had been stronger it would surely have led the United States to take a more proactive, and perhaps constructive, role in the negotiations over a Law of the Sea Treaty. Even where knowledge is not the issue, factoring can cause severe problems. From 1984 the CIA had critical data on Iraqi stores of nerve gas, but it failed to ensure that the US troops who blew up the bunker in Khamisiyah in 1991 were warned about their possible exposure to toxic agents (M. Walker, 1997).

- Secondly, bureaucracies cannot work without 'standard operating procedures' (SOPs – a key concept in Allison's *Essence of Decision*). That is, they need formal rules, almost always written down, which individuals are reluctant to overrule. Personal initiative is discouraged precisely because the *system* is seen as the source of efficiency. The rules usually only get changed under the pressure of a catastrophe which has already happened. Thus the Soviet Union's eastern air defences shot down the Korean civil airliner KAL007 in 1983 without proper reference to Moscow because they had orders not to allow hostile incursions which could be a missile attack on pain of their jobs – and possibly their lives (Dallin, 1985). It was easier to 'obey orders' than to take initiatives and to act on the basis of lateral thinking. The same was true in 1989 when policy finally changed in East Germany, with leader Egon Krenz signing an order to permit his people to make trips abroad. His administration could hardly believe the volte-face, and there was a serious risk that border guards would be ordered to fire on their fellow-citizens thronging the Berlin wall. Fortunately the guards themselves sensed the *Zeitgeist* and lowered their weapons. The most famous SOPs are those cited in explanations of the First World War: the Austrian need in 1914 to get the harvest in before calling up their reserves for war, together with the German Schlieffen Plan which led rigidly to the invasion of Belgium in the event of war with France, may between them have contributed to a limited conflict turning into a continent-wide disaster (C. Clark, 2013, pp. 292, 425–6, 531; Simms, 2013, pp. 292–3). Greater flexibility would at least have created more contingency plans and more political room for manoeuvre.

- Third is another iron law of bureaucracies – conservatism. Even at the level of basic competences, decision-makers are often unwilling to change the existing order of things. Thus the administration of EU development policy continued unreformed throughout the 1990s, despite its evident inability even to spend the funds allocated (Carbone, 2007). When problems are anticipated, change – in the form of retraining or new recruitment policies – can take decades to implement. The 'young turks' in the Italian foreign ministry had demanded reform for years before the measures announced in 1998 which began the slow process of modernization (Manfredi, 1998). In real-time foreign policy, behaviour conservatism usually takes the form of being 'risk-averse' and of over-insurance. Not wanting to be exposed as having failed to do the job, bureaucrats tend to stick to what they know has worked in the past and to err on the safe side. They often see their job as holding on to politicians by their coat tails to prevent fanciful initiatives. Of course it is thoroughly desirable to think things through and not to take stupid risks, especially with other people's lives and public money. But it can also be a fatal error not to change in time as the French armed services found with their attachment to the Maginot Line in 1940 and the entire communist bureaucracies of the Warsaw Pact discovered in 1989. Being self-consciously radical herself, Margaret Thatcher was accordingly disdainful of the Foreign Office 'where compromise and negotiation were ends in themselves' and even more of ministers who could not break free of its 'spell' (1993, p. 309).

- Fourthly, the quality of bureaucracy most prominent in the public mind – not always fairly – is pettiness. Most citizens associate their state with the administrative nightmares of long queues, unnecessary paperwork and officious behaviour. In foreign affairs the image is bad because of problems getting visas, passing through border controls and getting consular assistance – despite the fact that the first two of these are in fact not the responsibility of the foreign ministry. Behind the scenes the reality can indeed live up horrifyingly to the stereotype. The small-mindedness of the British officials in World War II who refused to accept the evidence before them of genocide against the Jews was staggering, rather like the wall of unseeing which characterized those who denied Serbian aggression towards Bosnia in the early 1990s (Simms, 2001). 'I was just doing my job' – the definition of the reliable bureaucrat – has unfortunately become a synonym for lack of imagination and humanity. Most of these errors are indeed committed by (relatively) good people doing nothing, to adapt Burke's phrase, about the triumph of evil. But bureaucracy does have its extreme case, summed up by Hannah Arendt in relation to Adolf Eichmann as 'the banality of evil'.

- Lastly, the comparative study of organizations highlights the inherent tendency of bureaucracy to expand when not positively checked. This can be termed elephantiasis. As Kissinger observed, 'the vast bureaucratic mechanisms that emerge develop a momentum and a vested interest of their own' (Kissinger, 1969, p. 144). Problems of coordination abound, particularly given the steady expansion of external relations and the information overloads evident in the second half of the twentieth century. The sheer technical problems of filing, copying, liaising and personnel management present formidable obstacles to efficiency in the biggest systems. Although computers can now sift vast amounts of data in an instant, at the same time the amount of transactions has vastly increased, while the need for encryption and other problems of secure communications can turn size and sophistication into a disadvantage. Managing an email archive is for most people no easier than organising a filing cabinet was for their predecessors.

Nor does privatization reduce the size and unwieldiness of bureaucracy. Although some ideas have been floated about subcontracting embassy work, it is hardly feasible to expect public policy to be conducted externally, often in highly political negotiations, by private interests. On the other hand states cannot avoid dealing with ever more private actors and substate entities. Whether in centralized or federal systems, the administration of foreign relations is complex and growing in proportion to the increased number of states, international organizations and private transactions that a foreign policy process has to track. At the extreme this can have dire consequences: the CIA is said to have received advance warning in 1981 that President Sadat of Egypt was going to be assassinated; there were, however, so many pieces of information to process that the warning was not read until after the murder had taken place.

Politicians and Officials: Can the Dog be Separated From Its Tail?

Given the theory of civil service deference to elected politicians, but the evident reality of officials' monopoly of expertise, detail and institutional memory, the question inevitably arises of whether the tail wags the dog. The work on bureaucratic politics has shown convincingly that in certain circumstances it is the administrative sector which sets the parameters of policy. It is, for instance, notoriously difficult for politicians to intervene in the processes of weapons development and procurement (Auger, 1996). Yet given the weaknesses of the BPM cited above we should also ask whether in the complex circumstances of modern foreign policy-making the dog can sensibly be considered separately from what has grown to be a very bushy tail. The American use of the term 'official' to cover both politicians and bureaucrats is revealing, placing both sets of people in the category of accountable public servants, with the implication that it is naïve to look upon professional administrators as being in some sense apolitical. Nor is this any longer a phenomenon peculiar to the United States. Recent British governments have tended to look sceptically on the notion of neutral advice from their top civil servants, and have made personnel changes to suit their ideology. More understandable was the ANC's determination in South Africa to get blacks into senior positions in the Department of Foreign Affairs and other ministries, at the same time as attempting not to alienate the existing white cadres.

The traditional view, whereby bureaucrats provide the continuity and expertise but leave strategic policy-*making* to the people's visible representatives, is therefore an ideal type – and as such worth aspiring to. It is idle to pretend that bureaucrats do not have a big role in making policy, even if their discretionary powers are more obvious during the vital implementation phase (Brighi and Hill, 2012; Smith and Clarke, 1986). The whole thrust of policy analysis as it has evolved since the 1960s has been to frame the 'policy-making process' as an integrated whole. In the context of foreign policy, Roger Hilsman (1964, 1987), the archetypal scholar-practitioner, formulated a model of concentric circles which accepts that there are different kinds of 'power centres' in the policy process, sometimes competing but also overlapping and engaged in a continuous search for consensus based on shared values. In this process some, both politicians and officials, will be closer to the centre of final decision than others, who orbit the inner group in varying degrees of proximity.

As Hilsman pointed out, 'policy-making *is* politics', and the bureaucrats responsible for high-level foreign policy decisions are political animals whether they recognize the fact or not. They are a key element of the elite which runs foreign policy, albeit with ever increasing pressures from domestic society. While divisions of view and interest within the elite are of central importance, they must not be mistaken for the more profound forms of politics which arise from the clashes between differing value-systems and sets of social interests. The range and depth of these differences almost always goes well beyond those apparent within the foreign policy elite, whether between bureaucrats and politicians or (more likely) between competing power centres containing members of both. From this point of view while the dog and its tail wag in harmony, the real problem is the tendency of the dog to escape its lead. As we shall see in Chapters 9 and 10 the populace still finds it difficult to participate in the process of setting directions in foreign policy, despite the potentially grievous consequences which flow for them from big decisions. We may conclude therefore that while politicians and officials share foreign policy agency, in terms of democracy they act only intermittently and ambiguously as agents of the people.

Notes

1   Here the term 'official' is used in its European sense, referring just to administrators, or what in France are known as *fonctionnaires*.
2   Figures obtained from <http://www.federaljobs.net>.
3   This does, of course, vary between states. In Japan, where diplomacy and image have been key instruments since 1945, the foreign ministry is relatively privileged in terms of resources (Komachi, 1999).
4   For a classic discussion of the role of military advice in foreign policy see Betts (1977).
5   See also an official account from the British National Archives (Twigge, Hampshire and Macklin, 2008). This would have been inconceivable before the Waldegrave initiative of 1993 to allow the release of selected intelligence files.

Further Reading

Allison, Graham and Zelikow Philip, 1999. *Essence of Decision: Explaining the Cuban Missile Crisis*. Second edition. The classic book on bureaucratic politics is reworked here, using new historical material.

Hocking, Brian and Spence, David, eds, 2005. *Foreign Ministries in the European Union: Integrating Diplomats*. This collection of essays provides an empirically rich analysis of 13 European ministries.

Ikenberry, John and Trubowitz, Peter, 2014. *American Foreign Policy: Theoretical Essays*, Seventh edition. This is a very useful collection of classic essays on the country around which most, indeed too much, of the FPA literature revolves. It contains the classic essays for and against the bureaucratic politics model.

Jervis, Robert, 2010. *Why Intelligence Fails: Lessons from the Iranian Revolution and the Iraq War*. Few are better placed than Jervis to provide a penetrating discussion of the political, organization and psychological factors involved in intelligence failures.

Neumann, Iver B., 2012. *At Home with the Diplomats: Inside a European Foreign Ministry*. As a senior IR scholar who has also served in a foreign ministry, Neumann's intriguing account is an example of participant observation.

Preston, Thomas and 't Hart, Paul, 2003. Understanding and Evaluating Bureaucratic Politics: The Nexus Between Political Leaders and Advisory Systems. *Political Psychology*, 20(1), pp. 49–98. This innovative article shows how the bureaucratic and leadership dimensions of foreign policy can only be understood in conjunction with each other, using cases from the Vietnam War.

Chapter 5

Rationality in Foreign Policy

Rationality is a central problem in social science, and it has figured prominently in the study of politics. Any attempt to understand or prescribe action has to reckon with the concept since it is the ideal type for both individuals and national systems. Indeed, the very idea of making 'decisions' and 'policies' is a modern notion indelibly associated with the attempt to exert rational control over events – as opposed to allowing destiny, God's will, chance or arbitrary power to determine one's lot. This said, it is a matter of debate as to how far human beings are capable of behaving rationally, how rationality is defined in the first place and whether what we deem rational behaviour is in any case so desirable. These issues have produced standoffs such as that between the profession of economics, where the idea of rationality has been of central importance, and other social scientists. For many of the latter the concept looks like a straitjacket imposed on the rich diversity of human motives and interactions, and one which assumes a greater degree of calculation (often quantitative) in the business of choosing futures than is possible or desirable. This debate is alive within political science, where rational choice approaches have made considerable inroads while encountering stiff resistance. Many are allergic to the idea that politics is best explained in terms of interactions between individuals – however self-interested – calculating the degree to which their preferences will be served by a given outcome – in short, through game theory and its variants (Nicholson, 1996, pp. 138–40).

Rationality in Policy-Making

Within IR the same issues are at stake, but with some particular complications (Kahler, 1999, pp. 285–6). In the first place, the classical rational actor model is too often blurred with realism, the historically dominant way of thinking about foreign policy and international politics. This is a mistake, for the two are logically distinct: realism privileges national security as the criterion for state decision-makers, whereas the 'rational actor' refers in this context to the idea of the state as unitary decision-maker – the actual criteria which the unitary actor might employ in

115

foreign policy are left open. In fact it does not follow that realism need operate by rational processes. It might, for example, involve leaders following their instincts as to how best to preserve their country's security. In the second place, 'rationalism' is a well-known label for the principal alternative to realism. Often termed 'Grotianism', and sometimes 'liberalism', it suggests both that states will often prefer cooperation to conflict and that they are gradually constructing 'a society of states' (Linklater, 1998, pp. 59–60, 209–10; M. Wight, 1991, pp. 37–40). This too need not entail rational decision procedures.

Lastly, where rational choice assumptions have made progress in IR, as with neorealism and neoliberal institutionalism, they have run into opposition not only from traditionalists and historicists, but also from the constructivists, whose argument that interests, preferences and values cannot be taken as given has attracted widespread support (Dessler, 1999, pp. 123–37). Preferences vary widely and are shaped by a range of personal, intra-state and international factors. From this viewpoint the main aim of foreign policy analysis is to probe 'the deeper questions of the formation of identities and the structural forces at the domestic level' (Waever, 1994, p. 256). There is an element of US–European difference in this rationalist–constructivist tension, but most good scholars acknowledge the need to draw on both lines of thought. The main need here is to clear the ground of the principal confusions which habitually attend the discussion of rationality and foreign policy.

After ground-clearing but before substance comes definition. In what follows, four fundamental tensions will be sketched out, between procedure and substance; the individual and the collective; efficiency and democracy; the normative and the positive. Thereafter the chapter is devoted to a more concrete assessment of what rationality means in the context of foreign policy, with special reference to the range of constraints on it which been extensively explored in the specialist literature. Although by the end of this discussion it may well seem that any hope for clear-sighted thinking in foreign policy is a mirage, the fundamental aim is to show that responsible agency is still possible even in uncertain, multilevel and intensely political environments.

Procedure versus substance

It was Herbert Simon who first made the formal distinction between procedural and substantive rationality, although it had been present in the writings of Max Weber and implicit in those of Adam Smith and J. S. Mill (Nozick, 1993, pp. 64–5). It can also be formulated as a distinction between process and outcome rationality (Simon 1955, 1982; Vertzberger, 1990, pp. 39–40, 367). Procedural rationality occurs when an actor engages in a systematic process, including reasoning, to enable him or her to achieve the goals which are already in mind. The focus here is on identifying the best means by which any given value may be optimised – or, more realistically, on avoiding those ways of behaving which seem likely to be counterproductive. Substantive rationality, by contrast, tells us the 'correct' outcome, given specified goals. Some argued, for example, that the 'only' rational path forward for Greece in its desperate economic condition after 2008 was to accept the discipline of the eurozone and to embark on a programme of austerity. Yet others viewed that option as doomed to failure, and therefore irrational. Such decisions hinge on judgements about the margins of choice and the capacity to force change. Czechoslovakia could have resisted Hitler in October 1938 despite the loss of Anglo-French support at Munich, but it would hardly have altered the ultimate outcome. Whereas Greece just as conceivably might do better if free to manage its own currency.

The trouble with such propositions is not just that they involve counterfactuals, but that they are barely distinguishable from normative statements. A more subtle approach is to stress the *link* between procedural and substantive rationality, with the former being a necessary but not sufficient condition of achieving the latter, while a form of 'action rationality' is necessary to make the connection: that is, proper information gathering and decisional procedures still have to be translated into action, which in turn will depend on both the values of the actor (that is, the criteria employed) and human judgement before a satisfactory outcome can be achieved (Vertzberger, 1990, p. 367). Foreign policy analysis is often confused and confusing because these basic distinctions are elided. For example an outcome might seem rational but have been reached fortuitously by non-rational means, such as a hunch; conversely, procedures might be meticulously followed but still of no use because the view taken of an adversary was fundamentally flawed. The classic example here is of US policy-makers in the late 1960s, who simply could not understand why they were losing the Vietnam War when the latest techniques of policy analysis were being used – not to mention an avalanche of weaponry (Gelb and Betts, 1979).

The individual versus the collective

The issue here is where to pitch rationality: is the unit whose behaviour is under the microscope the individual, or the group? If the latter, which group among the many possibilities should we choose? The answer is that rationality starts with the individual, because the latter is the ultimate source of intentional behaviour, but in politics it invariably extends to groups, where the problem moves to become that of the levels of analysis (Little, 1988). In this respect rationality epitomises the general problem of agency and foreign policy: who are the agents producing the decisions and actions? All individuals involved, politicians and bureaucrats, have to be assumed to be attempting to act rationally, in terms of both professional responsibility and personal interests (Hollis and Smith's (1986) 'roles and reasons'). Their pursuit of purely personal concerns is only likely to matter where they enjoy such seniority as to be able to exercise discretion to the point of impacting on policy. More significant is the problem of collective rationality. Does a decision-making group, let alone a state or other large entity, 'calculate', as opposed to relying on leadership, making compromises or just muddling through? Of course options get weighed. But does that mean that rational decision-making has taken place?

Research in FPA has blown holes in the notion of policy being made by a unitary collective actor. Theories of bureaucratic politics, of domestic politics and of competing perceptions have all suggested that it is very difficult for a state to aggregate the myriad attitudes of the human beings who constitute its 'agency' into a single and consistently pursued set of preferences (Carley, 1981, p. 63). Moreover, the inherent problems of collective action are magnified in international relations by the many levels of coordination and decision involved – domestic, national, intra-governmental, regional, international and transnational. If a firm is a collective not always in harmony with the interests of its employees, at least its goals are relatively limited: profit, growth, cohesiveness and so on. For foreign policy-makers the goals are plural, complex and subject to the inputs of many different participants. To understand the place of rationality in this context is a challenge indeed (Simon, 1976, pp. 41, 243–4).

Efficiency versus democracy

In a modern constitutional state there is a natural tension between the requirements of efficiency and those of democracy. Democracy may be desirable, but it is not in itself the purpose of foreign policy and may well be as a distraction from it. Elites may see the very security of the state, and certainly the policies in which they have a stake, as under threat if the notion of the sovereign people is taken too literally in the interests of democracy. If efficiency means the ability to achieve one's aims without unnecessary costs, then that must be closely related to procedural more than substantive rationality. For if ends are not related intelligently to means it seems highly likely that desired outcomes can be achieved, and that resources will be wasted.

Democracy, however, provides a separate set of compelling values, bringing substantive rationality into play. Certainly the need to follow democratic values will have opportunity costs. This is evident in the view that democratic states necessarily have one hand tied behind their back in international relations and therefore must strive to avoid disunity. This was Franklin D. Roosevelt's reasoning as he engaged in subterfuge with Congress in order to help a beleaguered United Kingdom in 1940 in what he saw as his country's own vital interests – while at the same time being unable to make strategic preparations for war. On the other hand some have argued that democratic debates make for a stronger and more resilient foreign policy in the long run (Waltz, 1967). Thus somehow we have to *incorporate* the need for democratic legitimacy into our definitions of efficiency and rationality in the first place. That is, policy will only be effective if it is seen to serve the values of the people as a whole and if it attracts their support. Equally, a policy which does not take into account the factor of legitimacy can hardly be deemed rational, in either the procedural or the substantive sense. Even in an autocracy it is likely to have only short-term success. This is broadly the position of the present book, although as we shall see, the phrase 'taking into account' begs a great many questions.

Normative versus positive

We have seen that substantive rationality is barely distinguishable from a debate over values, and it cannot be denied that the very notion of rationality carries within it a particular, contestable, view of the world. To the extent that this view derives from modernity, few are able to opt out of it, but in its emphasis on individuals optimising their preferences, it is divisive in many societies, especially in Asia and the Middle East, which start from very different religious and historical positions (Vertzberger, 1990, p. 270). This is not to imply that the West has a monopoly on rational behaviour – far from it – but rather that its procedural rationality is not the universal and self-evident good it sometimes seems. Even in the West there is room for disagreement about how much rational procedure is desirable in decision-making. As we shall see below many would regard excessive attachment to information gathering and the weighing of alternatives as counterproductive, preferring to rely on such assets as intuition, leadership or 'pragmatism'. There might even be occasions when decision-makers wish to employ the 'rationality of irrationality', which means convincing an adversary that one is irrational in order to deter them from pressing their case (Schelling, 1960, pp. 187–203).

Most Western decision-makers, however, do subscribe to one particular advantage of the idea of procedural rationality. That is the prescription that 'is' and 'ought' should be clearly distinguished, first so that a problem can be seen realistically rather than through rose-tinted spectacles, and

second so that when an 'ought' does not appeal it can be clearly identified rather than smuggled in via procedural language. Yet this is not the
case with some of the models which have been proposed as an improvement on classical rationality, to say nothing of the post-positivist view
that is and ought are impossible to disentangle. Some of the key critics of
the idea of rational decision-making, in their attempt to provide a more
accurate picture of what happens in the real world, tended to blur the
distinction between description and prescription, thus bringing in the
latter unacknowledged. This can be seen in the various ideas put forward
to deal with the weaknesses of the pure rational actor model.

Bounded Rationality

The problems of uncertainty, information overload and complexity
which confront any public policy-maker make it almost impossible to
live up to the ideal of rational method, with its clear subordination of
means to ends, and its assumption of what Simon has called 'a prepos-
terous omniscience' (Simon, 1976, p. xxvii). What is more, it takes only
a short acquaintance with actual patterns of behaviour to understand
that something well short of classical rationality is obtained in practice,
at both individual and collective levels. Beyond the pathologies of
bureaucracy, politics itself demonstrates that policy-making is predominantly a pragmatic business in which both planning and the sustained
control of programmes are at a premium, despite the conventional
rhetoric (Braybrooke and Lindblom, 1963, p. 77). Foreign policy is actually distinctive because it has a conscious tradition of avoiding excessive
abstraction and attempts at structural change, given the difficulty of
reshaping systems at the international level. Lord Salisbury's metaphor of
statesmen as canoeists, following the flow and avoiding the rocks rather
than being able to set their own course remains relevant (Joll, 1950;
Northedge, 1968, pp. 9–38).

Practical observations and metaphors have been given theoretical
shape over the past half-century through scholars in the area of administrative studies, first among them Herbert Simon and Charles Lindblom.
The former's notion of 'bounded rationality' and the latter's concept of
'muddling through' soon became part of the established vocabulary of
both academics and practitioners. What is their utility for our understanding of contemporary foreign policy?

The idea of bounded rationality arises from the futility of trying to
'maximise' one's values. Instead, it is more realistic to '*satisfice*', or
accept the outcome which approximates reasonably well to one's preferences. This, in the language of the psychotherapist Bruno Bettelheim, is

to be a 'good enough' politician (or parent) rather than striving for perfection, which incurs high costs and in any case is unattainable (Bettelheim, 1987). We do not know enough about consequences, and we cannot imagine all possible options well enough to optimize, even if there were the time and political space to do so. As Robert Keohane has pointed out, this fits well with the need in politics, particularly international politics, to compromise and to agree 'regimes' through which various issue-areas can be managed and expectations made realistic (R. Keohane, 1984, pp. 110–32). As with the SOPs of domestic bureaucracies, regimes discourage policy-makers from thinking of their agenda as a *tabula rasa*, on which to construct great monuments to their own memory. The temptation is great, as with the US ambitions for a 'new international order' after both 1919 and 1991, but most statesmen and women are more pragmatic, accepting the need to work within the limits of existing assumptions and institutions. In fact they have little choice other than to accept that goals such as 100 per cent security or a complete halt to global warming are simply unattainable.

Satisficing, however, only takes us so far down the road of how to make policy in an uncertain, intractable environment. In order to cope with this process over time, and with unpredictable change, many fall back on the idea of *disjointed incrementalism*, or 'muddling through' – terms which are almost onomatopoeic in conveying the fractured nature of the process (Braybrooke and Lindblom, 1963, pp. 81–110; Lindblom, 1979). This means changing policy by small steps rather than grand transformations – a version of the gradualist philosophy of English politics since 1689, articulated best by Edmund Burke. It also restricts the number of alternatives to be considered, using the methods of trial and error, accepting that ends and means are difficult to distinguish, concentrating on fixing problems rather than constructing 'positive goals' and, not least, ensuring that a consensus is built despite the many, disconnected points of consultation that exist in modern democracies. If agreement can be reached across the policy group, the theory holds, the option chosen must be the best in the circumstances on the grounds that: (i) two (plus) minds are better than one; and (ii) there is a better chance of being able to carry the policy through.

The attractions of this approach, as both description and prescription, are easy to see. Yet there is at least one significant objection to the theory of disjointed incrementalism, and one which brings us back to the understanding of rationality as an essentially contested concept. If rationality is too synoptic a notion, then incrementalism risks the opposite defect, of tunnel vision. Lindblom, for example, recommends muddling through as the preferred 'strategy' in policy-making, despite the apparent oxymoron. The same is true of satisficing, which Simon represents as a more realistic and useable notion than that epitomized by 'economic man' (Simon, 1976, pp. xxix–xxxiv). In this respect both models can mislead through their very realism. Accepting the virtues of muddling through can legitimize an unwillingness to ask fundamental questions, and to criticize the general direction of policy (Braybrooke and Lindblom, 1963, p. 105; Smith and May, 1980, p. 118). Arms races are incremental, by definition, once they have begun, but few would pretend that they are desirable, let alone represent an actual strategy. Another area where muddling through can be harmful through inhibiting change is economic policy. The British stumbled along with an overvalued pound for nearly 25 years after the Second World War without daring to do more than adjust economic policy marginally within a harmful stop–go cycle. When the inevitable crisis came, it had serious ramifications for defence policy as well as for sterling (Darby, 1973; Strange, 1971). The damage done by 'going with the flow' of easy credit from the mid-1980s until the crisis of 2008 is another such example. Similarly, the weakness of the satisficing approach was evident in the enthusiasm for European monetary union via a single currency, when it was clear from the launch of the euro that no economic government was in place to deal with the inevitable crises. In all these cases some attempt to look further than the immediate horizon might have led to major problems being avoided.

An awareness of these problems led some critics, including Lindblom himself, to suggest that a middle way can be found between the classical and the bounded versions of rationality. That possibility will be considered in the last section of this chapter. But it should also be noted that incrementalism can sometimes only appear to be cautious, when in fact it is making radical change possible by stealth, out of the visual range of critics. In a slow process broken down into small segments the full import of the cumulative change may not be apparent until it is too late. In foreign policy the prime example of this is the development of the EC. The key figure behind it, the French civil servant Jean Monnet, unusually combined a highly strategic vision with a pragmatic, subtle and gradualist method, never forcing the pace when that might have been counterproductive. Yet most of his successors preferred to deny the possibility of federalism while seizing any opportunity to push things incrementally in that direction under the cover of practical improvements. In this they have been helped by the prevalent ideology in the EC of neofunctionalism and graduated integration. Accordingly even their fiercest opponent, Margaret Thatcher, found herself supporting the Single European Act (SEA) for its initiation of the single market, when the SEA also introduced various institutional changes which ratcheted on the integration process towards the eventual Treaties of Maastricht and Amsterdam, which she found anathema.

Such processes do not depend on a conscious author, or conspiracy, to drive along some grand narrative; certain interests can simply nudge policy along in a direction which perhaps even they do not wholly understand at first. For instance the decision of 1997 in principle to enlarge the EU from 15 to 28 states locked governments into accepting large movements of poor people towards the richer countries, under the principle of the free movement of labour – a development not foreseen, and which led to serious unanticipated consequences such as the rise of the populist right. Ironically, enlargement was hailed to begin with as the triumph of strategic, long-term thinking – and indeed the geopolitical concern to stabilize east-central Europe was a major factor. But it turned out that much of the script was being written as the project went along.

Other examples of what might be termed 'self-deceiving incrementalism' are the creation of Bizonia in post-war Germany, sucking the US into a permanent commitment to western Europe, and the imperceptible start of the US commitment to South Vietnam between 1961 and 1965, with first advisers sent, then air support and finally ground troops. This was a case of what is known now as 'mission creep', that is of how undeclared small wars, producing major new commitments, come to pass. In practice the tendencies in policy-making towards drift and snowballing, as the downside of incrementalism, are all too common. They are typified by the long deadlock in the Doha Round of the WTO, where even those states with a strong interest in trade liberalization seemed unable to take a decisive initiative (Narlikar, 2010a), and by the move of Japan over several decades towards the status of a well-armed state, despite the limits imposed on its defence expenditure by the 1946 constitution. Japan has not kept within the 1 per cent of GDP guideline introduced between 1976 and 1987, but it would be a mistake to believe that governments in Tokyo have set out to transform the situation fundamentally (Hook et al., 2001, pp. 7, 132–6, 458).

There is one more important aspect of the theory of bounded rationality to explore, and this too raises the is/ought dilemma. John Steinbruner's theory of cybernetic decision-making (1974) has provided acute insights into the way the mind and organizations work, and has been illustrated in the context of foreign policy. Building on the work of other cognitive analysts before him, Steinbruner argued that because the human mind cannot cope with the mass of incoming information it develops repertoires for monitoring a limited number of variables, indeed often only one major variable. Abstract calculations are not made; rather, ends and means are blurred together and adjustments made on a semi-automatic basis. A good example is the way the brain adjusts to the roll of a boat at sea, so that when we step onto dry land, we feel unsteady until the next readjustment takes place. Similarly, if a tennis player consciously thinks about how to volley when at the net, the likelihood of success is diminished. In collective policy-making, the theory brings us back to organizational process, as when one armed service monitors its own well-being rather than security as a whole, but also alerts us to the fact that allowing those closest to events to make their own, parochial adjustments, may be the only way to get anything done, as with the Berlin airlift of 1948, when the US and Royal Air Forces found ways to achieve what some of their political masters thought both dangerous and impossible (Shlaim, 1982, pp. 242–6).

The difficulty with the cybernetic approach is that while it is convincing as an account of how the mind copes with complexity, its insights in relation to improving collective decision-making are more limited. It is difficult to find examples of the cybernetic process in politics which are not negative. There have been plenty of foul-ups in history through decision-makers being one-eyed, as with US Army intelligence being preoccupied with internal sabotage before Pearl Harbor, or the Soviet elite paying too much attention to the texts of Marx and Lenin, but it is more difficult to find successes relating to the ability to focus on a single key variable (Wohlstetter, 1962). Perhaps Churchill's wilful insistence on rearmament in the 1930s, or Helmut Kohl's ability to focus on German reunification in 1989 despite all the contextual difficulties, count. But even they are exceptional cases.

Thus, although rational foreign policy-making is restricted by the problems of information-processing and multivariate analysis, this does not mean that the cybernetic or the incremental approaches represent desirable replacements. There is a considerable difference between demonstrating that the rational approach to policy is deeply flawed, and proposing a working alternative, particularly when little care is taken to distinguish the descriptive from the prescriptive elements in the theory. We shall return to this problem after focusing more directly on concepts with a direct applicability to foreign policy.

Non-decisions in Foreign Policy

The concept of non-decisions has much to offer the study of foreign policy (Bachrach and Baratz, 1970; Crenson, 1971; Lukes, 2005). It has three dimensions, all of which have resonance for foreign policy behaviour. Firstly, a non-decision is simply a decision *not to act*, that is, to do nothing, even in the face of the need or pressure to act. This might be seen as the basic rule of prudence in international politics. An example might be the decision of the Arab friends of Hamas not to intervene militarily in Israel's onslaught on Gaza in 2014. Caution got the better of outrage.

Saddam Hussein, conversely, might have been better advised in 1980 to take Anwar Sadat's advice 'not to make war on a revolution' (Halliday, 1999, p. 256). His inability to resist exploiting Iran's weakness after its revolution led to the war of 1980–8, with devastating consequences for both sides, and for the region. Secondly, there is *decision avoidance,* or *the failure to act.* This is associated at the extreme with the paralysis of the decision-making system, as during Richard Nixon's Watergate period, but more common is the perpetual inability of countries to formulate clear war aims, either in the approach to conflict or during its evolution. This can be deliberate, in order to increase margin for manoeuvre, but it is likely to be just the result of policy drift. British policy was plagued by it in both world wars (Hill, 1991, pp. 188–223; Rothwell, 1971; Stevenson, 1988, pp. 87–138).

Third, and theoretically the most significant dimension of the concept of non-decisions, given its implicit critique of the pluralism dominant in policy studies, is the idea that *certain options are excluded* from the agenda, at times by sleight of hand but more effectively by what Schattschneider (1975, p. 69) called 'the mobilization of bias' in which '[s]ome issues are organized into politics while others are organized out'. Another way of looking at this is to note 'the weight of the existing order of things', which raises profound questions in history and political science about when change become feasible, and when not. For example, was it unrealistic for the colonialist countries to consider the possibility of withdrawal from empire before the Second World War? Why would any government in France and Britain even today find it almost impossible to dismantle their respective nuclear deterrents? When does the 'weight of things' become light enough to overthrow?

Given that all things come to an end eventually, it is fascinating to observe the 'unthinkable' finally becoming thinkable. The higher the wall of prejudice against change in the first place, the more dramatic is the eventual change. This was true of the sudden switch of American policy towards China in 1971 after two decades of hostility, of the revolution wrought by Gorbachev in Soviet foreign policy in 1985 and of the final loss of confidence by the apartheid state in South Africa in 1990. The power to ignore is one of the most powerful political (and indeed personal) weapons, but it can rebound decisively in the long term. It should not be forgotten that the attachment to gradual change of Burke, or in our own day of Michael Oakeshott, always included an injunction to anticipate events by intelligent adaptation, so as to avoid the eventual need for revolution. Policy analysis should never neglect the importance of time: some periods are more open to change, of a general or particular kind, than others. Policies can seem possible at one moment, but out of the question at another. Which is to say that while non-decisions can keep options open in principle, history (in the sense of wider movements) has a big say in providing opportunities for real change, and in closing windows of feasibility once events again start to congeal into stable patterns. The years 1945–1948, 1968–1979 and 1988–2001 may have been such windows, whereas between those years, and after 9/11, constructive foreign policy strategies proved difficult even for the major powers.

The idea of non-decisions has considerable applicability in foreign policy analysis because it takes us beyond process to the political and social structures from which power derives. More precisely, it enables us to link process to certain key structures, in the way that another neglected theory, that of elites, also does, but with more purchase on the ideas, and on policy itself, than the sociological approach, which concentrates on the identity and positions of office-holders (Parmar, 2000; Parry, 1969). As Steven Lukes (1974, 2005) has shown, when certain ideas are excluded from the policy agenda, or when attempts at change are systematically blocked, we need to ask not just the questions 'how?' and 'by whom?', but also 'why?', and 'with what differential consequences?' It may be that there will be no clear answers to such questions, but the serious ramifications of foreign policy decisions make it imperative that we probe beneath the surface towards the structures that might be shaping agency. If we are rightfully sceptical of conspiracy theories, then the concept of non-decisions is the most useful point of entry (Aaronovitch, 2009).

The Power of Historical Thinking

History provides politicians with a welcome form of structure amidst uncertainty, as well as a way of mobilising public opinion behind the government. If as individuals they have personal memories, as representatives of a political class they inherit certain dominant myths, rituals and pieces of conventional thinking which they use and abuse but are also themselves trapped within.

Most human beings constantly refer to the past as the best way to measure their progress and current situation. In this sense historical thinking is inevitable, and not a matter of choice. Those who are amnesiac, who literally have no sense of their past, cannot function in the world. Decision-makers tend to go further, looking for the 'lessons' to be drawn from history, while social scientists who reject the historical method nonetheless spend their lives seeking to discern patterns in history. Those working in the complex and diffuse world of international politics tend to put particular emphasis on the value of historical experience, and often on the seemingly timeless rules of realism. Yet scholars tend to stress that there are no clear lessons to be drawn from history and that, as Hegel said, 'we learn from history that we do not learn from history' (May, 1973, p. 179).

This is for a number of different reasons, some philosophical, some practical. Chief among them is the tendency of decision-makers to use over-simple historical comparisons and analogies, and then to end up in difficulty (Etheredge, 1985; Howard, 1991; Jervis, 1976, pp. 217–82; Khong, 1992; Vertzberger, 1990). In particular the crude use by British and American leaders of the spectre of 'appeasement' has been amply documented, with anti-Soviet policies inspired and justified by a fear of repeating the mistakes of the 1930s. Similar instances can be found in relation to the 'lessons' often cited of the Versailles Peace, the Great Crash, the Berlin airlift, the debacles at Suez and the Bay of Pigs, the Vietnam War, the Rwandan genocide of 1994 and many instances of counter-insurgency culminating in the 'war on terror'. It would be perverse not to draw some conclusions for the future from these and other traumatic events, but great care and sensitivity to context is required (Porch, 2013, pp. 332–4, 337–8).

We should look on history not as a store cupboard of off-the-shelf solutions but as something integral to ourselves and our sense of identity. If history is seen as perpetual flux, with familiar objects bobbing up regularly in the stream of change, the present becomes intimately connected to both past and future. It is then possible to be aware of both difference and similarity without attempting to follow a particular model. Ernest May and Richard Neustadt (1986) have provided intelligent guidance for decision-makers on how to be critically aware of history without falling into the traps of misleading analogies or of teleology. Even if it has to be doubted that leaders will often sit down during their weekends at Camp David or a Russian dacha to study their manual, there is a chance that its philosophy will filter down through education, staff training and generational change.

Much of the time decision-makers refer to history unselfconsciously. Often, however, they exploit it knowingly, to make a point in foreign relations or to mobilize domestic support by summing up a collective sense of the national past. Pageantry, anniversaries and history teaching in schools are grist to this mill, which are a form of soft propaganda. Defeats and crises, victories and revolutions, imperial pride and imperial guilt all provide fertile ground for connecting current policy to the most potent symbols of national life.

In any area of public policy those responsible have to strike a balance between being insouciant about the past and being dominated by it. It is not rational either to expect to wipe the slate clean or to deny the need for change. In any case, subjective conceptions of historical meaning will always have a significant bearing on what decisions get taken. Decision-makers would thus be well advised to distinguish between three kinds of legacy, in terms of their own freedom of choice and ability to act: (i) those so deeply engrained in institutions, dispositions or culture as to be virtually ineradicable by acts of policy – such as the United States' current position as first power in the world; (ii) those which are still deeply rooted but which might with a considerable effort be turned around within a political generation, as was Egyptian–Israeli hostility; and (iii) those which are either relatively recent, or superficially established, and can therefore be managed without too much difficulty, like French embarrassment during the Arab Spring over its association with the deposed Tunisian dictator Ben Ali. If a given problem is misperceived in terms of the depth of its rootedness in the past – too much or too little – problems follow, as Imre Nagy tragically discovered after his challenge to the Warsaw Pact's presence in Hungary in 1956. This was not simply a matter of underestimating Soviet power; Nagy got wrong Moscow's sense that history now demanded a buffer zone against Germany. Unfortunately for Hungary, the other central European states were the chosen instruments of this new history.

Own Goals

Foreign policy actors pursue different goals simultaneously, with varying degrees of self-consciousness and clarity. This is a major challenge for the idea of rationality. When pressed, decision-makers take refuge in the tired catchall of the national interest, which enables them to hide behind a screen of presumed unity and responsibility rather than examine the difficult trade-offs and feasibility issues which confront them.

The idea of the national interest is inadequate as a guide to foreign policy goals because it is tautologous. No policy-maker is likely to suggest going against the interests of his or her own state. If those officials in Britain's Department for International Development (DfID) who have privately said that they feel more answerable to the world's poor than to UK taxpayers were to go public with their view, it would cause a storm.[1] All politicians can be presumed to be pursuing their subjective versions of the national interest. The real issue is, following James Rosenau (1971), 'which interests are deemed to be national, and why?'. Ideology, values and private stakes all shape the competing views of how to define them. Thus the national interest cannot just be objectified in terms of power, security, prosperity and independence, all of which can be taken for granted as high level goals but which lead to disagreement as soon as discussion becomes more specific. Rather, its real use is as a measuring stick. On the one hand it enables us to judge whether a given policy is genuinely an attempt to serve collective *public* concerns, or whether it is serving instead a sectional interest flying under false colours. On the other, it should help us to see whether a goal or policy is really derived from an *interest*, in the sense of a stake which a given unit has in a problem, as opposed to being a value, preference or mere aspiration. Both sets of distinctions are vital, but yoking together the terms 'national' and 'interest' creates the same kind of confusion as the term 'nation-state'.

Decision-makers are not going to give up thinking in terms of the national interest overnight. But unless they engage in more self-analysis of their objectives they risk deceiving their publics. As a British newspaper observed of the US president during the phoney period of the Gulf War

> thus far Mr Bush's reasons for going to war have criss-crossed between a bewildering variety of causes from defence of oil fields, to upholding international law, to stamping on a new Hitler, to building a new regional security system and upholding American values. The latest reason, offered by an obviously frustrated Mr. Baker [Secretary of State], is 'to save American jobs'. (Pringle, 1990)

Even allowing for a certain amount of tactical obfuscation, this multiple reasoning betrayed a degree of policy uncertainty which undermined the legitimacy of the eventual decision to use force, particularly amongst those already hostile to the United States. To say that decision-makers should understand the taxonomy of their foreign policy goals is not to demand excessive rationality. If they have no sense of direction or priority they will be forced back on serendipity and chance. But at the very least they should be able to differentiate and prioritize among their objectives. There are four separate continuums to consider.

First, they should have a sense of the *time-frame* they wish to deal in. A goal such as 'defeating terrorism' or regaining lost new territory is something to consider only as a long-term strategy, and then with a suitable dose of scepticism; if it is sought even as a middle-term goal it involves high risks and costs. In relation to Taiwan, China understands what General Galtieri did not over the Falklands/Malvinas, namely that urgency is counterproductive when others' conceptions of vital interest are at stake. Vladimir Putin succeeded in annexing Crimea in 2014, but at the cost of destabilising the region and his own economy. Conversely, an overly long-term perspective can lead to missed opportunities, as when a sceptical Britain 'missed the bus' on the European Economic

Community (EEC) from 1955–7 and then struggled over the following decades in its relationship with Brussels. The most difficult assessments fall into the middle-range category, that is, within the maximum period of a democratic government's life. All new policies have to start somewhere, but if a government starts down the difficult road towards a destination which it has little chance of reaching, it must expect problems. The classic case is Turkey, which for many years pressed for membership of the EU with little chance of success. This produced angry disappointment at home, persistent conflicts with the governments seen as responsible for a veto on Turkey, and finally a nationalist reaction. Ankara might have been better advised to have accepted that entry was unlikely while extracting a high price from the EU member states for their duplicity.

The second continuum is that of *explicitness*. All actors display a difference between their declaratory and their operational goals, that is, between those they claim in public and those they are really pursuing. Nor is this a matter of the contrast between open, democratic regimes and deceitful autocracies. Few foreign policies have been more transparently clear in their ultimate aim than those of Hitler or Mussolini, while Britain, France and Israel each had well-disguised hidden agendas during the Suez crisis of 1956. More common than either extreme is the tendency for governments to be unaware that their actual criteria have drifted away from those they are publicly known for. It was no surprise that Joschka Fischer, Germany's foreign minister between 1998 and 2005, maintained the rhetoric of his Green Party origins while pursuing policies barely distinguishable from those of his Free Democratic Party (FDP) predecessor.

In terms of explicitness, goals fall into three main categories which in practice often become blurred: those which are taken wholly for granted, like the United States' world role; because they are part of the 'habits and furniture of our minds' (Danchev, 1993, p. 145); those gently floated but without any hope of realization, just as the idea of unification was kept alive by the FRG during the early Cold War; and those which are consciously pushed as major priorities, like China's current determination to be the major power in the South China Sea. Goals may move from one level to another, but if they do so it should always be with the appropriate degree of self-awareness and consensus. A large part of the problem that Britain has encountered over the EU in recent decades is the fact that significant parts of the governing Conservative Party have started to aim at withdrawal, while others are committed to remaining inside the Union, while negotiating better terms. In Egypt Anwar Sadat paid with his life because he shifted his country's foreign policy objective away from the destruction of Israel towards coexistence. In doing this he could not have been clearer, and the policy has endured, but he misjudged the extent to which such a change required advance preparation of the ground at home.

This brings us to the third continuum, that of the *values at stake*. Decision-makers, but also the citizens who criticize them, often fail to distinguish between their own state's particular stakes and those which involve all participants in the international system. This is Arnold Wolfer's distinction between 'possession' and 'milieu' goals, and is similar to (but not identical with) the difference between policies which for the most part can be pursued unilaterally and those which require multilateral action (Wolfers, 1962, pp. 67–80). At either level the policy can be revisionist or conservative. But it makes a huge difference, for example, as to whether a state's concern is principally to strengthen the United Nations as a pillar of international order by, say, reforming the Security Council, or just to maintain/acquire its own seat. Naturally leaders like to stress the compatibility between possessional and milieu goals, but this is as much public relations as serious political thought.

At this point the analysis can no longer be restricted to ends; means are inherently part of the equation, for few actors are indifferent to the way in which others pursue their aims, given that the means chosen can have major costs and knock-on effects. If the best way forward is seen to be the acquisition and insouciant use of power, then equal and opposite reactions will be forthcoming. At the opposite extreme, if considerations of power are neglected, not only is it unlikely that the desired aims will be achieved but it is quite possible things will get worse. Thus Belgium and the Netherlands in the late 1930s placed too much trust in the status of neutrality as their protection against German ambitions. In this context there is a continuum between what Wolfers called 'the pole of power and the pole of indifference', meaning power politics on the one hand, and introversion on the other (Wolfers, 1962, pp. 81–102). Neither, in these times, can be seriously counted as foreign policy strategies in its own right; but they represent tendencies which states variously lean towards, styles of foreign policy adopted in the hope of achieving more substantive ends.

Despite this qualification, decision-makers must consider whether or not a given value is particular to their state, shared with a like-minded group or of genuinely universal scope. All too often policies suffer from ethnocentrism through assuming that one's own interests coincide with those of the whole society of states, or the reverse when a general consensus fails to take account of the view of a state in a crucial position, as with the United States' lack of enthusiasm for the Kyoto Protocol on global warming. The most dramatic examples of this kind of category mistake come when a state decides to crusade abroad for its own set of domestic values. Attempting to export your own values on the basis of self-righteousness is always a recipe for conflict and often for disaster, whether conducted by a great power seeking to recast the whole system (Napoleonic France, the Wilsonian United States) or a smaller state in the grip of revolutionary fury (Gaddafi's Libya in the 1970s, Taliban Afghanistan in the late 1990s).

A more mundane problem is simply deciding on where the boundary of the like-minded, or your region, stops. The African Union (like its predecessor the OAU) has been weakened by uncertainties over the degree of common purpose shared by its sub-Saharan and north African members, just as the Organization of American States was riven by disputes over solidarity with Cuba. Arab states have long wished for unity, while pursuing policies which prevent it ever being achieved. The European Union has never clarified the extent of its external border, or where 'Europe' ends. In all these cases foreign policy has been launched more on the basis of rhetoric and hoping for the best than of a clear-sighted appreciation of costs and benefits. The very difficulty of deciding on identity, quite apart from distinguishing between ends and means, encourages the tendency to muddle through.

The last continuum of foreign policy goals is that of the specific *targets* of action, where similar problems occur. For any given policy it matters a great deal as to who or what is being targeted for influence. For example some states only woke up belatedly to the fact that if they wanted to shape US policy on the Middle East they needed to look to public opinion outside the Washington Beltway. In Europe British governments have struggled for years to find the right allies with whom to build winning coalitions in EU decision-making. Italian leaders, by contrast, perceiving their country's weakness accurately, clearly understood the importance of keeping open lines of communication to Paris and Bonn, and were accordingly able to play their hand more effectively.

The targets of foreign policy vary, from individual states to elements within a state, from whole groups of governments to transnational actors. What is important is to avoid blundering about in the dark as to those one is trying to influence. The point is the same as with the other three parts of the taxonomy of goals: nothing is fixed in stone – goals are in constant and necessary evolution. Serious blurring either within or across the categories mentioned will usually cause problems. If nuclear non-proliferation, or human rights, are thought to be desirable goals to be pursued in the long-term, but particular targets are then singled out according to the exigencies of the moment, a whole new raft of problems will suddenly spring up to do with double standards. Equally, if a short-term goal deemed urgent is pursued without its importance being conveyed effectively to the other party, as was the case with the Soviet attempt to assist Cuba with missiles in 1962, it is not surprising if a crisis results. Even retrospectively, in order to evaluate the success of a foreign policy we need to be able to know how seriously the policy was being pursued, in what time-frame and on what criteria.

Avoiding the Worst

Bearing in mind the many constraints deriving from their multiple environments – bureaucratic, political, psychological, external – it almost seems absurd to expect decision-makers to behave rationally. Certainly the classic picture of a group operating on the basis of clearly thought-through goals, leading to choices made on maximum information in conditions of calm, will only come near the truth on rare occasions. Even this method is no guarantee of success, let alone of ethical behaviour. Yet we cannot abandon the idea of rationality altogether. Leaders themselves believe they are acting rationally, and citizens have to trust that they are being governed on that basis. What is more, most governments set broad strategic directions within which bureaucratic and domestic politics take place. How then, are we to make sense of the tension between the persistent aspiration to rationality and the practical impediments to its achievement?

One way forward is to accept that substantive rationality is impossible to agree on. Who can say if it is inherently rational for a developing country like Pakistan to acquire nuclear weapons, or for a rich one like Switzerland to hold on to neutrality, given the political judgements which immediately come into play? Most politicians coming into office will operate on the basis of 'we are where we are'. Even lowering our sights to procedural rationality does not remove all the problems. In some circumstances we have to trust in the intuition and emotional capabilities of our leaders, which goes against the grain of the cerebral, knowledge-based, paradigm normally associated with the word 'rational'. The modernity which the West brought to the world is distrustful of instinct, chance, superstition and fate, and praises the ability to control actions and the environment. This approach has many achievements to its name, but even in natural science breakthroughs often occur by short-circuiting recommended procedures.

Research on foreign policy suggests that the best way out of this impasse may be to invert the usual process by seeking to identify those approaches to policy-making which are positively *irrational,* and for which the risks far outweigh the occasional benefit. This will primarily focus on good procedure, but there is also a certain convergence with substance, in that the extremes of subjectivity are associated with the tendency to base foreign policy on private prejudices, with a proclivity for hostility and suspicion towards the outside world. Most observers would regard this as irrational to a degree that goes far beyond miscalculations over the ends–means relationship.

Thus, although we cannot specify that any given decision-making technique – such as 'multiple advocacy' or the use of a devil's advocate – is inherently desirable, we are on surer ground in identifying forms of behaviour which will, more often than not, lead to serious problems in foreign policy (George, 1972; 1980; R. Keohane, 1993; 't Hart, Stern and Sundelius, 1997, pp. 311–33). The following fall into this category: acting on impulse, or whim; failing to ensure a basic level of interdepartmental coordination; screening out critical views; disregarding the need for good quality information and analysis; focusing only on the short-term; failing to communicate intentions and red lines to other actors; and failing to ensure domestic support. Naturally there is no simple correspondence between any one of these pathologies and policy failure. But persistence in one or more of them – and they do tend to go together – is very likely to be counterproductive.

This approach, of cutting out sloppiness and narcissism in decision-making, might be thought nearer to mere reasonableness than to rationality. Yet it is no trivial matter, for carelessness, arrogance and tunnel vision are likely to have serious consequences, not least for the foot soldiers and citizens who bear most of the costs of high-level foul-ups. In the twenty-first century foreign policy-makers are increasingly recognising their dual responsibility to their own citizens and to international society. As such they need self-awareness about how to take good decisions on potentially explosive issues. Linklater (1998, p. 211) puts this in a philosophical context by arguing that rationalism requires an acceptance of 'multiple communities of discourse [which] can promote new relations between universality and difference'. That idea might take time to trickle down, but if policy-makers consciously try to avoid approaches which downgrade thought, empathy, consultation and clarity, they will be demonstrating a commitment towards reasonableness and responsibility in this most dangerous of arenas. Perhaps this is a counsel of perfection, especially times of crisis. But as Vertzberger has pointed out, 'to recognize that decisionmakers cannot always be optimally rational ... does not preclude judging their responsibility. ... [T]he price of power and authority is responsibility, no matter what' (1990, p. 361).

We shall see in Chapter 11 how the ethic of responsibility pulls in different ways, and how the tension between internal and external constituencies cannot ultimately be resolved without a political discussion of the purposes of foreign policy. Nonetheless, decision-makers will still tend to cast around for a 'rational' approach, in terms of how best to translate their values into achievements. In this respect the FPA literature suggests two broad conclusions: first, that since it is so easy to confuse ends with means, and to blur objectives into each other, a degree of self-consciousness is essential, with basic assumptions being articulated and critically examined. Decision-makers would then stand a better chance of being able to hold to a strategy without being blown off course by the multi-layered politics in which they are perpetually engaged, or entangled in their own competing goals.

Second, they should adopt a form of 'flexi-planning', that is, setting broad strategies without specifying too much detail, and without being excessively committed to them where things are evidently not working out. Given the intractability and unpredictability of international relations a general openness of thought and process is desirable if obstacles are to be circumvented and new possibilities exploited. Who in 2009 could have predicted that a form of Caliphate would be proclaimed in Syria and Iraq only five years later? Yet collective action cannot occur without a sense of direction and a modicum of coherence, so that some form of medium-term, flexible planning is also indispensable.

Thus the notion of rationality need not be abandoned altogether, so long as it is not interpreted too narrowly or too prescriptively. In foreign policy the stakes are too high to risk downgrading the values associated with reason and rational process. There are many examples from the twentieth century alone of what happens when rationality gets out of proportion, at one extreme scorned and at the other elevated to the status of science. It should, rather, be seen as a vital background value, not a godhead to worship or destroy (Habermas, 1987).

Note

1   Private information from a senior ex-insider from DfID.

Further Reading

John, Peter, 2012. *Analyzing Public Policy*. Although containing little about foreign policy, this is a fair-minded survey of the various approaches to explaining rational – and less rational – policy-making.

Lucarelli, Sonia and Manners, Ian, eds, 2006. *Values and Principles in European Union Foreign Policy*. Lucarelli and Manners have brought together stimulating essays on issues of substantive rationality, identity and collective action.

McGrew, Anthony and Wilson, Michael J., 1982. *Decision Making: Approaches and Analysis*. While this unsurpassed collection of classic articles on rationality is currently out of print, it is easily available second-hand.

May, Ernest and Neustadt, Richard, 1986. *Thinking in Time: The Uses of History for Decision Makers*. This practical guide is the product of cooperation between a leading diplomatic historian and a political scientist who advised President Kennedy.

Steinbruner, John D., 2002. *The Cybernetic Theory of Decision: New Dimensions of Political Analysis*. Second edition. Steinbruner's classic and influential book explains why non-rational approaches often make more sense.

Vertzberger, Yaacov Y. I., 1990. *The World in Their Minds: Information Processing, Cognition and Perception in Foreign Policy Decisionmaking*. This comprehensive study provides an integrated treatment of rationality, cognition and historical learning.

Chapter 6

Implementation: Foreign Policy Practice and the Texture of Power

If the problem of agency in international politics is in the first place a matter of identifying the decision-makers who make a difference, the answers partly depend on the dimension of implementation. We must ask whether decisions once taken do get translated into the actions they imply, or whether what actually transpires is the product of delay, distortion and a further round of political conflict. A great deal of literature now exists which suggests the latter is far nearer to the truth than the former, which is, not unreasonably, expected by the public.

Implementation has two distinct aspects: first the capacity to do what is intended, given the capabilities and instruments at hand, and second the slippage between political decision and administrative execution. The second aspect is closely related to the problem of bureaucratic politics already discussed, so the current chapter gives more attention to the first. Yet before either can be tackled the relationship between action and implementation needs to be considered.

More than a Technicality

When confronting the problem of implementation we should always be aware of the fundamental misconceptions attached to it. The first is that implementation is not a technicality, consequent on decision-making. Rather it is integral to the whole policy-making cycle and very often difficult to distinguish from its other phases. At the least, implementation feeds back into the original decision and often begets new problems. The second arises out of the discussion conducted in Chapter 4: namely, the operations of the bureaucracy are central to the process of implementation, and vice versa; it was argued, furthermore, that it is not helpful to consider bureaucrats' and politicians' roles in foreign policy-making except in relation to each other. The third is an extension of the critique of classical rationality: when it comes to deciding how to put decisions into practice, the analogies of the surgeon choosing a scalpel or the golfer a club are inappropriate. The implementation of policy is not just a matter of selecting, precisely, the best tool for the job. In foreign policy there are a limited number of possible instruments – in broad categories the diplomatic, the military, the economic and the cultural – but they are almost always used either in combination or with some potential synergy held in reserve. The differential uses of these instruments will be analysed in the main part of this chapter, but except in a highly structured relationship between like-minded states (as in trade relations between the United States and western Europe) it is rarely possible to compartmentalize or to deny oneself recourse to the full range of possible pressures. Even in transatlantic relations there have sometimes been unpleasant surprises through action spilling out of the accepted channels, as with the US pressures on sterling over Britain's invasion of Suez in 1956, or European refusals to allow US overflights for the attack on Libya in 1986. In conditions of flux the choice of instruments becomes at once more uncertain and more crucial. The US's use of rendition to the Guantánamo base after 9/11, and Russia's subversive techniques in Ukraine during 2014, have both had destabilising consequences.

Such misconceptions flow from the tendency to see the foreign policy process in overly rigid terms. A flow chart typically represents it as starting with the identification of a problem, moving on to the collection of relevant information, enabling the formulation of options, until finally the point of decision is reached. The implementation phase, when the desired action occurs, is then something of a coda. Sequencing of this kind is a helpful starting-point, but it relies too much on the ideal-type of rationality qualified in Chapter 5, while also makes the stages of policy-making seem much more separate than they are in practice. For example, a problem can arise out of a state's mere proposals, or even surmised decisions, as with Iran's assertion of its right to a nuclear energy programme. This sparked fears and threats from those who saw themselves threatened long before any serious weaponized capacity was at hand. Tehran put itself at some risk by deliberately exploiting the international uncertainty, but it also skilfully used its new diplomatic leverage in relations with the European states anxious to avoid an Israeli pre-emptive attack.

Formal decisions are even more likely to be interpreted as actions, especially when made public, as when Prime Minister Romano Prodi of Italy announced in late 1996 that it was to throw all its energies into seeking entry into the European common currency, in the face of widespread scepticism. That expression of a major priority changed the environment for its partner states, particularly Spain and Greece, and made it much more difficult for Germany and France to keep Italy out. To that extent the statement of intention was a shrewd, self-executing, move. It shows that although the term 'action' implies a tangible set of activities it often takes a purely linguistic form. A declaration can represent a way of changing direction, or a form of pressure. Because it targets perceptions and others' internal politics it is no less a move in the international political environment than troop mobilizations or the selling of gold reserves (R. Cohen, 1987). Even decisions which are kept secret are actions in the sense that they ignite a new chain of events in the actor itself. When noticed by foreign intelligence agencies, they are taken particularly seriously, and then start a wider sequence of action-reaction (Rosecrance, 1977).

The Faces of Power

Power is a foundational concept of political science and a central pillar of international relations. Its relationship to foreign policy, however, tends to be subsumed in theories of international politics. Hans Morgenthau's *Politics among Nations* (1954) gave us 'a manual for state leaders' based on a theory of the drive for power in human nature (C. Wight, 2002), while George Modelski's *A Theory of Foreign Policy* (1962) made an explicit attempt to operationalize power as the currency in which foreign policy-makers deal. Kenneth Waltz (1979) puts power at the centre of his theory, but in the context of the security dilemma, and the uneven distribution of capabilities (Booth and Wheeler, 2007). Like most general theorists he is not interested in how leaders play the cards they are given or in the interaction between societies, collectively and transnationally. Only E. H. Carr (1939, 2001) and Raymond Aron (1966) have managed to square the circles of producing a theory of international politics which allows space for foreign policy as a variable and communicates something of the texture of policy dilemmas.

The practitioner acting internationally on behalf of a country faces three different dimensions of power: power as an *end*; power as a *means, or currency*; and power as a *context, or structure* (Boulding, 1989; M. Wight, 1966).[1] These themes have not always been distinguished, or connected up to the problem of agency. What follows seeks to correct this imbalance.

Power *as an end in itself* represents a popular view of politicians and their motives. Actors are seen as out to maximize their own personal power, for the psychological satisfaction involved in controlling others, and for the glory, money and opportunities that come with it. When acting on behalf of states they blur, in this view, the distinction between their own aggrandisement and that of the state and come to identify the fate of the latter with themselves.

Needless to say, this is largely a caricature. But it is not always false. Examples of Harold Laswell's 'mad Caesars', willing to subjugate whole peoples, even continents, in the pursuit of their personal lunacy, will always occur (Wolfers, 1962, p. 84). The twentieth century witnessed not just the excesses of Hitler and Stalin but also those of more mundane gangster-politicians, such as Saddam Hussein and Muammar Gaddafi. Corrupt dictators unwilling to relinquish power are commonplace in central Asia and parts of Africa. Nonetheless, increasing numbers of states are run by those who, however cynical, are essentially concerned with power as a means for achieving wider objectives. Even Hitler had far higher ambitions than the mere accumulation of personal power. He had a view, warped and bizarre as it was, of a particular kind of civilization to be extended across the globe, not least as the best way of destroying the twin evils of communism and international finance capital. Politics, he said, was 'a struggle of nations for life' (R. Evans, 2005, pp. 357–61). The advance of the Nazi Party was identified with this vision (R. Evans, 2004).

Even when leaders do pursue an improvement in their state's international power position for its own sake, there are always implicit questions to be answered about the extent and the nature of the expansion. How much power is enough? For the small number with a megalomaniac tendency the problem is that they are precisely incapable of such rational calculations; any gain simply whets the appetite for more. But those who pursue revisionist ends while understanding the limits are concerned with specific objectives and not with a drive for hegemony. Gamal Abdel Nasser, for example, leader of Egypt between 1954 and 1970, was intermittently demonized in the West as a threat to world peace when his actual concern was to reassert Egyptian interests and to counter the growing strength of Israel – policies unpalatable in many quarters, but perfectly compatible with a normal, instrumental, model of statecraft (A. Dawisha, 1976, pp. 102–7; Vatikiotis, 1978, pp. 325–47).

There is a fine line between power as a value in itself and *power as a means* to an end. While power-worship is about the desire to coerce and to dominate, any use of power involves some degree of coercion and domination. Thus some leaders begin with a vision, perhaps even noble, for which power is only the means, but which gets eventually subordinated to the determination not to relinquish power once gained. Lord Acton may have been right about absolute power corrupting absolutely, but even power in a democracy leads some to manipulate the rules to avoid relinquishing it – as we have seen with Vladimir Putin in Russia and Recep Tayyip Erdogan in Turkey. On the other hand in the context of foreign policy it must not be forgotten that those who seem intoxicated by power domestically are often capable of acting prudently in relation to other members of international society. Men like General

Pinochet in Chile or Paul Kagame in Rwanda have had a shrewd sense
of the limits of their external power. The model is that of the Bolsheviks,
who took power in Russia in 1917 precisely because Lenin understood
the need to surrender to Germany in the First World War if their domestic aims were to be achieved.

States and leaders vary considerably in how far they seek external
power and status. Many are cautious, even introverted, whether
through lack of capabilities or through political culture. Yet in an uncertain world all suffer to a greater or lesser degree from the 'security
dilemma' of which Arnold Wolfers (1962, pp. 81–102) wrote, following
Rousseau, namely that the craving for security entails an insurance
policy against unforeseen dangers, creating some margin of capacity
over that which would be necessary in a stable environment. This is the
justification for standing armed forces and for the whole modern apparatus of defence policy, currency reserves and emergency powers.
Whether it then follows that particular policies like France's nuclear
deterrent or US bases in the Persian Gulf are desirable and proportion-
ate forms of insurance, is a matter for political argument.

Power as currency deals explicitly with the question of the means to
serve other values. Modelski's metaphor of reserves of power, like dollar
holdings, can be turned on its head to see a strong economy as the ultimate asset in international relations (1962, pp. 27–30). If states have
both interests (I) and values (V) to promote, then together they lead to
certain *core concerns* (I + V = CC). These in turn revolve around one or
other of four universal issues – *security, prosperity, identity* and *prestige*
– which will be interpreted variously according to the context. All will
require both a measure of generalized power, and particular resources
appropriate to the purpose.

By *power as context* is meant the proposition that foreign policy
actors operate in an environment where they cannot sensibly disregard
power. It should be axiomatic, without implying the whole baggage of
realism, to accept that power is a central element in all social relations,
and, by definition, in politics. In international relations, moreover, the
uneven distribution of power goes a long way towards determining
outcomes. As the means of attenuating the exercise of power are still
only patchy, despite the hopes of interdependence theorists, it is a fool-
hardy person who writes it out of the script.

For their part practitioners may both overestimate and underestimate
the importance of power, including how much is at their disposal. A
state with many advantages on paper can still run into difficulties, as the
US did between 1951 and 1953 in its Korean stalemate with China, a
weak and predominantly agricultural country still adjusting to revolution. The opposite case is Afghanistan, which no great power has

managed to subdue – as shown by the humiliating Soviet withdrawal in 1989 and the retreat of the International Security Assistance Force (ISAF) in 2014 after 13 years of occupation.

Those who behave as if power disparities can be skirted are just as doomed to hit trouble. Mussolini, dazzled by the gains of war and by the dominance of his German ally, would not listen to the warnings of his more realist foreign minister, Count Ciano (Knox, 1982, pp. 46–9; Muggeridge, 1947). Ciano paid with his life for doubting that the Axis could win; Mussolini and thousands of others soon followed, through the Duce's blind faith in victory. Similarly, the Shah of Iran believed in the 1970s that the combination of repression and American support made his regime inviolable. In the event his arrogance simply heightened the violence of the revolution which overthrew him. A decade later the leaders of the Soviet Union trusted too much in the formidable apparatus of conventional power they had built up in Eastern Europe. The shock of its sudden unravelling destroyed a superpower. The fate of their regime is the greatest single testimony to the weakness of power politics as a guide to durable success in foreign policy.

The context of power also means understanding structures. Susan Strange argued that there were four principal structures in international relations, of security, money, trade and information (Strange, 1994). If, like the United States, a country is able to dominate one or more structures then it will have a decisive role in international affairs. This is a point of great relevance to the present argument, in that foreign policy actors not only have to cope with the hierarchy of power in a given structure, but also have to face the issue of who has the power *to set* the structure(s). Henry Kissinger (1994, p. 731) has said that 'structures are instruments that do not of themselves evoke commitments in the hearts and minds of a society'. They are abstract entities. Nonetheless, both the power to act and the ability to exert power over another require an understanding of the framework in which action has to take place (Sprout and Sprout, 1965). The problems of system-dominance and system-change will be dealt with in the next chapter of this book. For the time being it is enough to note that states vary enormously in their ability to shape the external 'milieu'. The very language of foreign policy – 'superpowers', 'great powers', 'middle-range powers', 'small states' and 'micro-states' – is a way of trying to express these differentials, but it does not do justice to the fact that world politics is also composed of diverse issue-areas and regimes, across which power is not necessarily cumulative. Thus while Germany is central to financial discussions it is more marginal in the diplomacy of arms control. The reverse is true of Pakistan.

The Texture of Power – Hard, Soft and Plastic

What counts as a reserve of power may change over time. Since the value of a currency depends on it being recognized by others, power always has a relational element (Strange, 1994). If an adversary does not fear your war paint, or your nuclear weapon, or if the world stops valuing gold, or membership of the UN Security Council, then your assets may turn out to be paper tigers. One of the best examples of this is the Austro-Hungarian Empire in the nineteenth century, when the waning mystique of historical monarchy could no longer inspire respect among subject peoples or abroad, leading to a spasm of self-assertion before the final collapse (Sked, 1989).

Just as money supply can be fixed or inflated so power in international relations is sometimes zero-sum and other times variable sum. If Ireland gains a given net sum from the European Community budget, then it follows that there is so much less money for everyone else in that partic-ular financial round. Conversely, those member states which are net contributors agree to be so because of their judgment about the long-term economic and political gains from the whole EU enterprise. Actors thus have to make continual judgements as to the nature of the game they are playing. When they attempt to translate strengths into action, they should be aware that power is not exercised in a vacuum, but rather *over* another party, *for* a specific purpose and in a given time-frame. Moreover, they need an understanding as much of limits as of possibili-ties. That is, at some point coerciveness loses its bite and dealing has to begin. If the possession of power means that one's own fate can always be determined to some degree, the question remains of to what degree and what kinds of compromises with others can be struck.

At one analytical level down from the general problem of power lies that of the instruments of foreign policy. This is not as straightforward as it might seem. To be sure, a taxonomy of means can easily be constructed while individual options, like economic sanctions, have been subjected to exhaustive research. But in practice it is difficult to isolate the impact of a single instrument compared to others. What follows tries to provide an integrative framework, in the form first of a continuum and second of a pyramidal model showing the interrelationships between the resources, capabilities and instruments of foreign policy.

The discussion of instruments is now dominated by the distinction between hard and soft power (Nye, 1990, pp. 29–35; 2004). Hard power is coercive, physical, targeted and often immediate. Soft power is indi-rect, long-term and works more through co-option, persuasion and the power of attraction. It has been defined as 'getting others to want what you want'. Some observers take the view that hard power is becoming increasingly redundant, while states are now racing to get ahead in the acquisition of soft power (J. Holden, 2013). Governments have come to recognize more explicitly in recent years that the capacity to shape images and values can have concrete pay-offs (Anholt, 2006). Be that as it may, there has always been a conceptual overlap between power and influence, and the hard/soft distinction is an evolution of that traditional relationship, as in Figure 6.1.

The continuum of power shows that there is no clear point where hard power stops and soft power begins. Sanctions – which can themselves take many forms – can be as much demonstrative as punitive, designed to encourage others to rethink their positions. Diplomacy is mostly associated with dialogue, but can be coercive when ambassadors are expelled or there is a veiled threat of tougher measures behind a request for cooperation. Propaganda is often difficult to distinguish from the simple burnishing of a self-image. Even armed services can be used to help in natural disasters or to train foreign military personnel without any particular quid pro quo being required – in which case they are not exerting hard power. Conversely the 'carrots' of financial aid or commercial privileges may seem like soft power when in practice they amount to inducements which cannot easily be refused given the weakness of the state in question. They thus become coercive in character.

If this argument is taken to its extreme it might be thought that all soft power, at least when mobilized by governments as opposed to that which emanates automatically from the very nature of a country and its culture, has to be ultimately coercive. This is perhaps what the Canadian Foreign Minister Lloyd Axworthy meant when he argued crudely that 'soft power does not mean wimp power' (Pearlstein, 1999). The use of slow-acting, opinion-shaping instruments can still be a form of coercion, albeit barely understood by the target, because actor X is seeking to change actor Y in directions which Y had not originally envisaged, even if the process is not technically against its will. This is the realm, at the international level, of agenda-setting, manipulation and 'hidden persuaders' (Packard, 1981).

We need not go quite this far. Because states are made up of multiple official units and millions of citizens they are not easily subject to brain-washing from outside. But soft power does aim at changing structures and mentalities over the long term, particularly through attracting others to one's own values and way of life. Thus the European Union has relied for decades (in the absence of a military instrument) on its 'civilian power', which has led to other regional organizations seeking to emulate it (for example, the African Union) and a queue of neighbouring countries seeking membership or partnerships (K. Smith, 2014, pp. 17–19). This is also an approach associated with pacific countries like Germany

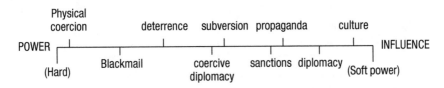

Figure 6.1   The continuum of power in foreign policy

and Japan (Maull, 1990), although they do hold hard power in reserve while also relying on powerful alliances for protection.

Any regime valuing soft power still thinks it too risky to dispense with hard power instruments even in peaceful times, taking their lessons from history. But the wider range of foreign policy instruments now available, and the way they confuse the issue of conflict versus cooperation, make decisions on which route to go down particularly problematical. Soft power always seems more reasonable, and cheaper, given that military hardware has become extortionately expensive. But it can be decried as a policy of weakness at home, and is often seen as cultural imperialism in target states. What is more an effective projection of image abroad may rest as much on a tacit respect for its hard power as on its soft power advantages. Thus there is an inevitably unresolved debate about whether the collapse of Soviet power was due more to popular recognition of the superiority of life under capitalism, or to the victory of the United States in a technology-driven arms race. Almost certainly both factors came into play, while neither was exactly useable as an instrument of foreign policy.

Most actors with the luxury of choice will prefer to have a range of instruments at their disposal. But measuring the costs and benefits of any instrument, hard or soft, is inherently difficult because of the multi-facetedness of foreign policy and the long time-lags often involved.[2] Leaders need to combine pressures and/or inducements while also think-ing about the uses of soft power for the longer term. As US Treasury Secretary Jack Lew said in responding to North Korea's supposed cyber-attack on the Sony film studios:

> we will employ a broad set of tools to defend US businesses and citi-zens, and to respond to attempts to undermine our values or threaten national security. (D. Roberts, 2015)

To use 'a broad set of tools' governments have to take an 'insurance policy' approach, whereby they decide how much cover they need against which eventualities, how much they can afford, and which time-frame is most important to them. They then adjust their policies and outlays as circumstances change, both for better and worse. Yet this brings us back to the limits of rationality. Major readjustments were widely expected after the Cold War, in the form of a 'peace dividend', but the inertia of alliance systems, bureaucracies and military–industrial vested interests limited the extent of change, as it so often does. To the extent that cutbacks were made in defence spending, notably in Europe, they were less the result of strategic planning than of budgetary pressure.

Combining the insurance approach with the management tool of 'risk assessment' could give executives and legislatures more of a handle on external policy spending. Going further, Joseph Nye has said that the false choice between soft and hard policy instruments can be resolved through his new concept of 'smart power' (Nye, 2008, pp. 43, 83). This involves mixing hard and soft power means according to context. It may be that hard power is riskier to use than soft power, but more useful to possess – as a deterrent, and a badge of status. Soft power takes longer to amass and works best when governments allow civil society to flourish, and to shape the country's reputation in the world (Hill and Beadle, 2014). Smart power is therefore not something which can be banked; it depends on leaders' judgement, and willingness to invest in long-term assets which they may not be around to use.

We return to the issue of striking a balance between the different instruments of foreign policy at the end of this chapter, after a more detailed discussion of specific instruments. But before either can be attempted there is one last theoretical issue to clarify. This is the pyramidal relationship between resources, capabilities and instruments. These three terms are often used as synonyms, which is a mistake. The distinctions between them are set out in Figure 6.2.

Resources are the elements, derived from history and geography, which constitute what Renouvin and Duroselle (1968) called the 'basic forces' of foreign policy, which determine the limits of a country's impact on the world – if not its ambition. These include the minerals in the ground, the fertility of the soil and the quality of the climate. Position, size (of both territory and population) and degree of development are all things which governments inherit and can only be changed over generations, if at all, assuming that territorial aggression is ruled out. French governments, for example, tried strenuously to increase their country's population size after 1870 but with very limited success. Resources matter immensely, but they are not in themselves operational instruments of foreign policy.

To reach the level of instruments, resources must first be operationalized into *capabilities*. These are the recognizable elements of a modern government's responsibilities where decisions may hope to have an effect, at least in the medium term. They include the armed services,

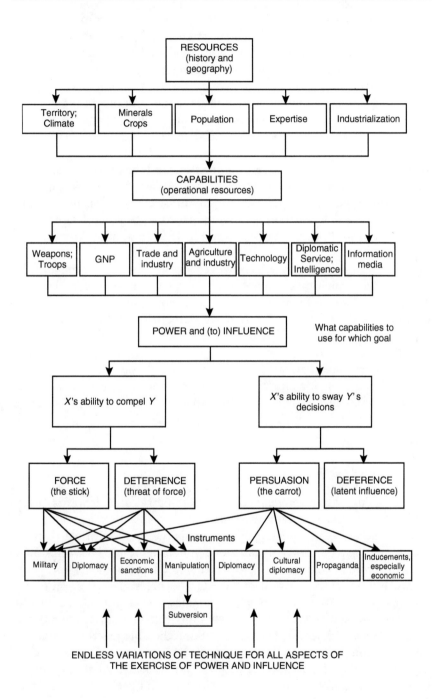

Figure 6.2   Resources, capabilities and instruments

technological capacity, levels of education, patterns of trade and diplomatic representation and the general strength of the nation's economy. Unlike power and its use, capabilities tend to be measurable, and to generate bureaucracies to enhance and develop them. Decisions on capabilities will usually affect foreign policy, but they do not always follow any foreign policy logic. Japan rebuilt its whole economy after 1945 for reasons of survival; the unexpected consequence was the emergence of an economic superpower. British financial retrenchment after 1979 incidentally damaged the effectiveness of institutions with a key external role, such as the diplomatic service, the BBC and the universities. On the other hand, the Soviet Union set out quite deliberately to repair its postwar technological vulnerability to its capitalist adversaries and by major (if ultimately self-defeating) efforts, managed to beat the United States into space, with both machine (Sputnik in 1957) and man (Yuri Gagarin in 1961).

Capabilities in themselves, however, do not constitute manageable *instruments,* which give states 'externally projectable power' (Puchala, 1971, pp. 176–84). Being both more numerous and more specific than capabilities they fall into four broad categories: military, economic, diplomatic and cultural. These are examined below in turn. Coercive (hard) strategies draw on instruments from the first three of these categories, and persuasive (soft) strategies may use all four.[3] Endless varieties of technique exist for any given instrument, none of which should be allowed to run ahead of the available capabilities. Each instrument therefore presents its own distinctive problems of agency.

The Military Arm

The front end of hard power is the use of military force. If war is always political, as Clausewitz famously asserted, then the other side of the coin is that behind much foreign policy there is the implicit threat of force. Not violent force necessarily, as the 'democratic peace' between OECD (Organisation for Economic Co-operation and Development) states illustrates. But some implication of threats and pressure is ever-present in international politics – even from weak states with their backs against the wall. This is, in effect, the message that any action in international relations risks incurring costs through the unpredictable reactions of others. Such reactions take many forms, from Israel's attack on the peace flotilla to Gaza in 2010, leading to the death of nine Turkish citizens (and then to Turkey's breaking of diplomatic relations with Israel), to Russia's military response to Georgia over Abkhazia and South Ossetia in 2008. Sometimes military force breaks right through the veil of diplomacy, and sometimes it merely rumbles over the horizon like a nearby storm. Either way, the two instruments often come close together. When they do so as part of a strategy it is termed 'coercive diplomacy' (George and Simons, 1994). As we saw with the theoretical analysis of power, threats to withdraw ambassadors, impose economic sanctions or subject a state's population to a barrage of propaganda are no less coercive in purpose than threats to invade or mount punitive air raids, even if the hope is to achieve a goal without the need to escalate. Those threats, by contrast, which carry an explicit reference to possible military action if the target does not comply always risk events spinning out of control. They gamble on big returns and big losses.

Where states are bound together, whether by formal pact or shared values, military force does not enter into their relationships. Geography is also a key factor. Where states are geographically distant, even if great powers are hostile to each other, an armed collision is unlikely (Mouritzen and Wivel, 2012). But there are still all too many places in the world where border issues, intercommunal conflicts, terrorism and historical antagonisms mean that the relationship between foreign policy and the possibility of violence is an intimate one. Even with rational policy-makers inclined to negotiation, the mere existence of sizeable armed forces and military expertise is a standing reminder of what lies in reserve if diplomacy does not work.

The work of many authors shows that although the threat of military force sometimes works, it can easily lead to its protagonists surrendering control over their own actions, as they become squeezed between unforeseen reactions abroad and expectations unleashed at home. 'Diplomatic history is littered with conflicts that escalated far beyond the goals either party initially perceived to be in conflict as a result of needlessly severe coercive tactics employed by one or both parties' (Lockhart, 1979, p. 146, cited in Lauren, 1994, p. 45). Force can be threatened in secret – as with what Lawrence Freedman (2005, pp. 84–6) called Prime Minister James Callaghan's 'undetected deterrence' of a possible Argentine move against the Falklands in 1977 by dispatching a small task force to the South Atlantic – but secrecy will rarely prove feasible for long.[4] President Kennedy conducted the first part of the Cuban missile crisis in private, but journalists got wind of the lights burning late in the State Department, and after a week some public announcement became inevitable. The possibility of humiliation in the eyes of the world thus became a dangerous extra pressure towards escalation (Allison and Zelikow, 1999; Dobbs, 2008; May and Zelikow, 1997). In the seven cases studied by George and Simons (1994, p. 291), only two (Laos in 1961–2 and Cuba in 1962) are seen as examples of successful coercive diplomacy. The other five (pressure on Japan in 1941 before Pearl Harbor, on North Vietnam in 1965, on Nicaragua under Ronald Reagan, on Libya in 1986 and on Iraq in 1990–1) display more evidence of dangerous complications than of productive results. At the most, the authors conclude, coercive diplomacy 'is highly context dependent'.

If this is true for the threat of military action, it is even more so for the actual use of force. One of the reasons why Saddam Hussein did not soften under the pressure of coercive diplomacy between August 1990 and 15 January 1991, or between April 2002 and March 2003, was that he did not believe that the US and its allies would risk the dangers of unleashing war. In this he was twice mistaken, and twice suffered rapid defeat by overwhelming force. Even so, the use of violence is evidence of the failure of diplomacy, and often of foreign policy. Its long-term consequences are often both harmful and unforeseeable. Military action may cut through the Gordian knot which diplomacy has failed to unravel, but it also rarely 'solves' problems in the sense of relegating conflicts to the history books. It more often exacerbates them and merely postpones their recrudescence.

Given that armed forces are a relatively crude instrument, for most states most of the time success consists in not having to resort to them. The age of military triumphalism has passed, which means that the military has become bureaucratized and as much a part of the decision-making process as a separate instrument to be used only in the field, albeit with an unusual degree of autonomy and a special claim on resources. Yet it does still present options for external policy which leaders find difficult to resist. These can be divided into the two categories of revisionism and deterrence.

So far as *revisionism* is concerned, or a state's ability to improve its perceived position, it is an unfortunate truth that military force does frequently work. Even in the post-1945 era there have been many examples: Israel in occupying and holding onto new territory from 1967; India in occupying Goa in 1961 and creating Bangladesh in 1971; Turkey in dividing Cyprus in 1974; the Western allies separating Kosovo from Serbia in 1999; Russia in annexing Crimea in 2014. These examples could be multiplied – just as they can be matched by many cases of the failed use of force. The Soviet Union's blockade of Berlin in 1948 and invasion of Afghanistan in 1979 both backfired; Britain and France were humiliated by the failed Suez expedition of 1956, as was the United States by the Bay of Pigs in Cuba in 1961, Vietnam between 1964 and 1975, and Iran in 1980; North Korea (1950), Egypt (1973), Argentina (1982) and Iraq (1980) all launched invasions which were then reversed. The invasion of Iraq in 2003 removed Saddam Hussein but turned the region into an even more dangerous trouble spot.

The conclusions to be drawn from this mixed record are fivefold: (i) the overwhelming, decisive and short-term use of force can work; (ii) initiating force is only an option for the already powerful, but even then success is far from guaranteed; (iii) the use of armed force is increasingly seen as dangerous and unacceptable by the international community because it sows dragons' teeth for the future; states are therefore ever more concerned that their actions should be legitimized, usually by the United Nations; (iv) force is more likely to work when the apple is already so ripe as to be about to fall – that is, when the target is already vulnerable; and (v) winning a war by no means guarantees winning the peace – in fact it often creates serious new problems.

Given these factors, decision-makers should regard the use of their armed forces more as an exceptional eventuality than as one of the principal instruments of their foreign policy. Conversely, it is foolish to take force off the table when an adversary is behaving aggressively, as Chamberlain did at Munich in 1938. The possibilities of threat and non-compliance which are implicit in foreign policy cannot always lie dormant.

The same considerations, particularly in relation to acts backfiring, apply to the variant of force which we call *subversion*. The assumption that even a superpower can manipulate the evolution of another society by covert means is a dubious one. In the long run subversion breeds as much antagonism and resistance as invasion and occupation. The US Cold War involvements in Latin America and in Iran left Washington with a legacy of anger and distrust that continues to nurture hostile regimes. For their part, revolutionary Iran, Libya and Afghanistan all overplayed their hands with their encouragement of transnational terrorism, a strategy which has exacerbated divisions within the Islamic world. Apartheid South Africa's ruthless interventions in the neighbouring black-ruled states probably hastened its own demise by reinforcing the solidarity of the frontline states and their links to the ANC. Subversion, in short, like most forms of violent attack, can succeed in the short run. But the costs are no less high for being delayed.

The military arm is more often deployed for reasons of *defence* and *deterrence*. Conventional arms fulfil both functions, but the term deterrence is particularly associated with nuclear weapons. Yet no more than nine states possess deliverable nuclear weapons, declared or undeclared, out of 193 UN member states. Why do they see nuclear weapons as indispensable, when most decide that they are irrelevant to their security? The answers are largely to be found in history and in strategic position. The United States, Britain and the Soviet Union acquired nuclear weapons as a direct consequence of the need to defeat Hitler. They soon became convinced of their indispensability and large vested interests have grown up around the nuclear armouries. In foreign policy terms they become an insurance policy which it seems risky to relinquish, and a badge of status – as in the case of Britain and France, needing to justify their increasingly anomalous positions as permanent members of the UN Security Council.

For its part, China acquired nuclear weapons as a consequence of its deteriorating relationship with the Soviet Union and the fear that Moscow might launch a pre-emptive attack. This two-party dynamic has been repeated in the symmetrical acquisition of nuclear weapons by India and Pakistan. North Korea and Israel also possess the bomb, although the latter refuses to confirm the fact. As a form of deterrence, against not only nuclear attack but also conventional invasion, it cannot be denied that the possession of nuclear weapons is a significant advantage. North Korea has deliberately cultivated the image of a state which would not be afraid to start a nuclear war if others moved against it, while Israel's neighbours have long foresworn the kind of coordinated attack planned in 1967 through fear of massive retaliation. On the other hand some, not illogically, have drawn the conclusion from events in Iraq and Libya that the possession of nuclear weapons is the only guarantee against external attempts at regime change – although that is not to say that they will be willing or able to acquire a nuclear capacity.

Most states, however, have given no serious consideration to the possibility, and indeed see every virtue in promoting the nuclear non-proliferation regime inaugurated by the multilateral treaty of 1968. Why is this? The answers are straightforward. First, even with modern technology, the costs of an advanced research programme on nuclear warheads, including testing, security and delivery are prohibitively high for all but the richest or most determined. Second, developing a nuclear weapon is a most dangerous step. It will create fear in neighbours, draw the attention of the great powers and possibly lead to the kind of pre-emptive strike that Israel carried out against Iraq in 1981 and has threatened against Iran. In recent years the United States and its allies have taken an increasingly strong line as self-appointed enforcers of nuclear non-proliferation, raising the political and economic costs for any state wishing to cash in on its theoretical sovereign right to acquire such weapons. Gaddafi notably backed off from the Libyan nuclear programme after the defeat of Saddam Hussein's Iraq in 2003.

Third, nuclear weapons have only marginal utility. They are not likely to be of use in coercive diplomacy given that the outrage caused by a nuclear power even threatening to use its weapons against a state not possessing them would be enough to plunge the world into crisis. They tend to be seen as weapons of last resort by regimes that imagine themselves in desperate straits. This is why the apartheid government in South Africa developed some limited nuclear capacity. Mandela's ANC

successor government soon renounced it, as did Ukraine in 1994, possibly to its subsequent regret. Even as a deterrent they would be of no use
against a great power itself possessing nuclear weapons, except in a game
of exceedingly dangerous chicken. And no weapon is useful unless it can
actually be delivered to its target, which in this case entails sophisticated
missile and guidance systems which are beyond the capacity of most
states (Sagan and Waltz, 2003; Solingen 2007).

Conventional deterrence is a far more common and useful instrument
of policy. When it does not work, then actual defence comes into play,
although states vary enormously in their ability to protect themselves
against attack, depending on the size and quality of their armed forces,
but also their inherent degree of vulnerability. Canada, for example, has
been content to depend on NATO, and the United States, for protection,
using its own military largely to support UN peacekeeping. But as the
waters of the Arctic have warmed, so the politics of the region have
heated up, leading to a growth in its naval forces and the perception of
specific national interests to defend.

For the most part, foreign and defence policy are intended to work
hand in hand so that a potential adversary always thinks twice before
risking aggression. This is certainly Israel's strategy, which has succeeded
beyond expectations. Despite its numerical inferiority with respect to its
enemies, the strength of Israel's conventional forces, demonstrated four
times in battle since 1948, has led Egypt and Jordan to make peace, and
Syria and Iraq to behave with great caution. Israel has reached the point
where it is immune from defeat on the battlefield by almost any likely
combination of enemies – independent of the strategic support which it
receives from the United States. A limited use of military power may also
be seen as necessary for admonitory reasons, as when China briefly
invaded Vietnam in 1979 to remind its assertive smaller neighbour of the
realities of the regional power balance.

In this way the defensive functions of military force all too easily
blur into its offensive side. The military instrument is qualitatively
different from the other instruments of foreign policy in the threat it
bears but also in the risks it unleashes. Even the build-up of apparently
defensive arms in peacetime can be seen as an act of aggression and lead
to unstable arms races or pre-emptive strikes. For this reason security
needs to be understood in a much wider and longer-term perspective
than that provided by conventional defence analysis. The history of
Alsace-Lorraine between 1870 and 1945, when it changed hands four
times between France and Germany, shows that neither elaborate
defence nor formidable offensive power necessarily produces more
than short-term gains. The problem was only finally resolved by the
complete remaking of western Europe in 1945, and by the use of other

instruments altogether, primarily economic and cultural, within the new structure created by unconditional surrender. Military power is therefore at once a dramatically effective arm of foreign policy and one which is peculiarly limited in its ability to shape political and social structures. This is a lesson once again being learned in the chaos of Afghanistan, Iraq and Libya.

Economic Statecraft

Economic statecraft is associated with international interdependence (Baldwin, 1985). But as Joseph Nye has shown, this is a misreading. It does not necessarily create cooperation. Nor is it just about foreign economic policy serving economic goals, important as that is (Hocking and Smith, 1997, pp. 7–22, 180–3). Given the starting point of linkage between politics and economics, between foreign policy and the pursuit of wealth, economic statecraft means analysing the extent to which economic instruments are at the disposal of the state and the whole range of its external goals, whether as carrots, sticks or forms of structural power. Even a carrot is a form of coercion, albeit in attractive form, because an inducement once accepted can always be withdrawn as a punishment, while any economic or financial help automatically alters the balance of interests within the receiving state (Nye, 2004, p. 31).

Most economic statecraft is a question of making some use of what is happening anyway, through trade, investment or development aid. In the economic realm, only sanctions represent a purpose-built foreign policy instrument, and even they cut across existing business, often with damaging effects on the subject as much as the object. The other economic vectors have to be nudged or exploited as and when possible without damaging too much their existing rationale. For international economic activity derives for the most part from the private sector, while foreign policy is the business of states.

There is therefore an uneasy public–private relationship at the heart of economic statecraft – even for a state capitalist system like that of China. Firms are often deeply unhappy about the restrictions imposed by boycotts and embargoes; governments see private industry as lacking any national loyalty, and capable of subversive sanctions-busting when it suits them. Yet public money can be used as sweeteners to obtain contracts for private enterprise where the 'national' interest may be less than clear, while 'trade' can blaze a trail which politicians are not yet ready to tread. Of course these ambiguities of the public–private relationship mostly concern those engaged in foreign policy or commercial expansion. From the viewpoint of the target societies they may well seem trivial in comparison to a perceived reality of external pressure, interference or neocolonialism.

However economic instruments are viewed there is no doubt that they are slow-moving in their impact and more complex to operate in an era of relative laissez-faire than one of autarky such as the 1930s, when politics and economics came together in such demonstrations of power as the Japanese Greater Co-Prosperity Sphere in East Asia, and the Nazi penetration of south-eastern Europe through tying currencies to the Reichsmark. In the post-war era the United States provided the liquidity vital for international reconstruction but exacted the price, through the Bretton Woods system and the Marshall Plan, of a system of free trade and exchange rates linked to the dollar. This commitment, far-sighted in itself, only gradually came to be understood as the way to insulate western Europe against communist influence and promote European integration (Gilbert, 2015, pp. 26–31). In the current international system, where capital moves globally and trade liberalization has become entrenched, it is far more difficult for governments either to act unilaterally or to disrupt the normal workings of the market for anything less than a national emergency. That said, the use of economic instruments has paradoxically been on the increase, as states have sought alternatives to the dangers of military force and the pressures for an ethical component in foreign policy have mounted. The use of sanctions in particular has become common, and hotly debated (Doxey, 1996; Elliott, 1998; Hufbauer et al., 2008; Pape, 1998).

Sanctions represent the sticks of economic diplomacy, and include the boycott of imports, embargoes on exports, restrictions on private business and travel and the imposition of price rises through punitive duties (see Table 6.1 below). Although commonly thought not to work, in the sense of not achieving their stated ends, they always impose some costs on the target and usually serve various ends beyond those officially declared (J. Barber, 1979). Moreover, there have been cases where sanctions have had a dramatic impact on international politics, even if they have not always been well controlled. The oil supply restrictions (directly and by price) imposed by OPEC in 1973 and 1979 focused world attention very clearly on the Arab–Israel conflict and its dangers for the rest of the world. The isolation of apartheid South Africa finally helped to bring down that regime, while the decades-long sanctions against Iran ultimately brought Tehran to the negotiating table (Ehteshami, 2014). Yet sanctions are not precise tools whose impact can be predicted with confidence. They can usually be parried, if the target is prepared (as they usually are, given the threat to their reputations for sovereign independence) to pay the inevitable price for defying states on whom they are dependent, and at times the whole international community. Cuba's capacity to defy a US blockade for half a century is a case in point.

Table 6.1   The range of economic sanctions (actions and threats)[5]

Trade	Capital
Embargo (ban on exports)	Freezing of assets
Boycott (of imports)	Controls on capital movements
Tariff increase	Controls on money-laundering
Tariff discrimination	Aid suspension
Withdrawal of 'most-favoured nation' (MFN) treatment (i)	Expropriation
Blacklist (ii)	Taxation (unfavourable)
Quotas (import or export)	Withholding dues to international organisations
Licence denial (import or export)	
Dumping (iii)	
Preclusive buying (iv)	

(i)   Ceasing to treat imports from a country as favourably as similar imports from other countries are treated – as required by the World Trade Organization
(ii) Ban on business with firms that trade with the target country
(iii) Deliberate sale of exports at below-cost prices, to gain market share or to disrupt the target's economy by depressing the price of a key export
(iv) Buying up a commodity so as to deny it to others, and/or to force up its price

Source: Adapted from Baldwin, p. 41 (1985)

It is the long-run use of economic power which has the most profound impact. Over the past 70 years it has proved to be the most effective way of pursuing foreign-policy goals – so long as you are rich, powerful and capitalist (Krasner, 1985). The sheer strength of the economies of North America, western Europe, Japan and now China has given them the capacity to penetrate every part of the globe and to project their values and ways of life onto other societies. This is partly through the use of carrots such as trade preferences, loans and grants on privileged terms, but mainly through the working of normal commercial expansion (Cassen, 1986, pp. 1–18). China and the Gulf states have used sovereign wealth funds to great effect, giving them investment holdings around the world and implicit political leverage. Britain, for example, is tied into uncritical relations with Saudi Arabia, as a major market for arms sales, and Qatar, whose investments in London have reached unrivalled heights.

Admittedly a hit-and-miss process, economic strength has conferred significant advantages which the leaders of rich countries show no sign of relinquishing, even under the pressures of recession. Indeed, developed Western states have steadily gained confidence in the historical rightness of their policies and way of life, to the point where they have made development assistance conditional on economic and political reforms being undertaken by the recipient (K. Smith, 1998). Yet as international relations is a competitive environment this in turn has given China the opportunity to use its own new wealth to offer deals to developing countries without such derogations of sovereignty – even if it is easy then to ensure that they use Chinese firms for their infrastructure projects (Alden, 2007).

Refusals, 'delinking' and ideological hostility are possible strategies for states facing this kind of soft blackmail. But there can be little doubt that spheres of influence have been constructed on the basis of the projection of wealth abroad, notably in Latin America, where the United States has managed to maintain a congenial order without significant military effort, and in eastern Europe, where the European Union's use of economic instruments makes it the key player in the region. Russia has its own weapon of energy supplies, which it can ration on political grounds, as Ukraine discovered. But since turning off the tap means forgoing its own major source of income there are limits to the utility of the sanction. This applies with any single point of pressure.

Not every wealthy state wants to use its potential for political impact. Japan and Germany long ago lost their post-1945 pariah status, becoming the third and fourth largest economies in the world. They have their own regional zones of influence, but are still cautious about using their economic leverage for political purposes, usually preferring to act in a multilateral context and to restrict their international activity. Perhaps this is wise, for while foreign policy can lead to the loss of wealth (through overstretch, war or simply an excessive sense of international responsibility) it can rarely create it (Kennedy, 1988; Strange, 1971). Conversely, foreign policy is not usually driven by simple economic needs. The argument that US foreign policy in the Middle East is driven primarily by the need to safeguard essential oil supplies founders on the facts that oil exporters need to sell their product regardless of the countries they are dealing with, and that Western support for the Gulf states shows no sign of weakening in the era of fracking and greater US self-sufficiency.

Of course oil and other energy supplies are not irrelevant. Anxiety about 'the tap being turned off' has been a constant refrain since 1973, as it has been over Russian gas supplies to Europe in the Putin era. The same underlying concern has led China to sign agreements with a number of African countries to obtain privileged access to raw material supplies of importance to its growing economy. In general therefore, while the liberalization of the world economy has led to the relative separation of economics and politics, they are still intertwined. In particular, economic sanctions, the politicization of overseas aid and human rights debates have all led to crossed wires between foreign policy, trade and development policy, to the irritation of the relevant officials – and thus to much bureaucratic politics.

Diplomacy

At the softer end of the continuum of foreign policy instruments lie diplomacy and culture. Diplomacy is the human face of protecting interests in international politics, as well as a crucial instrument for building international stability. In these two competing roles lies the source of much of the argument over whether diplomacy is anachronistic and reactionary, or peace-building and indispensable. The confusion is compounded because of the fact that most diplomatic agency is still the preserve of states, with the UN Secretary-General and other international civil servants outnumbered and limited by their dependence on the major powers (Barston, 2013; Berridge, 2010; Berridge and James, 2003; R. Cohen, 1987; Hamilton and Langhorne; 1994; Watson, 1982).

Professional diplomats do not have a monopoly on diplomacy. As we saw in Chapter 4, many parts of the state machinery, apart from the ministry of foreign affairs, now engage in international relations. As such, they are effectively required to practise diplomacy in their dealings with foreign counterparts. In this respect all agents of the state should in principle liaise with their diplomat colleagues. If Sierra Leone had had an effective diplomatic cadre, for example, its 27-year-old president would probably not have come within an ace of expelling the ambassador of its biggest aid donor (Germany) in 1993. For their part, the specialists are fighting a losing battle if they seek to preserve a monopoly over diplomacy. They need to work with their 'domestic' colleagues, not least because of the increasingly important domestic dimension of foreign policy (R. Cohen, 1998; Kennan, 1997).

As a means of implementing policy, weak states rely on diplomacy. With few resources they have no choice but to play a poor hand as skilfully as possible. Yet they are also the states with the smallest and least experienced diplomatic services. Major powers ensure that they possess large and effective foreign services and rely on diplomacy for the bulk of their external activity. Radical governments may start with Trotsky's aim of 'issuing some revolutionary proclamations to the people before shutting the shop', but they soon turn to conventional methods in the attempt to come to terms with an insistent outside world. For in practice diplomacy is always central to any kind of action, from crisis management through long-drawn-out negotiations to routine but sensitive matters such as diplomatic exemptions from parking fines. Only unsophisticated regimes rely on bluster and the delusions of power.

There are four functions which diplomacy performs for the contemporary international actor: communication, negotiation, participation in multilateral institutions and the promotion of economic goods. The four are related to those managed in home capitals by the foreign ministry (see

Chapter 4) but focus more on activity in the field, and therefore on the still critical role of embassies (Berridge, 2011, pp. 1–15).

The key function of *communication* is often assumed to mean, in practice, miscommunication. To be sure, any independent actor has to keep some information private. Key judgements on the timing of initiatives and concessions are simply not possible in conditions of publicity. But this produces ambiguity more frequently than deliberate deception, which does not make for good diplomacy. Routine foreign relations could not be sustained without a fair degree of trust. Harold Nicolson pointed out over 70 years ago that *policy* should be in the open even if negotiation required confidentiality (Nicolson, 1963). Indeed, if long-term intentions are not communicated clearly to both friends and adversaries the consequences can be disastrous. Robert Jervis (1970, pp. 18–40) has shown how actors read each other's intentions from a combination of signals (deliberate) and indices (inherent characteristics such as monthly trade figures). Unfortunately both are easy to misread even when not manipulated. Because ambiguity is inevitable across cultures governments need to be highly self-conscious about the signals they wish to send on matters of importance. The Australian Prime Minister Paul Keating got into a major row through what was for him normal plain speaking, but for Prime Minister Mahathir Mohamad of Malaysia showed a disgraceful lack of respect (Cohen, 1997, pp. 38–43).

Sometimes it is not clear whether the signal is deliberate or accidental. Did the United Kingdom, for example, intend to distance itself so significantly from the original six members of the forerunner to the European Economic Community when it sent only a junior official to the Messina Conference of 1955? When six years later the Macmillan government decided to apply for entry to the community it had an uphill struggle in part because of the negative messages conveyed by such oblique gestures. Conversely, when General de Gaulle shouted '*vive le Québec libre*' from the balcony of the Montreal City Hall in 1967 he intended to demonstrate support for French Canada but had probably not envisaged provoking the diplomatic crisis with Ottawa which ensued (R. Cohen, 1987, p. 21). Even more seriously, one can narrate the onset of the two world wars quite plausibly in terms of signals wrongly calibrated and misunderstood. Certainly the nature and timing of the outbreak of both conflicts owed much to failures of diplomatic communication (Joll, 1984; Weinberg, 1994, pp. 6–47).

As an instrument of policy, diplomacy represents the instinct for caution and sophistication in the face of the strong forces of nationalism and power politics. It provides ways of breaking log-jams and avoiding the costs of violence, so long as not everything is wagered on its success. Only patient diplomacy by Nixon and Kissinger was able finally to put an end to the damaging rupture between the United States and China, which in lasting from 1949 to 1971 had long outlived its original rationale (Kissinger, 1994, pp. 719–30). Without skilful diplomacy the Federal Republic of Germany would not have been able to launch Ostpolitik in the late 1960s and thus prepare the ground for eventual reunification – itself a triumph of imaginative negotiation. Through similar patience, key individuals, particularly in vulnerable locations, have been able to preserve their countries from potentially catastrophic consequences. It is easy to think what might have happened to Jordan, caught as it is between Israel, Iraq and Syria, without the ability of King Hussein to balance the impossible pressures on him in the region (Ashton, 2008, pp. 1–12). An Israeli intelligence report of 1980 described him as a man trapped on a bridge burning at both ends, with crocodiles in the river beneath (Shlaim, 2007, p. 609). In the wider international system, statesmen like Tito and Nehru had managed to loosen the structure of the Cold War and to give a voice to many smaller states by their creation of the Non-Aligned Movement. Diplomatic communication in this sense is a political activity of the highest importance.

The second function of diplomacy is the capacity to conduct *technical negotiations*, often of extreme complexity. Where a great deal hangs on the outcome, as with the Paris peace talks at the end of the Vietnam War, or the Dayton Accords of 1995 ending the Bosnian war, the identity of individual diplomats, and their degree of experience, may turn out to be crucial. In other negotiations, such as those between Britain and China over Hong Kong between 1982 and 1984, and again in the 1990s, considerable stamina is required, together with a deep understanding of the culture of the interlocutor (Cradock, 1994, 1997, pp. 203–5; Yahuda, 1996). Success is far from guaranteed, and often simply consists in preventing discussions from collapsing into violence, as in the long-running dispute over Cyprus. Even where success can be assumed, as in the EU's negotiations with future members, the range of detailed issues to be settled requires the coordination of a large number of complex dossiers.

What is more diplomacy is often physically dangerous. Diplomats have been held hostage and sometimes killed through their representation of a country's foreign policy – and through being the most obvious point of national vulnerability. The murder of the British ambassador by the IRA in Dublin in 1976, the four-month siege in the Japanese embassy in Lima in 1997, the killing of the US ambassador in Libya in 2012, and the regular bomb attacks on Western personnel in Afghanistan are vivid examples. Even in times of war and revolution diplomacy continues as long as it is possible to maintain the physical integrity of the embassy building, even if the ambassadors of the direct combatants get withdrawn. This presents serious challenges to those diplomats acting as mediators or conduits, and to the embassies of the belligerents in third-party capitals (Berridge, 2012). Negotiation in the international environment, in other words, is now less than ever a game for the gifted amateur.

Diplomacy in multilateral institutions is an important part of any foreign policy. States, and the non-state actors which also increasingly participate, have to manage an environment which requires balancing their own concerns with the purposes for which the IGO exists in the first place. Part of this means coalition-building and fostering diplomatic solidarity among like-minded states. Another part involves balancing private negotiation with the public posturing intended to win over hearts and minds, often across national boundaries. The large number of specialized multi-partner dialogues, such as the 107-member network linking the European Union and states from Africa, the Caribbean and the Pacific, or the 57-member Organisation on Security and Co-operation in Europe, cut across each other and represent a special challenge. From the viewpoint of the individual actor the aim is to achieve collective goals, such as the transfer of resources to the poorest LDCs (lesser-developed countries), or agreement on confidence-building measures, without compromising particular national interests. Success can require political as well as technical flair, as the Italian ambassador to the United Nations Paolo Fulci demonstrated with his effective coalition-building at the UN in the 1990s to derail the big powers' 'quick fix' plan to reform the Security Council by adding only Germany and Japan as permanent members (Pedrazzi, 2000).

Economic diplomacy is ever more important. It is conceptually distinct from the use of economic instruments for foreign policy goals discussed above. It derives from the particular need to promote national prosperity and to conduct a foreign economic policy to that end. Much of it operates through organizations like the OECD, G20, International Monetary Fund (IMF), World Bank, WTO and EU, and is subject to the conditions of all multilateral working. But in this context states also face the hegemony problem, or how to deal with the preponderant influence of key states, markets and courts. In extremis this means negotiating from a position of weakness in the pursuit of loans or the rescheduling of debts, as Argentina has discovered on several occasions. The dilemma is how to preserve sovereign independence without forgoing the desired help – a recipe for internal upheaval. The self-help system created by the states of western Europe has helped to buffer them against the Washington institutions and the vagaries of the world economy, but it still creates dilemmas. Since the onset of the major financial crisis in 2008 Greece has swung between following the rules of the eurozone and protesting against German dominance within it. Other regions have not got even this far in regional economic integration. Still, states such as

Japan, India, Singapore and South Korea have had success in trade and industrial diplomacy through developing expert national cadres and through avoiding the high costs of adventurism in foreign and security policy (Narlikar, 2003).

Most economic diplomacy focuses on the concrete objectives of boosting the export efforts of the country's enterprises and attracting the inward investment which will produce jobs. Japan was the most effective state in the post-war period at forging a public–private partnership in export promotion, but successive German governments have had outstanding success in striking the balance between liberal capitalism and the promotion of national enterprises. Britain under Thatcher and her successors was able to attract a surprising flow of inward investment, helped by a limited, but strategically important, number of interventions in areas such as aerospace, nuclear power, pharmaceuticals and the car industry, in all of which the international dimension is crucial. Furthermore, in order to get contracts abroad governments often resort to under-the-counter promises of development or military assistance – of greater or less subtlety, which risk legal and political embarrassment if the news becomes public – and thus work against transparency in decision-making.

For its part the private sector welcomes help from the state whenever it can be obtained, despite the rhetoric of free enterprise. Export credit support is effectively a form of subsidy, and diplomats often have valuable local contacts. Thus British firms successfully protested against cutbacks in embassy staff in the Gulf in 1993, knowing they would have support from arms exporters. Conversely, French commercial relations with Turkey were damaged by the bill which went through the Assemblée Nationale in 1998 recognising the Armenian genocide of 1915, and Danish trade in Muslim countries was hit by cartoons of the Prophet Muhammad published in 2005, and the government's perceived support for the cartoonists. For their part multinational enterprises have to engage in complex and often costly diplomacy in order to secure rights to build bridges, drill for oil, beam in satellite programmes and buy up parts of the economy deemed strategically important. It is no wonder that political consultancy, or risk analysis, has been one of the fastest-growing corporate sectors in the past 20 years. TNEs, like states, cannot do their business without engaging in politics – with each other, with regions and cities, and with states.

Culture

Culture is entwined with propaganda as an instrument of foreign policy, but the two are not identical. Propaganda has minimal cultural value, and genuine culture is a spontaneous affair, independent of political exploitation. Moreover, whereas culture is right at the soft-power end of the continuum, propaganda is coercive in its attempt to impact forcefully on the attitudes of its targets (Philip Taylor, 1995). There is an arrogance about the most self-conscious propagandists which clearly reveals the wish to control. Hitler said that 'by clever propaganda even heaven can be represented to the people as hell, and the most wretched life as paradise', while for Goering rallying mass support meant that 'all you have to do is tell [the people] they are being attacked, and denounce the pacifists for lack of patriotism' (Irving, 1977, p. 142; Wolfers, 1962, p. 94). Even a democratic politician like Senator Vandenberg could talk, at the start of the Cold War, of the need to 'scare the hell out of the American people' (R. Mann, 2001).

Cultural diplomacy, in contrast, is a form of soft power which governments mobilize without being too obvious about their intentions, and indeed taking a long view of the possible benefits. Like propaganda it targets public opinion in other states. The aim might be to undermine a hostile regime, to spread one's own values or simply to promote economic ends. Success therefore requires some evidence of internal changes in the target as the result of exogenous influence, and ideally without the subjects being aware that there was an element of external agency, let alone deliberate manipulation.

Didactic propaganda of the kind we associate with the 1930s is still practised by regimes which feel the world is against them. North Korea above all has abused its enemies and naïvely extolled its own virtues. Serbia, Libya and Iran have all had leaders in recent times prone to the same tendency. The Ayatollah Khomeini went so far as to send a letter to Mikhail Gorbachev in 1988 advising him (presciently) that communism was about to collapse and that the only hope for the Soviet Union lay in a mass conversion to Islam. Mahmoud Ahmadinejad notoriously called for Israel to be wiped off the map. For the most part no one takes this kind of thing seriously unless it suits them to do so, as it is mainly designed for domestic consumption. Much more effective was the soft-sell strategy the West became more adept at as the Cold War wore on, based on promoting desirable activities indirectly rather than preaching at high volume (Rawnsley, 1996). Although precise measurement is not possible it seems likely, for example, that the reputation of the BBC's World Service for impartiality, including on occasion criticisms of the mother country, does more to promote a sympathetic understanding of British positions, official and unofficial, than any amount of government handouts. Openness towards foreign journalists, encouraging educational exchanges and the glad-handing of elites through such events as the Königswinter or Davos meetings are other examples of the shrewd use of culture for broadly political purposes (Kunczik, 1997; Mitchell, 1986). With its new wealth China has followed the West down this road. It has opened more than 300 Confucius Institutes around the world to promote its language and image (Gil, 2009).

Sport has been a way of promoting national status at least since the infamous Berlin Olympics of 1936. More recently it has also been seen as having economic benefits, through attracting tourists and foreign investment. Together the political and economic motives have led to ferocious competition between states – and between cities – to host the major events. Those successful – like Qatar for the 2022 World Cup – automatically raise their profile and prestige, although the real test is the event itself. Whereas the London Olympics of 2012 were thought to have given a very positive impression of a cosmopolitan and dynamic British society, the Sochi Winter Olympics of February 2014 became mired in controversies over gay rights, and the Brazil World Cup of 2014 rebounded badly at home, with often violent protests over extravagance and incompetence.

Politicians must always tread carefully in their wish to exploit things which belong primarily to civil society. If they interfere with, or take credit for, what individuals do in a free society, they invite immediate reactions and bad publicity. They have little option but to encourage, to herd and to hope for long-term benefits. The confidence to do this and to see civil society as a good in itself brings results. The CIA was eventually damaged by the disclosure of the way in which it had secretly bankrolled publishing houses and serious magazines like *Encounter* (Saunders, 1999; Watt, 2000). The United States would have been better served by relying on the provision of its efficient library and information facilities to journalists and academics, as well as the appeal of its way of life and stated values to millions across the world. Who needs the Voice of America when you have Hollywood and CNN?

Any attempt at control is counterproductive in relation to the arts and intellectual life. The British Council or the Institut Français can facilitate tours by the Royal Ballet or the Comédie Française, but they cannot create art. Politicians' embarrassing attempts to associate themselves with popular or avant-garde culture invite ridicule. At least Anglo-Saxon societies can rely on the power of the English language and the hugely popular film and music industries associated with it, to disseminate themselves worldwide. The dilemma is more acute for societies like France, where there is the perception of an excessive cultural onslaught from English. Even here, however, Paris may be best advised not to fight an unwinnable global war, and to concentrate on reinforcing existing historical and economic links. This is what the German government has done in central and eastern Europe, where there is already a disposition to speak German as a second language. But success involves long-term financial commitments, and the nerve to take a hands-off approach towards cultural life.

In general people are more receptive to foreign cultural influence when those achievements already exist and simply need to be drawn to wider attention – and assuming they do not perceive the foreigners as hegemonic or hypocritical. Thus in less than two decades Japan was able to turn around its international image as a defeated, devastated, aggressor both because foreign consumers recognized the quality and availability of its products, and because of its newly pacific profile. It would have been even more popular had it taken full responsibility for its past militarism, as Germany has regularly done. Singapore did not have that problem, but it has risen above its small size and weakness to become a well-respected player in South-East Asian affairs through its prosperity, successful modernization and reputation for efficiency.

From this point of view, namely allowing economic and social achievements to speak for themselves, with the state only acting as a facilitator, cultural diplomacy is primarily an instrument of the developed West. More dirigiste regimes have to fall back on playing host to sports events, or ploughing money into subsidized student bursaries, language courses or prestige projects to attract the world's attention – but they have less attractive material at their disposal. That said, much depends on what the desired target of influence is. Egypt under Nasser engaged in an extraordinary campaign of radio broadcasting and cultural sponsorship across the Arab world in a largely successful attempt to establish its leadership role in the Middle East (Browne, 1982; A. Dawisha, 1976; Hale, 1975). Iran and Saudi Arabia have been mainly concerned to use their resources at the religious level in the rivalry within the Islamic world, although the latter has also funded mosques and study abroad (Leiken, 2012, pp. 68–9, 89). The small Gulf regimes have used their wealth by acquiring airlines and football clubs to demonstrate their modernity and connections. Castro's Cuba focused its resources in the developing world, where its provision of doctors was naturally welcomed.

For liberal or closed societies the same rule applies as with coercion: significant influence is unlikely to take place unless the target is already ripe for change. The Soviet Union may have been undermined by the yearning of its people for a better standard of living, but the lure of designer jeans and BMWs would not have been so seductive if its own economy had not been rigid, defence-geared and literally unable to deliver the goods over more than 70 years (I. Clark, 1997, pp. 172–9).

Seeking Balance

In the final analysis there are no rules for choosing and using foreign policy instruments. None should be excluded on *a priori* grounds, even military force. If states and some other international actors wish to protect core concerns, from time to time they will need to consider using violence, or at least the threat of it. To that end they will have to have considered well in advance the nature of the armed forces they might conceivably need, and to have made the necessary investments. There is no point in going to war without the means to fight it, as Britain and France did in 1939. Conversely, arms build-ups to a disproportionate level are expensive and create spirals of hostility with other states. In any case, no foreign policy instrument is a panacea. Economic sanctions have been a popular form of coercion from the 1980s on, but their success is highly case-dependent. Other economic means, notably the exercise of structural power in such policies as the Marshall Plan and EU enlargement, are difficult to manipulate in terms of specific consequences. They have important impacts, but of a long-term and architectonic nature.

As for soft power, the only form of attraction available to governments is cultural diplomacy, which is growing in importance while raising the same public–private dilemma so evident in the economic realm: when official policy-makers attempt to exploit the products of civil society they risk scepticism at home and abroad. And cultural assets, like defence planning, require long-term investments. Diplomacy, by contrast, which exists on the boundary between soft and hard power, is ubiquitous and unavoidable. It cannot be relied upon to implement all a state's goals in the face of intractable outsiders and circumstances, but it exists in every action taken by one actor towards another, and is not the monopoly of diplomats. It is capable of achieving far more than is generally thought, and is relatively inexpensive. It is, in fact, the epitome of international *politics.*

All instruments can backfire, especially if the elements of intervention and control are overemphasized. Policy-makers should take on board David Baldwin's insistence that the *means* of foreign policy, being inherently relational, need putting in the context not only of *ends* but also of the pattern of interaction between actor and target. They should also take it as given that action in international relations requires a mix of instruments, whether working together or held in reserve. The technical problem of foreign policy action is thus how to manage relations along a number of dimensions simultaneously. But from a wider, ethical, viewpoint, the challenge is how to pursue one's own concerns without demonising outsiders and without damaging the shared structures of international life. That is less likely to happen if means are not mistaken for ends in themselves. They need to be kept, as Clausewitz advised, under political control.

Notes

1   There are other ways of cutting this particular cake. Boulding distinguishes between threat power, economic power and integrative power. If rephrased, however, as being about assertiveness, resources and frameworks they are close to the version given here.
2   Although there is a great deal of data on the costs and composition of weapon systems, armed services etc., few have been interested in trying to measure their utility in political terms. Soft power, however, as a new and intangible concept, has generated attempts at measurement with a view to seeing where there might be value for money (McClory, 2010, 2011, 2013).
3   If it is doubted that soft power can include the military instrument, consider the Partnership for Peace system run by NATO since 1994 to help educate the military of the ex-Warsaw Pact states in Western approaches to civil–military relations and to build confidence.
4   'Undetected' because it is not clear whether Argentina was actually aware of the deployment of two frigates at three to four sailing days away from its normal search area, and of one nuclear-powered submarine which was to get closer. Callaghan's idea was that a hint could be given to the Americans who would then inform Argentina. Such are the subtleties of diplomatic signalling (Jervis, 1970).
5   Adapted by kind permission from David A. Baldwin, *Economic Statecraft* (Princeton: Princeton University Press, 1985), p. 41.

Further Reading

Berridge, G. R., 2010. *Diplomacy: Theory and Practice*. Fourth edition. Berridge is a leading expert on diplomatic history and practice, while his work is always readable and incisive.

Brighi, Elisabetta and Hill, Christopher, 2012. Implementation and behaviour. In: S. Smith, T. Dunne and A. Hadfield, eds, 2012, *Foreign Policy Analysis in International Relations*. Second edition, pp. 147–67. Using the strategic–relational approach, this chapter focuses on whether an 'implementation phase' of decision-making can be clearly identified.

Cohen, Raymond, 1997. *Negotiating across Cultures: International Communication in an Interdependent World*. Revised edition. Ranging over four continents, Cohen provides an innovative treatment of the importance of cultural differences.

George, Alexander L. and Simons, William E., eds, 1994. *The Limits of Coercive Diplomacy*. Second edition. The theoretical framework of this ground-breaking study, largely of US forcign policy in the Cold War, makes it of enduring relevance.

Lukes, Steven, 2005. *Power: A Radical View*. Second edition. Although not a book about foreign policy, this has hugely suggestive insights for politics in any context.

Nye, Joseph S., 2004. *Soft Power: The Means to Success in World Politics*. The founder and developer of thinking about soft power here rebalances the argument, towards 'smart power'.

Chapter 7

Foreign Policy in a Multi-Actor World

The focus in this book so far has been on the actors, but it is time to look more closely at the international context in which they operate and which shapes both thinking and outcomes. It is made up not only of the actors themselves and their interactions but also of the many economic, political and cultural forces which are out of their hands. In what Hedley Bull (1977) termed the 'anarchical society', elements of cooperation and conflict coexist uneasily, with the system looking differently according to an actor's location in it. This chapter looks at the interplay between material and human factors, and at the extent to which states are limited by the web of institutions, rules and expectations which they inhabit. Chapter 8 then moves away from the state system to analyse the other sites of agency which have arisen in international relations and the web of transnational relations which they generate.

The Outside World

One of the pioneers of FPA, Joseph Frankel, wrote that 'relations among single states are ... intimately related to the matrix of international society as a whole but the study of the latter is hampered by many difficulties and has scarcely made a start' (Frankel, 1963, p. 63). The situation has been almost wholly reversed since then. International society was launched as an idea in the 1960s by the 'English School' of International Relations scholars though it went back, as Martin Wight pointed out, to Grotius. Apart from Wight the key figures in developing the school were (in rough chronological order) Charles Manning, Hedley Bull, Alan James, James Mayall, Adam Watson, John Vincent and Robert Jackson (Dunne, 1998; Linklater and Suganami, 2006). Bull's book of 1977 soon became a key point of reference in the burgeoning subject of International Relations. It was therefore perhaps not surprising that a whole generation of scholars (at least in the Commonwealth countries) became preoccupied with the extent to which there was such a thing as a society of states, and if not, how they might otherwise characterize the overall pattern of international relations. It was fitting that when the school was revivified in the 1990s it was an Anglo-Canadian, Barry Buzan, who took the lead (Buzan, 2004).

Yet how the component parts of international society experienced its constraints, and how they behaved, was only of interest to the English School in so far as this threw light on the central issues of realism and rationalism, namely the tendency of states to go to war, and the conditions in which they might discover common interests. The normative dilemmas lurking beneath the surface were also beginning to be debated, in terms of what justice at the international level might look like. The more empirical questions, however, of how the dilemmas of choice played out in foreign policy-making, were generally passed over or left to the historians.

Things were not quite the same in the United States. While the British were understandably preoccupied with coming to terms with the pressures of the wider system, it was hardly possible for a country rising to the position of superpower to neglect the dilemmas of action. The emergence of classical realism after 1945, articulated by Hans Morgenthau, Reinhold Niebuhr and Arnold Wolfers, went hand in hand with an interest in statecraft and even issues of moral responsibility. Soon, however, the evident power of scientific rationality had spawned the behaviouralist movement, which focused among other things on foreign policy decision-making and hoped to extend the logic of microeconomics to the study of politics. This created what we now know as foreign policy analysis, but also increasingly distanced academic work from the substance of political argument.

The other main trend in the American study of international relations, which eventually overshadowed FPA, was the increasing sense of a bipolar strategic system, geared to the emerging logic of nuclear deterrence. The systemic perspectives won out in terms of a preoccupation with the idea of the balance of power, but in a far from classical sense. Once Kenneth Waltz had invented neorealism in 1979, American international relations focused on the dynamics of bi- and multipolarity and the strategies, derived from game theory, which seemed necessary to survive in a condition of self-help anarchy. Just as with the English School, but for very different reasons, foreign policy had become theoretically disconnected from international politics.

Waltz advocated this very disconnection. He did not shrink from criticising Morgenthau, Allison and Herbert Simon for their 'confusion' of the explanation of 'the results produced by the uncoordinated actions of states' (that is, the international system) with 'the tendencies and styles of different countries' policies' (that is, foreign policies). He accepted that the two levels were linked and that each therefore tells us something about the other – but different things (Waltz, 1979, pp. 122–3). As a result, the neorealists abhor 'reductionist' approaches which try to explain the pattern of international politics by looking inside states, and they use very parsimonious assumptions about state motivations (see Chapter 1, pp. 9–10). Their approach is really a variant of structuralism, which has dominated thinking about international relations for two decades, and by definition tends to play down the role of actors, states or otherwise. Neorealists tend to assume that states 'weigh options and make decisions based *primarily* on their strategic situation and an assessment of the external environment' (Elman, 1996, pp. 38–9). If they do not, they will 'fall by the wayside' (Waltz, 1979, p. 118). Even those who sympathize with this external–determinist perspective are likely to view it as an overly Procrustean approach to the kinds of complex pressures experienced by, say, Egypt as it operates simultaneously in the Arab League, the regional balance and the international capitalist system, to say nothing of coping with a complex set of internal challenges.

World systems theorists, and those who see social movements as the motor forces of world politics are also structuralists, in that they identify an overall framework, or set of forces, to which the component parts are ultimately subordinate. The same is largely true of those working with interdependence or globalization assumptions. In all these cases foreign policy gets bracketed out. The strong growth of interest in normative issues during the last decade or so has returned some of the focus to actors, but even here for many of those working in the field the key actor is the individual, and the framework that of 'cosmopolitan democracy' (Archibugi, Koenig-Archibugi and Marchetti, 2011; D. Holden, 2000). Foreign policy, or the collective political attempt to find a strategy for managing in the world, qua state or qua NGO, has seemed contingent or even a reactionary idea, to many general theorists of international relations.

For their part, while regional or country specialists continue to interest themselves in foreign policy, they rarely do more than take the international environment as given. Foreign policy analysts focusing on a particular country or part of the world assume that states and other actors are part of a system, based on regular patterns of interaction, feedback and homeostasis (Brecher, 1972; Kaplan, 1957; Snyder, Bruck and Sapin, 2002). But those located in area studies generally devote themselves to a high degree of local detail without much concern for the wider environment, whatever its degree of impact on their subject.

The majority of the various approaches to be found within the subject of International Relations do not focus directly, or even at all, on agents and what they do, let alone on foreign policy and its making. But a lofty neglect is simply not good enough given that we are studying politics, which consists of choices, conflicts, ideas and values, all of which are expressed by human beings in their various groups, within and across frontiers. It is good that FPA by definition is not guilty of this sin, but it is inherently undesirable that it should bear almost the whole weight of the discussion of agency in IR, with only the normative theorists as allies. Intellectual ghettoes do not serve the interests of those inside them or of the wider community.

If the challenge for IR is to think more about agency, however, that for the analyst of foreign policy is to understand how agency works in the context of the structures within which states and other actors are embedded. For some constructivists, the very idea of a discernible separation between the world and what goes on in our minds is problematic. For them, international reality is constituted less by physical constraints than by norms and beliefs, which result from the dialogistical processes of participation in the multiple levels at which international politics takes place. At least this places actors, and the ideas they have, at centre stage. But we need not go to the opposite extreme from the structuralists in believing, with the historian of thought Michael Donelan, that 'all is thought ... it is opinion which rules the world' (1978, p. 11).

For this book the starting points are not ideas, floating above and around political units, but the systems which affect those units' behaviour. We may justly debate how to characterize this world outside, as a society of states, multilevel governance or integrative globalization, but we should not pretend that there is no patterned set of processes outside the control of any one actor – or even that it can be summarized as the balance of power. It is difficult in practice to escape from the idea that interactions between the units of international relations form a web of networks which actors may or may not perceive accurately, with feedback reinforcing or challenging them according to the accuracy of their understandings and their ability to create an action–space for themselves within the system. For analysts this means both that there is a vacuum to be filled about the processes connecting actors and the system, and that the concepts of perception and misperception are of central importance (for reasons expanded on in Chapter 3). It is around these two points that the discussion proceeds, beginning with the idea of the 'external environment', so central to the whole decision-making approach, and its various meanings.

There are competing conceptions of the world in which states operate, some thick and some thin. That of an international society is at the thicker end of the continuum – although still short of an 'international community'. It sees states as developing common understandings and practices to the point where governments are constrained in their actions not just by considerations of prudence but also by a certain sense of common cause. This notion has been both attacked and extended, to the point where we now face a bewildering litany of alternative terms and interpretations (C. Brown, 2010, pp. 40–52). It has been attacked both for privileging the power of governments and for peddling liberal illusions over the obligations of states to promote human rights, political and economic. In particular the term 'international community', which is a term often used by Western leaders, has met with much scepticism. Yet there has been much serious discussion of an emerging normative sphere of international relations, driven by the UN conventions which came out of the Second World War, especially the growing concern with genocide, and by the mass poverty evident in the large number of newly decolonized states (Bull and Watson, 1984; Vincent, 1986a, 1986b).

What is clear to a significant extent, as Alexander Wendt has influentially argued, is that society (or anarchy) is what states make of it (Wendt, 1992, 1999, pp. 246–312). The outside world can amount to an iron cage but it can also be a realm which can be remade according to the will of actors, meaning their interaction and their ability to agree on new kinds of relationships. But, as we shall see, this needs to take into account not only ideas, perception and political will, but also material factors – some of which are susceptible to human manipulation, and others barely so.

The main need here is to indicate how the external environment impinges on foreign policy choices in terms of both power and ideas. A focus on the logic of the balance of power is no more adequate than the belief that states follow international law or morality. The neorealists have sacrificed too much in the pursuit of parsimony, while those interested in norms have too often neglected practical issues of geography, wealth, resources and domestic politics. If we return to the notion of the 'anarchical society' we see that behind Bull's elegant paradox lies the basic truth that elements of society coexist with elements of anarchy. That is, the world consists of cooperation and the desire for rules on the one hand, and unpredictability and untrustworthiness on the other. It makes no sense to choose between these two tendencies.

The coexistence of stability and indiscipline makes for tension and uncertainty among those responsible for policy. There is also a distinct patchiness about the international system. Variation is geographical, for western Europe is close to being a *Gemeinschaft* while other regions are not even *Gesellschaften,* and also chronological, in that zones like West Africa can go from stability to anarchy in a few years. Yet in general the system has not gone into reverse, despite the many new challenges which have emerged. The achievements of international law and organization in the past century were limited, but there has been a slow accretion. The failings of the League of Nations in the 1930s led not to the abandonment of universal organizations, but to the development of a more robust and extensive model after 1944. International law has steadily expanded its scope through providing practical benefits in conflict resolution, trade, intellectual property and many more areas.

Anarchy still has the alarming capacity to break through in the most unexpected ways, so that Kant's perpetual peace remains a distant dream. The descent of Yugoslavia into savagery was an existential shock to the postmodern societies of western Europe (Robert Cooper, 2003, pp. 59–62). The acquisition of nuclear arms by India and Pakistan has exposed the thinness of the constitutional provisions of international society. The terrorist attacks of 11 September 2001, followed at regular intervals by the slaughters in Madrid, London and Paris, put an end to the carefree lives of prosperous westerners. On the other hand, elements of solidarism now extend well beyond interstate relations, and indeed are to some degree independent of them. 'Cosmopolitan' networks between individuals or private associations may not live up to the expectations of fostering the unity of humankind often placed upon them, but they cut across the pretensions of states to speak always for their peoples, and fill in some of the gaps left by the sparse achievements of intergovernmentalism (Hurrell, 2007, pp. 57–94). By the same token they complicate life for official foreign policies through creating other sources of agency. In short, they represent elements of what some think of as a 'world' society.

Understanding the context in which action takes place thus requires a bringing together of the notions of international society and world society. As Henry Kissinger liked to say, everything is connected in reality. Decision-makers have to work in an environment in which transnational forces cut across the tidier world of diplomatic relations, and where domestic loyalty to a government can no longer be taken for granted. On the other hand they cannot be expected to take a detached academic view of the levels of analysis. They work under time pressure, attempting to make sense of a teeming mass of data and forms of activity. What then, does the 'international' mean for the actors which encounter it? What intellectual shorthands help them, and citizens, come to terms with a world which is at once superficially familiar and bewilderingly complex?

The most accurate response is that decision-makers tend to perceive international relations as a *system*. That is, that they are part of a regular pattern of interactions between separate societies, across most of the issue areas affecting human life, disrupted at times by war and other sources of fear, but of a more stable and civil character than in the era of world war. Some of these interactions operate in more established channels, and more intensively, than others. This activity covers the whole globe now that virtually all its territory is politically accounted for, and isolation is only possible at high costs. The units of the system are now accepted to be not only states but also other actors and communities which cut across national frontiers. Its boundaries are twofold: those where human activity encounters the physical world of climate, topography and so on, and those (more blurred) where international transactions stop and the domestic life begins.

The system has various different levels, and it is here that the analyst has the advantage over the practitioner, who will focus on issues rather than waste time on rules, regimes and competences. It would be wrong to call them 'subsystems' because that would imply that we can identify the primary system from which others flow. Despite the arguments which rage over this very question, which is over whether to privilege security and states over capital and firms or over knowledge and technocrats, the fact is that we are in an epistemological blind spot. We have no way of *knowing* the origins and direction of the causal flow. Without that certainty we have no option but to conceive of a model – like the globe itself – with no top, bottom, sides or centre, girdled by different bands of activity, distinct but overlapping. Each band may be shaped or animated by different forces, including states, social movements and historical trends. A hierarchy may be observed or predicted – whether dominated by the abstraction of global capital, or a superpower – as with talk of this being 'China's century' (Beckley, 2011). Many assert that politics and economics will eventually have to bow before the ecosystem. All we can usefully assume is that patterns of power and causation come and go, as in a kaleidoscope.

The assumption made here is that the world has three distinctive logics: the logic of economics (including structures of trade, production and investment); the logic of politics (which is the competition over how the world is to be organized and resources to be allocated); and the logic of knowledge, which is an autonomous realm because of the impossibility of confining ideas, which flow like water through every crack.[1] Naturally economics is a major preoccupation of politicians, while economic actors sometimes play politics. Scientists and thinkers deal in everything. The point is not that subject matter can be sealed into separate compartments. Rather, economic, political and intellectual behaviours each have their distinctive priorities and dynamics, which can be influenced from outside but not eradicated. If one becomes too dominant, as with laissez-faire economics under the Chilean dictatorship, or Stalin's destruction of peasant agriculture, harm – and policy problems – tend to follow. For its part scientific knowledge usually has to struggle against political and religious interference, as both the persecution of Galileo and national firewalls against the internet remind us.

This multi-banded system, in a condition of constant flux, is far from the metaphor of a (primitive) society of states with which we began. It encompasses the whole range of competing actors on the world scene, together with varying patterns of conflict and cooperation, fragmentation and solidarity. Different dimensions, and issue areas within them, exhibit different patterns of authority or dominance. Some are chaotic, some well enough organized to constitute 'regimes' (Krasner, 1983). The only thing certain is that from all this comes bubbling up an endless supply of new events, initiatives, problems and ideas. This is the tumult of change which many see as defining the postmodern world, and which James Rosenau captured in terms like 'turbulence' and 'cascade' (Rosenau, 1990; Rosenau and Cziempel, 1989). Whether you work for Apple, the Muslim Brotherhood or the European Union, it makes international decision-making a challenging business.

This is only a sketch of what the modern world system means. From the perspective of agency and responsibility in foreign policy it is important to look at how the system works, in terms of openings and pressures. What follows is based on the strategic-relational assumptions laid out in Chapter 2, namely that actors both constitute certain structures in themselves and interact with the structures in which they themselves are embedded. Thus while they move across and within the various bands of the international system, and are constrained by them they also give life to the system. Indeed without the actors and their actions there would be no international system, only ecology. On this basis, the analysis will begin by assessing the material, or relatively unchanging aspects of actors' environment; the semi-material aspects where human intervention takes place, including political geography, political economy and knowledge; and the political aspects, of behaviour, institutions and ideas.

The Politics of Geography

The various dimensions of human action are played out in a physical world which is as independent and slow-changing as anything can be in history. This is why in FPA geography is often included in the category of the external environment, despite it being evident that territory, resources, airspace and territorial waters are at the disposal of states and constitute part of their internal configuration. It is the *pattern* of geography, with its distribution of features, which is independent of political action. A contoured map of the world, naked of political divisions, looks much as it would have done, had cartography been up to the task, in 1492, in 500, or even in the age of Thucydides, the fifth century BC. Physical features are difficult to change by human action even where sovereign control is undisputed. Decision-makers have to cope with this fact, even if they still compete ferociously to take advantage of the material world.

Some major changes have been made to nature by human action, some intentional, some not. The most dramatic were the opening of the canals at Suez and Panama and of the Channel Tunnel, but of equal importance have been the Alpine road and railway tunnels between Switzerland and its neighbours, great bridges such as that between Demark and Sweden, or over the Bosphorus, and the trans-oceanic cables laid from the mid-nineteenth century onwards. These engineering achievements are vulnerable to interruption by subversion. But the fact remains that they are very rarely blocked, even by war. The Suez Canal has twice been put out of action, but only once for any length of time, between 1967 and 1975, while the Panama Canal has never been seriously threatened. Such human constructs soon become perceived as part of the geographical givens themselves, not least because the great powers usually have a powerful interest in keeping them open.

It is also the case that we have changed the meaning of our physical environment without fully intending to. The advance of science means that air and space have become crucial dimensions of life and politics while mountains and rivers are less important as barriers. The industrialization of much of the globe, meanwhile, has placed a premium on resources such as oil, uranium, water, fish and manganese, with the result that the seabed, over-flying rights and access to secure energy supplies have moved to the top of states' concerns. By contrast, grain, coal, iron ore and gold have become less critical than they were. The ecosphere has dramatically come into play as an issue in both domestic and international politics. Burning forests no less than drilling for oil invites instant foreign interest. Not only has the quality of our air and food been placed in question through a combination of increased dependence on external supplies, and microbes which are no respecters of frontiers, but the world's climate and sea levels are now at serious risk.

The physical world, therefore, consists in much which we inherit and must live with, plus other phenomena which we have collectively created but are no less difficult to manage. Together these things shape security concerns, in that they present states with distinctive problems according to position, size and period of history. The military balance and the economic league tables are intimately connected to a society's physical patrimony. In the first half of the twentieth century some influential work on geopolitics suggested that this matrix had a decisive effect on a state's foreign policy, and indeed on the global balance of power. Various factors were identified at different phases of this work; when taken up by policy-makers they became semi-fulfilling prophecies, ultimately with disastrous results. All revealed the obsession of the times with a neo-Darwinian view of international relations as struggle and survival which reached its nadir in Nazi-fascism (Parker, 1982). This is why the

term 'politics of geography' is preferred here; 'geopolitics' has such difficult historical associations, with power politics and worse, that it creates
immediate preconceptions, often leading people to shy away from what
is a vital subject – the influence of position and resources on politics.
Even realists suffer from what has been called 'spatial blindness'
(Mouritzen and Wivel, 2012, pp. 7–8).

Nonetheless, geopolitical theory cannot be ignored, given its historical
impact. Of the main proponents Alfred Mahan (1890) was the first to
influence policy, through his stress on the importance of sea power and
President Theodore Roosevelt's subsequent decisions to build up the
Navy and to ensure US control of the new Panama Canal (in the
Hay–Bunau-Varilla Treaty of 1903). The most malign, if scarcely intentional influence, was exerted in combination by the Englishman Halford
Mackinder (1919) and the German Klaus Haushofer, whose contrary
belief that power had now shifted to those controlling great land masses,
and in particular the 'heartland' of the 'world-island' of Eurasia,
provided Hitler with some of the conceptual architecture he needed for
the policies of *Lebensraum* and world domination. The madness of
1939–45 discredited these overtly geopolitical theories but it did not
prevent ideas like the 'iron curtain', 'containment' and 'the domino
theory' perpetuating the belief that foreign policy had to follow strategic
imperatives deriving from the territorial distribution of power across the
earth's surface.

This kind of grand strategy seemed irrelevant after the end of the Cold
War. Even before 1989 it was not the central reality for the majority of
states. Although the arrival of intercontinental ballistic missiles meant
that the increasing numbers of new states had little stake in the 'great
game', local and regional balances of power continued to exist, with
geography being of huge importance – as the stories of Cuba, the
Falkland Islands, Finland and the Sudan demonstrated, among many
others. But for once some lessons had presented themselves, and been
half-learned. The crudity and dangers of grand geopolitical explanations
had been fully exposed, and rejected.[2] Unfortunately the futility of any
single-factor explanation had not yet been grasped, as the fashions for
the end of history, globalization and 'the clash of civilisations' in the
1990s showed. Fortunately, like all headline-grabbing ideas they soon
had to give ground before events (Jean, 1995). Insofar as foreign policy-
making is becoming a more sophisticated and well-advised process,
decision-makers are at least now aware that their environment is
complex and multifaceted.

Geography affects political action in much more subtle ways than was
previously allowed. In place of the classical notion of 'natural frontiers',
which only ever applied to a few locations, we now focus on 'border

regions' overlapping legal frontiers, where economic and cultural life changes only gradually over hundreds of kilometres. This approach is important in relation to societies' senses of identity, which are inevitably complex: differences may seem less sharp in the context of a common regional identity, or climate and topography, held in common, while many new states are highly artificial in terms of the way they divide communities and trade patterns which have endured for centuries.

The power struggles which have superimposed frontiers on the planet mean that states vary enormously in size, mineral wealth, access to the sea, vulnerability and cohesiveness. This is the meaning of modern political geography. Some come under great pressure through being in difficult physical circumstances, such as Bangladesh. Others, like the United States, seem to possess every card in the pack. Both extremes are the product of geography in conjunction with history and political action. The United States was created by immigration, imperialism, war, political creativity and economic vitality. Bangladesh is in the situation it is because of the artificiality of the divided Pakistan created in 1947, and the dangerous international consequences which would have followed any attempt to absorb East Pakistan into India in 1971. Its leaders face enormous challenges, but their own administrative incompetence and internecine political conflicts have worsened them. States have to work with the political geography they have, however unjust. They cannot be indifferent to it, yet they can only change it at the margin. The physical characteristics of a state have important implications for all areas of public policy, not least foreign policy. Many thought that distance had been rendered insignificant by technology, but degrees of proximity certainly matter, as has been evident in Russia's regional dominance in relation to Georgia and the Ukraine (Mouritzen and Wivel, 2012).

The costs and benefits of size and location are not straightforward to calculate. Bigness expands the number of neighbours, and thus potential problems, but does not necessarily bestow great resources. It depends on terrain and population, as the histories of Russia, China and India show. Conversely smallness can be made to work to advantage, as in Switzerland and Singapore. States, through their decision-makers and ultimately their peoples, always have choices about how to interpret their physical situation, although these choices can only be implemented over a long term, through intergenerational consensus. Perceptions, skill and determination are all important. As R. G. Collingwood argued, it is how people living on an island respond to their situation that determines their degree of insularity. Conversely, a land-locked state can behave in an insular way (Sprout and Sprout, 1969, p. 45).

On the one hand the physical environment imposes costs and constraints. If a government tries to ignore the vulnerability of its borders, or gambles on always getting good harvests, it may be severely punished by events. On the other, the physical world provides varying kinds of opportunity. This is not the anthropomorphic 'beckoning' of what the Sprouts (1969, pp. 44–6) called 'environmental possibilism', but the simple recognition of the fact that states have to respond to their neighbours, their region and their resource problems. Once created, the territorial state becomes more a material than a contingent fact. Thus Turkey is persistently torn between European, trans-Caucasian and Middle Eastern patterns of friendship, while communist Cuba, for years at odds with its giant neighbour, had little option but to seek support from outside the Western Hemisphere.

The particular choices made are not inevitable. What matters is the long-run pattern of reactions to the matrix of constraints and opportunities which the material situation provides, and the available technological and economic resources. Through successive phases of domestic politics state orientations evolve, as the number of geopolitical anomalies testifies. Yugoslavia, for example, was the paradigm case of an artificial state, created by treaty in the face of geographical and ethnic obstacles, and ultimately foundering. But one should also ask how was it that such a state managed to survive between 1919 and 1992. To which the most plausible answer is: through a combination of international political necessity and domestic leadership. Other examples of politics (and technology) flying in the face of geography are the European seaborne empires, and the fact that Italy remained fragmented rather than united between circa 455 and 1861. All such cases raise as many questions as answers, suggesting both the complex interplay of human and material factors and the tendency of geographical chickens to come home to roost when states can no longer bear the costs of inherently difficult enterprises. A contemporary case might be thought to be the Gulf sheikhdoms. So long as the price and supply of oil is sufficient, these statelets will be wealthy enough to make gardens in the desert, and to build up sophisticated armed forces. If that circumstance should change, their basic vulnerability will lead to an upheaval in the politics of the region. In short, while the material environment in itself does nothing, it must always be factored into decision-making. If is discounted it may in time make itself cruelly felt.

The emphasis so far has been on political geography, but this needs extending into the study of international political economy (IPE). For the physical world also impacts hugely on the process of wealth creation, over which states compete fiercely. Foreign economic policy actors encounter a wide range of semi-material requirements when engaged in the pursuit of wealth. Features such as ports or international airports can be built and structures improved, although they are usually a long time in the making. Frankfurt may be gradually becoming a rival to London as a financial centre and airline hub, but it takes decades to achieve supremacy in such matters.

Technology, however, does determine the pace of change. Even major oceans and mountain ranges hardly represent the same obstacles as 100 years ago given the jet engine and the ubiquity of air travel. The great motorway networks which link most of western Europe have helped to integrate the single European market, while China's construction of a rail link to Lhasa in defiance of the high altitude was designed to emphasize its control over Tibet. India is very well connected to the outside world, but is trying urgently to overcome its lack of an internal transport infra-structure. The creation of virtual networks through high-speed comput-ers has had an even more dramatic impact. As a result some see the impact of geography as having been effectively neutralized (Cairncross, 1997). This is too extreme. What has happened is simply a change in relative costs; if a society can afford to pay the costs of air freight it can import exotic foods to eat with the same freshness as local producers. If not it has to do without. The same applies to other options, such as the projection of military force or the ability to be represented at official international gatherings. Computers can only substitute for part of this kind of capacity, not least because they too consume expensive resources, including highly educated labour. North Korea may be able to hack into American networks, or even make a nuclear bomb, but the opportunity costs for its economy and society are severe.

In the same way, the possession of key physical resources such as minerals, water and fish stocks only takes on significance in relation to the ability to exploit them – and to the premium put on them by the global system at any given point. Mines and oil rigs are opened or shut down with considerable flexibility according to the market. If the indige-nous capacity does not exist, then multinational companies are only too eager to step in – assuming strategic sanctions are not in place. What are less amenable to change are capabilities which provide a market advan-tage because they are relied on by a substantial proportion of other members of the international system. These key factors of modern production revolve around skilled labour, plus services such as educa-tion, finance, transport and culture.

In practice the socioeconomic attributes needed to establish stock markets, banking centres, transport networks and tourist industries can only be acquired slowly, taking on a material solidity which cannot easily be substituted. Indeed, there are limits to the extent to which they can be created by official design. Thus the People's Republic of China recog-nized the valuable international asset that was Hong Kong, and conducted negotiations with Britain so as to preserve and incorporate it.

Similarly elites in the developing world have had to look to the old metropoles such as Paris and London for investment services, freight forwarding, medicine, secondary and tertiary education, sport and entertainment, consultancies and technical standards. The City of London, the Dow Jones Index, Volkswagen, the Nobel Prize Committee, the English Premier League and the Académie Française are all examples of institutions which set the highest standards and provide services which are difficult to replicate. They therefore constitute the semi-material parts of the external environment in which states and other international actors have to work.

From the point of view of international political economy as much as classical security it still matters where on the earth's surface an actor is located. Despite their many advantages, the cities of Latin America do not figure prominently in the provision of key services in the international political economy. Although these days the question is all too rarely asked as to why not, it is difficult to resist the conclusion that the centre-periphery model introduced by critics such as Raúl Prebisch and André Gunder Frank in the 1950s does have some descriptive power. It is revealing that skilled labour continues to drain from those places where it is sorely needed to those in which it already exists, as with the flow of qualified Indian medical staff into the US and UK.

In the agricultural sector position and physical conditions matter even more to the quality of human enterprise, and thus a state's relative success. The examples of the Soviet Union and India show that where the climate is adverse and social organization inadequate, it is immensely difficult to produce food surpluses at affordable prices. States which then get locked into the cycle of expensive imports and weak currencies fall into various forms of dependency, such as that of Iceland, rich but over-reliant on fish. Those, by contrast, which enjoy the temperate conditions supposedly ideal for human life to prosper not only incur fewer costs but given an effective social system may also generate surpluses to exchange for other resources (E. Huntington, 1924; Toynbee, 1972, pp. 95–6). Clearly Poland's harsh environment creates costs which California, say, does not have. On the other hand the limits of this single-factor explanation are exposed by the evidence of the Scandinavian countries' ability to prosper despite their cold climate. And since 2004, when it entered the favourable environment of the EU, Poland too has progressed significantly on all fronts.

A state needs a combination of features if it is to be in a position to create a favourable human geography. The lack of one crucial element such as population (in particular a large skilled workforce) will restrict a state's international influence. Canada and Saudi Arabia are cases in point, despite their wealth. India, Nigeria and Brazil, which suffer from poverty and problems of infrastructure, have more long-term potential to become power-centres. That said, such predictions have been made for many years, and these states demonstrate the importance of intervening social and political variables in determining influence in both the international political economy and the international political system. What is more, how long is the 'long term' in international relations?

The external environment in the widest sense is therefore vital to an understanding of all foreign policy decisions. 'External' does not mean just those things outside the territorial boundaries of an actor; it means all those things which are outside the social and political processes by which the actor comes to its choices. Some of these things, while material, occur inside territorial limits, as with topography, climate and mineral resources. Even more of them are semi-material, created by human interaction with the physical world over a long period but by the same token very slow-changing. In this context the scope for agency is limited.

Political Interdependence

The political layer of the international system is a human product, and exists largely in the minds of decision-makers. In material terms it can be glimpsed in the form of the various institutions where states come together, or where judgements are made on their behaviour. Of these the most important are the buildings of the United Nations in New York and Geneva, and the International Court of Justice, plus the new International Criminal Court, in The Hague. The regional institutions, notably those of the European Union in Brussels and the striking new African Union building in Addis Ababa, are also manifestations of the structure of international politics.

An observer who expected the outputs of these institutions to reveal the workings of the system as a whole, however, would be sadly misled. Although they now total over 400 in comparison to only 37 in 1909, intergovernmental organizations constitute only one of the five main sources of political constraint and interdependence at the global level (Zacher, 2001).[3] The others are: international law; informal norms; other states' foreign policies, and in particular the hierarchy of states; and transnational processes, including INGOs. Before each is discussed briefly in turn, the notional character of political interdependence needs further explanation.

Any set of relationships with a regular pattern and characteristics that go beyond the sum of its parts constitutes a significant structure for the constituent units, even if the relationships are only lightly institutionalized.

Thus the international political system, despite being patchy, contested and dependent on the expectations of its participants, is nonetheless an important structure for those responsible for foreign policy. It both constrains them and shapes their opportunities. Despite its notional quality it is not random or evanescent. On the contrary, beliefs, procedures and expectations accumulate over generations, increasingly in written and institutional form. There are few enforcement mechanisms but equally no single actor can easily change the system. In the context of foreign policy-making, most actors factor it prominently into their decision-making, sometimes to the intense irritation of domestic critics who think too much notice is being taken of external considerations. What is more, as we shall see in Chapter 9, states' own identities are increasingly shaped by their political contexts.

Actors expect elements of both anarchy and order in their external environment, and are thus plagued by the dilemmas of trying at one and the same time to: (i) accrue benefits; (ii) achieve protection from actual and potential threats; (iii) minimize the costs and constraints imposed from outside; (iv) uphold what are perceived as the basic rules of order and (v) build a degree of international solidarity – for its inherent value and for the technical advantages in specific fields like non-proliferation. This is a perpetual balancing act, often simplified in the concept of interdependence.

Interdependence is a concept mostly associated with international economics, but it is also at the heart of the idea of an international political system (Mastanduno, 1999). Its key attributes have been identified as sensitivity and vulnerability (Keohane and Nye, 1977, pp. 11–19). That is, when change occurs in one actor others also experience some disturbance because their internal system is partially plugged into that of the outsider. This will show itself either through the 'sensitivity' of immediate but manageable reactions (such as the transfer of price inflation) or in a more serious 'vulnerability' to actual dislocations (such as reduced oil supplies during war in the Gulf). Both the examples given are from political economy, and many more could be cited, particularly in relation to the environment and to debt rescheduling (no one wants to risk the ripple effects of even a small country like Greece exiting the eurozone).

Politics often operates in the same way. One state's domestic 'solutions' can easily be another's problems, as the history of revolution demonstrates (D. Armstrong, 1993; Halliday, 1999). The French and Russian revolutions spread alarm far and wide beyond their frontiers (partly through hysteria, but that is another story), precipitating two decades of war. The mechanism of interdependence works in the first instance through direct knock-on effects inside domestic society, but these cannot easily be insulated from foreign policy and soon complicate relations between governments. This is particularly so where states are intensively connected, whether through a regional community, or even an adversary partnership. An example of the former is the Association of Southeast Asian Nations (ASEAN), where despite the importance of sovereignty as a founding principle, any upheaval in one member state closely affects the others – although the smaller members are more at risk than the bigger, interdependence usually being asymmetrical. An example of this is the Indo-Pakistan relationship. When the Bharatiya Janata Party (BJP) came to power in New Delhi in 1996, with its militant Hindu rhetoric, it caused alarm in Karachi and exacerbated the problems over Kashmir, which ultimately led to nuclear testing on both sides. Perhaps learning from this experience, when the BJP returned to government in 2014, Prime Minister Modi immediately extended an invitation to attend his inauguration to his Pakistani opposite number, Nawaz Sharif.

This is, however, only one face of political interdependence. The other derives from the common membership of the society of states. The effects of the latter in shaping the attitudes and behaviour of foreign policy actors should not be underestimated. They derive from the five sources of interdependence mentioned earlier, and it is to these that we now turn.

The first is the *institutional web of international organizations*. Whatever the variable performance of these organizations, the norm for states is now participation. All states are members of some, and most take part in many, whether they are universal or regional, technical- or security-related. This shows both that such institutions serve functional purposes and that states are concerned not to be left out of a common system. Together they represent a complex and growing network which generates a vast range of bilateral and multilateral diplomatic exchanges. Various socialising and constraining effects cannot be avoided, which is why some states have exerted their right not to join, as with the refusal of the Swiss people in 1985 to join the UN (finally reversed in the referendum of 2002), and Norway's referenda decisions in 1972 and 1994 to stay out of the European Community. But such opt-outs are becoming rare.

The weak feel the socialising effects of intergovernmental organizations more than the strong, as with the imposition of structural adjustment policies on developing countries by the Washington institutions, but even the strong accept the need for some mechanisms of negotiation and compromise. The presence of the UN General Assembly in New York is a standing reminder to a sceptical US Congress of the importance of international organization, with its annual September plenary bringing world leaders together on a single stage. Moreover while the Security Council was designed to give a privileged position to the victors of 1945, it and the General Assembly provide many opportunities for weaker states and controversial causes to be heard, and thus picked up in the world's media. This is precisely why the permanent members have insisted on vetoing resolutions which go against their own policies – to deny a position legitimacy and international momentum.

New international organizations also provide platforms for ideas that the bigger powers dislike, such as the critiques of neocolonialism which grew up in the Group of 77 (soon 120 plus) in the 1970s, encouraged by the setting up of UNCTAD (the United Nations Conference on Trade and Development). The demands for a 'new international economic order' changed the agenda of international politics. Even if that new order was not forthcoming the pressure still contributed to the growing confidence of various new states and transnational political groups in challenging Western hegemony. This could not be ignored, as the subsequent activism of states like Libya and Iran on the one hand (confrontational), and Malaysia and Singapore on the other (reformist), demonstrated.

This role in agenda-setting was also evident in the ability of the smaller and more progressive Western countries to push environmental and human rights concerns through special conferences like those on the environment in Stockholm in 1972 and in Beijing on women in 1995. Such states have also found regional groupings of great usefulness in raising their individual profiles and projecting their own concerns. Ireland barely had a national foreign policy before joining the European Community in 1973. Its national profile became much higher, paradoxically, through participation in collective diplomacy (D. Keohane, 2001). In a similar vein Canada's distinctive commitment to UN peacekeeping has helped it to emerge from the shadow of its powerful neighbour and ally.

International law is much better understood as a source of political interdependence than as a framework of governance. Whereas international law is too basic and patchy to be 'obeyed' by states its gradual evolution has produced a set of agreements and principles that operate as points of reference across the variety of ideological viewpoints in the international system. After all, international law largely derives from states themselves and serves the vital function of formally establishing and delimiting their sovereignty. Beyond this, it draws them into a process of common dialogue and shared procedures which makes them, in Stanley Hoffmann's words 'system-conscious' (Cassese, 1993, p. 442). More particularly, as Louis Henkin pointed out, foreign ministries become 'treaty-geared' because they cannot afford to risk a possible disadvantage if new law is left to be made by others (Henkin, 1979). In game-theory terms this is a prisoners' dilemma. It leads governments, companies and INGOs to appoint ever more international lawyers. States with limited bureaucratic resources have to hire freelance top-guns for important disputes – as for both parties over the issue of a divided Cyprus at the International Court of Justice (ICJ).

On the other side of the coin, states always feel the need to justify any breach of international law, and usually to find some legal justification. As Reus-Smit (2003, p. 592, cited in Byers, 2008, p. 625) points out, this sense of obligation is also the very reason they try to avoid too many legal entanglements. A country can always choose to ignore the ICJ and its judgments, but it thereby gives its critics a potent argument which may take decades to recede, as the United States did in its unwillingness to accept the court's 1986 ruling against it over Nicaragua. The Soviet Union's gradual isolation in international politics after its invasions of Hungary in 1956 and Czechoslovakia in 1968 came about through its inability to convince most states that the 'Brezhnev Doctrine' of limited sovereignty was a desirable innovation in international law, let alone a retrospective justification (McGwire, 1991, pp. 174–86). Tony Blair, and to a lesser extent George W. Bush, were anxious to get UN Security Council authorization for the attack on Iraq in 2003 (Booth, 2007, pp. 434–5).

Ultimately, states – and increasing numbers of private actors – also need international law for practical reasons: to conduct transactions; to regulate specialist areas like intellectual property or civil aviation; for protection against illicit interference; and to establish the principle of reciprocity. Although they are inconsistent, bypassing or distorting laws while observing others, decision-makers are well aware that the legal dimension is central to their ability to manage their external environment.

Closely related to international law, but not synonymous with it, is the third source of political interdependence, namely *informal norms*. These can run ahead of formal rules, or lag behind them. Indeed between formal 'black letter' law and norms there is a grey area in which arguments run over whether law should be extended, how it is to be interpreted and who has what rights in international society (Byers, 1999). By 'norms' is meant the general principles and working assumptions that states acknowledge in their routine relationships. They are in a condition of evolution, and head in various directions simultaneously. Among the most prominent are: *pacta sunt servanda*; the illegitimacy of aggressive war, the value of peaceful coexistence; the rights of non-intervention and to self-determination; the illegitimacy of terrorism; the right of interested parties to an action to be consulted; the right to sell goods abroad. Many of these principles are articulated either in the UN Charter or in some particular international convention. Yet law is only part of their legitimacy; international politics ultimately generates the discourses which determine whether a principle becomes accepted.

Such discourses are generated by intergovernmental relations on the one hand and the cosmopolitan processes eating away at state monopolies on the other. Yet these two things cannot be kept in separate compartments. Much of the thinking about human rights which has become increasingly prominent in the past fifty years derives from what the victorious states did at Nuremberg, at San Francisco in 1945 and in the Universal Declaration of Human Rights in 1948. The commitments made then have taken a long time to ferment, but that is precisely the point about discourse and norms. In the international political system it is not enough to announce a new principle; it has to become internalized and achieve a consensus before it will appear in actions. That will only happen through the slow process of interaction and debate between governments. NGOs are increasingly actors in this process, as over civil rights in eastern Europe, where spontaneous resistance to Soviet authoritarianism was given a considerable boost by Moscow's agreement to the final principles of the Helsinki Accord of the Conference on Security and Cooperation in Europe in 1975. Almost without noticing, the Soviet government had acknowledged the legitimacy of human rights concerns and given its dissidents crucial international footholds in their ascent towards liberty.

In this process of establishing norms, publicity and transparency are of crucial importance, as Kant foresaw two hundred years ago: 'all actions affecting the rights of other human beings are wrong if their maxim is not compatible with their being made public' (Kant, 1795, p. 126). In the modern world it is much more difficult to keep deeds out of the public eye. Accordingly, what is referred to optimistically as 'world opinion' casts perpetual judgement on decision-makers. Despite its vagueness world opinion clearly means something to those active in international affairs, as the term is in constant use (Hill, 1996b). To the extent that actors show concern for world opinion they reveal themselves to be acknowledging the build-up of judgements across frontiers, as expressed by both official and private voices. They display the value of not wishing to alienate people in other countries unnecessarily, or to be unduly isolated. There may be moral reasons for this, but also practical ones, such as wishing to quiet a storm which is only giving encouragement to domestic critics (Rusciano, 2006; Rusciano and Fiske-Rusciano, 1998). On occasions, for example, regimes such as those in Jakarta, Riyadh and Tehran, have backed away from inflicting harsh punishments in the face of international outcries. On others they have proceeded with them, precisely so as to demonstrate their independence of general opinion.

World opinion may be linked to the idea of *confidence*, which we know is crucial in currency markets and can also affect the operation of the fragile international political system. When confidence breaks down, long-established patterns of alliance or stability may be called into question. Even a major player like the United States can lose the confidence of its friends when policies, such as those on Iraq after 2003, are generally thought to be misconceived. The standing of an individual leader, as we have seen with Boris Yeltsin, Silvio Berlusconi and François Hollande, can drop away with alarming speed when domestic and international doubts start to snowball.

International politics, and especially the idea of international society, also entails some notion of civilized behaviour which no decent government would wish to transgress. The fact of regular transgressions does not invalidate the idea; rather, it helps to stimulate discussion as to what its content should be. The UN Charter laid down a skeleton of rules about international relations, notably the prohibition on aggressive war. These have had some effect, if only by leading governments to use indirect and more covert methods, as Russia has done in the Ukraine, and by delegitimising the idea of empire. It also established many common standards to aspire to, in relation to the pacific settlement of disputes, economic cooperation and trusteeship. Subsequent conventions extended the timid challenge to state sovereignty by laying down standards on universal human rights. These, particularly the concerns over genocide and/or enforced population movements, have provided a slow-burning example of how international norms can evolve and shape behaviour. In this context that means a global 'human rights culture' which regimes can defy but hardly ignore (C. Brown, 2010, p. 179).

Although the international community still fails to prevent cases of genocide, as in Rwanda in 1994, states no longer feel able to avert their gaze on the grounds of non-intervention and cultural relativism. The NATO action against Serbia in Kosovo in 1999 (without the authorization of the United Nations Security Council (UNSC), given the prospect of a Russian veto) was an indication that the Western states at least were afraid of being accused of allowing another round of atrocities only a few years after Rwanda and Srebrenica.

These two scars on the idea of post–Cold War progress in fact created great pressure for the acceptance of a specific new norm, the 'Responsibility to Protect' (R2P), via the adoption at the General Assembly in 2001 of 'the Report to UN of the International Commission on Intervention and State Sovereignty'. This was the result of activism by a number of key players in and out of government, notably UN Secretary-General Kofi Annan, Lloyd Axworthy (Canada), Francis Deng (Somalia) and Gareth Evans (Australia) (G. Evans, 2008). Despite the huge distraction of 9/11 and the 'war on terror', the UN World Summit of 2005 adopted a document whose crucial provision in relation to genocide and crimes against humanity was that:

> When a state manifestly fails in its protection responsibilities, and peaceful means are inadequate, the international community must take stronger measures, including collective use of force authorized by the Security Council under Chapter VII.[4]

Since the 2001 initiative various crises have demonstrated the inability of the 'international community' to live up to this injunction, notably the disastrous conflict in Syria from 2011. But in almost all there has been fierce debate about a possible obligation to intervene on humanitarian grounds, which is a discourse very different from that of the Cold War. Arguably the humanitarian argument tipped the balance in the Anglo-French decisions to mount an operation in Libya in 2011 and France's move into Mali in 2013. Most states now have to factor into their foreign policy calculations the qualifications to sovereignty given such authoritative international backing, even if they oppose and resent them. The same goes for the possibility of leaders being arrested on charges of crimes against humanity, since the setting up of the International Criminal Court in 2002. Given that 122 states have signed its founding Rome Statute, figures like Henry Kissinger and Tony Blair may have to be careful in their travel plans. So far, however, all formal investigations have involved African states, which feeds existing scepticism about the existence of an 'international community'. On the other hand the International Criminal Tribunal for Former Yugoslavia in The Hague has been operating since 1993, and has shown itself to have teeth through the 161 Europeans indicted for 'serious violations of international humanitarian law', including famously Slobodan Milošević and Ratko Mladić.

In contrast to R2P most foreign policy is routine and rule-bound in the narrow sense – with the rules generated as the result of incessant international dialogue and painfully agreed upon conventions. Here the gradual internalization of shared norms is far more significant than any fear of incurring sanctions. Diplomatic practice, for example, functions extremely well. Even declared enemies can communicate thanks to the established practice of using interest sections in third-country missions. States have a common interest in being able to communicate, to trade and to protect their citizens abroad. This has led them to work out, through trial and error, a range of procedures and understandings which all can live with, such as immunity for diplomatic personnel accused of crimes, respecting embassy property, and generally observing the rules of extradition. When such norms are violated, the culprit is regarded as a pariah. More positively, the sending of emergency aid in natural disasters, even when there is no likelihood of reciprocity, is another sign that there are certain values which are diffused among states even where they are not codified or enforceable.

The fourth source of political interdependence is the *hierarchy of states*. This is not a mere synonym for the balance of power, which is too crude a notion to cover the richness of relations between 193 states of widely varying character. In any social environment the units have to understand their relative positions in the system, but the international relations pecking order is not straightforward, given that power comes from different and incommensurable sources. Subnational regions, and indeed companies, dispose of more wealth than many states, while not all rich states dispose of military strength. Some nuclear weapon states are actually weak on other indices. The system is thus characterized by a hierarchy consisting of a single superpower (that is, one with the capacity to act globally and influence the lives of everyone on the planet), a few 'rising powers' with some potential for a global role, a small number of ex-great powers still possessing wealth and diplomatic clout, and around 48 'least-developed countries' (LLDCs). Between the last two categories come the majority of the members of the United Nations, around 130 small- and middle-range states, both developed and developing, whose roles are largely confined to their own neighbourhoods.

In day-to-day diplomacy states know their place quite well, in the sense that they understand where they can exert influence and where they cannot. Decision-makers do not follow any formal classification of wealth or power, along the lines of the OECD indicators or a football league table, but they still need some way of representing the international system to themselves and their citizens. They therefore think of their state as operating in a particular region or issue area, and do not pretend to the global role that the United States takes for granted. Geographical proximity or notions of comparative advantage provide guidance and shape choices.

No doubt cautious by disposition, foreign policy-makers rarely display signs of radical revisionism, and when they do they come up against the weight of the existing order of things. The hierarchy of states presses strongly down from the top, and rebellion against its ordering principles is difficult. Only the most determined and reckless leaders, of whom Napoleon and Hitler are the archetypes, rise to the challenge. Fortunately the drive for world hegemony is rare, and tends to unite a winning coalition against it. More common is the desire to alter a particular aspect of the informal hierarchies which exist within IGOs, in the international political economy or over the right to acquire nuclear power. But here too a revisionist has to expect powerful opposition from those who act as the self-appointed keepers of the status quo.

Given all this it is misleading to describe international relations as anarchy. Its arrangements may bear little resemblance to what goes on inside a state, but the system possesses not only a structure but an implicit pecking order and set of dominant assumptions which is intensely frustrating to those who did not help form them, and feel disadvantaged by them. Even the beneficiaries of the system, which are for the most part the states of West, are at times ambivalent about the 'responsibilities' which they assume. The US has often demanded that others step up to the plate in terms of paying for and contributing to global security – though in practice that would only be acceptable on its own terms. Since the collapse of the Soviet Union it has become even more difficult for any smaller state which might want to defy Western-generated orthodoxies, especially in foreign policy. The price of the sovereign independence valued by all, but particularly by small and/or weak states, is keeping a low profile in international politics. Seeking to preserve one's existing position, meaning the simple fact of statehood and its associated status, is the most that the majority of states can aspire to in terms of their contribution to the international system. In times of flux, or when a major power is in difficulties, some states may see tempting possibilities for change, but the onset of a major crisis usually throws into stark relief the limits of such aspirations. The stalemate over Palestine, despite the innumerable efforts to reach a peace settlement made by many parties from inside and outside the region, is a compelling example. The system moves exceedingly slow, and all states – including the great powers – have to dance to the music of time.[5]

Opting Out and Other Forms of Resistance

Although the international system displays considerable elements of interdependence, both political and economic, this does not mean that there is no way for individual actors to retain or create space for themselves. There have always been cases of states managing to defy the great powers, if only for a period, not least because the system is too big, geographically, and too complicated to be fully policed, and because competition between the great powers creates opportunities for others. Thus there are always differing strategies available and a wide range of possible responses to the same conditions. The external environment looms large, but it is not *determining*. Apparent anomalies like the survival of Castro's Cuban regime may be explained by reference to the balance of power (although support from Moscow ended in 1991) but cases like Ceauşescu's Romania, whose foreign policy defied its Soviet neighbour, do not fit into that mould. Nor did Nyerere's Tanzania, which pursued its own model of development independent of pressures from East and West, led by a distinctive figure who simultaneously coruscated capitalism and translated Shakespeare into Swahili.

Many states choose to cope with the pressures of the system by conformity – to the wishes of a powerful neighbour, to an alliance or other form of diplomatic coalition, or to the general rules set by a combination of consensus and hegemonic leadership. Those who do not fit into these categories – and many states change their positions over time – still have a number of different ways of manifesting their independence. They may be summarized as non-alignment, self-assertion, isolationism and eccentricity.

Non-alignment takes a wide variety of forms. It overlaps but is distinct from neutrality, which has the technical meaning of staying out of armed conflicts. It covers the wide range of approaches used to avoid commitments to the major groupings in international politics. The Non-Aligned Movement started in 1955 as a way of achieving solidarity among those who resisted the gravitational pulls of the two Cold War camps. Despite its lack of institutionalization (and the disappearance of one of the camps) it still fulfils a need for its 120 members (including all the states of Africa, and most of Asia), who use it to stress their lack of alignment with the West without actually being confrontational. In Europe the group of neutral states which included Austria, Finland, Ireland, Sweden and Switzerland has gradually been eroded by the absorption of four of them into the EU, although echoes of their neutral traditions still survive in their national foreign policies. Yugoslavia collapsed not because of its non-aligned foreign policy, which functioned successfully until 1989, but because the end of the Cold War brought its bubbling internal tensions to the surface. It had in effect been held together as a state by international politics.

Self-assertion is far less common than huddling together in non-alignment. Great power rhetoric makes it appear that maverick states regularly emerge to endanger international order. In practice, very few countries risk drawing hostile attention to themselves by challenging the status quo, certainly in general terms but even on issues of importance to themselves. When a state does behave in a self-assertive and unmanageable way, it soon finds itself a pariah, which tells us something about the conformist nature of the international system (Litwak, 2000). In the Cold War a state attempting to defy a sphere of influence usually found support from the other side, only to find it evaporating when the chips were down, as with Dubcek in Czechoslovakia in 1968 and Allende in Chile. More free-floating dissidents, like Libya and post-revolutionary Iran, avoided this fate. They partly chose their status and partly had it thrust upon them. Having an unpleasant internal regime like South Africa under apartheid can outrage the 'opinion of mankind' in Woodrow Wilson's phrase (Geldenhuys, 1984, 1990). But it is usually the perception by the dominant powers that a state represents a threat to the existing order, as with the prospect of North Korea's acquisition of nuclear weapons, or Venezuela's challenge to the US in South America, that confirms the image. It then becomes difficult to reverse the process, so as to come in from the cold. Not wishing to freeze change, the Obama administration preferred the term 'outliers' to 'rogue states', although this diplomatic subtlety has so far had little reward (Litwak, 2012).

Isolation can go with being a pariah, or it can be deliberately sought (Holsti et al., 1982). Albania, Burma/Myanmar, Cuba, North Korea and Syria have at various times preferred to be shunned rather than submit to external pressure – or rather their governments have. Their peoples usually have no choice, since isolation requires authoritarianism to enforce it. Few actively seek out isolation, given the economic costs, but it is easy to get locked into an aggressive–defensive spiral with external criticism producing the perception of illegitimate interference or cultural contamination. Robert Mugabe took Zimbabwe down this path for a decade, although as he managed to keep lines open to fellow African leaders he avoided total purdah, and eventually saw off sanctions. In its way such an approach is an assertion of agency in an ever more confining international environment. The 'ourselves alone' image is very powerful, as embattled Serbia demonstrated in 1999. On the other hand, isolation, like neutrality, is never absolute. There will always be some contact, or some trade deal, which will be quietly welcome (Berkovitch, 1988). Finally there are a few isolated countries which desperately wish to escape the condition, usually through diplomatic recognition. The Turkish Republic of Northern Cyprus is the best current case in point, although as with Taiwan, the practical problems of isolation are alleviated by having a powerful patron.

Eccentricity, in the sense of going against conventional expectations, is a less durable strategy for resisting the weight of the international system than the other three. It is mostly associated with individual leaders and particular policy concerns. In the 1980s New Zealand's Prime Minister David Lange rather startlingly departed from its normal pro-Western quietism to denounce French and American nuclear tests in the Pacific. The consequence was to raise the profiles of both New Zealand and nuclear testing, but at a political price then imposed relentlessly at home and abroad. New Zealand exerted its sovereign right to ban visits from nuclear weapon-carrying ships, but lost its US security guarantee, and domestic opposition to the government was stirred up from outside. This was a considered choice, like that of Slovakia to separate from the richer Czech Republic in 1993 – which many Slovaks subsequently regretted. National independence might have been served, and the beliefs of Vladimir Meciar and his party, but the standard of living of the Slovakian people was clearly damaged for the next decade. And as Czech Foreign Minister

Karel Schwarzenberg has said wistfully, 'the international weight of both republics together is less than [that of] the former Czechoslovakia' (G. Campbell, 2013).

Only the peoples of these states, and history, can judge whether the various strategies employed to resist, opt-out of or merely diverge from the orthodox paths in foreign policy have been worthwhile. What is certain, however, is that there remains plenty of scope for divergence among the actors of the international system despite the pressures for conformity and conservatism which it contains. It largely depends on which set of costs a community prefers to incur – assuming the political choice is clearly and democratically set before them.

System Change

This chapter has argued that the external environment is central to the foreign policy of any state, large or small. Yet the 'outside world' has various dimensions with separate functional logics arising from the overlapping of the society of states with transnational relations. It remains external in the sense that it is outside the control of any given actor, and because it consists to a large degree of material and semi-material conditions, which may be misperceived but which inevitably make their presence felt at some stage or other of the decision cycle.

The question then remains of how the international system changes. It is not static and some actors are far more able to influence it than others. Is the system driven by impersonal historical forces? Or is it pluralist, the sum of all its parts in perpetual interaction? Is it 'run' by a small group of privileged players? The three possibilities are not mutually exclusive, and they all have an element of truth. What is difficult to deny is that while the world can move a surprisingly long way in a mere half century, it is at no one's particular behest. Imperialism aroused increasing opposition in the 1930s, but no one imagined that almost all the European colonies would disappear between 1947 and 1964. The sudden collapse of the USSR and its empire at the end of the 1980s was a systemic shock. The United States completely failed to foresee a second Pearl Harbor at the hands of Al Qaeda.

History is always on the move, and one of its key manifestations is the changing international political system, where individual agency, even at the level of powerful states, has only a limited role. Philosophers and commentators from Marx and Lenin to Huntington and Fukuyama have sought to unlock its secrets and to identify the reason of change. But there are no short cuts to understanding this massive system in which national foreign policies and the strategies of transnational actors (TNAs) provide the only avenues for action, responsibility and (at times) accountability. In effect policy-makers take a series of bets on the opportunities presented by their international situation, and on the forces which might consign their policies to the rubbish heap. When they oversimplify or misinterpret external 'realities', which happens all too often, the results are disastrous.

Notes

1   These categories are influenced by the four 'structures', or power–authority nexuses posited by Susan Strange (1994, pp. 235–40): security, production, finance and knowledge.
2   John Mearsheimer (2001), however, has made the argument that the 'stopping power of water' (that is, the sea as a major line of defence) is a critical factor in international politics. See the discussion of this in Little (2007, pp. 225–30).
3   It is difficult to agree on the criteria for identifying an intergovernmental organization, as that depends on the degree of institutionalism and permanence. The number of 400 is a significant underestimate if a relaxed view is taken of the candidates (Kegley and Blanton, 2012, pp. 149–50).
4   Language used by the International Coalition for the Responsibility to Protect, available online at <http://www.responsibilitytoprotect.org>.
5   The reference is to Nicolas Poussin's great painting, in London's Wallace Collection, *A Dance to the Music of Time* (1634–6). The title was subsequently used by Anthony Powell for a 12-volume sequence of novels.

Further Reading

Aran, Amnon, 2009. *Israel's Foreign Policy towards the PLO: The Impact of Globalization.* This fascinating case study tests the impact of globalization on international politics by analysing one of the world's most intractable security disputes.

Cooper, Robert, 2003. *The Breaking of Nations: Order and Chaos in the Twenty-first Century.* This is a lucid and influential study of a changing international order, and the different kinds of states which inhabit it.

Litwak, Robert S., 2012. *Outlier States: American Strategies to Change, Contain or Engage Regimes.* This careful analysis examines the rules of the 'international community' and the states which spurn them, from the perspective of US foreign policy.

Mouritzen, Hans and Wivel, Anders, 2012. *Explaining Foreign Policy: International Diplomacy and the Russo-Georgian War.* This is both an excellent case study of foreign policy strategies and a powerful argument against neglecting geography.

Wendt, Alexander, 1992. Anarchy is what states make of it: The social construction of power politics. *International Organization*, 46(2), pp. 391–426. Wendt's article is a key reference point for launching constructivism. In doing so, it draws attention to the interactions and shared understandings which constitute the international political environment.

Chapter 8

Transnational Reformulations

The international system has always had a transnational dimension. Indeed the proportion of transactions controlled by governments was much lower in the past – as during the Reformation and the Counter-Reformation – than it is now (Krasner, 1995; Northedge, 1976). The world of people has always been separate from that of rulers, with a detachment from the state and its borders summed up in Eugen Weber's account of the process of turning 'peasants into Frenchmen' (1976). Even the rise to dominance of nation-states, which often stopped the movement of people, could not stop ideas, goods and loyalties from finding their own ways across their policed frontiers. And with globalization and the end of the Cold War these transnational links have burgeoned once more.

Yet states monopolize political decision-making, and civil societies tend still to have a strong sense of their own distinctiveness. Accordingly we need a framework of analysis which takes into account both transnational relations and state foreign policies. Figure 8.1 does this in the form of a four-box quadrant. The vertical axis distinguishes between states and peoples, while the horizontal axis separates the internal from the external (for both societies and states). The boxes indicate the actors and the activities characteristic for each conformation, namely: inside the state; the state's external activity; everyday life at the local or national level; and popular relations internationally.

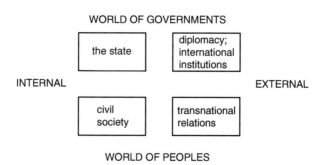

Figure 8.1   Governments, peoples and international relations

Where governments dominate internally, the state is powerful; where they dominate externally, they produce official diplomacy, inter-governmental institutions and war. Where peoples have more scope, they produce a strong civil society inside the state and transnational relations internationally. Since no quadrant is sealed off from the others, and positions vary on both axes, all the phenomena noted are subject to influence from the others. Politics both within the state and outside it thus need to be conducted with some sensitivity to the proximity of other forces and kinds of activity.

In terms of IR scholarship the focus on transnational relations began in the early 1970s with the work of Rosenau (1969) and Keohane and Nye (1971), all of whom wanted to refine the government-to-government model of interactions. The immediate effect was to focus attention on the issue of 'sovereignty bay', or how far states were in decline (Vernon, 1971). This elided the distinction between structure and agency in international politics and diverted interest away from the issue of how TNAs and national foreign policies interact. This is the gap tackled in the present chapter, with regard both to political activism across borders and to foreign economic policy and its relationship with the private sector. Much of the latter is 'external relations' more than classical foreign policy, through being apparently depoliticized. Just as many actions of transnational actors (TNAs) have no particular political relevance, so not all the state's activity abroad fits easily into the category of foreign policy – or is run by the foreign ministry. Foreign economic policy and foreign policy may serve the same ultimate ends but often come into conflict over tactics and priorities – as over economic sanctions or trade promotion. Development policy, which is an area where TNAs are particularly prominent, can cut across both.

Relations between TNAs and states vary in their nature. Sometimes they take place largely inside the state, and relate to economic and social life through such matters as the siting of factories or the criticism of a human rights record. At other times they will take place in the international sphere, relating to high-profile debates on such matters as arms control, the negotiation of a multilateral investment agreement or the international whaling regime. Finally, they can involve a direct clash between a state's foreign policy and the TNA. This chapter examines such issues on the assumption that while it is not as difficult to distinguish between the domestic and the international as many contend, the two are inherently interlaced – in part by the activity of transnational actors which complicate the efforts of governments to manage in either sphere (Clark, 1998). It does so by describing the nature of the transnational environment, then moving on to a taxonomy of the actors which operate within it, before suggesting a model to help us understand the conflicts and dilemmas which arise on both sides of the government–TNA relationship.

A Transnational Environment

For decision-makers the external environment is holistic, including geography, the state system and an inchoate mass of links between peoples, groups and private individuals which make up transnational relations. The definition of the latter is relatively straightforward. Keohane and Nye (1971, p. xi) said that *transnational relations* consisted in 'contacts, coalitions and interactions across state boundaries that are not controlled by the central foreign policy organs of government'. Forty years later Vertovec (2009, p. 3) agreed: they are 'sustained linkages and ongoing exchanges among non-state actors based across national borders'. *Transnational actors* are those private groups or individuals who, while they rely on physical facilities inside states, do not need governments in order to conduct international relations. They relate directly either to other TNAs or to states without needing any intermediary. Transnational relations are not to be confused with the trans-governmental contacts referred to in Chapter 4, which operate only between official bureaucracies. There is, however, certainly a grey area.

The quality of the transnational environment varies greatly – over time, and between the three bands of the international system identified in Chapter 7, of economics, politics and knowledge. While states have to assume an increasing role for global trends both for good (inventions, inward investment) and ill (terrorism, health epidemics) it cannot be assumed there is a linear progression towards increased transnationalism and reduced state roles. Those who seem to operate easily across state borders are not free from their own constraints, as with journalists taken hostage and killed, or terrorists being hunted down by state authorities. It is important to understand that states and TNAs share a multilayer environment, and one that changes over a longer time frame than the career of the average politician.

The conventional way of describing this environment is now through the lens of *globalization,* already touched upon in Chapter 1. The advantages lie in the fact that the term has now become part of our everyday vocabulary, connecting up to the experience of those who might lose their jobs because of an economic downturn on the other side of the world, or who watch a distant crisis on live television then to find traumatized refugees from that conflict turning up in their own neighbourhood. Given the way we live now, globalization has become both a necessary shorthand and a dominant elite construct.

The academic literature on the subject settled down into two tendencies identified by David Held as the 'hyperglobalist' and the 'transformationalist' schools. The hyperglobalists believe that the emerging world market dominates most aspects of our life on the planet and renders nugatory attempts to pursue distinctive, let alone reactionary, paths of development. The transformationalists are more cautious, arguing only that the present is an epoch of rapid and wide-ranging change, driven by global socioeconomic processes which are loosening, if not destroying, the bonds of traditional political communities (Held et al., 1999, pp. 1–28).

The implications of both schools for foreign policy are clear enough – not addressed in the globalization literature itself, but now increasingly picked up within FPA by those who do not just focus on decision-making (Alden and Aran, 2012, pp. 10–11, 78–91; Baumann and Stengel, 2014; Beach, 2012, pp. 198–212). The globalization perspective sees action by governments which does not try to harness globalization as doomed to failure, meaning that traditional foreign policy, with its stress on the primacy of politics, is steadily losing relevance. This is because both hyperglobalists and transformationalists adhere to two basic propositions: first, that a single world market is coming rapidly into being; second, following Marshall McLuhan's argument of the 1960s, that information technology and social media have created a global village, where we share the same news, concerns, gossip and consequences across the full range of human activity (McLuhan, 1964, 1989). In this second sense globalization goes far beyond the economic indicators with which it is often associated. We are all thus members of an immanent world community, which changes the nature of the politics which can be conducted within it. States increasingly have to give ground to other actors more adapted to the new realities.

What value do these two central propositions have, and how far should our understanding of international politics be based on them? The first certainly has a good deal of force. Those working in finance, trade and labour markets now operate in a global market. They are aware of the regulatory role of governments, but also that this is more played out through multilateral negotiations in conjunction with private enterprise than by unilateral action. The disciplines of the global market are felt inside every producing country, damaging the ability of national trades unions to protect jobs.

Yet global trends are far from uniform and the market is never a level playing field, both factors which create space for governments to assert themselves, especially on a collective basis (Chang, 2003) – if they have the ability and willingness to act. In itself the globalization thesis suggests little about where agency should be expected, and indeed it is fatalistic about the political management of globalization. It says little about foreign policy, even foreign economic policy, because it assumes that the state is giving ever more ground to the private sector and will come to see the futility of attempting to intervene.[1] As a hypothesis, it points to an ever smaller area for public policy, with economic sovereignty effectively transferred to those who control the major capital and investment flows known as 'the market'. States may be exhorted to manage the market better, especially through multilateral cooperation and regional integration, but the problem of the differences, and competition, between existing territorial communities is left to one side.

The second proposition remains the same general insight it was 50 years ago, reinforced by the prominence of Facebook, Instagram and Twitter. But this hardly amounts to a step change in political terms. The idea of a global community at present does not extend much beyond the media and consumerism. We may see on TV deprived African children wearing fake Real Madrid shirts made in China, or we may agonize over the fate of Ukrainians, but the implication that we all have the same stake in the same events is not convincing. For a superficial awareness of events in Ethiopia or the Crimea is a very different thing from the politically crucial attributes of caring, acting and influencing. As the state exists in part so as to buffer us against the tide of happenings in the world, we expect it to act as a filter, advising on whether we need, or are able, to do anything about them. We want the state to set an agenda, and to help us make sense of a challenging world, so that we may collectively *choose* whether or not to get involved in matters outside our own community. This is why immigration has become such a difficult issue for many developed countries. Where elites have often worked on the laissez-faire assumptions of market principles their citizens have expected them to manage effectively the endless flow of politically and economically desperate people understandably seeking a better life for themselves.

It is commonly said that 'we have no choice' but to be involved in *x* or *y*, but this is disingenuous. Every year new crises and tragedies come to the world's attention, but this does not mean, for any given state, that 'something has to be done' (Brown, 2001; Erskine, 2001). It depends on who 'we' are and what capabilities, or other priorities, we have. Furthermore, any engagement will necessarily have different goals from those directly involved. Thus even if there is an increasingly shared global set of social and political processes, with a widely diffused awareness of problems, globalization does not produce uniform responses – perhaps the reverse, through reactions against it. If we are to understand the evolving world system we shall need to focus at least as much on differentiation as on homogeneity.

In the end the globalization thesis both misleads and claims too much, especially in the domain of international politics. This is revealed interestingly by its most ardent opponents. Those who believe enough in globalization to take to the streets against it display a baffled anger as to who might be responsible for correcting its abuses. Calls for the UN or World Bank to act are made without conviction, given the power of key states to direct them. They would be better advised to cast their understanding of the transnational environment in less general terms, and to focus on coordinating pressures on governments so as to stimulate them to use foreign policy to work multilaterally, in harness with some transnational actors as a form of 'hybrid foreign policymaking' – and against others (Baumann and Stengel, 2014, pp. 495–9).

How has the development of transnationalism and the rhetoric of globalization affected the idea of international society? We have seen that the environment of all international actors is one of constant change and mixed actorness. In practice the mechanism of state diplomacy, together with the legal and practical powers of governments over territory, means that the state system still provides the formal framework of international relations. Its evolution over 400 years has involved managing change and accepting the arrival of new forces, which, rather than undermining the structure of the system, tend to make it more elaborate (Jones, 1999). The system has therefore had both progressive and conservative elements, in that it has allowed for change while also often legitimising a particular order against demands which have seemed too radical or disruptive to the major powers of the day. Given that most states have a vested interest in preventing the system's complete breakdown, it is also conservative in the sense of being fundamentally slow-moving (Watson, 1992, p. 318).

For their part TNAs cannot help but be part of the system, and to adapt to its terms. They cannot ignore states, for their rationale is often to change state policies. In cases like that of climate change where they cannot push state decision-making far enough and/or get Green parties elected to power, they face immense frustration. Thus they piggyback on intergovernmental conferences by sending observers and arranging parallel NGO meetings at the same time and place. The major UN conference planned for Paris in December 2015 will attract 20,000 delegates and 20,000 other attendees (Roger, 2015). For their part, governments will be punished by events if they assume that international politics consists mainly of negotiations with other states, with occasional glances in the rear-view mirror at domestic politics. In effect the two-level game has become triangular. In each policy area they now have to calculate the mix of different *kinds* of actor they need to deal with, and what kind of coalition to assemble so as to influence the relevant elements of civil society and private enterprise, which increasingly participate in inter-governmental institutions as well as exerting pressure bilaterally. As Hocking and Smith say, policy thus has to be conducted 'through a variety of bilateral, multilateral and plurilateral channels' (1997, p. 13). It is accordingly difficult for any actor to have a clear sense of whether their actions are making much of a difference to the overall environment.

The transnational part of that environment is the result of a quantitative shift which may now have become qualitative. That is, there have always been non-state actors and transnational political forces. It is just that now the number and degree of organization of TNAs has put them on a more equal (but still not a substantively equal) footing with states. Whereas anyone running a church, pressure group or corporation assumes that governments will be their interlocutors on many issues, the truth of the converse took longer to dawn in official bureaucracies. Yet while politicians and public officials still look first to their peers when engaging in international deal-making, the growth of conferences like that at Davos is an acknowledgement of change.[2] The greater willingness of publics to criticize authority means that governments can hardly afford to ignore organized opinion, even that which is transnational. However, this very fact means that decision-makers are often confused as to the nature of the system they are working in, anxious about its seemingly constant quality of change, and uncertain about the diverse sources of power. This explains the attraction of one-stop ideas like globalization, whatever their scientific deficiencies.

A Taxonomy of Actors

The range of transnational actors is surprisingly wide. All kinds of different entities of varying sizes now 'act' in international relations with 'private foreign policies' which complicate the environment of states. A first step in the process of trying to make sense of this variety and the activities being pursued is to construct a taxonomy of the TNAs.

The most straightforward way to do this is to distinguish the main types of transnational actors from each other, namely churches, multinational corporations, trades unions, political parties and terrorist groups. This is helpful in terms of giving us a sense of the breadth of the overall category, but what it cannot do is give guidance on their roles or significance. Another approach would be simply to rank TNAs in terms of size and/or power, producing an equivalent of the hierarchy of states, and a sense of the major rivals to states. Yet this also soon becomes unsatisfactory, since the comparison is rarely of like with like. How, for instance, can the activities or impact of the Roman Catholic Church be compared to those of Volkswagen, or of Oxfam?

A more useful basis for categorization is to distinguish between those TNAs which are (i) *territorial*, that is, they either use or seek to achieve some territorial base, like states; (ii) *ideological/cultural*, since they promote ideas or ways of thinking across national frontiers; (iii) *economic*, because their primary focus is wealth-creation. This tripartite division has several advantages: virtually every TNA fits into it; the powerful but rather particular group of transnational corporations gets its own category; while those actors which do not fundamentally challenge the state and the state system, but rather wish to participate in it, are not confused with those for whom states are either the problem or an irrelevancy.

The *territorial* group contains the primary and the most formidable antagonists of individual states, if not states as such. Zionists, Armenians, Palestinians and Kurds are the best-known cases of peoples who have worked over long periods through politico-military organizations with de facto foreign policies to achieve the clear goal of statehood. They have at times alarmed even the most powerful states. Because of their threats to the status quo they are often dismissed as terrorists, but this is not helpful. Relatively few acts of violence have arisen from a nihilist attachment to terror in itself, as demonstrated in 2014 by the savagery of the self-styled Islamic State in Iraq and Syria. Most, however cruel and unjustifiable, have been committed in the pursuit of a political cause, with clear objectives. What is more, they are not infrequently successful, although whether the end can ever justify these means is another matter, and an issue for political philosophy. It is revealing that actors in this category so often live down their association with terror, as with many anti-colonial fighters, the leaders of the Irish Republican Army (IRA), and – for a time – Muammar Gaddafi of Libya.

Success in its endeavour means that a territorial TNA stops being a TNA. On the other hand those who do not manage to replace a regime or create a new state find it difficult to continue an international campaign indefinitely. Israel has exploited Palestinian divisions to keep the idea of a two-state solution on the distant horizon. In these circumstances it is remarkable that the Palestinian Authority has managed to sustain such an active international campaign and high profile. The Kurds are still struggling to establish a state of their own despite the autonomy they have gained through the fragmentation of Iraq. Actors of this kind sometimes form pragmatic coalitions, as with the IRA and its contacts with Libya and other radical Arab groups in the 1980s, while Sinn Féin, the IRA's political wing, attracted political and financial support in the United States and other supposedly anti-terrorist countries.

The other kind of territorial actor to be found is the sub-national unit. Cities, regions and units inside federations have all produced 'local' or 'municipal' foreign policies (Hobbs, 1994; Hocking, 1993a, 1993b). They have done this for diverse reasons, even if all share a dissatisfaction with the monopoly of central government over foreign policy. Some city mayors become well-known international figures who exploit their profile for domestic political advantage, and conversely use their strong constituency base to exert influence abroad, whether to please a local ethnic minority or for some wider motive. The mayor of New York has an Office for International Affairs which liaises with the local UN community, but also with 100 cities worldwide. The last two London mayors, Ken Livingstone and Boris Johnson, have both been extremely active outside the UK (Elgot, 2013). Johnson even visited Kurdish Iraq in January 2015, being photographed aiming an AK-47, presumably to help promote himself as a future British prime minister.

Less instrumentally, the German *Länder* have a constitutional role in foreign policy, while individual Canadian and US states, notably Quebec, Florida and California, have been quick to take their own positions on international issues close to their own interests – in this case *La Francophonie,* Cuba and immigration from Mexico respectively (Goetz, 1995). Regions tend to focus mostly on commercial self-promotion and other aspects of political economy, being wary of treading on central government's traditional prerogative over foreign policy, but cities have been more political, and not just through publicity-seeking mayors. They have engaged in such long-term policies as twin-towning, nuclear-free zones and self-promotion through hosting global sporting events. This activity may seem to be self-indulgent, but it does create new transnational networks through which to influence civil society over time. Municipal foreign policy may be too grand a term to describe it, but the combination of a territorial base, significant resources, political legitimacy and a high profile means that major cities do possess a form of soft power outside the control of governments (Alger, 1977, 1990; Farquharson and Holt, 1975).

The second category into which we may group TNAs is the *ideological/cultural.* This in turn contains various kinds of actor. What they all they share is a commitment to spreading ideas, or sharing values, without relying on the conventional sources of power.

Groups which are more ideological than cultural in character are inherently more competitive with states, which they need to help them achieve their desired ends. Some are single-issue 'cause' organizations, promoting one particular end internationally and losing prominence once it is achieved – or seems impossible. A notable example is the anti-apartheid movement, which mobilized opposition to the white regime in South Africa most effectively for three decades (S. Thomas, 1996). Less political, but still a considerable factor given its five million members and work in 100 countries, is the World Wildlife Fund, which attempts to help (or shame) countries which do not protect their endangered species.

More wide ranging but also more contested TNAs are those which proselytize, seeking to promote a vision of the good life. Here we find churches and religious sects, the Socialist and Communist Internationals and their modern imitators in the form of the Liberal and Christian Democratic international networks. There are also principled, sometimes idealist, groups of various persuasions, including Amnesty International, the Green movement, neo-conservatism and the Muslim Brotherhood, which move beyond pressure group origins to promote a whole way of life. They may at times get close to government or even take power, though they will struggle to hold onto it – as the Brotherhood found out in Egypt during 2013 – unless they can broaden their appeal beyond the already committed. These actors are hoping to construct a common global discourse on politics, through convergence between different societies around their preferred values.

The churches, and in particular the Catholic Church, are not only the transnational actors with the longest historical roots, they are older even than the idea of the state. They have had to come to terms with the power of states, as with the Gallican compromise in France, but they retain extensive transnational networks, and a claim on the ultimate loyalty of the believer (Johnston and Sampson, 1994). Nor is this a matter solely of private faith. The views and character of the man acting as Pope influences the attitudes of millions in poorer countries such as Mexico and the Philippines on such issues as birth control or homosexuality, while local priests have bravely stood up against injustice and organized crime in many countries from communist Poland, through El Salvador to contemporary Italy – sometimes without support from the Vatican. No other Christian church has such a wide reach, but the moral standing of Archbishop Desmond Tutu in South Africa should remind us of the legacy of protestant missionaries in Africa, where a 'black theology' has grown up that cuts across already artificial state boundaries, and where evangelicalism has taken hold in certain regions.

The transnational qualities of religion were long underestimated by secular-minded state decision-makers in the West (Rubin, 1994). Where the historical pattern of communities of faith does not coincide with state boundaries (as it rarely does, in fact) there is potential for serious conflict, as has been evident in Bosnia and increasingly in both East and West Africa. In places this takes the form of fundamentalist fanaticism with often brutal consequences for those designated unbelievers, but it is just as likely to take the form of political identity becoming manifest through religion, whose transnational reach and structure are particularly threatening to states already fragile and lacking in resources.

Transnationalism does not, any more than statehood, imply uniformity or homogeneity. Jews worldwide have suffered the consequences of being stereotyped as a people without loyalty to the states in which they live. The culmination of this persecution is that probably the only thing which unites Jews everywhere is a determination to defend the *state* of Israel, seen as the Jewish homeland. Some fundamentalist Jews have, nonetheless, operated transnationally in attempts to move Israel in their favoured, theocratic direction, and to push Western foreign policies into a commitment to an expanded 'eretz Israel'. In doing so they have demonstrated the divisions within the world of Jewry, for they have been fiercely opposed by liberal Jews both inside and outside Israel.

Islam is also often thought by outsiders to be a single entity, and even to have a crusading character, as if it were like the Vatican but with a guerrilla army at its disposal. In practice, the world of Islam is as variegated as that of Christianity, with a wide range of different positions held on politics and international affairs (Halliday, 1996, 2000, pp. 129–36). Furthermore, Islam has no central institutions which dispense authoritative leadership. The Organisation of Islamic Cooperation (OIC), created in 1969 and now with 57 members, is resolutely intergovernmental rather than transnational, albeit powerfully influenced by the patronage of Saudi Arabia. Yet the fact that Islamic theology sees church, state and civil society as integrally connected means that there is much potential for political activism, and long before Al Qaeda the cross-border activities of organizations like the Muslim Brotherhood, Hezbollah and Hamas made governments tremble, notably in Egypt (with the assassination of Anwar Sadat) and during the civil war in Algeria of the 1990s. The Arab Spring uprisings of 2011 in particular highlighted the transnational element of this activism, although the powerful (if competitive) reactions against them from the Gulf States made clear the limits of its political effectiveness. Where internal opposition has turned violent, however, as in the Syrian, Iraqi and Libyan civil wars, the transnational factor becomes critical – indeed leading distant European states to fear serious blowback from those of their own citizens who leave to fight.

It is thus important to distinguish between Islam as an important factor in the interaction between domestic and foreign policies, where it will always have an important role because of its refusal to see society as separate from matters of faith, and Islam as a transnational actor, in which capacity it exists in the form of specific and highly differentiated groups. To the extent that there has been any movement to create an Islamic 'world society' it has arisen out of the collective efforts of Muslim *states* in the OIC, which seeks to 'galvanize the Ummah into a unified body'. Within that group, however, states compete to lead the Muslim world, notably through the fierce political and theological rivalry between Shia Iran and Sunni Saudi Arabia, which spills over state boundaries (Matthiesen, 2015). Only the murderous attempt by Daesh to create a new caliphate has led them into common cause. And here again we confront the paradoxes which transnationalism can generate: Daesh is a movement across state borders which aims to create a new state, which on the basis of controlling 15 per cent of Iraq's oil wealth in principle it could do. At the same time because of its crusading and violent nature such an enterprise threatens the very basis of the current society of states – sovereignty and fixed borders.

Political proselytizers come and go, transnationally as they do nationally. In the democratic world the links between political parties are in any case always stronger when the parties in question are in government, especially if national trends coincide, as sometimes happens among the member states of the European Union, where victory in a key state like France or Germany by either the centre-left or the centre-right can have a snowball effect across the continent. Between the wars this tendency was seen in extreme form through the rise of extreme right-wing politics in Italy, Germany and then Spain. The current period of economic austerity has seen populist reactions, mostly of the left, emerge in Greece, Italy and Spain, again feeding off each other. But transnational impact is not the same as solidarity, which is usually brittle, as in the failure of international socialism to prevent war in 1914. The workers of the world could not unite, even if they had cast off their chains. The European Union has encouraged the creation of transnational parties, but even in these favourable conditions little progress has been made. The political groups of the European Parliament are still only loose coalitions containing diverse entities still closely tied to their national political environments.

Party operations may be transnational but they are also parastatal. The German party foundations have made all kinds of links with their equivalents abroad, at both ends of the political spectrum, but only with the aim of encouraging another state to adopt similar values (Bartsch, 2001). They do not want to transcend their own state, let alone statehood as such. The same is true of the powerful US parties and ideological foundations, which operate transnationally but primarily aim to export the values of the United States.

This is not true of organizations like Amnesty and Greenpeace, which began with limited, functional goals and have grown despite themselves into de facto international parties, far in advance of single-issue politics and with the ability to influence political policy-making in states of many different types. Oxfam is another pressure group that has become a brand name, with the capacity to raise voluntary taxes worldwide and bring both technical expertise and political activists into the field in the pursuit of developmental goals. The changes in Western policies over the last two decades in the areas of both development and human rights owe a good deal to the persistent campaigning and ability to harness transnationally the resources of these major organizations. On the other hand as their range and expertise have expanded so governments have started to work with them, creating the danger of co-option. This is not only a risk to their political independence, but also poses a threat to workers in the field, who are regularly accused of being the agents of Western governments. Some have paid with their lives for this blurring of external perceptions.

More at the cultural than the ideological end of the transnational spectrum are diasporas, which have become a significant form of international actor as migration has increased through improved communications and the pull of labour markets in rich countries. It takes generations for ethnocultural minorities to become so integrated in their new societies that they lose interest in staying in touch with those left behind. Indeed, the sending of remittances 'home' is often a key part of their practice and value-system. Given that the homelands they have left are also often riven by conflict and poverty, it is natural that minorities in developed countries should display much more concern for international affairs than the majority with no transnational links. Their activism can have a significant effect on their homelands, which does not go unnoticed by governments at either end of the chain (Lyons and Mandaville, 2012).

Another example of cultural transnationalists is those in the knowledge business, who have an interest in spreading information and ideas without specific political aims. They constitute the 'knowledge band' of the international system. Much of this is functional activity not relevant to the environment of foreign policy, but some certainly is. The medical community's transmission of knowledge about AIDS (in conjunction with the World Health Organization) became highly political. The Nobel Peace Prize has enormous international resonance (despite such clangers as the awards to Henry Kissinger, Le Duc Tho and Barack Obama). This was evident in the Chinese government's hostile reaction of 2010 when the prize was won by the dissident Liu Xiaobo.

Even more striking was the impact of senior US and Soviet scientists on arms control negotiations between the superpowers. Fear of nuclear war led to the starting of the transnational Pugwash conferences in 1957 and, despite the security problems, figures from both sides managed to stay in touch through the Cold War – partly because they represented potentially useful back channels for Moscow and Washington. It has been argued convincingly by Matthew Evangelista (1995) that these transnational networks were crucial in making possible some of the breakthroughs in nuclear arms control of the 1980s. The Soviet Union then demonstrated how a state which is difficult for transnational actors to penetrate can change quite quickly under their impact once access has been gained.

Thus on occasions these 'epistemic communities' (Haas, 1992, 1997) transmute into political actors. International media campaigns are not unknown on relatively 'soft' subjects such as famine relief, but on anything more controversial they tend to be forestalled by editorial diversity. Effective humanitarian action is more likely to be mobilized by ad hoc coalitions of specialists, preferably with wide reputations and operating out of universities. Médecins Sans Frontières is an organization produced by doctors concerned with the relief of suffering in the Third World, founded in 1971 by the French humanitarian activist Bernard Kouchner who left in 1980 to set up Médecins du Monde, with a more political take on the relief of suffering. Both have helped to push French foreign policy towards humanitarian concerns. Kouchner's reputation eventually led to his appointment as foreign minister by his ideological adversary Nicolas Sarkozy.

Less structured have been the groupings of environmental scientists which have kept up the pressure on governments to acknowledge such problems as the polar holes in the ozone layer, not least by suggesting constructive responses. They have worked hand in hand with pressure groups, and have determined the agendas of intergovernmental conferences, as well as influencing public opinion in the developed countries (Giddens, 2011; Keck and Sikkink, 1998; Risse, Ropp and Sikkink, 1999; D. Thomas, 1999). The ability to keep up the pressure even after failed summits like that in Copenhagen in 2009 is a credit to the expertise of environmental specialists and activists. Helped by natural disasters like the tsunami in South-East Asia of 2004, they have managed to keep governments focused on the need for action, despite the powerful countervailing interests, both private and public, in the status quo. This led the United States and China to an agreement in 2014 on the limiting of carbon emissions, even if this is far short of what will be required to limit global warming.

A final, but significant, example of an epistemic community achieving policy impact is that of the economics profession. As economists became sceptical about the benefits of Keynesian, demand-led economic policies, particularly in the United States, so they turned to supply-side analysis and followed through the logic of liberalism by recommending monetary discipline, privatization and free trade. These ideas were taken up by parties which had previously abhorred them. The profession still covers a range of views but it is striking how much convergence there has been, both intellectually, and politically, around the neo-liberal consensus. This can be seen as the triumph of reason and expertise, but few other social scientists would be willing to accept such a naïve view of the role of ideas in politics (Chang, 2010). There are many causes of the revolution in economic policies which occurred after 1980, but one of them was the power of the top university departments in the United States to engineer a new consensus among academic economists. In Thomas Risse-Kappen's phrase, ideas are not 'free-floating' (1999). This is true, indeed, of transnational phenomena in general.

States find that while they can intervene and even control some areas of knowledge-development – nuclear weapons and outer space are prime examples – much of the rapidly changing scientific environment leaves them with little choice but to adapt. The advance of communications technology is the prime case. The internet has transformed the transmission of knowledge, affecting all governments and causing some to react strongly – as with the 'great firewall of China', and the restrictions imposed by many others on their citizens' access to this reference library of incredible dimensions (Hughes, 2010). Once a story breaks it is impossible to confine it, given the speed with which information moves and the way the world's media now feed off each other.

The international news agencies and TV companies have adapted to the technology to retain a key role in deciding on news priorities and shaping debate. This led at first to a widespread belief in the 'CNN effect' (meaning that governments had no choice but to follow the agendas set by 24/7 worldwide news organizations, capable of bringing far-flung events into every sitting room). It became clear that this phenomenon had been grossly exaggerated, but it remains true that a regime can no longer avoid opposition or embarrassment just by closing down its own press and TV (Gowing, 1994a). The media giants no longer monopolize the field. The long-standing power of word of mouth, which used to rely on underground publications like the *samizdat* which used to circulate round the Soviet Union, has been amplified by the extraordinary take up of social media, through which large numbers of people communicate instantly and cheaply. Not surprisingly they have been used to organize political demonstrations which easily keep one step ahead of the authorities. This was the case in Egypt in 2011, and in both Turkey and Hong Kong in 2014. Only when governments are willing to use extreme force – and thus suffer a loss of legitimacy – are these spontaneous movements halted.

The third and last category of TNAs is the *economic*. This now includes both manufacturing and service sectors, which increasingly overlap, just as the distinction between the private and public sectors has become blurred through such things as government support for defence sales and energy companies (Charillon, 1999, pp. 123–4). Apple's design brilliance has led to mass production lines in China, and mass consumption worldwide. Toyota's successful hybrid car, the Prius, is a response to social and governmental pressures (and tax incentives) for more green vehicles. It is a favourite with taxi fleets. English football's Premier League is a global billion-pound business, supported by a government World Cup bid, while the Russian state energy company Gazprom is a major sponsor of the UEFA Champions League. These enterprises and more long-established names such as Shell, McDonald's, General Motors and Philips directly impact on the lives of millions, and they are a central factor in the making of state economic policy. Transnational crime and money laundering suck huge amounts from national tax income. It is not surprising, therefore, that the issue of the possible decline of the state, and the difficulties of modern government, are so often linked to their power. The issue here, however, is different and more specific: in what respect are transnational businesses independent actors in international politics?

At one level the answer to this question is disarmingly straightforward. Within the international economy transnational enterprises (TNEs) are very big players. Given that they share certain values and interests they are able collectively to exert powerful pressures in favour of trade liberalization, tax incentives and havens, favourable regimes for the free movement of labour and the exploitation of minerals. They did, for instance, manage to undermine the project for the mining of the seabed in the common interests of mankind (D. Armstrong, 1999). Occasionally, they assist in engineering change in particular states, as famously happened in Guatemala in 1954 with the United Fruit Company and Chile in 1973 with ITT (Guardiola-Rivera, 2014). TNEs represent a heavy weight in favour not just of capitalism, but of a particular variety of capitalism associated with free movement across the international system. In relation to their interests they play politics persistently if often indirectly.

The other side of this coin is that the TNEs are inherently competitive amongst themselves and rarely work together on the model of state multilateralism. In general they prefer to work with states where their relatively narrow range of objectives, relating to profit, expansion, stability and modernization, coincide with the needs of local governments. Thus in the Caribbean, offshore financiers cooperated with the region's microstates in a struggle with the OECD over tax evasion, money laundering and the funding of terrorists (Vlcek, 2008). It is when TNEs go beyond this background role to take on parastatal social responsibilities that they are likely to find themselves out of their comfort zone, as with Blackwater's controversial security role in Iraq after the 2003 invasion.

Corporations are often accused of being only interested in profit, with an amoral attitude towards the values of the regimes they deal with. In consequence they cultivate an image of 'corporate responsibility' and make public relations a priority, but their capacity for agency in international politics is very restricted. As international actors they influence, and often have privileged access to, interstate discussions on aspects of the international political economy such as trade, the environment and intellectual property. Yet on the classical issues of war, security, international institutions, border disputes and human rights they have little to contribute. The old arguments about the arms manufacturers with an interest in war have been overtaken by the profits to be made in selling arms which states never use, and by the fact that profitable business is often seriously disrupted by international conflict, through violence and chaos on the one hand, and economic sanctions on the other.

This is not to say that TNEs, legal as well as illegal, do not cause security problems for states. The proliferation of private security companies and dealers in small arms rarely encourages peace and stability in the crisis states to which they are attracted, while the traffickers in human misery responsible for the huge increase in irregular migration have exploited the inability of sending and receiving states to manage the problem together, whether in the Mediterranean, Australasia or on the Rio Grande. Even major firms can disrupt the foreign policies of states to which they are otherwise favourably disposed, as with resistance to sanctions on Iran or Russia. In these cases the business-as-usual instinct cuts across political strategy.

On the positive side of the balance sheet organizations like Eurovision or UEFA have done more to create a sense of shared experience among the peoples of Europe than the rhetoric of a thousand politicians. But this is only a by-product of their normal activity, a case of functionalism in action (Niemann, Garcia and Grant, 2011, pp. 1–22). It is not in the nature of TNEs to set out to achieve such ends; consequences and intentions must always be distinguished. In this the media provide a special and paradoxical case, however, for they consciously further a global news agenda, while also – depending on the issue and the outlet – indulging in forms of nationalism which then complicate inter-state relations.

Economic actors in the transnational environment enjoy considerable autonomy in their own business, the conduct of which will largely determine the health and the direction of the international economy. States have some influence over prosperity, but in a capitalist world it is difficult for them to second-guess the market. TNEs also have some impact on international politics, but usually indirectly and rarely by design. In both contexts they need to be analysed in terms of their interaction with states. In particular, although multinational businesses are broadly independent of control by governments, they are a powerful shaping force on the culture and values of the relatively small number of rich societies from which they spring, and which determine the pace of growth for the rest. This means that states and 'their' TNEs often end up pressing in the same general direction – as with European anxieties not to allow relations with Russia to deteriorate too far in the wake of Moscow's aggression towards the Ukraine. Yet this case also shows up the differences between the two sets of actors. While European leaders, and particularly those in Berlin, were concerned for the economic damage which sanctions against Moscow would entail, that was not enough to trump their wish to send a clear signal about their opposition to President's Putin's revanchism. Since the business and the priority of states is politics, they are still the agents with the capacity to make critical choices on the great issues of international political life.

Foreign Policy and Transnational Actors: A Model

Distinguishing the different types of transnational actors helps us to appreciate the range of activity which goes under the heading of international politics, and the varying nature of the challenges they pose to states. It is now time to focus more directly on the nature of the relationship which exists between states and TNAs in the international realm, given their contrasting aims and responsibilities.

Three forms of this relationship may be observed. They derive from the problems which arise for state foreign policies, and from attempts of TNAs to conduct equivalent strategies, but they may also be applied to state-TNA relations in general – with the proviso that weak, poor states are at a particular disadvantage in their relations with corporations. The three forms are: (i) normal, bargaining relations; (ii) competitive, power relations and (iii) what can be called, following Samuel Huntington (1973), transcendent or parallel relations. Their structures and implications are set out in Table 8.1.

The first of these relationships is termed '*normal*' more because it represents the possibility of a functioning relationship, than on any assumption that it describes what happens most of the time. The number of actors and issue areas involved is too large for us to be able to generalize safely about what sort of relations are prevalent. In this context the TNA envisages being able to coexist with a state's foreign policy, but wishes to negotiate about some specific elements. It thus lobbies a government directly. The state in turn is relatively relaxed about dealing with the TNA (which will not be seen as 'foreign' if it has a foothold in the state's own society) and thus engages in dialogue. It may even seek to incorporate the TNA in some way, and exploit its channels for its own

Table 8.1   TNA–state relationships in international politics

	What TNAs may do	What states may do	Nature of interaction	Examples	Advantage with?
1. Normal bargaining relationship	Request policy change; lobby	Accept legitimacy of input; engage in dialogue; co-opt; exploit TNA for own purposes	Compromise; deals; possibly cooperative ventures; SOPs	Foreign aid ventures; WTO negotiations; electoral monitoring	Balanced
2. Competitive power relationship	Act directly in domestic environment, to stir public opinion; encourage new pressure groups, even cells; divide and rule states; create transnational coalitions	Ignore; use powers over legislation, tax and borders to weaken TNA or even deny access; stir up nationalist reactions; intergovernmental cooperation; suppression; remote military action	Mutual hostility, with zero-sum elements; unstable, especially when public opinion divided or states at odds with each other; TNAs can be out of their depth politically	Human rights clashes; disputes over local restraints on trade, or technology transfer; diasporas with political concerns; terrorism	Varies – ultimately with states
3. Parallel relationship	Focus on their specific business; tend to disregard frontiers; states not main interlocutors	Find it difficult always to ignore, but try to move issue to 1 or 2 in the event of problems; often exhibit confusion; try to get involved in soft power	Uneasy; mutual wariness but distance; diverging assumptions and priorities	Churches; many TNEs; epistemic communities; many diasporas and ethnocultural groups	Usually with TNAs

advantage. In consequence, deals are struck, and even when they are not, relations proceed on a routinized basis. For example, states, corporations and lobbies interact well enough, despite the endless manoeuvring on all sides, in major power centres like Brussels or Washington and in a range of multilateral fora.

The second kind of relationship is *competitive*. It involves a more overt use of power in a struggle for advantage that may involve one or both sides contesting the legitimacy of the other. The TNA sees little advantage in dealings with certain governments and therefore goes behind their backs to speak directly to domestic society. At its most provocative this behaviour may be deemed subversive, but more usually it involves the strengthening of local organizations, appeals to public opinion and attempts to weaken the hold of governments by opening up the discussion of policy options. The food corporation Monsanto has done this over a long period in Europe, as part of its attempt to get acceptance for genetically modified crops – but strong and effective resistance from green groups has tied the hands of governments which might otherwise have given way.

The more sophisticated TNAs may try to play states off against each other. In response, governments have a range of options at their disposal. They may call the TNA's bluff by ignoring their activity, reinforcing the strength of their position by coordinating with other states or by appealing to public opinion. For more serious threats they may use their powers to control frontiers or to enact legislation as ways of denying a TNA freedom of movement. At the extreme end of the continuum autocratic regimes may use security forces to suppress the interfering 'foreigners', while democratic governments have responded to transnational terrorism by striking bases abroad or adopting draconian controls over the movements of people and money.

The consequence of this mutual suspicion is escalating hostility, with conflicts increasingly polarized. The relationship is at best unstable, with states likely to overreact as a result of the pressures of having to play a two-level game, and TNAs beginning to get out of their depth in head-on conflicts with states, sometimes becoming involved in issues – such as political authority structures – which they are not equipped to handle, and which touch on the most sensitive spots of state sovereignty. The classic case was the determination of Greenpeace's *Rainbow Warrior* crew to intrude on French nuclear testing areas in the Pacific, which produced a state terrorist response. Equally drastic was the decision of the new Egyptian government in 2014 to imprison journalists from Al Jazeera for doing their job of reporting news – a common reaction from autocrats towards their own press, but relatively unusual with foreigners. It is all too easy for governments to see threats even in the activities of functional organizations, such is the diversity of values which still characterizes our 'globalised' system.

By extension any TNA with a territorial or explicitly political claim is automatically on a collision course with the state in its sights. And states generally hold more cards in this kind of situation. In overt conflict their powers are more concrete and extensive – that is, if they are not in a fractured condition to begin with, as in Lebanon where Hezbollah has an established fiefdom, or post-Gaddafi Libya where jihadists have faced down the army. In political economy terms, small and/or weak states have similar problems resisting the pressures of powerful TNEs, as with the Central American countries' dependence on the US fruit-growing companies which led to the pejorative term 'banana republics' – although, with the help of 'cause'-oriented TNAs such as the Fair Trade movement these countries have acquired more leverage in recent decades. But the need for investment and markets makes self-assertion difficult. Even the European Union, with its common commercial and competition policies, struggles to control the activities of Google and Amazon on privacy, competition and tax issues.

The third kind of relationship, termed *'parallel'*, is more subtle. Samuel Huntington (1973) argued that the real strength of transnational actors was that they 'transcended' inter-state relations because they operated in another dimension. From this viewpoint TNAs are simply uninterested in many of the things states do. In pursuing their own goals – whether profit, the dissemination of an ideology, or the protection of fauna and flora – they act as if a world society were already in existence. Frontiers are a marginal irritation, to be circumvented without difficulty by technology and by the free movement of people, goods and ideas, which states themselves have come to treat as international public goods. Governments are not then the principal interlocutors.

When faced by TNAs in 'transcending' mode governments may well feel unmoved and opt to do nothing. Equally, if they feel threatened by the actions they will try in effect to move the issue into category *one* or *two*. That is, they will either try to engage the TNA in straightforward negotiation, or to take countermeasures. Yet the very nature of the problem means that they may not succeed in the manoeuvre, either because there is no obvious point of responsibility with which to engage or because the TNA has no interest in either a deal or a confrontation. In this case a government will probably exhibit signs of confusion. The more astute will learn how to play the TNA game by using private groups or individuals based in their own society to counter transnationalism in its own terms, or through taking its ground by adopting certain policy stances as their own.

In general, a transcending relationship is like the sound of one hand clapping, as diverging assumptions and modes of agency make

engagement inherently difficult. A good example of this form of relationship was the West's initially baffled reaction to the international
resurgence of the Islamic faith, which to secularists seemed to go against
the tide of history. When parallelism turned into conflict through attacks
by jihadists, the instinctive search was for governments to take responsibility. The view that states had sponsored, and thus could eliminate, Al
Qaeda led to more than a decade of war and chaos in Afghanistan and
Iraq. Even when the transnational dimension is acknowledged there is a
tendency to target a few groups or individuals as bogeymen, while
assuming that the moderate mass can easily be detached from the
'extremists'. This reveals a misunderstanding of Islam and its political
role. Although most individual Muslims have nothing to do with
jihadism, and the religion consists of many diverse strands, its world
view does inherently transcend state boundaries. At the same time it challenges the Western tendency to separate church and state. In certain
conditions, therefore, some adherents to particular versions of Islam will
present a transnational challenge to state authority.

These conditions have mostly arisen through the international
encounter between the secular West and Muslim countries in the Middle
East, with military interventions perceived as hypocritical because they
do not address the great grievance over Palestine. This was bound to
alienate Islamic opinion worldwide. An intelligent foreign policy needs to
discriminate not only between the faith and those who are carrying out
unjustified atrocities in its name but also between those things which
anger most Muslims and those things which they can accept or ignore. In
the twenty-first century this means thinking domestically as well as
geopolitically.

The relationship which governments have with transnational business
is not so dissimilar. Although intermittent engagement is inevitable it
would be a mistake to assume that they are continually locked in a struggle over sovereignty and control of the international economy.
Corporations defend their profits and expansion plans vigorously but
otherwise they want governments to get on with running society. For
their part governments vary in the degree to which they can (or wish to)
control TNEs, but in the age of privatization they have mostly come to
accept that their role in business is limited. They need, as Stopford and
Strange (1991) pointed out, to negotiate with firms over investment sites,
tax breaks and regulation, which is complex and time consuming. But
this is hardly the sum total of international relations, and very often gets
overshadowed by issues of security and identity. On many key questions,
such as the collapse of order in the Balkans or the Middle East, world
poverty or religious conflict, governments and TNEs simply do not have
much to say to each other.

Epistemic communities and cultural movements are the best example of actors which transcend conventional interstate affairs, even if their actorness is rather fuzzy. While they are capable of engaging governments to good effect, their rationale is quite otherwise – the sharing and extension of knowledge with other experts independent of nationality. Scientists sometimes follow their own conscience in breaking off links with a given country, but in general professional ties survive unless governments actually prevent travel. This happened at times of tension during the Cold War, with both sides denying visas to academics, or suspending the exchange clauses of cultural agreements. In these circumstances democratic governments are faced with the prospect of restricting the freedom of their own citizens in the pursuit of a foreign policy goal, which goes against their very ethos. French governments have wriggled on this hook for decades in their attempts to insist on the use of the French language in the face of English-dominated films, computing and the like which the French people have an inconvenient taste for.

In more authoritarian states the issue seems clearer, but only in the short run, as governments ultimately want the benefits of knowledge transmission and even external recognition of their culture. In Iran the Ahmadinejad regime cracked down on both the interest of its youth in Western music and clothes and the ability of women to attend sports events. At the same time the government in Tehran was negotiating with the British Museum to borrow the historic Cyrus Cylinder, which it duly returned despite some internal pressure to retain it. It also needed Iranian doctors to be in contact with outside medical and pharmaceutical expertise in order to meet its people's healthcare expectations, and thus gave some ground on the nuclear issue under the pressure of sanctions. Short of complete isolation and the puritanism on show in North Korea, even radical regimes accept the need for their specialists to be part of an international community of experts.

Thus much transnational activity takes place on a plane where governments do not belong, and find few levers to pull even on issues which trouble them. In the 'transcending' or parallel relationship between states and TNAs, the latter have the advantage. For once, they are playing on home ground.

Linkage Politics

The transnational dimension of the international environment is now significant. Governments have no choice but to coexist with a wide range of different actors, and the state system is tangled in a net of transnational connections. But how exactly do these TNAs penetrate states, impacting upon civil society and at times causing governments significant problems? James Rosenau (1969) labelled the whole process 'linkage politics', to be distinguished from the advocacy of linkages in diplomacy, which is the standard technique whereby one government pressurises another by bringing an unrelated matter to the negotiating table.

Linkage politics in Rosenau's sense is a way of conceptualising agency at the transnational level; that is, the ways in which TNAs operate, creating links between the international system and the domestic environment. Foreign policy-makers may realize that they need to take domestic politics into account, but they do not always realize that the domestic realm itself is not insulated from the outside world, or how far that transnationalism occurs outside their sight line. The politics of linkage increasingly demonstrates that any aspiration a government might have to be the gatekeeper of its people's international connections is doomed to failure.

The original definition of linkage politics envisaged 'a recurrent sequence of behaviour that originates in one state and is reacted to in another'. This needs adapting through replacing the word 'state' with society' (Rosenau, 1969, p. 45). Rosenau himself abandoned his over-complex taxonomy of linkages and moved on to grand generalizations about 'cascading interdependence'. Yet the scheme was basically sound in the first place. It revolves round a set of simple but sharply defined concepts which are well adapted to the growing coexistence of states and other actors.

Rosenau distinguished between three kinds of linkage: reactive, emulative and penetrative. *Reactive linkages* occur when an event in one society leads to spontaneous reactions in another, unprompted by governments. An early example was the demonstration in London in 1851 in favour of the visiting Hungarian liberal exile Lajos Kossuth, which contributed to the dismissal of Palmerston as foreign secretary (Taylor, 1993, 58–9; Woodward, 1954, pp. 236–9). The equivalent today would be the support shown around the world for the Russian feminist group Pussy Riot, imprisoned for an anti-government demonstration in the Cathedral of the Orthodox Church in Moscow. Given modern conditions, transnational reactions to an outrage are almost guaranteed, especially if co-nationals are involved. Thus the treatment of Tamils in the last stages of the Sri Lankan civil war led to mass demonstrations by Tamils living in a number of Western capitals. Even when the national link is absent, a reactive linkage can take place, as when three Danish diplomatic missions were sacked by crowds angry at the publishing of cartoons of the Prophet Muhammad by a Danish newspaper. One hundred thousand people attended a demonstration in Sana'a, the capital of Yemen (Hill, 2013, pp. 81–3). Fellow feeling takes many forms.

Not infrequently these actions, while genuinely independent of governments, are not unwelcome to them, as they send signals to another state without the need for official responsibility. But they can also be embarrassing, even damaging, to the coherent conduct of foreign policy. Thus when the state legislature of Massachusetts passed a 'selective purchasing law' barring firms doing business with the repressive regime in Burma, it was seen by the federal government as a challenge to its own and Congress's powers to conduct foreign policy and regulate foreign trade. This could not be allowed to pass, and the law was challenged successfully in the US Court of Appeals (Denning and McCall, 2000; Philips, 1999).

An *emulative* linkage is what the economists call a demonstration effect. An event takes place in one society and is soon picked up on by the citizens of others, like the 'Mexican wave' in a stadium. Once again the demonstrations in Eastern Europe in 1989 are the best example. After decades of repression, the coming of crowds onto the streets in the German Democratic Republic, and the movement of refugees to the west through Hungary, detonated similar events in Czechoslovakia. The subsequent peaceful demolition of the Berlin Wall on 7 November was an event of the greatest symbolic significance, and made any continued repression impossible given the unwillingness of the Gorbachev government to sanction bloodshed as Khrushchev's government had done in Hungary in 1956. But it was also clear that the societies of Eastern Europe felt themselves linked by common experience, and were reacting spontaneously to each other regardless of particular governments. Thus the Ceauşescu regime in Romania suddenly collapsed in December 1989, despite the fact that it had always advertized its independence from Moscow. Even the Italian 'First Republic' felt the tremors reverberating across Europe, leading to the collapse of the cosy *partitocrazia* of the Socialists and Christian Democrats.

The year 1989 was a 'world historical event' in Hegel's terms, and revolutions almost always spawn some emulative, band-wagoning behaviour of this kind. The sixteenth-century Reformation spread rapidly across societies, as did the abortive revolutions of 1848. The potential for emulation is the very reason why foreign governments are often hostile towards the prospect of revolution in any country, as with the Holy Alliance of 1815 or the intervention in Russia in 1918. There tends to be an exaggerated fear of political contagion. Nonetheless, spill-overs of this kind do take place, *when the underlying conditions are favourable*, and of all political colours. This happened with the spread of colonial independence and the creation of 40 new states between 1957 and 1964, the speed of which was unanticipated. Harold Macmillan's Cape Town speech of February 1960 announcing a 'wind of change' was both perceptive and influential in helping to create the conditions for movement.

The third kind of linkage is *penetrative*, by which is meant the deliberate attempt on the part of elements from one society to enter, influence and, on occasions, manipulate another. This may be aimed ultimately at a government, and indeed may sometimes be difficult to distinguish from the operations of government agents. But the transnational dimension is prominent. Historically various forms of imperialism and neo-colonialism have occurred through the direct operations of missionaries, traders and soldiers of fortune. Allowing for changes of context, they continue to do so. American foundations, and German parties, spend a great deal of money in third countries spreading their various ideologies.

Terrorism is the most obvious form of penetrative linkage. It has been one of the major security challenges for most kinds of regimes over the last four decades. The more fanatical of the current wave of jihadists think they can actually overthrow decadent modernity in the West, but the more sophisticated of them employ cold rationality to the task of exerting pressure on Western governments by inflicting pain on their civilian populations. Either way, their activity brings forth a strong state reaction, as does some perfectly peaceful activity deemed subversive by a given government, such as Christian evangelism in China or gay rights activism in Uganda.

The accumulation of these three different kinds of linkage has produced changes in the nature of both domestic and international politics, with concomitant complications for policy-makers at home and abroad. The prevalence of transnationalism demonstrates that however important the state system it can only be understood in a wider context, with agency located in a range of sources and operating in a number of different ways. Figure 8.2 shows how the funnel model, which represents a common view of how foreign relations used to work, has been made redundant by the processes described in the linkage politics model. The arrows provide examples of the kind of political transactions which can take place between societies, and between groups and foreign governments, without going through parent governments. Where countries start to give up parts of their sovereignty, as in the European Union, a third model arises, that of overlapping jurisdictions. Societies and governments then become structurally interlinked.

Linkage politics is prevalent because transnational actors, and individuals, are proactive, reactive and imitative. Following their own agendas leads them to engage with each other and with states. Their actions are far from always designed to cause problems for governments – indeed, the two sides increasingly find ways of working together. As a result of this mass of varied activity most societies in the world are directly linked into others, unsystematically to be sure, but with sufficient continuity to ensure that governments have come to assume a high

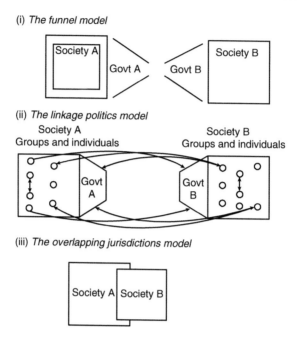

Figure 8.2   Intersocietal connections: three models

degree of autonomous interaction between societies whatever policing powers they enjoy. Inevitably this perception has led governments to seek ever more powers of surveillance and control. Societal linkages and state watchfulness are two sides of the same coin.

On the face of things most transnational channels of action are legal, banal and innocuous – connecting everyone from art dealers and steam train enthusiasts to experts on rare diseases. Only some of them produce political difficulties, usually because of competing views about how society should be organized or resources distributed. The transnational dimension adds extra tensions over the issue of who may legitimately participate and over where the authority to act lies. Moreover, what the law allows is one thing; what is regarded as politically acceptable quite another. There is a fine line, for example, between fraternal assistance to a like-minded party in an election campaign, and unacceptable interference in another society's internal affairs. This will be even truer where the TNA is prepared to break laws, and/or operates in societies where it behaves in a way not permitted to local citizens. Hence the tensions between Western journalists and the authorities in Russia over the 2014 Winter Olympics in Sochi. Raising questions over local disruptions, the conditions for migrant workers, or gay rights were all perceived as acts of hostility.

Confusing Responsibilities

The web of linkage politics feeds back constantly into all the bands of the international system. It constitutes a distinctive form of agency in itself and thus exerts distinctive pressures on the agency of states. As a result, it is becoming increasingly difficult to know what decisions are being made, where and by whom. This has implications both for our understanding and for democratic accountability.

Actors and citizens are themselves confused as to where power and authority lie in multilevel world politics. States tend to overstate and TNAs to understate their respective roles; the one not to have their responsibilities diminished, the other not to attract unnecessary attention. A specific case will make the point clearly. By 1995 the tragic civil war in Algeria had already taken tens of thousands of lives, with neighbouring governments apparently either powerless to intervene or uninterested. At this point the Rome-based Catholic pressure group Sant'Egidio – known by some as 'the UN of Trastevere' – began an attempt at mediation between the Algerian government and its fundamentalist opponents which soon made the headlines.[3] After prolonged efforts, including a preliminary meeting, the effort was rebuffed by the military government, but over the eight years of war it was the single most constructive external intervention (Giro, 1998).

How are we to interpret the actions of Sant'Egidio, of whom few non-Italians had heard before these events? Both realists and conspiracy theorists would waste little time in concluding that the TNA was probably a convenient front for the Italian government, and possibly behind them others which did not wish to be seen as active. A believer in international civil society, by contrast, would stress the autonomous will and capacity of Sant'Egidio in the vacuum created by the indifference of the neighbouring states. More likely than either of these competing interpretations, however, is one which combines the two and accepts the messy character of such events. The Italian government was certainly aware of the actions of Sant'Egidio, and was almost certainly backing them. The same can probably be said of its major allies such as France, the United Kingdom and the United States. A strong degree of official encouragement had probably been forthcoming. On the other hand the government was not in a position to control the intervention once begun, and was vulnerable to the political damage which ensues from failure, or even success, on the wrong terms. There seems, indeed, to have been much argument inside the Italian foreign ministry about the activities of Sant'Egidio (de Courten, 2003). In this delicate and dangerous environment, where religion and human rights were as prominent as oil and patronage, all actors were groping in the dark and were, to a degree, mutually dependent.

Whereas governments are responsible for the welfare of their people and have to make multiple trade-offs, transnational actors focus on a particular concern. Yet their increasing prevalence bestows a legitimacy that states have to acknowledge. Some TNAs are co-opted – because they are so useful – into the processes of policy implementation, while others have an important role in standard-setting. The more this happens the more they will come to take on bureaucratic roles similar to those of states, and the more necessary it will become to find ways of holding them to account. External policy traditionally allows executives much freedom of manoeuvre but civil society is now more reluctant to leave world politics in the hands of governments. States thus face a double bind in trying to manage both foreign policy and transnational relations within recognizable democratic processes.

Notes

1   The speeches of Tony Blair, notably in Chicago in April 1999, to the Labour Party Conference in October 2000 and in Bangalore on 5 January 2002, arguably constitute the most serious attempt yet to articulate what globalization implies for foreign policy.
2   The World Economic Forum, in Davos, Switzerland, is attended by the world's business elite, private and public. See <http://www.weforum.org>. For the transnational anti-globalizers, see Houtart and Polet (2001).
3   Trastevere is the area in Rome south of the Vatican, on the west bank of the Tiber.

Further Reading

Baumann, Rainer and Stengel, Frank A., 2014. Foreign policy analysis, globalization and non-state actors: state-centric after all? *Journal of International Relations and Development*, 17(4), pp. 489–521. This article is a good survey of the literature dealing with the intersection of FPA and transnationalism.
Held, David and McGrew, Anthony, eds, 2003. *The Global Transformations Reader*. Second edition. This extensive collection of essays, on every aspect of the globalization theses, gives proper space to critical views.
Lyons, Terence and Mandaville, Peter, eds, 2012. *Politics from Afar: Transnational Diasporas and Networks*. This collection of strong essays covers both the conceptual and the empirical aspects of one of the key types of transnational actors.

Risse-Kappen, Thomas, ed., 1995a. *Bringing Transnational Relations Back In: Non-State Actors, Domestic Structures and International Institutions.* This was an influential book in the second wave of interest in transnational actors, after Keohane and Nye's initiative in 1973.

Vertovec, Steven, 2009. *Transnationalism.* Vertovec's text offers a concise but comprehensive introduction to definitions of transnationalism and its various dimensions.

Chapter 9

The Domestic Sources of Foreign Policy

Those responsible for foreign policy have to face many different directions at once: towards the states and transnational actors of the international political system, but also increasingly inwards towards the citizens who pay their salaries. They must accept that policy outcomes are vulnerable to internal events and pressures just as, conversely, foreign policy impacts upon domestic politics. The current chapter discusses the theoretical relationship between the domestic and the foreign, with special reference to the domestic 'sources' of foreign policy, meaning the impact of domestic politics, institutions and types of regime. Chapter 10 moves the argument in a more normative direction, by considering how far foreign policy is meaningful to modern citizens, and the extent to which they can participate in debates about foreign policy. If most political action now has an international dimension, then the problems of choice between responsibilities inside and out, or over where to use scarce resources, become even sharper than in the days of autarkic or Keynesian states. Given the challenges posed by globalization to sovereignty, to identity and to ethics, foreign policy represents the primary space where a given community encounters the world and can consider its options for action.

Sources, Constraints and Actors

Starting from the position that the domestic and the foreign are inextricably interconnected, Robert Putnam (1988) formulated the concept of the 'two-level game' whereby 'chiefs of governments' are seen as playing politics simultaneously on two boards (Moravcsik, 1998). Accepting that foreign policy decision-makers are always 'Janus-faced' enables us both to avoid the errors of single-factor explanation and to observe what space might be available for leadership to make a difference. The different logics of the two environments impose choices about priorities and the management of complexity. In the rationalist conception of Putnam and colleagues, a leader can manipulate the 'win-set', that is, 'the set of potential agreements that would be ratified by domestic constituencies in a straight up-or-down vote against the status quo of "no agreement"' (Moravcsik, 1993, p. 23). Yet the set is not self-executing, requiring in fact considerable effort, skill and political creativity. Given (i) that foreign policy is now more about negotiating agreements than about issuing unilateral edicts, and (ii) that even in non-democratic states it often involves discussions with domestic stakeholders, this model may be assumed to be generally applicable in international relations.

The scheme of two levels, however, barely does justice to the nature of contemporary foreign policy. Its sources are multiple, requiring actors to play on many multilateral chessboards simultaneously in the external environment, as well as dealing with the transnational actors catalogued in Chapter 8. To some extent this stream of influences from all directions provides structure and continuity for decision-makers' calculations, as even if one set of relationships deteriorates states are embedded in many more. On the other hand the expectations and rules of these games are diverse. In particular, voters have very tangible concerns about local or national issues, which do not easily map onto the concerns of those meeting in international venues on a range of issues, local, regional and global.

The contrast in priorities or perceptions often creates disjunctions in the conduct of public policy – an issue to which we shall return. More straightforwardly it is clear that the foreign policy dimension is now not immune from the impact of pressures generated internally. No one now believes that foreign policy is just about the dynamics of diplomacy. The billiard ball and chessboard metaphors have been discarded by all but diehard traditionalists, with even neorealists conceding that there are important things which cannot be explained by the balance of power (Hill, 1996a, pp. 5–11; Owen, 2010). In practice observers have been pointing out since the 1920s that the very nature of the modern state impinges on foreign policy, with its elements of mass mobilization, populism and economism. Most critics of fascism or of Soviet communism predicted that domestic authoritarianism would spill over into external aggression, and events bore them out. On the democratic side the idea that US foreign policy was at the mercy of domestic opinion became commonplace after the disavowal by Congress of the Treaty of Versailles and the passing of the neutrality legislation in the 1930s. It then became a self-fulfilling prophecy as successive presidents became convinced that they could only take on major international commitments by either deceiving the public or scaring it. Franklin Roosevelt's insidious pressure on Japan, the communist spectre summoned up in the early Cold War, and the deception of the Gulf of Tonkin Resolution on Vietnam all exemplify the executive's assumption that it needed to head off domestic scepticism at the pass.

In some instances, usually starting in key states, domestic forces become transnational, washing over the wider international system

(Halliday, 1999a, pp. 133–60). This happened with both the French Revolution and the Third Reich where national upheaval soon led to foreign policy change. It is then natural to conclude, as Eckhart Kehr (1977) did in anticipating Fritz Fischer's interpretation of the origins of the First World War, that we should accept *das Primat der Innenpolitik*. But to ascribe causal primacy to either internal or external factors is to be far too crude. Better is the nuanced conclusion of Alexander Wendt (1999), that 'foreign policy behaviour is often determined primarily by domestic politics', or of Richard Haass (2013), an experienced practitioner, whose book is entitled *Foreign Policy Begins at Home* but who wishes to argue only that US power will be undermined unless it puts its own house in order, fiscally and socially.

In a democratic and relatively self-sufficient country like the United States, it may well seem that the balance of influences on foreign policy comes down on the domestic side. The complex politics of Capitol Hill, in interplay with the teeming numbers of lobbyists, have significant influence on its international relations. Against this, it is remarkable how much continuity there has been over decades in American foreign policy despite the vicissitudes of electoral politics, which would seem to lead us back to the notion of system dominance. But either way, the United States is untypical. On the one hand its constitution contains unparalleled opportunities for the legislature to check the foreign policy powers of the executive, while the powerful anti-government tendency of its political culture puts pressure even on strong presidents. On the other, it has been the most powerful state in the world for 75 years, with global commitments which set limits to the changes which domestic opinion can bring about.

The majority of states have both a less vibrant domestic debate and a less engaged foreign policy than those of the United States. But there may still be '*domestic sources*' of their external behaviour. Electoral change or domestic turbulence can lead to stances which affect outsiders, as when the pressure for land reform from disgruntled war veterans in Zimbabwe, combined with President Mugabe's need of an election-winning gambit in 2000, led to the occupation of white farms and a crisis with Britain which dragged on for a decade. The victory of the radical party Syriza in the Greek elections of January 2015 put it on a direct collision course with the German government of Angela Merkel, which continued to insist on tough conditions for any assistance towards the relief of Greece's chronic debt problem. The stronger a government's – or a society's – sense of its distinctiveness, the more likely it is that its foreign policy will seem unpredictable to outsiders operating on the basis of shared rules for the international game.

On the other side of the coin domestic society can also impose stable *constraints* on foreign policy-makers, in the sense of known limits to their freedom of manoeuvre by virtue of the particular community they represent in international relations. No British government, for example, can overlook the importance of financial services to the economy in its negotiations with its European partners. Nor can the United States or France overlook their powerful farm lobbies in trade negotiations. Leaders get seduced into making international affairs their priority, but the elastic which connects them to their domestic base is always liable to pull them up sharply. This is partly a matter of intra-elite disputes, and the lack of resources with which to pursue ambitious plans, but it can also be the result of running ahead of opinion. Although it depends on the nature of the state, certain groups have a veto power in the sense that an initiative in their domain will require their 'ratification' (to use Moravcsik's term) if it is to have credibility abroad. The military are the traditional case in point, but in foreign economic policy banking and investment circles both home and abroad will be equally crucial, affecting as they do the confidence which sustains a national currency.

Even mass opinion can have a braking effect of this kind, as the French and Dutch governments discovered in 2005 when they subjected the draft European constitution to referenda with damaging results. Thus an intelligent government will anticipate likely opposition at home and build into its foreign policy a sense of what the country will stand – something that the Soviet leaders, too used to assuming the obedience of their people, failed to take into account in 1979 when launching the war in Afghanistan, which turned sour at home through the impact of 70,000 killed or wounded. The withdrawal ten years later took place for strategic reasons, but first among them was Mikhail Gorbachev's conclusion that the war was incompatible with vitally needed domestic reform.

The constraints which domestic politics imposes on leaders are sometimes used effectively in negotiations with other states through the 'my hands are tied' tactic which, however, tends to work only when the third party is disproportionately keen to reach an agreement. Otherwise it encourages direct intervention in one's own domestic politics, so as to 'untie the hands', or it produces a waiting game in the knowledge that domestic political constellations always change in the end (P. Evans, 1993, pp. 402–3). Conversely, the prospect of a change in government, democratic or otherwise, makes any foreign policy-maker cautious about what it is plausible to promise in negotiations. Ultimately no government can tie the hands of its successors on the major issues of foreign policy, whatever the particular constitutional provisions.

The domestic environment is hardly monochrome, for it throws up a variety of sources of foreign policy and constraints on activity. But it also contains different kinds of *actors*, best conceptualized here in terms of concentric circles (Hilsman, 1964, pp. 541–4). When Snyder, Bruck and Sapin (1962) first conceived of the notion of a foreign policy decision-making system they put official leaders at the centre of their model. This remains valid, but those who followed – notably Michael Brecher (1972) – added the other necessary circles of activity. Chapters 3 and 4 of this book dealt with competing elites and bureaucratic interests. Moving outwards into domestic society, we encounter the four Ps: parliaments, public opinion, pressure groups and the press (used as shorthand for all the media). These are mainly covered in Chapter 10 in relation to the 'constituencies' of foreign policy – that is, those to whom leaders feel practically and morally responsible. What is more, there are other forces which a pluralist approach neglects, namely social class and regime type. Both are dealt with in this chapter as instances of determining domestic factors, although there is a grey area between the individuals or groups which possess some degree of conscious agency and therefore participate in the policy process, and those elements of society which may affect policy but have no clear voice or mechanism for mobilising their interests. Thus 'the peasants', the 'working class', some religious communities and large ethnic minorities (such as 'the Hispanics' in the US) may all have the potential to affect foreign policy, but they are not close to having the collective self-awareness and common positions which are the prerequisite of agency. Yet while their influence is difficult to gauge, they may still represent important forms of structural constraint over a longer term. Here again, actors and structures shade into each other.

More evanescent are the individual actors which can emerge from almost anywhere, with an impact of unpredictable nature and duration. Who would have thought that Princess Diana would have become a crusader against land mines, causing controversy inside her own state on a matter of defence policy? Or that a young girl in Pakistan, speaking out against the Taliban before and after being wounded in an assassination attempt, would tour the world inspiring young and old with her speeches before becoming the youngest winner of the Nobel Peace Prize?[1] These are cases of strong-willed individuals, but the emergence of more durable political forces such as the Greens in western Europe, or Hindu nationalism in India, can also come out of left field to surprise conventional thinking. Analysts on international relations have to cover the whole system and rarely know about more than one or two countries in depth. Given that every domestic environment is unique and in perpetual movement it means there are always regular surprises even for the best informed.

Interactions

Since a sizeable number of the world's nearly 200 states lack stable administrative, political and social systems, it is not easy to generalize about the relationship between foreign policy and the domestic environment. Where we find weak, failed, 'quasi' or 'prebendal' states we shall probably find weak, erratic and dependent foreign policies.[2] It is notable how low a profile Lebanon has in its region, compared to equally small states such as Jordan or Georgia. The same is true of many African states. The penetration of the Taliban Afghan state by the private interests of Al Qaeda soon exposed that country to devastating foreign intervention. By contrast, where the military take power it is often a sign that the state has failed; the new regime then aims to restore effective statehood, together with a predictable foreign policy. Of course human rights suffer, especially when the 'temporary' restoration of order turns into an all-too-predictable failure to organize democratic elections.

Foreign and domestic politics are separate but not separable (Yaniv, 1979). Many actors busy themselves in both arenas, either because their belief systems do not acknowledge state boundaries or because their business activities go beyond the national level. Issues do at times present zero-sum choices between domestic and external goals, but more often they reverberate across the policy boundary. The interconnection is most obvious in resource questions, but it also appears in relation to political culture and to the consequences of domestic change. Each of these three dimensions deserves further discussion.

On the *resources* front the issue involves the detail of public expenditure decisions as well as the long-term allocation of resources. Foreign policy is not the most expensive area of state activity, at least until diplomacy fails and serious conflict begins. But its associated instruments, of defence, trade promotion and overseas development assistance, are far more costly. They provoke regular controversies over value for money, which all too easily degenerate into 'us' versus 'them' polarities. Do we need: another aircraft carrier, far-flung bases, embassies in capitals where nothing much seems to happen, a national airline, membership of UNESCO or more consulates to help out citizens in distress? Especially when the alternatives seem to be more hospitals, schools and roads, or simply mouths fed and children vaccinated against killer diseases. The issues are more complicated than these stark choices. But there is no avoiding the facts that big commitments in international relations do imply fewer resources available for state expenditure at home, and that public debate often sets up the problem in this kind of way – charity begins at home, elections are won on the tax issue, and other commonplaces of domestic political life.

The more debate proceeds the more evident it becomes that domestic society is itself divided on the need for what might be termed 'spending beyond borders'. There are divisions between consumers, who generally favour tax cuts, and producers, some of whose jobs will depend on the arms industry, the military or the various other forms of government-subsidized international activity. Producers may have privileged access to the bureaucracy which is so important in the policy-making process, with arms sales seen as critical to employment and export earnings. A point can be reached, nonetheless, where high expenditure on external goals imposes a crippling burden on a state, leading to foreign policy decisions taken for domestic financial reasons. Economic recession inevitably throws such choices into sharper relief. Even the United States had to reverse its whole foreign economic policy in 1971 as the result of domestic stagnation brought on by the huge costs of the Vietnam War (W. Cohen, 1993, pp. 198–201). Defence spending by European states generally dropped in the first decades of the twenty-first century, despite complaints from the military concerned about the demands made on them through the increased interventions in Africa and the Middle East, and growing worries about Russian revanchism. An effective foreign policy should avoid getting to the point where major decisions have to be taken in one realm for reasons more to do with the other.

Essentially the pressures coming from the domestic and international environments are of contrasting types. The former can be insistent, practical, but also the product of relatively ephemeral political rows. Yet as a misjudgement can lead to the fall of a government even trivial domestic problems loom large on the horizons of democratic decision-makers – while autocrats tend to overreact to any hint of a challenge to their position. International pressures, by contrast, may well be ignored in favour of domestic concerns, yet ultimately may have greater long-term significance. This is when they are thought to be central to the state's very survival, through the need for defence and alliances on the one hand and the creation of a favourable international milieu on the other. Bearing in mind that foreign policy-makers are often bound together internationally by common concerns and personal contacts, it can be seen why heavy domestic costs, both financial and political, are often incurred for external reasons – as with Australia's dispatch of troops to help the United States in Vietnam, or the support of French elites for a nuclear deterrent. In the first case the need to avoid alienating Washington was seen as so strong that Canberra accepted the political cost at home. In the second the assumption that French prestige and security absolutely require an independent *force de dissuasion* means that the financial and fiscal consequences go almost unquestioned.

While acting as a free-rider sometimes works – as when the US does not pay its dues to the UN or Sweden does not join NATO – for most there is a perpetual balancing act to be conducted between the external and internal aspects of resource allocation, with some commitments relatively inelastic. Despite the powerful lead it could give in terms of reduced oil consumption the United States will not consider serious taxes on petrol, because of the noisy domestic protests which even a rise in price of a few cents provokes. The federal tax on gasoline has not been raised since 1993. Two decades of taking cheap oil for granted did come to an abrupt end after the Middle East war of 1973, which taught the lesson that foreign sources had to be diversified and domestic explorations increased. But domestic demand, and imports, continued to rise until the fallout from wars with Iraq, which stimulated the 'fracking' revolution which in 2015 helped to lower the price of world oil. This then had foreign policy ramifications, weakening the position of energy exporters like Russia and Saudi Arabia. And so the dance goes on.

Big powers tend to regard spending on foreign and defence policy as sacrosanct, whatever the costs for their citizens, with cutbacks only at the margins. The exceptions, such as the failure to rearm against Germany by Britain and France in the 1930s because of deference to a pacifist public opinion, usually lead in time to a reaction in favour of rearmament – in this case perforce, but in that of Russia after the 1990s, through nationalism. Whether justified or not, however, there are always costs attached to any decision to prioritize either the domestic or the international sides of public policy. The Israeli public accepts the need for some sacrifices at home given the perception of its overriding security needs. Conversely, the members of the European Union have not been prepared fully to fund the European Security and Defence Policy (ESDP) about which there is much political rhetoric. Their subsequent dependence on NATO means that they have little scope from distancing themselves from the United States.

That foreign policy is subject to the twists and turns of domestic politics can also be seen in relation to *domestic culture*. Here, certain social attitudes and political forces feed back to affect future foreign policy choices, often with serious consequences. The most prominent case of modern times was that of white-ruled South Africa. The regime in Pretoria tried to separate domestic and foreign politics, by denying the legitimacy of foreign criticisms of apartheid and seeking to engage in diplomatic business as usual. It also sought to use classic realist tactics by dividing its opponents abroad. In particular, this meant wooing the few leaders of black African states willing to deal with them, notably Felix Houphouët-Boigny of the Ivory Coast and Hastings Banda of Malawi. This approach had some temporary success but in the long run was brought down by the impossibility of keeping apartheid in a sealed domestic compartment. The oppression of the black majority in South Africa ultimately conditioned South Africa's external relations, both through transnational groups and because most governments, encouraged by their own peoples, came to see apartheid as doomed as well as repugnant. If it took time for this view to become established that was because domestic and foreign politics tend to run at different speeds.

South Africa under white rule may seem an exceptional case of a social system incurring international costs, but in modern conditions any autocratic regime will face similar pressures, especially if it fetishises sovereignty and the autonomy of domestic politics. China is already under cross-pressures for this reason, although it currently has the wealth and self-confidence to withstand them. In pluralist states the impact is more likely to come from dominant attitudes and collective memories. In Greece, for instance, the anti-German feeling dating from the savage occupation of the Second World War quickly rose to the surface during the negotiations over debt relief in 2014 and 2015, when the Merkel government, backed by public opinion, showed little sympathy for the Greek people and little willingness to reopen the issue of historical responsibility.

Switzerland is an interesting case of a different kind. This is a country which hosts various international institutions, whose banks provide key services for private international finance, and with over 20 per cent of its population consisting of immigrants. Yet it is inward looking to the point where it stays out of the EU and resists most involvement in multilateral initiatives. At the opposite end of the developmental scale is Afghanistan, where the persistence of internal tribal and warrior traditions make the country both extremely difficult to subjugate and an uncomfortable ally, as the Soviet Union, the United States and Pakistan have variously discovered over the last 35 years. The Afghans' long experience of external interference has produced a fierce culture of independence – and internal divisions – which make its foreign relations highly unpredictable (Halliday, 1999b; Reuveny and Prakash, 1999).

The impact of *domestic change* on foreign policy has spawned a great deal of literature, particularly within the positivist tradition of comparative foreign policy. Rummel (1968, p. 208), for example, confirming Sorokin (1937), argued that conflicts inside and outside the state are unrelated. That is, foreign policy is not affected by internal upheaval, and vice versa. This finding is counter-intuitive – and contestable, given the difficulties of coding 'conflict events'. In the same vein the more traditional scholar Geoffrey Blainey (1973, pp. 70–1) pointed out that half of the wars between 1815 and 1939 were preceded by major internal turmoil in at least one participant. This obviously meant that the other

50 per cent had no such precedent, but more importantly the fact of preceding an event does not mean causing – or even triggering – it.

More convincing are careful generalizations like that of Miles Kahler (1997, p. 12): namely that 'if a near-revolutionary situation exists internally, foreign policy paralysis and quiescence are more likely than belligerence'. The corollary is that once a revolution has settled down, the twin consequences of its own fervour and the hostility of external conservatism can spark a powerfully assertive foreign policy and equally strong reactions from others (Halliday, 1999a, pp. 135–40). It is striking that of the major states of the Westphalian system to have undergone violent revolution, the majority (Britain, America, France, Russia, China and Iran) have found themselves engaged in serious warfare in the decade after their revolution succeeded.

Civil war, by contrast, inevitably paralyses foreign policy while making it the more vital, to cope with the outsiders who are tempted to meddle. In fact civil conflicts create situations of great danger both for the state concerned and for the international system, as shown by the costly intervention of the Western powers in Russia between 1918 and 1920, which contributed to the subsequent siege mentality of the Soviet regime (Little, 1975). In our own time the incendiary condition of Syria since the first uprising in 2011 has destabilized the whole Levant and drawn the West into a conflict with the self-styled Islamic State.

Even routine political turmoil can undermine the credibility of external policy, as was the case with the many short-lived Italian governments in the second half of the twentieth century (Santoro, 1991, pp. 177–246). The similarly hamstrung French Fourth Republic managed to sound the death knell in 1954 of the European Defence Community which France itself had initiated in 1950. The severe crisis then occasioned by the Algerian war of independence eventually brought down the fragile political system, to be replaced by the very different model of the Fifth Republic, with a strong executive and consistent foreign policy as its prime objectives (Pickles, 1962).

Whereas for a small country a period of internal instability only matters if it provokes intervention from the outside, for a major power it can reverberate through a range of key foreign policy problems. The United States found that the weakness of the second Nixon administration resulting from the Watergate scandal made its difficulties with the Soviet Union, the Middle East and even its European allies even more problematical. It was no coincidence that this was the era in which Henry Kissinger talked a great deal about 'linkage politics'. By linkage Kissinger meant the trading off of different diplomatic issues, and never far from his mind was the weakness of his own position in international negotiations (not least in the end-game of the Vietnam War) occasioned by the chaos in Washington. On the other side of the Cold War conflict, foreign policy often had to be put on hold for the quite long periods when ageing leaders were incapable either of action or of stepping down. The same painful saga was played out by Boris Yeltsin in the second half of the 1990s. Its immobilism meant that the Russian political system cut a poor figure abroad, with Moscow virtually powerless to oppose NATO enlargement.

Internal events, therefore, like domestic culture and debates over resources, are perpetually connected to foreign policy in a two-way flow of influence. The scopes, issues and actors of the two arenas do overlap, which makes it sensible to talk at times of 'intermestic' politics or of 'policy modes', as in the EU (Brenner, Haney and Vanderbush, 2008, pp. 67–83; H. Wallace, 2000, pp. 71–2). Yet inside and outside can still be distinguished. The contrasting rhythms and legal-normative structures of the foreign and domestic mean that they each retain the capacity to surprise, upset and divert the best laid plans of the other.

Constitutional Structures

Few things are more important for any entity than its basic constitutional structure, usually outlined in a foundational document. This is even true for states which do not pretend to be 'constitutional' in the sense of subscribing to the principle of the supremacy of the law, and of liberal notions about the rights of the people (R. Jones, 1979, pp. 83–7). While no formal constitution is ever fully lived up to, even under autocratic systems there are specified rules – and often statements about democracy – which create expectations as to what proper conduct should be.

In foreign policy the elements of the constitutional structure which most affect outcomes are those dealing with executive–legislative relations. In this context the axes around which systems revolve are: federal versus unitary states; pluralist democracy versus centralism; and parliamentary control versus the division of powers. These dyads provide various combinations, represented in different states according to their history. The nature of the constitutional solutions found, and the ways in which they are implemented, affect both the style and the substance of a country's foreign policy. This can be seen by reference to influential states like Britain, China, France, Japan and the United States.

In federal systems the relations between central government and the constituent states are of importance for foreign policy despite the fact that it is one of the areas most clearly reserved for central government – indeed, security and external relations provide the rationale for an otherwise decentralized body. This means that in principle the non-central government (NCG) parts of the constitution are not permitted to have their own international policies. This varies, however, according to the nature and maturity of the system. The new German Reich after 1871, for example, allowed the *Bundesstaten* as well as the federal government to have foreign relations. Thus, following Bismarck's view that the centre should not have more power 'than is absolutely necessary for the cohesion of the whole and for the effect presented to the outside', large *Staaten* like Bavaria and Wurttemberg retained some of their diplomatic legations (Leonardy, 1993, p. 249). The German state subsequently turned through a full historical circle, with federalism suspended by the Third Reich only to be reintroduced by the Basic Law of the Federal Republic in 1949. The *Länder* were then restrained by circumstances from asserting themselves in international relations, but then so was the federal chancellery itself.

Over the past few decades it has become clear that the widening agenda of foreign affairs has both enabled German foreign policy in general to be normalized and brought the *Länder* into more direct international involvement. Central government has had to accept that the consent of the *Länder* must be obtained for the conclusion of treaties which touch on matters normally under their competence – as do, for example, the treaties establishing the European Community (Leonardy, 1993, pp. 237–41). Conversely, the *Länder* have been increasingly active in direct relations with other subnational units, following a general trend which is mostly limited to commercial and cultural activity but does have the effect of squeezing national foreign policy in certain areas between global, regional and local pressures. On environmental issues, for example, where it is vital both to agree globally and to act locally, the regions are indispensable partners (Hocking, 1999).

A federal structure both reins in potential actors (units like Quebec or California clearly could be effective nation-states if given the chance) and privileges them, in the sense that it acknowledges their distinct identities, visibility and administrative structures. All three qualities make some kind of international actorness feasible. Thus some US states have been able either to frustrate central government's external relations (as with Washington's inability to compel full domestic compliance with the provisions of the US–UK Tax Treaty) or to build up pressure for a change in official foreign policy by engaging in human rights-motivated embargoes of countries like Burma or Iran, despite the conflicts with world trade rules or the ultimate supremacy of national foreign policy (Fry, 2009, pp. 302–5; Whitten and Phelps, 2011). The struggle between federal government and the states over aspects of foreign policy naturally increases with demands for devolution, and with any divergences in wealth between the regions of a state. Thus even in non-federal systems like Britain, Italy and Spain there has been regional unrest (in Scotland, 'Padania' and Catalonia) over the costs and political associations of a foreign policy made in London and Madrid.

Federal systems can operate either on the basis of a separation of powers between the executive and the legislature, or on that of a parliamentary system, with the executive dependent on a majority in the assembly. In the first case, exemplified by the United States, the division of responsibilities in principle acts as a check on the executive's freedom of action in foreign policy. The Congress can complicate and slow down the conduct of the US foreign policy through its formal role in the ratification of treaties, the appointment of ambassadors and its budgetary powers. Barack Obama's ability to reach agreement with Iran on nuclear technology was inhibited by congressional threats to impose new economic sanctions (although that also has helped the president's external negotiating position). Much of the post-war history of the US, however, illustrates the presidency's ability to enlarge that freedom by the use of executive agreements, by exploiting its power of initiative in crisis and by appeals to patriotism which play on the natural wish for national unity. At times there is a major reaction against what is seen as the abuse of presidential power, as with the enforced withdrawal from the League of Nations (1919), the televised Senate Foreign Relations Committee hearings into the Vietnam War and the War Powers Act of 1973. But in foreign policy the presidency has structural advantages which soon return to the fore. Presidents have also learned to avoid formal declarations of war and the need to ask for congressional approval.

Such characteristics are also to be seen in some measure in other federations, for the very limitations on central government tend to emphasize the importance of its foreign policy prerogatives. Countries like Australia, Brazil, Canada, India and Nigeria display a more conventional pattern of executive dominance over foreign policy. Even where the constituent states have tried to take the opportunities of direct international participation, the executive has usually managed to limit their incursions, generally backed up by the courts' interpretation of the constitution (Hocking, 1993b). But as constitutional structures are in a condition of perpetual evolution it is quite possible that the units of their federations will gradually acquire a higher international profile, especially in the pursuit of economic interests. In a detailed comparative study Hans Michelmann (2009, p. 333) and colleagues found that in eight of 12 states the 'constituent units have been accorded foreign relations powers or increased foreign relations powers'. This is particularly the case in states with large land areas and/or populations, where central authority has its inherent limits.

Beyond the variations of circumstance it is clear that the specific legal provisions of a constitution do make a difference. Australian federalism gives the foreign policy executive advantages compared to that of the United States and this is facilitated by the Westminster model of an executive enjoying a parliamentary majority which in principle will last until the next general election. Yet the same is true of the Federal Republic of Germany, where despite proportional representation and the consequent reliance on coalition governments of various combinations successive chancellors have provided stable government and a consistent, if cautious, foreign policy. In part this has been through the device of allowing the minority member of the coalition to hold the office of foreign minister, as with the Free Democrats Hans-Dietrich Genscher and Guido Westerwelle, the Green Joschka Fischer and the Social Democrat Frank-Walter Steinmeier.

Unitary states vary just as much in how their constitutional structures affect foreign policy-making. General de Gaulle precisely cast the constitution of the Fifth Republic so as to strengthen the executive, creating a separate presidency far freer from legislative constraints. He saw the parliamentary system of the Third and Fourth Republics as having led France to disaster through an inability to take difficult foreign policy decisions, and which made the country 'the sick man of Europe'. The change had meant that 'today [1962] its influences and prestige are recognized throughout the world' (de Gaulle, 1971, p. 319). Italy has been making efforts for more than 20 years to break out of the same trap. The endless governments of the 'First Republic' set up after the Second World War have been replaced by some more durable administrations, although the aim of German-style stable coalitions based on clear electoral victories has yet to be achieved. Part of the motivation for change has come from foreign policy, with a growing frustration at the invisibility of Italy due to the political system's chronic political introspection and instability (Brighi, 2013, pp. 121–47). Part of the thinking of recent prime ministers Enrico Letta and Matteo Renzi is that Italy needs serious constitutional reform if is to be seen as 'a serious country' – that is, one with strong, stable leadership where foreign policy is not hostage to domestic politicking.

In Israel, by contrast, whose system combines elements of the British model with some characteristics of the French Fourth Republic, we see that the constant difficulty of putting together a majority government in a multiparty system, combined with the unusual salience of foreign policy in the day-to-day politics of the country, makes for a high degree of immobilism, as minority parties have an effective veto over change. That this would become ever more problematic for Israel (and by extension for those trying to negotiate with it) was predicted long ago by Avi

Shlaim and Avner Yaniv (1980, pp. 256, 262) when they pointed out that 'the extraordinary publicity given to cabinet discussions and the complete absence of secrecy facilitate pressures, since parties can observe their representatives hewing to the party line'. They concluded that the compounding of intra-party divisions by inter-party ones produced 'a complex multiple fragmentation of all mainstream political forces' which would continue to damage Israeli foreign policy. This analysis has been borne out by the tortuous history of the peace process since Camp David. Since then it has proved impossible to assemble a winning coalition for anything other than a risk-averse strategy of dependence on overwhelming military might. On the other hand, it starts from the liberal position that defence and deterrence will not be sufficient in the long run for Israel's needs. Conservatives might respond that in practice there has been much continuity of the key security issue, despite the constitutional difficulties, because of the wider consensus in the country at large.

The last example of how constitutional structure affects foreign policy relates to one-party systems. There are two modes in which single parties can dominate domestic politics. The first is through a socialist or communist approach in which the popular will is supposed to be served not by the competition for votes, but by a dominant, monolithic, party which claims to embody that will and operates through delegation rather than representation. The major historical examples here are the Soviet Union and the People's Republic of China. One-dimensional views of these countries see them through the lens of either power politics or communist ideology, with little or no reference to institutional or other domestic factors. More sophisticated interpretations combine all these elements. In the Soviet Union the dominance of the Communist Party was the single most important factor in foreign policy-making, but that only tells us so much. The interplay with the institutions of the state such as the military, the KGB and the scientific establishment is also critical to our understanding, as is the way Moscow was able to dominate the other republics of the USSR despite the huge distances and multiple time zones involved. Even within the party the variation in the roles played by the general secretary and the Politburo over time was vital information for outsiders trying to penetrate what Churchill dubbed 'a riddle, wrapped in a mystery, inside an enigma', leading to the scholarly sub-specialism known as 'Kremlinology'.

The Communist Party and its leading role disappeared with the fall of the Soviet Union. Russia adopted a new constitution in 1993 broadly on the model of Western democracies although it left room as it turned out for the eventual emergence of a new kind of authoritarianism. China's foreign policy system, however, continues to follow the classic communist model. The unchallengeable rule of the Communist Party certainly makes it possible to take the long view in foreign policy – as has been evident over both Hong Kong and Taiwan – which might not have occurred under an alternative regime. The structure of the Chinese political system ensures top-down decision-making, not least because this is a highly centralized country despite its size. The 'autonomous regions' are anything but, and even Soviet-style federalism is ruled out. On the other hand the roles of state institutions like the People's Liberation Army cannot be assumed to operate simply on the basis of party diktats. Furthermore the constitution, which spoke of socialism under 'the people's democratic dictatorship' was amended in 2004 to allow for private property rights.[3] This may have been an ex post facto change, given the way the party had allowed capitalist enterprise to flourish, but it demonstrates that even autocratic systems display variations and change which have to be taken into account by outsiders seeking to deal with them.

The other mode of single-party dominance suggests even more strongly that constitutional structure needs understanding in conjunction with political culture. This is the kind of system which is democratic in most respects, and in which governments may fall with some regularity, but where the same party dominates for decades on end. This was the case in Italy between 1947 and 1992, when the Christian Democrats were always the principal coalition partner. Despite (or perhaps because of) the regular collapse and reformation of cabinets, they usually occupied the key posts of prime minister and foreign minister. Key individuals like Giulio Andreotti or Francesco Cossiga continued to bob to the surface whatever the particular political storm. An even more revealing example is that of Japan. Here a fairly stable democratic system emerged in the post-bellum with none of the apparent weaknesses of the Italian state. Yet the Japanese Liberal Democratic Party (LDP) remained the governing party right up to the economic and corruption crisis of 1993. The constitution allowed for change, but the people, embedded in a corporatist political culture which valued continuity, consensus and discipline, regularly returned the same party to power. The effect was to make politics within the LDP more important than that between the parties. In the case of foreign policy it reinforced the caution and pro-Americanism which had been the watchwords since the renunciation of the sovereign right to make war in the new constitution of 1946, and the San Francisco Peace Treaty of 1951 (Pempel, 1978, pp. 145–57). Thus foreign policy and domestic order went hand in hand, which was hardly surprising given that both were the products of the victors' peace imposed on Japan, and that it was followed by an era of unparalleled prosperity (Katzenstein and Tsujinaka, 1995). They continue to do so (Zarakol, 2011, p. 177).

Constitutional structure is therefore an important factor in shaping foreign policy conduct. It bestows strengths and weaknesses which an executive has to deal with in the light of the issues that come along. An effective foreign policy may be achieved despite constitutional problems, but only by skill and self-conscious effort. This will apply whether the problems are those of an over-weak or an over-strong executive. Although at first sight it may seem that constitutions are a marginal factor in foreign policy the examination of particular countries shows that, in interaction with other domestic factors, the legal basis of a polity matters greatly, through allocating powers and helping to frame identity. Where effective constitutions (and constitutionalism) are lacking altogether, as is still sadly the case in some parts of Africa, the chances of achieving the continuity and accountability implied by the term *foreign policy* are low (S. Wright, 1999, pp. 10–19).

The Regime Factor

An extensive academic literature now exists about the links between foreign policy and the actual character of a regime, that is, not the constitutional theory but the reality. This is the 'democratic peace' hypothesis, which harks back to Kant and was formulated by Michael Doyle (2012, pp. 54–77). It states that democracies are a force for peace, or at least that their mutual relations are peaceable. The debate has been productive in that it has brought empirical and normative work together, just as it has joined up IR, political philosophy and comparative politics. Strangely, it has not attracted many foreign policy analysts, despite the fact that the impact of the internal nature of a state is a central question for FPA (Brown, Lynn-Jones and Miller, 1996; Kahler, 1997; Risse-Kappen, 1995b; Rummel, 1995; Russett, 1993). In fact the issue was identified at an early stage but many were put off by the sterility of behavioural attempts to give a definitive answer (Weede, 1984).

If it could be established that democracies are less war-prone, or more cooperative, or indeed that they display any particular pattern of external behaviour, it would demonstrate conclusively that the domestic factor is of central importance in international relations – *pace* Waltz (1959, 1979) and other international structuralists. Unfortunately the question is not quite as straightforward as it seems. There are two major caveats to note before any conclusions can be drawn.

The first is that the problem can be set up in subtly different ways, with the result that much debate takes place merely over whether findings are commensurable. Some focus on whether or not democracies are *intrinsically* pacifistic; others only on how they behave towards each other. Some restrict their interest to the problem of war; others are interested in whether democracies are as 'constitutional', or respectful of law, in their external relations as they are in internal affairs. Lurking behind the whole debate are the issues of whether historical period makes a difference, and of the distinction between those democracies which proselytize and those which steer clear of moralising and intervention. Thus there exist various possible lines of argument, some much more ambitious than others. All, however, presuppose a significant link between domestic regime and foreign policy behaviour.

The second caveat is that the categories of 'democracy' and 'non-democracy' (for the debate necessarily involves the discussion of both sides of the coin) are more elusive than might be supposed. Despite the common tendency to include classical Athens in the former category, and to talk as if the democratic era began in 1816, it is highly dubious as to whether we can justify talking about established democracies until after the First World War. This is because of the de facto disenfranchisement of the black population in the United States (which arguably continued until the 1960s), the lack of votes for women in Britain (and even of votes *by right* for men) before 1918 and the strongly authoritarian nature of Wilhelmine Germany. Republican France between 1877 and 1945 only qualifies as a democracy if women are written out of the script. Thus we have barely a century's experience to go on, a period in which war regularly led to the suspension of normal rights, and in which the number of new, unsteady states was rapidly growing. This is not a basis for grand generalization.

Defining democracy also raises the problem of what kind of democracy, and how much of it, we are talking about. We may decide that we mean liberal democracy, with its stress on political competition, individual rights and a free economy, rather than the one-party democracy claimed by socialist states. But that still leaves a great deal of variety to take into account – between degrees of mass suffrage (for both men and women), between degrees of efficacy and between systems where the economy is wholly 'free' and those where the state controls some or all of the movement of capital, goods, persons, information and services. Is modern Russia, with its oligarchic capitalism grafted onto Putin's clientelism, truly a democracy? Is Singapore, with its paternalist-guided democracy of efficiency and clean living, to be counted in the same category as messy, individualistic Britain or stable, participatory Canada?

One approach has been to ask whether coalition governments, which are inherently pluralist but to varying degrees, behave more aggressively. Jack Snyder argued that major regimes in the period of imperial expansion, including the Cold War, produced 'myths' which sustained expansion because vested interests were able to capture coalitions through 'log-rolling' (by exchanging favours and cutting deals), especially where the system was 'cartelized' (that is, with a relatively narrow set of groups involved). Juliet Kaarbo, 20 years later, focused more on actual coalitions of political parties, finding that coalitions did tend to pursue foreign poli-cies which were more 'extreme' (meaning assertive, 'not moderate') than single-party governments, but that they were not necessarily more peace-ful or more aggressive (2012). Neither approach, however, allows much space for the actual ideas and interests at stake in a particular historical period.

Non-democracies also present category problems given the grey area between them and democracies. So many states are in transition, or display elements of autocracy and liberalism simultaneously. And can any group which contains totalitarian North Korea and Morocco's rela-tively benign monarchy really be a good basis for generalization?

Despite these difficulties, there are three conclusions to be drawn from the democratic peace debate with respect to the role of domestic factors in foreign policy. The first is often seen as the most 'robust' empirical finding in all international relations, namely that established democratic states do not tend to fight each other. This proposition can only be qualified at the margins, by including minor affairs like the four Anglo-Icelandic 'cod wars', which in truth were not shooting wars. The reasons why democracies would not wish to fight each other can be speculated over at length, but it is highly unlikely that international factors alone, such as the need for unity against a common enemy, can explain the persistence and universality of the norm. Certain aspects of democratic life do seem to predispose towards peaceful conflict resolu-tion with others of the same kind. These aspects do not relate only to the political system. It is quite probable that civil society, through the rule of law, attitudes to violence and standards of living, are at least as impor-tant.

The second finding is that democracies do not hold back in their will-ingness to use violence against those they regard as 'Others': that is, not of their own type. Although such statements subsume complicated debates about the responsibility for starting the major wars of the twen-tieth century, what can be said is that democratic states have been willing to declare wars, that they may sometimes have created the conditions in which war was likely and that they have often pursued war with grim vigour – as the tragic slaughters in Korea and in Vietnam testify – when it was not so infeasible to consider a negotiated peace. This argument has been put even more strongly: namely that the (Western) democracies are hypocritical in their foreign policies since they often treat non-westerners in a ruthless, even racist way, and continue to engage in various forms of oppressive imperialism (Barkawi, 2008). At the least one must conclude that the proposition that democracies have an intrinsic aversion to war as such is plain wrong.

This does not mean that democracies have no option but to switch into cynical realism when they step outside relations between 'like-minded' states – *pace* Robert Cooper's (2003) distinctions between the postmodern world of peaceful democracies and the modern or premodern worlds of other kinds of states. Indeed domestic factors play their part here too, in that the sense of rectitude so common in liberal states can lead to civilising missions, whether anti-communist, anti-fundamentalist or simply against a failed and unstable state. This has been one of the most paradoxical aspects of the Western debates about the varied problems arising from Kosovo, Iraq, Libya and Syria. War has moved from being the epitome of failure or domination to being a necessary instrument of humanitarianism, even at the risk of great human damage. It is a switch which has left many, on both right and left, confused.

The third and last point arising from the democratic peace debate is that non-democracies do not necessarily engage in aggressive or uncooperative behaviour internationally, however unpleasant they may be towards their own people. That they were inherently dangerous was a common assumption among Western scholars at the height of the Cold War, especially those who identified 'totalitarianism' as a distinct phenomenon, and the hawks who saw the Soviet Union and its Third World friends as the successors to the Third Reich in posing a threat to world peace and to democracy (usually equated). The collapse of the Soviet bloc strengthened this view but meant that new sources of potentially bellicose behaviour had to be found. Those who resisted the Hegelian spirit of history, it seemed, would be a danger to the international community as well as to their own people.

In practice this was, and remains, a political position. There is no convincing evidence which suggests that autocracies necessarily pursue their ends through aggression, terrorism or general uncooperativeness. Because some examples can easily be found of tyrants who do so behave does not justify the larger statement. There are just as many cases, perhaps indeed a majority, where a deeply illiberal regime has behaved with great caution, even propriety, in its foreign relations. Many Latin American states in the 1960s and 1970s, Spain under Franco, and Iran under the shah are examples. The People's Republic of China has been another, although it took the United States 22 years to accept that it could conduct normal diplomatic business with Beijing, conditioned by its view that communist autocracies were inherently more dangerous than right-wing ones (Kirkpatrick, 1982). But this was a projection from the fear and dislike of communism as a political and social system which lingers today, combining with a fear of China's rising power to create a new wave of insecurity in Washington.

Military regimes, likewise, are far from being inherently militarist. The armed forces increase defence spending, to be sure, and usually degrade the societies they control, but on balance they are more cautious over external adventures than are their civilian counterparts (Jensen, 1982, pp. 130–5). It is easier to suppress the enemy within – usually the reason for taking power in the first place – than to unleash unpredictable international conflicts.

The result of this survey of the democratic peace problem is one positive statement – that democracies shy away from war with each other – and two negative propositions, about democracies not displaying any particular pattern of behaviour towards other states, and non-democracies not behaving in a distinctive, let alone a uniformly aggressive, manner. Taken together the three findings suggest that the nature of a regime is only significant in the relatively narrow circumstances of inter-democratic relations. This would, however, be too restricted a conclusion. Foreign policy is not only about the war problem, and the nature of a regime also matters in terms of how closely states are prepared to work together – contrary to traditional views of the inconstancy of democracies, it may be that they are capable of considerable continuity in their alliances and other commitments (Gaubatz, 1997). Conversely, an autocratic regime by definition imposes fewer restraints on unstable or incompetent leaders, which can have difficult consequences for outsiders as well as the citizens of the state concerned.

When we move beyond the single-factor approach and add in a sensitivity to historical period or to the extent to which the regime in question has universalising aspirations (as some do, independently of their democratic or undemocratic character), we may see that the nature of any domestic political system does affect the direction of a foreign policy (Barkawi and Laffey, 2001). In part this is merely to impart the truism that when governments change there may well be an impact on foreign policy; more profoundly, it suggests that certain regimes evolve historically, through the very interplay of domestic and external forces, into international actors which are assertive or introverted, cooperative or domineering, ineffectual or responsible. And once institutionalized, this mix of regime and policy will take time to change. Ultimately, the constellation of domestic and international factors particular to a country represents a powerful, evolving, matrix which determines its 'place in the world'. A good example is the limits on modern Germany's foreign policy activism, despite Nazism and the Second World War being long gone. It follows that too much external pressure to change is likely to prove counterproductive. The post-communist regime in

Russia, for example, is now 25 years old, but is showing ever fewer signs of conforming to a Western model. This is hardly a surprise, for it has centuries of turbulent and distinctive history behind it, little of which leads Russians to trust outside advice, quite apart from the recent memory of the humiliating loss of status in 1991. Russian foreign policy has been since then a key point for the domestic system to process external influences and to express its identity, in an overbearing world. Regimes need foreign policies, and Putin has used his for domestic and international reassertion.

Social Forces

Beyond regimes, constitutions and politics lies the broader social and economic context of a state. The possible impact of society on external relations is both a neglected subject and one too large to do more than introduce here. But foreign policy cannot be fully understood if it is abstracted from the society and productive system which it serves, particularly as economic goals are central to modern government and since civil society now has an increasingly transnational dimension (Hopf, 2002). What follows gives a brief sketch of the social forces which impinge on foreign policy, however indirectly, namely class, nationalism, religion, gender and development.

The twentieth century produced a great deal of talk about 'socialist' or 'bourgeois' foreign policies – evolving from John Bright's nineteenth-century view that diplomacy was 'a gigantic system of outdoor relief for the aristocracy' (Bright, 1858, p. 204). Most of this was mere rhetoric. It is difficult to imagine that any socioeconomic class would have strong and distinctive interests in a particular policy of war or peace, cooperation or nationalism – witness the divide among US entrepreneurs over the desirability of the Marshall Plan, or within the British Conservative Party over the EU. Even the fact that foreign policy, like most other aspects of government, is inevitably conducted by an internationally mobile and sophisticated elite, does not mean that it will reflect the interests of a particular social class. The elite is small, and the classes below it are big. This has been a familiar problem in the debate over Marxian analyses of society, and few would now argue for a straightforward relationship between class and politics in any area. The most that can be said is that a persistent 'ruling class' can be normally identified in terms of socio-educational backgrounds and internal networks. This may well tend to certain attitudes and the exclusion of others, but the subsequent balance of actual benefits and losses will be difficult to draw in social class terms (Snyder, 1991, p. 16).

On the other hand, it does stretch a point to assume, as liberal commentators tend to, that the views of the masses are automatically represented in democratically elected governments. It is rare to find a person of working-class culture (or even extraction) in high office, let alone dealing with foreign policy. The outlook or interests of so-called 'ordinary people' (which include a very wide range from company directors to the homeless on the streets) are interpreted by politicians who are elected every four or five years at best, often with a large minority not voting. There may be no realistic alternative to this, but it does mean that it is easy for leaders to get out of touch with the wishes or needs of their constituents. There are other ways in which public opinion can make itself felt, as we shall see in Chapter 10, but those who make foreign policy do have a considerable freedom of manoeuvre, which can lead to a disastrous divergence between policy and the popular will. This was most evident in Russia in 1917, when war exhaustion enforced surrender and then revolution. There can be little doubt that in Britain too at that time a referendum on Lord Lansdowne's compromise peace proposal would have met with a much more positive response than it got from Lloyd George's government – especially if those in the trenches had been able to vote.

Thus while it is difficult to analyse foreign policy in terms of social class, one should always bear in mind the possible divergence between elites' view of the 'national interest' and how the voiceless masses might interpret it, given the chance. Referenda are rare on international issues (except in Switzerland) because politicians rightly fear that the results would be at odds with their views on the 'necessities' of foreign policy. When given the chance, as they have been for example in Denmark, France, Ireland and the Netherlands, citizens in various European countries have often voted against their leaders' recommendations for new treaties.

In the immediate aftermath of a successful revolution a new elite, usually with very different social origins, enters power. It then wishes to put its stamp on foreign policy. Having to deal with the continuing dominance of traditional diplomatic caste across the rest of the international system tends to diminish their radical ardour sooner rather than later, but in the period before socialization takes place some unusual moves may be made. The Soviet Union soon learned to play the diplomatic game after Trotsky's early threat to 'shut up shop', but continued for some time to behave as if diplomacy was a supplement to secret intelligence, rather than vice versa. The style of Chinese diplomacy after the 1949 revolution was parochial, ideological and somewhat hectoring, at least until after Mao's death in 1976 (Kreisberg, 1994; Levine, 1994). For most of the Gaddafi period Libya's 'People's Bureaux' were bases for various kinds of subversive activity including terrorism. Eventually, however, revolutionaries settle into the status of a governing class, coming to see the advantages of conventional participation on the international scene.

Class is not the only way in which to approach the social origins of foreign policy. *Nationalism* and populism figure prominently in the history of foreign policies. It is not difficult to think of examples where assertive, even xenophobic, campaigns have been conducted against other states, or have undermined attempts at international cooperation. Some of this can be put down to the cynical exploitation by elites of the popular factor so as to justify acts of aggression, and/or to distract their disgruntled populations. But some derives from the very nature of 'nation-states', independence and nation-building. In that respect foreign policy and nationalism always feed off each other (Göl, 2013). The origins of the European nation-state were associated with the creation of conscript armies and the idea of 'the nation in arms' to defend the French Revolution, making nationalism a sociological phenomenon with a mass element (Polk, 1997, pp. 118, 226). Moreover, although the idea that the nation is the highest good need not entail xenophobia, it is difficult for professional diplomats to contain the effects of populism and high emotion, especially in difficult times. Just as within a society minorities will be the first victims of a nationalist resurgence, so foreign policy is structurally vulnerable to exaggerated and defensive fears of the outsider.

Two examples can make the point. In India the dominance of the Congress Party after independence produced a foreign policy of pacifistic non-alignment, qualified only by a powerful assertiveness where borders were in question, in Kashmir, Goa, Bengal and the Himalayas. There seemed no interest in becoming a great power or in acquiring the relevant military strength. From the late 1980s, however, the Congress Party, weakened by the failings of any dynastic order and by the sharpening contradictions of modernization, was increasingly under challenge from the BJP, which came to power in 1996. This militant Hindu party arose from nowhere on a tide of discontent with corruption and stagnation, but it also soon developed a distinctive foreign policy, in part genuine and in part an effective way of accusing the old order of not having defended India's interests. The result, by 1998, was that India had taken the momentous step to explode a nuclear device. This immediately led to a tit-for-tat Pakistani explosion, but it was wildly popular in India. The nationalism of the BJP had thus taken India's foreign policy very rapidly down a new and risky path, compelling other parties to jump on the bandwagon if they wished to survive (Sen Gupta, 1998, pp. 40–1). In 2004 it lost power, only to return in a landslide in 2014. This time the nationalist element was present in its assertiveness about India as a 'rising power', but a learning process must have taken place in the interim, as there was a marked lack of associated xenophobia. Indeed a charm offensive towards the country's neighbours was soon under way.

The second example is the case of the Austrian far-right nationalist Jörg Haider. Although only the governor of the province of Carinthia, Haider's populist appeals to a notion of a pristine Austria free from the contamination of immigrants and other forms of external 'interference' meant that the Freedom Party gained 27 per cent of the vote and was taken into the governing coalition in February 1999. This in itself would not have changed Austrian foreign policy, but the strong reactions from fellow member states of the European Union, and their imposition of sanctions on Austria (in the form of exclusion from meetings) eventually forced Haider from office. On the other hand it evoked a further nationalist reaction which in the long run reinforced Euroscepticism in Austria. The Defence Minister Werner Fassalend (from the conservative People's Party) immediately replied that 'we absolutely reject the possibility of accepting that foreigners can make decisions over us' (Karacs, 2000).

The most extreme form of nationalism is fascism, which went beyond autocracy to engage in violence, messianic nationalism/racism, and mass mobilization behind a crusading disrespect for pluralism (Woolf, 1968). Nazi fascism was a historical phenomenon of a particular period, but there is always the possibility that it could return in some form. In that event we should be alert to any state in which there is considerable domestic upheaval, demanding *Lebensraum* and/or producing a xenophobic regime. That would be likely to have contempt for its neighbours and for any notion of international society. By definition, fascists are not interested in realpolitik and coexistence. They are revolutionaries with a commitment to an aesthetic of violence, at home and abroad. Their sense of historical rectitude and supremacy means that their agitation is unlikely to stop at their own frontier.

If nationalism, even in its more benign forms, spills over into foreign policy the same is true of *religion,* although as argued in Chapter 8 this has a transnational as much as a national dimension. Occasionally a state shows a theocratic tendency, as in Iran and Saudi Arabia. Israel is more an ethno-cultural state than a theocracy, but has it has become ever more torn between the influence of ultra-orthodox Jewry and more secular principles. In these circumstances foreign policy will always be affected, partly through particular codes of morality, but also through parallel diplomatic practices. Italy under the Christian Democrats sometimes harnessed its foreign policy to that of the Vatican, and in Iran's pursuit of the *fatwa* against Salman Rushdie it was almost impossible to distinguish the roles of politicians and *imams*. German Catholics had some influence over Germany's concern to recognize Croatia. When religion is important domestically, there will always be a limit to what can be tolerated abroad. Muslim states cannot be indifferent to the sufferings of Bosnia, or to the Palestinian position on Jerusalem. This is, however, a long way from saying that they will act, even in a crisis, for religion is more a background factor than a driver of foreign policy.

Gender is a social dimension which can bear on foreign policy, but more indirectly than nationalism or religion. The concern with gender which has burgeoned in IR has primarily been normative and philosophical. There are important cases to be made about the differential sufferings of women in development, and about their neglected roles in war. The view that orthodox thinking about international relations has been too suffused with masculinist values also has a great deal to be said for it (Grant and Newland, 1991; Steans, 1998). In terms of an analytical approach to the impact of the gender dimension on foreign policy, however, either in general or in particular states, there has been less research done. Clearly in almost all states women have found it difficult to rise up the diplomatic career ladder, although some progress has been made over both promotion and recruitment in recent years, particularly in the states of northern Europe (Neumann, 2012, pp. 129–68). Women and men divide to some degree on gender lines in terms of attitudes to war and nationalism, with women displaying a marginally more pacific tendency. Famously, the Greenham Common women's movement against nuclear weapons had a wide impact on public attitudes, well beyond Britain. The United Nations has promoted awareness of gender-specific human rights concerns.

For the most part, however, discourse changes more than facts. The desolation of the mothers of the disappeared young people in Argentina or of the sailors drowned in the *Kursk* submarine, is only acknowledged after the event, and at best helps to forge better intentions for the future. The scandal of sex tourism to the Third World is publicized, but left largely untouched. It should not be forgotten, either, that there are just as many fathers mourning their lost sons, from Verdun through Stalingrad to the Iran–Iraq War, and that the horrors of invasion, displacement and civil war do not discriminate. The issue then becomes less that of the impact of gender on foreign policy than whether there is any scope at all for 'the voice from below' (Hill, 1999).

Development is another point at which domestic society and foreign policy meet, and another where a vast literature fails to give much coverage to the intersection. Yet it is important to say something, however brief, about the relationship between *levels* of development and foreign policy.[4] The question revolves around whether or not the least-developed countries (LDCs) manifest particular kinds of foreign policies given the self-evident handicaps under which they labour.

The category excludes those countries which have 'graduated' from poverty, such as South Korea and Singapore. It includes the largely agricultural states whose per capita income languishes far below that of the OECD world. These poor states constitute about a quarter of the 193 members of the UN, and have a per capita income (GDP) of less than $1,000 a year.[5] Paul Collier, whose phrase 'the bottom billion' has focused attention on the LDCs, thought that the category contained around fifty-eight states, the majority in Africa, comprising one billion people, or a sixth (now less) of global population (Collier, 2007, 2010). The other criteria for qualifying as an LDC are weakness in human resource (for example, educational level) and economic vulnerability to upheaval, internal and external. If the income criterion were to be relaxed, however, to the level of $5,000 per year (bearing in mind that the EU average in 2012 was $32,000) this would add another 40 countries to the total, meaning that nearly half the world's states struggle with poverty, and are structurally on the defensive in their foreign relations.

Not only do such states lack the resources to be proactive in international affairs, with such things as interventions or major contributions to multilateral institutions being out of the question, but they also find it difficult to protect themselves against external interference. All too often they are subject to war washing across their frontiers, so that the distinction between civil and international conflict becomes meaningless – as in the Horn of Africa, or around the Great Lakes (Kaldor, 2013). Their foreign policy is dominated by the need for economic development and financial assistance, but also by the need for assistance in conflict resolution and nation-building. Diplomacy in these circumstances is successful if it can widen the negotiating margin of manoeuvre of a supplicant, but an effective diplomatic cadre and the resources to support it is usually one of the things which these states lack. Although many of them have wasted precious resources on building armed forces and absurd prestige projects (often encouraged by cynical rich states) they actually have little use for the military instrument. Even internal order is often at risk because the armed forces become a law unto themselves.

These generalizations do not fit all LDCs or all phases of their history. Countries do develop, reducing their vulnerability and making possible more self-assertion internationally. Jamaica's Michael Manley consciously reacted against the perception of dependence in the 1970s, and attempted to use foreign policy to break out of it, as had Kwame Nkrumah and Julius Nyerere, but with the same largely counterproductive results (Beshoff, 1988). Cuba did the same for half a century, incurring the heavy costs of the US embargo, and Venezuela under Hugo

Chavez used its oil resources to follow a similar path. Paul Kagame's authoritarian leadership of Rwanda, privileging good relations with the West, has turned a small country devastated by war into a self-confident and stable system hailed by some as a model for Africa. But most of the LDCs are still in very difficult situations. They do not have the options of the average developed state, that is of a relaxed independence with some free choice over association and cooperation with other states. In theory they have five options, but in practice their domestic situation makes only the first of them viable – that of accepting the disciplines of structural adjustment presented by international economic institutions, and not seeking to rock the boat by too much political activism. The other four are all unattractive or costly in various ways:

(1) A strategy of *solidarity* with other poor states. This looked like the way forward in the 1970s with the Group of 77; now the divisions within the group are too great.

(2) *Trailblazing*, rhetorical or practical. This was a line pursued variously by China, Cuba, Iran, Iraq and Libya. The costs require states to have secure sources of funds, and an impregnable domestic basis; only China has been strong enough to continue successfully on its own path.

(3) *Clientelism*, or attaching the fate of the state to a more powerful friend. Cuba and South Vietnam followed this path, only to discover their vulnerability to changes in internal patterns of power or in the regime of the patron. Microstates seem to have little other option (Wivel and Oest, 2010).

(4) *Isolation*, of which North Korea is the unattractive paradigm case.

All of these options are relatively extreme, and illustrate how LDCs have to make big sacrifices if they wish to assert their political values and independence. It is not surprising that most do not try, or are forced to change course after a costly attempt. More often than not the combination of poverty with an unforgiving external environment (witness the dragging of feet over the cancellation of Third World debts, and the protectionism of Western agriculture) ensures limited choices in public policy. Inevitably it is the elite rather than the people of these states who determine the trade-off to go for and the distribution of costs – and those elites do not always have a strong sense of public responsibility.

This said, it should not be assumed that LDCs are totally dissimilar from other states. They face the same general foreign policy issues, of security, regionalism, balancing the internal with the external, and ideology. It is just that their constraints are more pressing, and that foreign policy also has to be used for nation-building, and for consolidating the borders and governance of the state itself. In time, the same kind of decision-making issues and domestic pressures will occur in LDCs as in richer states: bureaucratic politics, groupthink, domestic factionalism and even public pressures are not the preserve of the developed alone (Hill, 1977). These syndromes are just more spasmodic and embryonic in the poorer countries, whose domestic and international environments tend to blur into one around the needs of development. Yet even the LDCs vary within the group, between large and microstates, the land-locked and the islands, those with resource potential and those which might be obliterated by rising sea levels. Not all, furthermore, are irrelevant to the global balance of power. When poverty coincides with a key geopolitical position, or some other form of wider value, the foreign policies of the resulting 'pivotal states' may be of great consequence for themselves and others (Chase, Hill and Kennedy, 1999, pp. 1–11).

Foreign Policy as Output – and Choice

The domestic environment undoubtedly impacts upon foreign policy. The issue is the significance of that impact. Generalization is difficult because of the unpredictability of the interplay with international factors. Both are filtered through the decision-making process, itself a domestic variable. This process then produces a set of positions and attitudes which may over time congeal into a discourse, or tradition. It represents the continuity of foreign policy and becomes institutionalized in processes, language and institutions (R. Cohen, 2001).

From this point of view foreign policy is an *output*, driven to a degree by domestic factors. Foreign policy traditions, while they represent a history of encounters with the world, have a rationale which is primarily national. Moreover in practice foreign policy is often severely constrained by domestic forces and actors. None of this, however, is enough to justify statements about the 'primacy of domestic politics' for single countries or particular periods, let alone across the board. The domestic factor is frequently central to our ability to understand foreign policy, and in some sense it provides its ultimate purpose. Nonetheless, the output here is 'foreign' policy and cannot be regarded simply as the external face of pre-packaged domestic positions. Because the interplay between inside and outside is perpetual and complex, in terms of causation the two sets of pressures cannot always be fully disentangled. It means also that in some cases the consequences go well beyond foreign policy, as was evident in relation to fascism. A more relevant example for the present day is that of the many 'transitional

states' in the international system, where the very process of constitution and reconstitution involves simultaneous attention to problems of
borders, recognition, regime, aid and nation-building, all of which face
both ways (Göl, 2013).

It is thus misleading to think of domestic *or* international explanations
of foreign policy (Snyder, 1991). We need to pay attention to a persistent
set of causal loops and overlaps. At the normative level, however, the
domestic dimension directs us to the question of choice; that is, how far
can a people control their own leaders, and how much influence can they
exert over the content of foreign policy? What are the most important
means by which domestic participation is made possible – and how far
does practice vary? In dealing with these issues the chapter which follows
prepares the ground for the book's conclusion, which attempts to make
sense of the changing place of foreign policy in our political and ethical
life.

Notes

1   Malala Yusafzai won the Nobel Prize at the age of 17 in 2014. She had
    started speaking out in favour of girls' education in Pakistan at the age of 11.
2   For the concept of a prebendal state see Chapter 2, p. 39.
3   Article 21 of the 14 March 2004 amendment to the Constitution of the
    People's Republic of China.
4   An exception is Tayfur (2003), which focuses interestingly on the 'semi-
    peripheral' cases of Greece and Spain, for whom European Community
    membership provided a boost to both development and political indepen-
    dence.
5   According to the United Nations Conference on Trade and Development
    (UNCTAD). There are currently 48 on UNCTAD's list.

Further Reading

Barkawi, Tarak and Laffey, Mark, eds, 2001. *Democracy, Liberalism, and War:
    Rethinking the Democratic Peace Debate.* This set of critical essays takes to
    task the ahistorical character of the democratic peace paradigm.
Brighi, Elisabetta, 2013. *Foreign Policy, Domestic Politics and International
    Relations: The Case of Italy.* Brighi's exemplary case study applies the strategic–
    relational approach to policy evolution over a full century.
Haass, Richard N., 2013. *Foreign Policy Begins at Home: The Case for Putting
    America's House in Order.* As a senior US practitioner, Richard Haass
    concludes that his country's foreign policy has been seriously undermined by
    neglecting the domestic foundations of power.

Halliday, Fred, 1999. *Revolution and World Politics: The Rise and Fall of the Sixth Great Power*. In one of his best books Halliday demonstrates the major impact revolution can have on international politics, using a wide range of historical examples.

Michelmann, Hans J., ed., 2009, *Foreign Relations in Federal Countries*. This is an authoritative comparative study on the increasingly active international roles of subnational units of federal states.

Chapter 10

Politics, Society and Foreign Policy

A democratic decision-maker is always aware of his or her responsibility to the society which lies behind the political process. But responsibility is ambiguous and relational because of the many constituencies which must be borne in mind: at home there are colleagues in government and party, the constituency voters who brought you to power in the first place, sponsors of various kinds and ultimately the electorate as a whole. In the international realm there are the allies, neighbours and colleagues in various cross-cutting networks, together with obligations undertaken to the international community as a whole – to say nothing of any sense of responsibility to future generations.

Feelings of responsibility do not necessarily coincide with others' expectations. In any case both are highly variable according to context, and difficult to identify empirically. This is partly because of the obscure nature of the evidence about the extent to which domestic populations are concerned about foreign policy. Little research has been done on this question, although much has been presumed. While it is clear that a growing number of people and groups now have stakes in external policy, at the same time there is much which remains specialized, arcane and remote to the silent majorities rooted in their particular societies – until the world smashes unexpectedly into their lives, as it did so literally and horribly for the people of New York and Washington on 11 September 2001.

In the rich countries we have become used to a peaceful, undisturbed life in which the world is ever more present, but mostly as a source of colourful stories and added value through trade and tourism. Occasional waves of indignation about excessive immigration, or even terrorist shocks, do not really disturb the sense of distance from the lived experience of those in other countries. Opinion polls regularly reveal a surprising, indeed shocking, level of factual ignorance about world geography and international affairs. Thus we cannot assume that there is necessarily a growing awareness of the great issues of foreign policy and international politics. The tragic upheavals of war and totalitarianism destroyed or rearranged the lives of hundreds of millions between 1914 and 1989. Yet for the grandchildren of those who suffered this is now history. The Battle of Stalingrad is now as much in the past for a student of today as was the Franco-German War of 1870 to the soldiers of 1942. The experience of occupation, or even of being conscripted to fight, is just as remote.

Of course this is an OECD-centred perspective. Across the world only a minority can truly harvest the benefits of peace and globalization. The populations of the Middle East, Indo-China and parts of Africa know only too well how the international can tear into their lives through war, environmental degradation, alien ideologies and the continuing consequences of imperialism. The attacks of 9/11 in the United States led quickly to the occupation of Afghanistan and less than two years later to the invasion of Iraq which in turn has destabilized the whole Middle East. The citizens of Israel live with the constant threat of missile attacks, while Palestinians in Gaza have suffered devastating losses in Israeli reprisal attacks. The dispute ripples out to disturb relations between Muslims and their fellow citizens in states across the world. Rising sea levels, desertification and excessive resource extraction threatens the well-being of millions in developing countries.

This chapter investigates the relationship between foreign policy and the political constituencies which lie behind it. A path is steered between the traditional paternalist assumption of an elite running foreign policy for the general good, and the implication of globalization theory that social movements and transnationalism have rendered foreign policy an empty vessel in any case. The following questions are posed: first, for whom is foreign policy conducted, in principle and in practice? Second, by what means are decision-makers held to account? The analysis begins with the formal mechanisms of foreign policy accountability, building on the discussion of constitutional structures in Chapter 9. This is followed by a survey of the channels which connect decision-makers to wider society, namely public opinion, interest groups and the mass media. The chapter ends by addressing the changing nature of civil society under conditions of increased mobility, analysing how degrees of diversity affect both national identity and foreign policy.

Accountability versus the Security State

Accountability is not the same as responsibility. Responsibility is about the awareness of acting for others as well as oneself; it begins with perceptions and values. Accountability is more formal, and refers to the ability to make those in office answerable for their actions, and to make them pay a penalty if their account is unsatisfactory according to the prevalent rules. In foreign policy the issue of accountability was brought to the fore by the First World War, meaning that we have now had over a century to wrestle with the problem. In few countries, however, have clear mechanisms been established, and even where they have, actual practice often does not live up to theory. Indeed, it can be argued that provisions for accountability have often been deliberately sacrificed in the presumed interests of security and of a credible executive – with legislators being more willing to go along with the attenuation of their powers in foreign policy than in any other area. When one adds in the dimension of the enormous growth in the bureaucracies of foreign, defence and intelligence policy-making in the twentieth century, it is easy to see how difficult democratic accountability is to achieve in practice, against what is too often a bloated, secretive and overbearing 'security state'.

Liberal democratic states make it an article of faith to restrain executive power and to seek a popular consensus for public policy. Even one-party systems, however, usually have formal provisions for some degree of answerability and participation in foreign policy-making. The Supreme Soviet had powers over the ratification of treaties (Aspaturian, 1971, pp. 592–5, 676–83), and the Chinese National People's Congress (NPC) likewise (Shambaugh, 1994, p. 215). That in practice they performed the function of rubber-stamps does not mean that their constitutional powers were meaningless. The NPC gets petitioned on issues such as human rights, the environment and information, but it works mainly through committees and is hardly a forum for open debate (Economy and Oksenberg, 1999). In the cumbersome pyramidal system of communism, views occasionally filter upwards through the transmission-belt system of party delegates, but are rarely controversial or short-circuited by media debate. The political systems of the Soviet Union and of the People's Republic were forged in war and revolution and found it difficult to evolve beyond their original command culture. The first collapsed, but the second has survived and shows some signs of slowly loosening up.

In many other states, even liberal democracies, parliaments are equally ineffective on foreign policy, being passive, inadequately informed and easily manipulated. The boost to democracy given by the end of the Cold War, and the apparent reduction in security concerns, has led to some changes, but it is a slow process. There are two interrelated dimensions at stake: *parliamentary control* and the verdict of the electors. Members of parliament (MPs) are representatives who exercise powers in the light of the views of the voters who gave them power, but they also follow the dictates of party and conscience, both of which (the first in particular) tends to take precedence over constituents' wishes – assuming they can be discerned. In foreign policy-making MPs have few constitutional levers to pull because of the presumption in most constitutions that the executive needs a free hand if the state is to be effectively protected. Still, parliaments are powerful symbols of popular political control, and make focal points for both insurgents and nervous leaders – as Boris Yeltsin revealed when suspending and shelling the Russian Supreme Soviet in 1993, and as the Egyptian military did when dissolving parliament during the Arab Spring (Abdelrahman, 2014; Light, 2000a).

The United States is an exception to most generalizations about democratic process. In terms of basic powers over foreign policy-making the US Congress has no rival (Ambrose, 1991–2; McCormick, 2012). It has considerable powers of its own, which the president cannot ignore. Thus accountability in the US can amount to legislators threatening the executive with their own, parallel, foreign policy if the president does not take their concerns into account. This was the case throughout Obama's negotiations with Iran over nuclear weapons, which took place against a backcloth of congressional threats to maintain or even increase sanctions (although that also helped the president's negotiating position with the government in Tehran). Difficulties like these seem to bear out Richard Neustadt's (1991) influential view of a relatively weak presidency forced to share power.

Congress also has the crucial power of the purse which keeps the president perpetually on a short lead when appropriations for defence or new commitments are needed (foreign policy purposes are not excluded, as in Britain, from the requirement to be specified in a budget for legislative approval). Congress extended powers further towards the end of the Vietnam fiasco by approving the War Powers Resolution (in 1973) which sets limits on the period in which the presidency can pursue an un-declared war. In practice, however, the presidency has little difficulty in finding ways round the war powers constraint, as was evident during the crises over Kosovo in 1999 and Libya in 2011. Furthermore major crises usually produce a solemn national consensus over going to war, as in the years immediately following 9/11, with the president's role as commander-in-chief in a time of emergency granting him much freedom. Thus while accountability to Congress hangs like a perpetual shadow over the White House, in practice it is a very uneven process with much depending on the issue. The president's ability to pressurize Israel has been fettered for decades. But its diplomacy in relation to many other actors, notably China, the EU and Russia, is broadly unconstrained.

Other democratic systems, mature or not, do not have such extensive provisions for parliamentary control. In some the executive is notably cautious about not running too far ahead of the legislature, for historical reasons. In the Federal Republic of Germany the Basic Law of 1949 does not in so many words forbid the use of troops 'out of area', but the political interpretation until the Federal Constitutional Court ruling of 1994 was that it did (Baumann and Hellmann, 2001). The Bundestag must still authorize action but in recent judgements the notion of a 'parliamentary army' has been qualified by giving the executive more operational freedom, especially in times of crisis (Aust and Vashakmadze, 2008). The French National Assembly voted down the European Defence Community in 1954 just as the US Senate had done with the League of Nations 35 years before. The Japanese Diet in 1955 threw out the idea of an extension of the Japanese–American security treaty, despite Foreign Minister Shigemitsu having signed a joint communiqué agreeing to it (R. Cohen, 1997, p. 132; Destler et al., 1976, p. 15). The House of Commons has given British governments a hard time over every treaty relating to accession to the European Communities and their development. After the Iraq War of 2003 it also, finally, began to assert itself over military interventions (Strong, 2014).

What is common to these cases is not the formal powers which parliaments have over foreign policy; these vary considerably, not least in their implementation. More important is the interpretation of the law, which itself depends partly on political culture and partly on particular circumstances. Given the number of occasions when even those parliaments with relevant powers do not assert themselves to halt treaties or to interrogate defence budgets, it is clear that it will take an unusual combination of circumstances for the executive to have a major foreign policy derailed by parliament at home. Even in the United States there will need to be both a deep lack of confidence in the government of the day plus a high degree of salience and concern about the issue concerned – probably the result of a long sequence of frustrations. Thus both President Carter and the Congress had had enough of Soviet behaviour in the Third World by the time they ended the second round of Strategic Arms Limitation Talks (SALT II) after the Soviet invasion of Afghanistan in December 1979. But the Congress was ready to throw out a treaty whatever Carter decided, and it is the knowledge of its *potential* power which is most inhibiting to a president. The same applied to Clinton's signature of the Kyoto Protocol on climate change towards the end of his time in office. He was fully aware that this was a symbolic gesture given the cross-party hostility to the measure in Congress.

At times, given these are two-level games, the potential obstruction can be useful to an executive. The German government was relieved in 2011 to be able to fall back on the need for parliamentary authorization when faced with the issue of an intervention in Libya. At other times, the blind eye tactic suits the legislature itself. The Congress was generally opposed to President Reagan's covert actions with the Contras in Central America, but at much the same time was prepared to overlook the arming of the *mujahidin* in Afghanistan. More constructively, where a legislature has a significant role in foreign policy-making, as with the

Danish Folketing, it creates a greater certainty, both at home and abroad, that commitments once entered into are legitimate and will hold – precisely because they are more difficult to achieve in the first place (Martin, 2000).

One neuralgic point where legislative activism can be expected is where a treaty agreement has implications for sovereignty, in terms of ceding powers or territory. The Israeli Knesset introduced a law in 1999 at the behest of the settlers in the Golan Heights specifying that no territory can be ceded to another country without a majority in the house (Navot, 2014, p. 46). This is the ultimate power of a parliament which makes any democratic leader cautious; legislators exist to make law, and increasingly the law bears on external relations. In the US *only* the Congress can acquire or cede territory. The UK government, well aware only two years after the Falklands War of how sensitive an issue the cession of Hong Kong to China would be, ensured that the Westminster Parliament had plenty of opportunities to discuss the Sino-British Agreement, even though only the Queen's signature was constitutionally required for ratification of a treaty, which technically this was not (Cradock, 1994, pp. 214–16; Hinton, 1994, p. 355).

Apart from legal considerations, parliamentary divisions stimulate public awareness and pressures on government. When legislation was sought in the New Zealand parliament to enshrine in law the ban on visits by nuclear-armed ships, it stirred up debate and precipitated a serious clash with the United States. The outcome was that the US suspended its guarantees, and the ANZUS (Australia, New Zealand, United States Security) Treaty, between 1986 and 1994 (Jackson and Lamare, 1988, pp. 175–6). Similarly, once the European Parliament had acquired in 1987 the 'power of assent' over association agreements concluded by the European Community, debate on the policy-making of external relations became notably more substantial.

Against these cases may be set a greater number, equally 'high politics' in character, where executives have been able to circumvent parliamentary powers without difficulty, or simply to drive a coach and horses through gaps not covered by the constitution. With sufficient hubris, the law is sometimes just broken, as Reagan did when continuing to arm the Contras in defiance of the Boland Amendment, or as Nixon and Kissinger had done through the secret bombing of Cambodia – which certainly breached the spirit, if not the letter, of the War Powers Resolution (Ambrose, 1991–2, p. 127). At least the latter had closed the loophole exploited by President Johnson nine years before, in 1964, when he got almost unanimous congressional support for the Tonkin Gulf Resolution, and thus a free hand to prosecute a war against North Vietnam, on the basis of the most flimsy, indeed fabricated, *casus belli*

(Ambrose, 2012, pp. 199–200). In the United States much depends on whether the president's party has a majority and/or on whether he is already in difficulties with Congress. In Britain and France, by contrast, war may still be undertaken by executive fiat, although the lofty disregard of parliamentary support may later come home to haunt leaders, as during the Suez crisis of 1956–7. Mrs Thatcher was wise enough to allow an emergency debate in the House of Commons on a Saturday (3 April 1982) before sending a task force to the Falklands three days later. Tony Blair was desperate to get a vote in favour of his war in Iraq in 2003. Both succeeded, but David Cameron got a nasty surprise when calling for a vote on military action against Syria in 2013.

Even the power over the purse strings may be circumvented – this is precisely what Colonel Oliver North was doing for President Reagan in arranging the secret arms deal with Iran which funded the Contras in Nicaragua (Tower et al., 1987). British governments have persistently slipped through the necessary funding for upgrading the nuclear deterrent via general defence estimates placed before the House of Commons. In Malaysia in 1988 the leader of the opposition demanded that full details of a proposed $1 billion arms deal with Britain be made public; his speech in the budget debate was not even reported in the local media. The Italian government moved in the 1990s to being one of the major contributors to UN peacekeeping efforts, with the Chamber of Deputies barely noticing (Andreatta and Hill, 1997, pp. 78–9).

On a day-to-day level, parliaments relate to foreign policy less through the exercise of formal powers than through supervision, scrutiny and investigation. Here too their capacity to constrain and participate is limited, but it is growing as foreign policy becomes ever more central to normal political life. Representatives usually have some means of questioning the executive on its activities. In the Westminster model, in use in various Commonwealth countries, this occurs through scheduled question-and-answer sessions. Unfortunately, civil servants soon become skilled in briefing ministers on how not to give away information, and on how to use the occasion for sending signals to other states as much as to their own citizens (Carstairs and Ware, 1991). Elsewhere, foreign ministers may be brought more regularly under the spotlight and cross-questioned on particular themes. But this will normally rely on the existence of a lively and independent foreign affairs committee (FAC).

It is now the norm for legislatures to have a committee specialising in foreign affairs on the American model, although it was not always so. All member states of the European Union now have FACs, and they are also well-established in the major Commonwealth democracies and in Japan. Unfortunately they are too often perceived as 'a nice club of honoured personalities who are satisfied to have regular exchanges of views with the foreign minister without claiming directly to control and influence the government's strategy' (Stavridis and Hill, 1996, p. 71). They also provide opportunities to travel abroad, leading to reports which go unnoticed or are out of date by the time they appear. As in the relatively infrequent plenary debates which take place on foreign policy in national assemblies, it is evident that only a small proportion of members is informed and interested about foreign affairs, of whom many will be pursuing special interests, such as the need to gain a particular defence contract for their own constituency.

Granted the deficiencies of parliamentarians in relation to foreign policy, it is the FACs which represent the best hope of exerting sustained pressure on an executive. Governments are still sensitive to reports which may be noticed abroad and used to embarrass them – as with a 2015 House of Lords report which characterized the UK and the EU as sleepwalking into the Ukraine crisis. It was almost immediately followed by the (anticlimactic) announcement that 75 troops were being sent to help train the Ukrainian military. FACs can at least build up the expertise over time with which to challenge the diplomatic specialists. They may, if able to insist on the presence of ministers (and even better, the release of documents), expose errors and dissimulations. Their reports – especially those investigating policy fiascos – carry the weight of a public body and will often be taken up by journalists and scholars. So long as the committees can avoid being recruited into the process of diplomacy itself – for example by acting as spokesmen abroad – and free up their membership from the control of party managers, then they will at least be able to engage the executive in a meaningful dialogue. Although the foreign relations committees of the US Congress are now less in the public eye than during the Vietnam War, in conjunction with others such as the committees on appropriations, armed services, commerce, and intelligence, they keep up a remorseless pressure on the White House, which knows that if it wants to get measures approved it needs to invest in a major political effort, involving side-payments and concessions. This is particularly evident in foreign trade policy, where the lobbies proliferate, but it can also happen on purely political matters, since key groups can exert a veto on official policy by the threats of publicity, filibustering and withdrawing electoral support.

No other national system yet has the resources to rival the US effort (the total staff of the two houses of Congress is around 16,000), but most parliaments are coming to realize that detailed forensic work through committees is the essential precondition of plenary debate and ultimately of the very principle of democratic control (Peterson, Reynolds and Wilhelm, 2010). Otherwise accountability is left to special interests, which claim all too easily to be representing 'the national interest'. This was the case with the Falkland Islands in the late 1970s and early 1980s, when a small group in the House of Commons was able to talk out a government proposal for a negotiated solution with Argentina. The British government simply decided not to invest the political effort in overruling it, and paid the price later with a major crisis. If expertise is spread more widely, enabling a sizeable minority of MPs to debate foreign affairs on a regular basis, then it puts governments on the *qui vive* in relation to the substance of an issue as well as to domestic difficulties.

The second way in which formal accountability is exercised over foreign policy is through *the verdict of the electors*, who can make governments pay the price for errors or simply decide to change direction by voting in a new party or coalition. At one level it is difficult to see how elections do give citizens a role in foreign policy. They take place only every four to seven years, and represent crude choices between the large package deals offered by the main parties. Voters usually prioritize tax and welfare issues, and in any case there is not often on offer a clear choice on foreign policy strategies given that the parties cluster round the status quo as the safest option. In periods of war, when voters might actually wish to have a say in the foreign policy questions deciding their fate, elections are often suspended. At best there will be pressure not to undermine the government by voting for peace parties.

In this context it is not surprising if election outcomes seem to have little to do with foreign policy. In the 1983 German election, for example, the conservative Christian Democratic Union of Germany (CDU)/ Christian Social Union in Bavaria (CSU) party was returned to government at a time when there was considerable unrest in the country over the Euromissiles affair. In 1992 and 1996 Bill Clinton deliberately campaigned on domestic issues alone, partly because he genuinely wished to concentrate on internal priorities but also because he correctly deduced that foreign policy was not a strong suit for the Democrats in general, and (certainly in 1996) for himself in particular (Galston and Makins, 1988). The case can be made that conservative parties generally find it easier to 'wrap themselves in the flag' and to portray progressive parties as 'soft' on the national interest. On the other hand this would suggest that conservatives ought to campaign on foreign policy questions more frequently than seems to be the case. The arrival of human rights concerns on the foreign policy agenda may have reversed this advantage to a degree, but the more likely result is the consolidation of the progressive vote and the erosion of bipartisanism.

Even in the past voters have occasionally distinguished between foreign and domestic policy – and in making such distinctions they show themselves to have the capacity for *judgement*, which is a different thing from expertise. In 1945 the world was astonished to see the British people vote out of office, in a landslide victory for the Labour Party, the war hero Winston Churchill. This result did not arise from any disapproval of Churchill's conduct of the war but was the product of years of discontent with the old social and political order. Having made the huge effort for victory, the British people were determined to reap some reward at home. In that they thought that the war had been brought on by the failures of the Chamberlain government in 1938 and 1939, voters were punishing the Conservative Party, and not Churchill, who had himself been marginalized in the 1930s (Addison, 1975, pp. 266–9; Calder, 1971). This degree of sophistication was also evident in the election of Clinton in 1992, which was a slap in the face for the Republican presidents who had been in office from 1981, and who had 'won the Cold War' so dramatically. It also showed no inclination to reward President George H. W. Bush for his victory in the first Gulf War.

Only in countries with (1) active foreign policies and (2) well-established democracies will foreign-policy debate emerge at election time. It is the kind of higher order activity that is difficult to achieve even in mature systems. Yet it is also true that 'foreign policy is ... a prism through which voters judge the basic soundness of a candidate to govern the country' (Galston and Makins, 1988, pp. 3–4). The ability to run a foreign policy safely and successfully in a dangerous world is an attribute which contributes significantly to general images of competence. It is therefore played on by the spin doctors who have dominated elections since at least the arrival of President Kennedy's 'Camelot' in 1960. Kennedy was untried in foreign policy at one of the most dangerous times of the Cold War, a weakness which was reflected in his victory over Richard Nixon by the narrowest of margins. Other American elections, such as those of Eisenhower in 1952, Reagan in 1980 and George W. Bush in 2004, were also determined in part by the image of a president who was strong in foreign policy (Nincic, 2004). More recently Vladimir Putin has built his popularity around the idea that only he can restore Russia's international image as a country to be reckoned with (Light, 2000b). Elections are always an opportunity to play up the gravitas that comes with office and the opportunities for international statesmanship.

It may be just as well that personality and world events both have their roles, for there are very few occasions when voters actually get a choice in key foreign policy issues. In 1968 there was a crucial opportunity for the two main American parties to offer the voters a choice of strategies at the most difficult time in the Vietnam War, when Lyndon Johnson had withdrawn from the race in a funk, and the best way forward was genuinely uncertain. In the event, neither Nixon nor Humphrey gave a clear lead as to peace or war; both promised vaguely to achieve both peace and honour, but without specifying the policy implications. In office Nixon then escalated the war while trying to scale down the number of US troops. This was a major failure for democracy. Foreign policy does not need to dominate elections often, but this was the obvious exception. Neither party trusted the American people, or indeed itself.

The same is true in other states. The United Kingdom has had 18 general elections since the Second World War. Arguably in three of them (1964, 1983 and 1987) the Labour Party was damaged by having an image of being unreliable on defence, in particular through association with the Campaign for Nuclear Disarmament. The second two of these were lost, not least because the two leaders of the time, Michael Foot and Neil Kinnock, were effectively characterized as being unsound on defence. Foot held few cards on foreign policy; indeed he was proud of never having visited the United States. For her part Mrs Thatcher had just conducted the victorious campaign in the Falklands. Labour ran scared and actively tried to avoid giving the voters a clear foreign policy choice. In most of the other elections, despite some obvious possibilities for debates on international matters (Korea in 1950 and 1951, Suez in the 1959 campaign, east of Suez in 1970, the Middle East in 1974) the campaigns were almost wholly domestic in tone. Voters would have had difficulty in obtaining information on the parties' foreign policy differences.

There are structural limits on the extent to which foreign policy accountability can be achieved through democratic elections, which are both inherent in the complexity of the process and the product of a security state ethos among elites. There are, however, some signs of change which might at least raise the profile of foreign policy at elections. One is the blurring of foreign and domestic issues, which makes it less easy in an election to seal off foreign policy into a separate, bipartisan, compartment. Another is the way in which the politicization of foreign policy weakens both bipartisanism and internal party discipline, aided by the end of the Cold War but predating it in origin. Thus Tony Blair's Labour Party suffered losses at the polls through the discontent of its own supporters with the war in Iraq, reducing the size of the 2005 victory and probably contributing to the defeat of 2010. Some external issues even cut across parties, leading to political turmoil, as with the various debates over Euroscepticism, immigration and humanitarian intervention in many EU member states over recent years. The process may not create clear electoral choices, but it does weaken the ability of parties to manage the argument.

Elections are, therefore, likely to offer more of a platform for debate on foreign policy. But given the range of bread-and-butter issues at stake, and the sensitivity of many external relationships, voters will be able to do little more than to indicate broad preferences. Even when new radical parties emerge, as with the Movimento Cinque Stelle (M5S) in Italy, which curtly rejects the usual foreign policy consensus, the international dimension tends not to be the first concern. Yet democracy is unpredictable by definition, which keeps executives guessing. Although foreign policy-makers exploit the lacunae they find in the processes of accountability, an embarrassing row over foreign policy, in parliament or at election time, is to be avoided if possible for the damage it can do to personal or party reputations. Thus US foreign policy virtually shuts down in an election year because of risk-averse candidates. Whether justifiably or not, public opinion looms large in their minds as a potential constraint.

Public Opinion

Politicians often argue that their hands are tied by public opinion, or at the least that they have to work within the limits set by it. Campaigners also set store by this belief. The *Anti-Slavery Reporter* in the nineteenth century claimed that public opinion, 'strongly expressed', was 'the steam' which would enable Parliament to 'annihilate Colonial Slavery at one majestic stroke' (Lean, 1998), which the remarkable Jubilee 2000 campaign to cancel the debts of the poorest countries took as its inspiration, shrewdly using sound bites from rock stars to get global publicity and mobilising the grass roots through the churches (including the Pope).[1] Thus even in foreign policy a wave of concern can sometimes lead to change. For the most part, however political scientists tend to be sceptical and to side with critics who complain that while public opinion gets lots of lip-service it is in practice ignored. All these positions need scrutinising within the special context of foreign policy.

The concept of public opinion is difficult to pin down. It refers at once to an actor in the political process and to an object of influence. Academic writing has, however, done a good deal to establish the parameters of the problem over the past 40 years. On that basis there are four preliminary conclusions which may be drawn.

First is the by now familiar but fundamental distinction between mass and attentive opinion, central to any issue which cannot even be made sense of without specialized knowledge (compare, for example, the state of the nation's hospitals on which most people have a view, derived from experience, with the technical problem of international cooperation over epidemics). This is not the same as a distinction between elite and mass, as the latter includes all sections of society, from the illiterate to Nobel Prize winners. But it does differentiate between the whole, which will only rarely be sufficiently focused on a foreign policy issue as to display a collective animus, and the minority, which takes a persistent and knowledgeable interest in international affairs (Almond, 1950). The latter will vary in size according to the location, culture and degree of development of a country, but even in western Europe it is unlikely to be more than 20 per cent of the adult population, and may be much less – in a Eurobarometer opinion poll in 2013, 77 per cent of Europeans said that they had never heard of the Millennium Development Goals, which were formulated by the UN in consultation with around one thousand NGOs to provide focal points for assisting the large proportion of the world's population which is trapped in poverty (European Commission, 2013a). This does not mean that people are unconcerned or ungenerous – in fact the same survey showed that 48 per cent would be willing to pay more for their groceries to help producers in developing countries. It is just that interest goes up and down according to the salience of an issue, which will depend on the initiatives of politicians, on the media and interest groups, and on the turn of events. The 'attentive' group can swell quickly, especially in times of crisis. Otherwise interest is latent or passive. More particularly there is a contrast between the priority which the majority gives to domestic affairs, and the generally more internationalist attentive public. In a US poll in the 1990s 84 per cent of 'the elite' were willing to go to war to defend South Korea from an invasion by North Korea, but only 45 per cent of the general public took the same view (Alterman, 1997). Against this Destler and Kull (1998) argued convincingly that Americans tended to hold more internationalist views than they were given credit for, with the implication that the right kind of leadership would be able to build support for the kind of multilateralist policies more associated with the European Union.

The second proposition which most students of foreign policy would accept is that there is a widespread degree of ignorance about the details of international affairs, and even the basics of geography. It is difficult to form an opinion about the European Union if you do not know the names of its member states, or where to find them on a map. In the midst of the arguments raging in the early 1970s about Britain's entry into the European Communities only 17 per cent of those questioned in the UK knew that the EEC had nine members, and the location of its headquarters (Jowell and Spence, 1975, pp. 1–7). At the end of the decade, in 1979, only 60 per cent correctly identified what the initials EEC stood for. The figures for NATO and the IMF were even lower, at 33 per cent and 44 per cent respectively, although interestingly the UN was identified by 85 per cent of people and the IRA, whose actions were very much closer to home, by 75 per cent (Hastings and Hastings, 1981, p. 89).

There are, however, some indications that things are improving. In 2013, 71 per cent of those sampled in the EU knew that Switzerland is not a member state, and 69 per cent knew that the Union had 27 states (European Commission, 2013b). In the United States, whereas in 1988 one in five could not name a single European country and only one in three could find Vietnam, where nearly 60,000 Americans had died, in 2014, 67 per cent knew that Daesh was operating in Syria and 60 per cent that Ukraine had once been part of the Soviet Union (*The Economist*, 1988; Pew Research Center, 2014). Respondents from smaller countries with a higher proportion of graduates, such as Sweden or Luxembourg, do better on these kinds of tests, but it is possible to be cautiously optimistic that the decades of 24/7 news and ever more school and college courses on international affairs may be starting to have beneficial effects.

Most people do not have the knowledge of world politics taken for granted by diplomats or journalists, but that does not stop them having opinions or making judgements, nor should it. In a developed democracy, at least, people can improve their knowledge quite quickly if they so wish. But lack of knowledge does undermine individuals' confidence in their ability to participate in the political process, and heightens the elite perception of an ill-informed mass whom it would be irresponsible to trust with decisions. In China or Russia there is no question of any serious debate being permitted on foreign and security policy, but even in liberal democracies, with the exception of Switzerland and rare referenda elsewhere, the main lines of international policy are not presented as being open for choice.

This is the third of our general conclusions, that the public are inevitably followers, not leaders, when it comes to shaping policy. Citizens' passivity between elections, plus a tendency to be fatalistic about the possibilities of change, means that public opinion can be ignored or have its name taken in vain. Decision-makers hold four vital cards: (i) the power of initiative; (ii) the capacity to define external threats; (iii) control over information and propaganda and (iv) the ultimate power of the state to coerce. Leaders issue the cues and the public tend to pick them up. France is the best contemporary example; despite its tradition of political literacy and intellectual ferment, to say nothing of setbacks like the Arab Spring, there is remarkably little debate about the direction of French foreign policy, which a confident elite continues to direct.

Occasionally it becomes clear that there are risks in taking an apparently content and suggestible public for granted. In 1999 the UN conducted what it claimed was 'the largest survey of public opinion ever conducted – of 57,000 adults in 60 countries, spread across all six continents'. This found that while most people thought elections were fair, 'two-thirds of all respondents considered that their country was not governed by the will of the people. This opinion held even in some of the oldest democracies in the world' (UN General Assembly, 2000, pp. 9–11). This shows that the conditions of distrust and cynicism exist for occasional resistance. When a government ignores the actual feelings of its people, as opposed to its perceptions of their views, a political earthquake can ensue, with unpredictable consequences, even over foreign policy.

When this happens it is because of the impact of the last of our four parameters: the tendency on the part of government to confuse the voice of the people with a particular channel through which opinion is being expressed. Decision-makers naturally look to the most articulate elements in society for evidence of what the public is thinking. They may assume that silence means consent, or they may take the hubbub in press and television to be widely representative – a transmission belt of democratic feeling, rather than one particular source of opinion. The same is true for parliamentarians, who are representatives not delegates (Burke, 1774, pp. 63–70). In modern conditions leaders are particularly likely to interpret the activity of attentive opinion, in the form of pressure groups, as the voices which matter most, because they seem to care most. Pluralist theories of politics make the same assumption.

Steven Lukes (1974) and others have shown that this distorts the truth. The politically active may have a better idea than most as to grass-roots opinion but they have their own special interests and perceptual blinkers. It is all too easy for decision-makers and their privileged partners to lock arms in a closed circle of complacency as to what politics is about. They assume that the passive and the silent are content to act as spectators to democracy. Then, on occasions, they get taken by surprise (Enloe, 1996, p. 189; Hill, 1999). The bitter outpourings in Russia in the summer of 2000 against the arrogance of the military in not seeking foreign help early enough to save the crew of the foundering submarine *Kursk* was a sharp lesson for Vladimir Putin, previously insulated from the people by his past as a KGB officer and by his facile entry into office. The greatest lesson of all was administered by the peoples of Eastern Europe when they finally managed to throw off Moscow-imposed communism through peaceful revolution. That this was possible only in 1989, and not in the abortive risings of 1956 in Hungary and 1968 in Czechoslovakia, tells us something about the need for conditions to be ripe before popular resistance can succeed. But it also demonstrates the immense strength of the people when united and facing a government whose will to use force had been weakened through a loss of legitimacy. It was spectacular evidence of how even elites disposing of the fullest apparatus of internal surveillance can misperceive the feelings of their own citizens. Their sonar had picked up 'merely the echo of their own propellers' (B. Cohen, 1973, pp. 178–9).

There will always be cases of misinterpreting public opinion badly. Neville Chamberlain was so entranced by the welcome he received at Heston Airport on his return from Munich in October 1938, and by his overwhelmingly favourable postbag, that he came to believe in the myth of his ability to know what the people wanted. Thus when he received a critical postbag after taking Britain into war in September 1939, he interpreted it as the product of an unrepresentative minority. He could not believe that the majority had not followed his own change of direction (Hill, 1991, pp. 116, 295).

Some indicators of public opinion are evidently more objective than others. Unless amounting to wholescale revolution, demonstrations will always be subject to the kind of cognitive dissonance displayed by Anthony Eden in 1956, when citing a bus driver's letter to the effect that 80 per cent of a hostile demonstration in London over Suez was composed of foreigners, and therefore did not count (Eden, 1960, p. 546). Tony Blair and his advisers were, however, rattled by the huge demonstration of 15 February 2003 against the Iraq War even if they concluded that this just showed the country to be divided (A. Campbell, 2007, p. 667). Referenda and opinion polls, however, are more difficult to overlook. The latter have been used increasingly after 1945, as party managers have sought to discover how best to woo voters, and how to stave off embarrassing media criticisms. Referenda are still unusual on foreign policy issues, and they always contain the dangers of manipulation and populism, but turn-out tends to be high, suggesting that they are welcomed by citizens. The results set the outline of policy for the medium term and make backsliding by government difficult. The Swiss, for whom referenda are a way of life, could not possibly enter the EU without popular approval in a referendum. Indeed, in 1985, 75 per cent of the poll voted against Switzerland even entering the United Nations, with all 26 cantons voting against. After that few could be in any doubt as to public opinion on the issue, until the question was raised again in 1997, leading to acceptance of entry in the referendum of 2002. The vote in 1997 by 74 per cent against opening accession negotiations with the EU made it impossible to reopen the question in the foreseeable future. On the other hand in 2009 the extension by a bilateral agreement of the freedom of movement principle to Bulgaria and Romania was approved by 56 per cent, giving that policy a legitimacy it has lacked in some actual EU member states. Referenda in Denmark, Ireland and France on aspects of European integration over the last 30 years have forced the governments of these countries to take on board the concerns of their populations about sovereignty, defence and enlargement.

After such setbacks governments become even more cautious about embarking on referenda, and about their wording, with good reason. For a referendum made legitimate by a good turn-out makes it impossible for a government to interpret the public's wishes on that issue in a cavalier way, and will always increase circumspection. That is why there have been moves in the Israeli parliament to ensure that those parts of the occupied territories which have been annexed by Israel (East Jerusalem and the Golan Heights) can only be relinquished in any peace deal, failing a two-thirds majority in the Knesset, by a national referendum.[2] This will naturally tie the hands of Israeli negotiators in future diplomacy, which they may or may not welcome.

Attention to opinion polls represents either a fetishising of the *vox populi* or a fiendish instrument of political spinning, according to one's point of view. Polls, like any statistics, are certainly not inherently neutral and reliable. Vladimir Putin's approval ratings have always been high, often going over 80 per cent. It is anyone's guess as to the extent this figure reflects respondents being afraid to reveal hostility. More accurate, paradoxically, are the private samplings taken by governments, such as the police reports on censored letters which Mussolini saw in 1942 and 1943, showing clearly the extent of popular disillusion with his rule (Muggeridge, 1947, pp. 519, 527). These are what Jervis (1970) called an 'index' of actual attitudes or behaviour. Although polling, which George Gallup began in the United States in 1935, has become a refined and indispensable instrument of government in the past few decades, it is only recently that it has become routinely used to measure attitudes on foreign policy. In this the arrival of the surprisingly accurate internet polling firms, which can access large numbers of people easily and quickly, has opened up the process. What is more, the growth of interest in international affairs through media attention and the interpenetration of home and abroad, has made governments more sensitive, and less confident about a domestic consensus behind their diplomacy. Foreign policy crises have always been tests of a government's competence, but now even some routine foreign issues achieve daily visibility, thus becoming potential sources of embarrassment and vote losers.

There are transnational elements to governments' concern for public opinion. Israeli Prime Minister Benjamin Netanyahu's advisers concluded that his best chance of reaching the Russian immigrants in his country was to appear on the Russian-language TV shows which most of them watch on cable. Accordingly Netanyahu's trip to Georgia, the Ukraine and Moscow in March 1999 was 'first and foremost a campaign trip'. Given the forthcoming general election, and the large number of immigrants from the ex-Soviet Union, this reaped dividends in terms of the 'reams of articles, stacks of photographs and many minutes of campaign time dedicated to Netanyahu and his pitch' (Harman, 1999). Diasporas play important roles in and for particular countries. Thus

Nicolas Sarkozy held an election meeting in London in 2012, aware not only that it contained around 113,000 French people with the right to vote in the 'Third Overseas Constituency', but that many were high-flying opinion formers working in the financial sector.[3] In this context, however, voting is less than half the story. Governments are increasingly anxious about transnational diaspora ties leading to the fragmentation of public opinion, with damaging consequences for foreign policy through demonstrations, social disharmony and even terrorism (Hill, 2013; Vaïsse, 2010).

Despite this trend decision-makers still largely focus on public opinion as part of their own and others' domestic environments. Thus it is common to come across discussions of how Europeans and Americans may be growing apart because of divergences between their respective publics (Robert Cooper, 2012; Kagan, 2003). The existence of sovereign states based on separate political communities means that is natural to conceptualize of public opinion as being distinctively national. This why references to wider constituencies, such as Atlantic, Asian or African opinion, have less political traction. Europe is a strange exception, inviting generalization because of the European Union, but is still internally diverse enough to make Kagan's comparison between the US as Mars and Europe as Venus seem facile.

Framings of public opinion matter, for ultimately it is a 'notional constraint' (Hill, 1979, p. 378). By this is meant a pressure which exists at least as much in the minds of decision-makers as it is embodied in substantive elements like law, institutions, demonstrations. However much statistical evidence is provided, its political importance means that public opinion always has a 'constructed' element. On any given foreign policy issue decision-makers will have an image of the public's view, degree of interest and mood which may or may not be supported by 'the facts'. Indeed the nature of the facts is inherently contestable, given that the public is large, amorphous, divided and reliant on transmission belts. Democratic politicians may obsess over daily opinion polls on their electoral chances, and rely on focus groups for broader issues. But their preconceptions, reinforced by personal encounters, also play a large part.

If a view of what the public wants (or abhors) is held strongly enough it may become a self-fulfilling prophecy in that decision-makers will feel inclined to bow the knee, and the myth of an influential public is born. This happened after the Vietnam War, from which the US is commonly thought to have withdrawn because of opposition at home, but where there is evidence to show that public opinion was not ahead of official decisions, and indeed was generally permissive (Herring, 1987, pp. 39–55). Yet ever since one of the most prominent 'lessons' of Vietnam has been the need not to 'test the endurance of the American public to a point where the outcome can no longer be sustained by our political process' (Kissinger, 2007). In the long term the myth did not stop future interventions, but it certainly made George H. W. Bush cautious about an Iraqi occupation in 1991, and Bill Clinton averse to sending ground troops into the Balkans, and Somalia, in the decade which followed.

Democratic leaders do not always exploit the inherent passivity of the public to the extent they might. They are, after all, immersed in their country's political culture like everyone else, and are themselves members of the public. They want and need to believe in accountability because it relieves them of some responsibility, and because it avoids the cognitive dissonance which comes from speechifying about democracy while behaving like Stalin. On any given occasion this does give the alert politician the opportunity to have it both ways, but for the most part decision-makers keep a close eye on the shadow flickering in the cave behind them.

Interest Groups and Foreign Policy Corporatism

Even attentive public opinion requires organization, if it is to be an actor in the policy process. Risse-Kappen's study (1991) concluded that in established democracies the more decentralized the system and the stronger the social groups capable of mobilising public opinion, the more opportunities the latter had for influencing policy-makers. It is evident that the groups seeking to influence foreign policy have multiplied since 1945, even if they are hardly as new a phenomenon as is often assumed. They are more visible, and have acquired a degree of informal legitimacy in the political systems of complex societies, where governments require dialogue with their citizens on an increasing range of issues, many of them intermestic. As a result, in some cases they can be drawn into a form of corporatism, whereby interest group leaders and government officials have more in common than either have with their rank and files. The revolving door of appointments between the two professional worlds makes this more likely.

Interest groups by definition start with their own specific concerns, relating to particular 'stakes' in society or distinctive cherished values, but they also, to a greater or lesser degree, transmit mass opinion to the centre. A double distinction must be made at the outset, between interest groups and pressure groups, and between interest groups and cause groups. Many interest groups will wish to influence policy and are therefore also pressure groups. But some exist simply to enable citizens to mobilize themselves around common interests – sporting federations are a good example – and will only occasionally need to take on the role of pressure group. Cause groups are a subset of pressure groups, without being interest groups. They exist in order to change the world, but instead of defending stakes which the members hold jointly, whether as car workers or hikers, they arise out of common value positions, and a desire to achieve a given good independent of their connection to it. The groups in rich countries which devote themselves to helping developing countries are a prime case in point. Thus, cause, interest and pressure groups are interconnected but distinct categories (Milbrath, 1967).

Many of these groups have developed considerable expertise, resources and (as we saw in Chapter 8), transnational scope. The more important, like Amnesty, RAND (Research and Development Corporation) or the Stockholm International Peace Research Institute, target many governments and their influence must be assessed on a regional or global basis. They also act as much on civil society, nationally or transnationally, as on governments (Stone and Denham, 2004). But there are still important national organizations. The Foreign Policy Association of the United States, founded in 1918, and doing a huge amount of work to spread knowledge of international issues among schools, colleges and citizens' groups, is a foremost example – even if other countries struggle to emulate it.

In terms of individual issue areas, pressure groups can be effective, although there is much variability according to historical and national context. There can be little doubt that the rise in British overseas aid levels, to the point where the UN target of 0.7 per cent of GDP is now being enshrined in law, owes much to the persistence of the many pro-development groups active in the UK. More negatively, nationalist groups in Japan have made it very difficult for governments to envisage accepting public responsibility for the aggression and atrocities of the 1930s and 1940s, as Germany has done and as they have often been advised to do by their diplomatic partners. There are thus still significant obstacles arising from the past to the development of relations with Japan's two most important neighbours, China and South Korea.

In particular sectors where the government either rates the issue low on its agenda, or is concerned not to engage in a public struggle, groups may have a veto on the way in which policy develops. Various national and ethnic groups within the United States are seen as having this capacity, particularly the Cubans, the Greeks, the Irish, the Jews and the Poles, although matters are rarely so simple (T. Smith, 2000). While these groups are better organized and have more electoral clout, than, say, the Native American population, it is by no means clear that US policy in relation to their concerns would be any different without their input. In any case, the more a group's influence is celebrated, the more others try to counterbalance it. This has happened with the Cuban lobby, whose conservative nature frustrated the new generation of Cuban-Americans wanting to open up the island, and who increasingly made their voice heard in Washington. The Obama administration was receptive, but without a change in the lobby a new policy would have been very difficult. Similarly, where one national lobby seems to have an inside track it is not long before its rivals are hiring consultants to help counterbalance them. Thus Turkey, noting the activity of the Greek-American diaspora, but also desperate to counter the Armenian lobby's attempts to get Congress to label the huge number of Armenian deaths after 1915 as genocide, spent millions of dollars to improve its own influence on the Hill, with some success in that a genocide resolution was never formally voted on (Narayanswamy, Rosiak and LaFleur, 2009). In a pluralist system groups compete in the political market and can cancel each other out. This is particularly true of economic groups, which are amongst the most active given the international dimension of most economic issues.

Even powerful lobbies may be outflanked by governments when they choose to ride out a public storm, as they often can, given the relative infrequency of elections. All American presidents have to tread carefully when they consider withdrawing support from Israeli actions, for the American Israel Public Affairs Committee (AIPAC) is always on the alert for any signs of shifts in US Middle East policy and is able to mobilize significant pressure at short notice. Support for Israel is strong in Congress even without AIPAC's sophisticated lobbying, as evident in the three invitations to Prime Minister Netanyahu to address joint sessions, in 2011, 2012 and 2015 – the last a blatant boost to Netanyahu's own election campaign.[4] But the very strength of a lobby eventually breeds a reaction. According to *Fortune* magazine in 1997 AIPAC was the only foreign policy group in the top 25 lobbies, and the second most powerful in the country after the American Association of Retired Persons (T. Smith, 2000, pp. 110–15). Since it has hardly become weaker since, the Israeli lobby is widely believed, especially outside the US, to determine American policy on the Middle East, a perception which has important consequences.

On the other hand a strong critique of AIPAC did belatedly emerge from establishment circles as well as the American left. In 2006 the senior academics John Mearsheimer and Stephen Walt (2006) published a robust analysis of how the Israeli tail was wagging the American dog in foreign policy. This appeared first in London, as their original New York publisher had backed off its original agreement, and caused a predictable storm of controversy – as did the subsequent book version (2007). There is no doubt that despite the criticisms which were made of their thesis, some merited, but many merely political, the intervention by Mearsheimer and Walt both gave voice to, and helped to catalyse, a growing concern about the disproportionate influence of this very well-funded and connected lobby group, as about the strategy of unconditional support for Israel with which it was associated.

When key values are at stake, or where there is a risk of serious upheaval, some groups have to be heard. No Greek government could have ignored the nationalist outrage against the former Yugoslav Republic of Macedonia, for having taken the name of Macedonia on independence (Veremis, 1995). Similarly, it was impossible even for the centre-left elements in the government of Concertación Democrática in Chile in 1999 not to protest to the British government over the arrest of General Pinochet (Menesis, 1999, pp. 23–5). In a dangerously divided country, the organized right was simply too strong to be allowed the luxury of painting the government in anti-patriotic colours. But on matters less central to the character of the state, governments can usually find ways of averting pressure from sectoral or cause groups.

It is in their collective impact that societal groups have most impact on foreign policy. Pluralism creates a web of activity in which governments as well as interest groups get caught, and in which a number of groups may act in broadly the same direction even if not in an actual coalition. In foreign policy this has produced a number of examples of the cumulative impact of a range of groups operating in parallel to box a government in. For example the number and extent of the foreign aid lobbies in the Netherlands and Scandinavian countries ensure that their Overseas Development Assistance (ODA) spending remains at a high level even in times of financial retrenchment. With more dramatic consequences was the persistent pressure from organized peace groups on the Conservative administrations of Stanley Baldwin and Neville Chamberlain in the 1930s, meaning they had little incentive to rearm or to abandon appeasement. This was despite the freedom bestowed by their huge majority in the House of Commons (Ceadel, 1980). Just as significantly the French right, acting through various extra-parliamentary groups, some violent, some not, brought down the Fourth Republic over the Algerian crisis in 1958, while the wide range of companies, trades unions and towns with a vested interest in defence spending reinforces the political disposition among US decision-makers for a global military role. In such cases collective pressure does not even need to be brought to bear on policy. After a while a tacit consensus is established between pressure groups and officialdom which becomes a structural feature (Held et al., 1999, pp. 137–9).

Organized opinion focuses on getting close to the seat of power. By the same token it may be drawn in too close, and lose some of its independence. If this becomes a permanent arrangement groups become what has been called 'parastate organisations', effectively serving the functions of the state while remaining private (Eisenach, 1994; Parmar, 1999). In such form they may be subsidized directly or indirectly by the state, and develop common definitions of problems and solutions. Inderjeet Parmar (2012) and others have argued from a Gramscian perspective that while ideas, groups and individuals make a difference, if they come to share the same 'state spirit', the necessary tensions between those in power and those seeking accountability will become lost in a form of intellectual (and sometimes institutional) corporatism. It is certainly no accident that in most countries the principal institute of foreign affairs is close to government, and often significantly subsidized by it. Even when no money changes hands, as is currently the case with Chatham House (the Royal Institute of International Affairs) in London, it is difficult not to take cues from officialdom via research projects, conferences and visiting speakers.

Such institutes are perceived abroad as being staffed by what Chadwick Alger (1962) labelled 'external bureaucrats' (Parmar, 2004). The Council on Foreign Relations in New York is the most studied example, and indeed one which has been important in creating and reproducing consensus over American foreign policy, particularly during the move away from isolationism and during the Cold War. Such a privileged position, however, carries with it the inevitable risk of becoming detached from wider society, and overtaken by powerful new ideas and groups. Thus the Council was seen by the radical right as part of the very East Coast establishment which needed supplanting, and struggled to have influence over the neo-conservatives who came to prominence in the 1990s through developing their own think tanks (Abelson, 2009).

If there are to be democratic struggles over the direction of foreign policy, expert officials can only be engaged by those with a degree of knowledge and professionalism. Accordingly, pressure groups become a career choice like everything else, and their permanent staffs can end up in too cosy a relationship with their erstwhile targets. They create for decision-makers the sense of being in touch with public opinion, when in practice the boundary between ins and outs may simply have been moved a little further out. This process can be seen in the way the Blair government in Britain encouraged human rights and development groups to enter into structured dialogues with officialdom, and came to rely on them for help with policy implementation. The risk, as with the Green Party in Germany which entered the governing coalition in 1998, is that the process of taking responsibility alienates natural supporters without convincing general opinion. The whole point about interest groups is that they offer alternative definitions of responsible behaviour; once in partnership with decision-makers they imperceptibly change roles and the pressure for accountability must come from elsewhere. Nonetheless the general public has little choice but to rely on these groups to keep governments up to the mark. The same is true of another and even more important social institution.

The Media and the Construction of 'Spectacles'

In the age of the 24/7 news cycle the mass media look like kings. They seem to be the key to influence over public opinion, and they have the ear and eye of government. With real-time broadcasts from even remote spots in the world to hundreds of millions of homes, what was quickly called the 'CNN effect' – of foreign policy shaped by the latest media feeding frenzy – is palpable (Robinson, 2002, 2012, p. 179). If the press was the 'fourth estate' so television is now the fifth – the political constituency with most informal power. This view is unsurprisingly propagated by the media themselves. Journalists play up their insider access while politicians like to paint themselves as boxed in by constant media pressure. In contrast academic work tends to qualify the picture of the dominant media. As Simon Serfaty (1990, p. 229) has said, on foreign policy issues the media 'are neither hero nor villain'.

Historically the 'age of the masses' and the growing importance of the media go hand in hand, the one fostering the other. If print was important in fostering first the emergence of the state, and then the imagined communities of nationalism, the development of rapidly published and widely disseminated broadsheets was fundamental to the organization of modern industrial society (Anderson, 1991). The daily newspaper was soon recognized as a key instrument of the mobilization of the mass, whether for constructive or manipulative purposes. Nor did it take long to become apparent that the flow of influence went in two directions – from the top down but also from the public via the press to government – or that the press itself could be a formidable independent factor. As early as 1922 there was an example of a politician using the press, when Colonial Secretary Winston Churchill in Lloyd George's cabinet let journalists know during the Chanak crisis that he would be calling on military support from the Dominions before the governments of those countries had received the telegram of request – thus exploiting the advantage of time zones and print deadlines. This ill-judged form of pressure only hastened on the determination of Dominion leaders not to have their foreign policy run by London (L. Smith, 2014, pp. 274–5).

After the Second World War, with the proliferation of war correspondents, film crews and 'star' reporters this kind of 'media event' became commonplace. A constant struggle takes place for advantage between journalists (of all kinds) and those responsible for official policy. At one moment the former will have the advantage, creating embarrassment or setting the agenda. At the next government 'spin doctors' will be planting a story or distracting attention from the real issue of the day. It also happens not infrequently that the two sides develop a common way of looking at the world, behaving in an incestuous way which closes the circle against public involvement. Common to each of these three patterns of relationship has been the tendency to create foreign policy 'spectacles', or dramas for a mass audience, which may fascinate and motivate people, but which usually do not lead to the full ventilation of the important underlying issues.

The power of the media is exerted in two distinct ways: over public opinion, and then over decision-makers, including indirectly via the political class. There is no doubt that in foreign policy the media have a key gatekeeping role with respect to the public. Such public debate as exists is focused on the notice boards provided by newspapers and television. Public meetings, word of mouth and internet blogs have some impact, but even they do not exist in isolation from the dominant discourse conducted by the big battalions. It is not difficult to think of cases where the media have created almost out of nothing a mood of concern which has then rebounded onto government. African famines have produced some such moments in Western societies, but in recent times more have revolved around the fate of hostages, where the media in parent countries, stimulated by desperate families, keep up a constant drumbeat of concern which makes it difficult for governments to stand aside – or to engage in back-channel diplomacy. Kidnappers quickly came to appreciate the role of the media, and have exploited it by releasing increasingly sophisticated images of victims on the internet. This process reached its nadir in the revolting images of executions released by Daesh during their attempt to create a Caliphate. The spectacles were designed to create terror and to set the Western political agenda, in which cause they temporarily succeeded.

Image does often predominate over information and analysis. This is not always a superficial matter, since an emotional and visual appeal can leave a more lasting effect than metres of the written word, as with the pictures of a lone demonstrator before tanks in Tiananmen Square in 1989. But it is usually evanescent, and unless followed up leaves the reader or viewer ill-equipped to make serious judgements. The position is worsened by the fact that even serious newspapers only devote 33–45 per cent of their space to international affairs (Clarke, 1992, pp. 319–28). Television news does the same, but as Theodore Sorensen (1986, p. 92) points out, '45 per cent of the 22 minutes of news contained in a 30 minute newscast does not convey enough words to fill one-third of one page of a standard-size newspaper'. Hard-headed journalists assume that most readers and viewers are not much interested in foreign affairs – even if this is gradually changing, as mobility increases and societies become increasingly interconnected. Distance also counts, in the sense that without some involvement of 'our people' only the most massive events will halt the tendency to switch off, literally, or more likely, psychologically. Thus much of the media will play up the simplistic and even the xenophobic aspects of their coverage to ensure the attention their proprietors and advertisers require (Carruthers, 2011, pp. 9–10; Sorensen, 1986, pp. 92–3). This has a dumbing-down effect, but even more insidious is the opportunity cost of denying clear information and analysis to voters. Politicians may distrust the judgement of the public, but there is no evidence to suggest that their own is superior when judged over the long term.

The role of the media as an actor in the policy-making process is exerted through the notice board it provides for communication between foreign policy professionals and the attentive public. Decision-makers may not have much time to read the press or watch television but they employ advisers to summarize who is saying what, so that anything which shows a weakness or starts a trend is soon spotted. Key opinion-formers, like Josef Joffe of *Die Zeit* in Germany or Martin Wolf of the *Financial Times*, do not go unheard. In this respect the media have the capacity to influence political argument by ventilating debate which might otherwise stay behind closed doors, by subjecting the party line to critical scrutiny and by tilting the balance in favour of one position over another. What is for the average citizen the arcane subject of TTIP (Transatlantic Trade and Investment Partnership) has produced extensive debate in both press and legislative circles. The interaction between these two sets of experts (not to mention swathes of lobbyists) means that the outcome can never be taken for granted by those engaged in official negotiations. This is a highly technical subject but one of considerable importance in citizens' lives, which deserves more ventilation than it gets.

This example indicates the kind of issue which the media rarely succeed in bringing properly to wider attention. The case of the large-scale enlargement of the EU, canvassed from 1993 onwards, and the subject of incremental commitments from governments before its final implementation in 2004–7, is another. There is no doubt that enlargement had, for good or ill, significant effects on both on the project of EU integration and the everyday lives of Europe's citizens (Majone, 2009, pp. 111, 218). But the amount and level of the debate before the fact was generally abysmal. This was because the timetable was long and shifting, the permutations endless and the issues multiple. In this situation even the serious press failed to identify the main outlines of a debate, let alone ensure one took place. The problem was compounded by the need for a

Europe-wide debate, whereas the press is still predominantly national in its focus, and by the tendency in a complex issue to take cues from governments – which in this case, although for diverse reasons, manufactured a consensus in favour of the principle of enlargement. The issue was presented as closed, with only the timing of implementation at stake. Without a 'spectacle' to conjure up the media lost interest – at least until after the fact, when the consequential mass movements of workers predictably led to a polarising and emotive treatment of migration. By this time, of course, a rational consideration of the various policy options was beside the point. As James Reston once said of the US press, 'we will send 500 correspondents to Vietnam after the war breaks out ... but we will not send five reporters there when the danger of war is developing' (Serfaty, 1990, p. 14).

If media influence over foreign policy is to be expected in the democracies, on many occasions their role has been exaggerated. This is the conclusion of Halliday's (1997) study of the first Gulf War, and of Carruthers' (2000) survey of other cases in the 1990s, including Somalia, Yugoslavia and Rwanda. It is also the view taken of television in the research done by Nik Gowing (1994a, 1994b, 1996), himself a distinguished TV reporter. What is more the media can be more easily manipulated by policy-makers than the general public realizes. The press has long been used to launch diplomatic trial balloons, and not infrequently information is released which has only the most tenuous relationship to the truth. Particularly in war-time, actual disinformation is frequently reported faithfully by the media. Whole squads of public relations experts have now moved into the foreign policy area in order to present parties in the best light. Many foreign trips are essentially media events, designed to use press, radio and television as instruments of projection, at home and abroad (Dickie, 1992, pp. 82–5, 247–8).

Thus in many respects the relationship between the media and government suits both sides very well. Publicity and the two-way transmission of information are exchanged for privileged access and (often) seats on the presidential or prime ministerial plane. Some critics have concluded from this element of collusion that the press corps is structurally rotten and part of the self-serving elites it is supposed to be scrutinising (Herman and Chomsky, 1994; Pilger, 1992). It is certainly true that some journalists have subverted their own independence by acting as diplomatic 'couriers', or even as actual spies. Nervous governments often assume that foreign journalists are agents of influence. Systematic subordination is a serious problem in autocracies, but in democracies it is a relatively small problem compared to the structural difficulty of developing foreign policy themes in an ever more commercial and trivialising environment.

In any case, on many of the problems confronting us, like the Middle East peace process, climate change and the fate of the eurozone, it is simple-minded to suppose that there is an obvious line which elites are united on and which serves their interests most. Human beings' inability even to know their own best long-term interests produces divided opinion inside both officialdom and the media. The latter could be much more alert, sceptical and creative in their approach to the reporting of international affairs, but enough exceptions exist to demonstrate that free comment still has some power. The press in some countries, for instance France and the Netherlands, remains serious and not dominated by tabloid values. Key individuals like Daniel Ellsberg, who released the 'Pentagon papers' on the Vietnam War to the *New York Times*, and Edward Snowden who leaked around one million National Security Agency documents, enabling *The Guardian*, *Le Monde* and other newspapers worldwide to expose the extent of surveillance by US intelligence, have broken open some major conspiracies of silence. The same is true of some campaigning journalists, like John Pilger himself, but they have often been pushed to the margins of the media industry.

The media are, after all, hardly a flawless example of pluralism in action, given the power of the big proprietors like Murdoch, Berlusconi and Springer, and the combination they represent of conservative views and profit-seeking. This leads to serious critical assessments of official orthodoxies being confined to late-night slots and fringe publications. It is true that there is still competition in the treatment of foreign policy issues, and that press, radio and TV can bring new issues to the public's attention, link up debates across borders and put governments under pressure. The difficulty is that the process is hit and miss, with little continuity. For the most part short-termism and the addiction to sensationalism means that complex issues are rarely done justice, while the basic assumptions of decision-makers too often go unquestioned. Debate about foreign policy too often takes place within narrow limits, with both policy-makers and commentators accepting the same conventional wisdoms. Moreover the costs of running modern media mean that once a pattern of ownership, and a culture, has been established, it can be changed only slowly, if at all.

For this reason many have taken refuge in the view that the internet is the saviour of democratic accountability. Certainly it provides a wealth of easily available information, and a means of feeding back responses almost instantly to politicians. This has led autocratic regimes from China to Iran to clamp down on its availability, although they are probably fighting a losing battle. Western governments have to take the different approach, of participating in the information wars via public diplomacy and more or less subtle attempts to shape debate. They too run scared of the social media campaigns which can take off like forest fires on unpredictable subjects. But for the time being there is no sign that on the major issues of foreign policy, such as the level of defence spending or a decision on interventions, the internet is enabling greater pressure to be exerted on governments than occurred in the era of Suez or Vietnam. What can be expected is that the rapid transmission of news and views in the 'blogosphere' will create much stronger transnational opinion coalitions (Drezner and Farrell, 2004). What can also be hoped is that over the long term the internet will lead to greater public education on international politics and thus the confidence to participate more effectively in policy debates.

Civil Society, Diversity and Identity

An important new dimension of the domestic environment is the emergence in many countries of more diverse civil societies as the result of growing human mobility. People are increasingly moving for work, as rich countries' labour markets pull in poor migrants, and mobile professionals go where globalization takes them. Pensioners in developed countries follow the sun or their emigrant children and grandchildren. World poverty is a constant driver of mobility as people search for a better life. The wars in Afghanistan, Iraq, Syria and the Maghreb have produced waves of refugees. All movement in its turn creates pressures for family unification. The outcome of all this is a breaking up of such homogenization as had been achieved through the model of the 'nation-state', and the arrival in an increasing number of states of what is loosely called 'multiculturalism', or more accurately ethnocultural diversity.

The relevance of this large and complex subject here is that foreign policy-makers can no longer take for granted not just support from their home base but even any consensus on what sorts of values and interests provide the criteria for their decisions. This is not at all because the ethnocultural groups which form as the result of mobility are working against the interests of their new countries (though acts of home-grown terrorism show that a very small minority in some countries have been) but because they naturally have an interest in events in their original homeland, often establish diaspora links and sometimes create lobbies which push for privileged relationships, or particular causes. In short these minority groups, or at least their leaders, tend to be more interested in foreign policy than the majority population, for whom personal connections to abroad are likely to be more limited (Hill, 2013).

In consequence governments may find that a foreign policy issue can take on an unexpected importance because it resonates with a particular minority, as when Tamils in Europe and North America staged demonstrations to publicize the plight of their community in Sri Lanka towards the end of that country's civil war, and to urge their governments to take diplomatic action. Conversely, a problem of international politics can rebound into the domestic sphere unpredictably, as when the war in Syria led to a sudden rise in the number of young European Muslims leaving to join the struggle, presenting their governments in due course with the problem of returning jihadists and a possible new security threat.

Governments have long attempted to influence public opinion in other societies, as we saw in Chapter 6 when discussing cultural diplomacy. But they have to be careful not to stir up minorities for fear of exposing them to accusations of treason, and themselves risking a breach of international law. Neither of these concerns weighed heavily with the Russian government in 2014 when it engineered a referendum in the Crimea to justify its annexation, or when it encouraged an armed uprising in the Russian-speaking areas of eastern Ukraine. Fortunately this kind of subversion, crudely disregarding international norms, is more the exception than the rule. Most states limit themselves to public diplomacy, which while also an attempt to manipulate another society is generally perceived as legitimate. This is because it builds upon an implicit recognition of shared, or at least overlapping, constituencies between separate states. Issues such as the future of genetically modified food, or capital punishment, play differently in different societies, but they stimulate enough of a common debate for governments to accept that they are involved in dialogues not just with their own publics, but with opinion more broadly.

We therefore face an apparent paradox in the interplay between inside and outside in world politics. On the one hand transnational developments and the corresponding tendency of governments to speak to foreign publics as well as their own are slowly creating a bigger and more inclusive forum for debate on international affairs. On the other, multiculturalism and the growth in the number of minorities within states are leading to the multiplication of voices in the domestic public sphere. But it is only an apparent paradox because in practice both developments have a similar effect, that of challenging the ability of a government to speak exclusively and authoritatively for all its people. Moreover if leaders can no longer assume a distinctive, settled, national identity then inevitably they are less clear as to the criteria on which to conduct external relations.

In this situation of flux governments may be tempted to react by using foreign policy to reinforce (their view of) national identity. Vladimir Putin has been a classic case in point, starting with a determination to restore Russian pride and reputation and becoming steadily more assertive (Zarakol, 2011, pp. 230–9). The Chinese government sees the demands of its Uighurs and Tibetans for more autonomy as a threat to its national security, and cools relations with any state which shows signs of supporting these demands. Spain has refused to recognize Kosovo's independence for fear of the internal repercussions, with Catalonia and the Basque country already resentful of Madrid. Indeed, the Spanish government watched with anxiety as Catalan nationalists travelled to support the Scottish National Party in the referendum campaign of 2014 over independence from the United Kingdom. In their turn Conservative administrations in Britain since the days of Margaret Thatcher have treated their partners in the EU as troublesome outsiders. They have played the nationalist card in the hope of gaining votes, heightening their own domestic legitimacy, and holding an increasingly shaky United Kingdom together.

Such tactics do not always work, and indeed may be seen as trying to reverse the tide of history. British policies on both the EU and the nuclear deterrent, for example, have steadily increased the desire of Scots to be disassociated from London. The participation of various countries in the coalitions which went to war in Afghanistan and Iraq did nothing for national unity, calling up indeed the spectre of fractured identities within civil society. Much more effective at both the domestic and the international levels at reinforcing community and identity are substantive achievements, such as Ireland's self-transformation from a poor agricultural backwater to thriving postmodern economy, and then a second time after the bubble burst in 2008. The same is true of Iceland, which in the midst of financial crisis had seen salvation in applying for membership of the EU, but with its economic well-being restored no longer feels the need for an external solution.[5] Word of mouth – which today means the internet – has transmitted the new images around the world, in Ireland's case with the aid of the diaspora.

Finally, the changing character of civil society raises two further issues in relation to foreign policy which have an ethical as well as a political dimension. The first is about the public's right to know, and to campaign. When officialdom neglects its duties in relation to information and accountability, citizens increasingly assert themselves through direct access to sources abroad, often mobilising against their own government. They also do not feel an automatic loyalty to their own country if it is shown to have breached basic standards of decency, as in the row about surveillance which arose from the revelations by Edward Snowden. Governments then face the dilemma of whether to see this as a threat to national security, with possible consequences in terms of restricting access to the internet, and to foreign journalists, diplomats and academics. Well-grounded political systems have little to fear from this cross-fertilization, but they are not in the majority. In an age of terrorism even democracies succumb to restrictive measures.

The second issue revolves around the ethics of intervening in the internal affairs of another state. The more diverse nature of modern societies means that governments will be faced with pressures both from refugee groups wanting intervention against the regime in the land from which they have fled, and from minorities deeply opposed to the consequences of a foreign policy action for their co-nationals or co-religionists in lands where they may still have family and friends. The issue here is whether to follow some overall *raison d'état*, or to give particular weight to the intensity of the preferences on the issue felt by a concerned group. This is not a trivial problem, as the recent history of Pakistan illustrates. Supporters of the Taliban have persistently attacked, often violently, Pakistani governments over their support for the United States during the 'War on Terror'. Elsewhere the dilemmas may be less traumatic, but the underlying difficulty remains: an intervention is always likely to lead some to respond 'not in my name'.

In Conclusion

While Chapter 9 dealt with the issue of how far foreign policy was primarily a domestic formation, this chapter has been concerned with the more directly political dimension of decision-makers' answerability to their domestic constituents. It is clear that with respect to foreign policy the function of intermediary institutions between government and public is even more significant than usual. Individual citizens have few opportunities to get to grips with the substance of foreign policy, for all the obeisance paid by politicians to public opinion. Given the usual weakness of constitutional provisions they have to rely on their parliamentary representatives, pressure groups and the media. In their turn decision-makers have to deal with a range of different institutions and interests, in which concern for the common weal is continuously blurred by special interests.

The foreign policy process has an inherent element of pluralism, even where societies are not fully developed economically or liberal in their politics. Except under conditions of terror there will always be some domestic inputs from those with special degrees of concern for, or knowledge about, the outside world. Yet this is not at all to say that even in established democracies the processes of foreign policy scrutiny work well. They do not. Formal accountability usually amounts to a light and loose set of obligations on the executive, and the day-to-day influence of interest groups and the media works only in a patchy, indirect and post hoc way. Actual participation in foreign policy-making is still immensely difficult even for the informed and articulate, who continue to be in a small minority. Yet decision-makers tend to look nervously over their shoulders, even when there seems little to be concerned about. Politicians and officials do internalize an ideology of accountability – 'the notional constraint' – and as a result they sometimes aim off for fear of anticipated opposition or accusations of illegitimacy.

This Gramscian picture, of elitism fleshed out by a sense of duty and the need for consensus, must be qualified to fit modern conditions. First, the relationship between foreign policy-making and its domestic constituencies is unpredictable, and can erupt in ways which disturb both the governing elite and the pattern of international relations. The nature of civil society on the one hand, and the rapid increase in personal access to information and contacts through the internet and social media, mean that a conjuncture of forces can at times empower the citizenry, cutting decisively across the normal pattern. This was what happened with the 'Orange Revolution' in the Ukraine of 2004–5, which began the train of events which culminated in the further social upheaval of February 2014, with dramatic international consequences.

Secondly, historical and geographical contexts matter a great deal. In many states foreign policy is still such an elite domain that any attempt to participate is regarded as insubordination or worse. Although citizens may have more means of getting information and encouraging outside sympathizers, in these traditionally statist regimes they have no chance of directly influencing foreign policy. But in other, looser, systems there is now a noticeable trend towards greater domestic interest in international affairs, not least because the scope of foreign policy has expanded to include much of what is familiar in everyday life. We thus observe a heightened activism, especially in developed liberal societies, deriving from the view that foreign policy is normal politics, and should not be treated as if it exists in its own (a)moral realm. Foreign policy has always mattered to a people. It is now increasingly seen to matter, and to be part of the public space.

Notes

1   The Jubilee 2000 campaign was launched by two academics, both Africanists and Christians, Martin Dent OBE and Bill Peters, an ex-diplomat. The quotation included here is from Dent, the leading Jubilee Campaigner, cited in 'Meet the debt-busters', *Independent on Sunday*, 17 May 1998. The original quotation may be found in the *Anti-Slavery Reporter*, 1830, Supplement, May (60), p. 225. The Jubilee 2000 campaign

snowballed, culminating in extensive demonstrations at the G7 summit in Birmingham in 1998. Dent and Peters drew the lesson from the anti-slavery campaign that influence was only possible on the basis of 'a simple and radical goal', and they succeeded in moving official opinion.

2   The law to this effect was passed in the Knesset on 22 November 2010. See *Haaretz*, 23 November 2010, and Navot (2014, pp. 45–6).

3   In fact turnout was low at 18 per cent, and it was the Left which did best in the constituency. But it is the perception and the profile which count.

4   For a list of what AIPAC itself says are its most significant lobbying achievements see http://www.aipac.org/about/what-weve-accomplished (accessed 20 March 2015).

5   Iceland applied for EU membership in 2009 and withdrew its application in 2015.

Further Reading

Carruthers, Susan L., 2011. *The Media at War*. Second edition. This updated version holds its place as a standard work on the subject.

Everts, Philip and Isernia, Pierangelo, 2015. *Public Opinion, Transatlantic Relations and the Use of Force*. Europe's two leading experts on public opinion and foreign policy focus here on differing attitudes about going to war within the Atlantic community.

Hill, Christopher, 2013. *The National Interest in Question: Foreign Policy in Multicultural Societies*. This is the first study to appear of the relationship between ethnocultural diversity and foreign policy in Europe.

Parmar, Inderjeet, 2004. *Think Tanks and Power in Foreign Policy: A Comparative Study of the Role and Influence of the Council on Foreign Relations and the Royal Institute of International Affairs, 1939–1945*. Parmar's work goes beyond his interesting historical focus to throw light on the inherent role of foreign policy institutes in linking elites to public opinion.

Smith, Tony, 2000. *Foreign Attachments: The Power of Ethnic Groups in the Making of American Foreign Policy*. Smith's innovative study is an important contribution to an often-debated issue in US foreign policy.

Zarakol, Ayşe, 2011. *After Defeat: How the East Learned to Live with the West*. Zarakol's comparative study of Japan, Russia and Turkey focuses on issues of change, status and stigma in international politics.

Chapter 11

Foreign Policy and the Revival of the State

On the face of things foreign policy in the twenty-first century involves a shift from the realism of the great power conflicts of the past into the ideas of liberal interdependence which many policy-makers came to espouse in the 1990s, after two decades of discussion in academic and business circles. Yet the sensational events of 2001 turned this supposition around, leading to an obsession with security concerns in government and a revival of security studies in the academy. This book has attempted to go beyond such pendulum effects by showing that just as it was simplistic in 2000 to relegate the state and foreign policy to history, so it is unjustifiable now to overlook the impact of transnationalism and the challenges to coherent state actions. Apart from anything else, there is no straightforward relationship between changes in the immediate pattern of world politics and the slower-moving forces which shape events. Changes in thinking about international relations should not therefore respond too hysterically to events, however dramatic. The recent return to realism in many quarters, especially in the form of neoclassical realism, is an advance on the lofty Waltzian disregard of foreign policy, but it is still not enough. As an explanation of the huge variety of foreign policy behaviours, from crusading nationalism to abstract cosmopolitanism, realism is necessary but insufficient.

All the central notions of modern politics are implicated in the conduct of foreign policy, which is an activity employable on behalf of most of the preoccupations of the modern state. And it is therefore a mistake to regard it as a specialized form of conduct, sealed away from the rest of public life. Civil society, the state and the values which they serve are implicated in foreign policy and affected by it in turn. In an era where most societies are touched by globalization and oriented to popular concerns this is even truer. Foreign policy faces the impact of structural economic forces which if left to themselves have a homogenising effect, but which individual political communities exist to mediate and diversify. It must also cope with not just greater public interest in external policy but also an increasingly direct participation by citizens in international relations, fuelled by the knowledge that their 'domestic' concerns may be difficult to satisfy at the national level alone. This heightens and makes more complex the political and managerial responsibilities of foreign policy-makers.

This chapter brings the book to a close by focusing on the evolving place of foreign policy in our political and ethical life. It does this through three concepts: action, choice and responsibility. *Action* is the missing link in much academic work on international relations, which tends to privilege theory or system-wide trends. *Choice* is the central issue in any consideration of decision-making, itself a necessary concept if we are to probe beneath the surface of events and political dissimulation. *Responsibility* is a crucial notion because it connects technical issues of democratic accountability to wider concerns over the effects of public policy, including those outside the constituency of a particular state.

Because governments dispose of considerable assets on our behalf, and exert major powers over everyday life, we have to consider where and how they may *act*, and with what effect. They have to *choose* between those problems in which they might make a difference and those where their involvement might prove counterproductive. And they need some reasonably coherent notion as to whom, in a chaotic world of competing claims and demands, they are *responsible* and to what degree. Since even the most powerful states have no choice but to work with others towards their goals, foreign policy is a perpetual process of engagement in degrees of multilateralism. It is also political theory in perpetual motion, for principles over intervention, genocide or development tend to be forged through individual events in which interests and values jostle each other confusingly. Only the distance attained by theory, or by the historian's rear-view mirror, provides some eventual clarity of vision.

Action: Who Acts, and for Whom?

Immersed in the swirling events and conflicts which make up politics, leaders are faced with the need on any given issue to locate the decisional space – that is, what is to be decided, and in which forum – and to assert themselves in it whenever their primary concerns are at stake. They may not always be aware that this involves judgements about the purpose of foreign policy, and its role in linking a society to the wider world community, but it does. What is more, their actions in the foreign policy arena may well turn out to have significant implications for the kind of polity, even the kind of society, they are developing at home. Conflicts with the United States and France over nuclear power had radicalising effects on domestic politics in New Zealand; the second Gulf War stirred up identity politics in Europe; the proximity of the conflict in Afghanistan has imposed deep fractures on Pakistan.

Ultimately, foreign policy is purposive action, on behalf of a single community. Its concerns will be particular and self-regarding but they also inherently relate to the wider milieux in which the state is located. The hopes, fears and values which lie behind such purposes overlap with those of other political communities and occasionally may generate collective action. Thus analysing a foreign policy is a significant intellectual task. It involves outlining the parameters of actions and choices and the ways in which polities formulate their underlying purposes in relation to the wider world. It requires an understanding of how states use international politics to achieve their goals and how far their very identity derives from the nature of their interactions with others. Lastly, it means reflecting on the *proper* purposes of foreign policy, a discussion where philosophers and public debate will set the tone. Here some balance has to be struck between communitarian and cosmopolitan concerns.[1] Foreign policy has to be at the cusp of this great debate, as John Rawls acknowledged when he set himself the task of elaborating the 'foreign policy of a liberal people' (1999, p. 82).

Whatever a country's size or weaknesses, its conduct of foreign policy can 'make a difference'. Both realists and liberal globalists have underestimated this capacity, with their respective emphases on military force and market integration. Practical decision-makers have fewer doubts. Australia's first white paper on foreign and trade policy, for example, stressed the 'contribution that foreign and trade policy makes to the advancement of Australia's core national interests: the security of the Australian nation and the jobs and standard of living of the Australian people' (Department of Foreign Affairs and Trade of Australia, 1997, p. ii). And this from one of the most progressive foreign policy elites, which since 1972 had stressed the need to abandon the old UK-centric verities. For their part the 'rising powers' of Brazil, China and India have all seen foreign policy as integral to the modernising and strengthening of their countries. It is a path both to coping with competition and creating effective partnerships.

For those carrying public responsibility, foreign policy seems to have become an even more critical site of action and choice than ever before. All states, including those unrecognized, and indeed some purely transnational actors, have a foreign policy in some form. What is more, since there are now nearly four times as many states as there were in 1945, there are proportionately more foreign ministries, more diplomatic missions and more diplomats employed across the world. Up-to-date comparable data is difficult to come by, but in 1988 it was estimated that the 159 member states of the UN maintained between them 18,400 missions at various levels, employing over 100,000 diplomatic staff – national and local (McClanahan, 1989, p. 141). At the end of 2014 the United States alone employed 72,000 such staff, in more than 270 posts (US Department of State, 2014, pp. 8–9). In 2011 four small EU states (Austria, Denmark, Finland and Ireland) between them employed 1,171 staff just for bilateral relations within the Union (Department of Foreign Affairs and Trade of Ireland, 2013, p. 30). These examples, from either end of the scale, suggest that even in an age of financial retrenchment, there is still a great perceived need for diplomatic personnel at all levels – political, commercial and consular.

Part of this comes from the proliferation of multilateral institutions, which instead of reducing numbers through economies of scale has created a demand for staff to coordinate national positions. The expansion of the subjects now counting as international relations (prefigured in 1945 by the UN Charter, with its stress on the economic and social conditions of peace) has worked in the same direction. Thus international cooperation, and the internationalization of domestic politics, tends to place more of a premium on diplomacy, not less.

Diplomatic activity, however, only amounts to foreign policy once coordinated across the piste. It is understandable that some should see the involvement of functional experts and bureaucratic rivals as outflanking the role of the professional diplomats, formally responsible for foreign policy. Certainly the idea that foreign policy-making is a discrete area with sharply distinct boundaries must be abandoned. It is, rather, now a broad area of interface between the public policies of one state or community and a multilayered external environment. States thus need to make conscious efforts to pull together the strands of their external relations, and are stimulated to do so by a concern for their country's reputation and 'brand'. Their distinctive historical, geographical and ethical concerns push in the same direction. But to work well a foreign policy needs to ensure both that diplomats, the military and domestic civil servants are pulling in the same direction, and that strategy is coordinated with 'like-minded' countries.

It is a temptation to think that many states are simply not up to such a challenge. Yet although states vary – in size, development, coherence and power – it is not the case that only the major powers are capable of significant actions such as war-making, maintaining complex programmes of international assistance or building an alliance. Some are capable of none of these things but still manage to pursue consistent damage-limitation strategies of various kinds. Only a very few are so splintered or ineffectual, perhaps through external interference and/or civil war, that they have no foreign policy worth the name.

What, then, does 'the state' mean in today's foreign policy context? In Chapter 2 we saw that although there are 'outside–in' as well as 'inside–out' accounts of states' emergence and purposes, they have rarely touched on issues of foreign policy (Poggi, 1990; Tilly, 1976). To say more about this relationship we need to return briefly to first principles. If we take it as given that the territorial state 'has not succumbed to transnational or localist influences', and that it still provides an 'arena in which individuals can decide or at least influence their collective fates', then it follows that some collective means of relating to other such arenas will be necessary (Rosecrance, 1999, p. 211). The state furnishes a people with a means of bundling its concerns together when that entails dealing with outsiders – at its most extreme in war or other issues of high politics, but more routinely in discussions over borders, travel, trade and various public–private joint enterprises. Very often full bundling will not be necessary or possible, but broad coherence remains the ideal type.

The growth of the world economy, and of the private sector within it, has tended to obscure this fact. Even those who study foreign economic policy tend to be at arm's length from political scientists studying FPA (with the fault on both sides), with the result that the divide between economics and politics is preserved among analysts as well as in practice. But it is evident both that states and firms are deeply intertwined in the mutual pursuit of prosperity and that problems of security or diplomacy always have an economic dimension – witness the debate over reparations after the First World War, or the importance of oil supplies throughout the last hundred years. That there are problems in connecting up the economic and political complexities of these issues is a challenge to foreign policy not a death blow to it.

In analysing foreign policy both the liberal, night-watchman version of the state and the realist emphasis on collective strength and identity have things to tell us (J. Hall, 2001). The first requires the state to perform some external political functions, such as ensuring stability and the honouring of agreements, but also helping to promote domestic enterprises abroad and what Rosecrance (1999, p. 211) calls 'supervising and protecting the market'. Conversely the second, especially in neo-Hegelian versions with the state embodying the national will, must allow for mediation between internal and external dynamics, and variation across issue areas – which is where foreign policy comes in, as the formal means whereby societies engage with each other, and attempt to mediate their differences (Der Derian, 1987).

A focus on foreign policy and international politics also points up key dilemmas which other perspectives may miss or get out of context. Among the more important are:

- *How far external pressures which threaten the state may be relieved by helping to build a safer, more durable milieu*, thus in turn enabling new domestic developments.
- *What costs to bear on behalf of the international system*, say by operating a reserve currency or acting as a world policeman. Here the notion, implicit in liberal contract theory, that the state exists primarily to serve its own citizens, gets reversed.
- *What new obligations or orientations to take on*, through alliances, treaties or foreign friendships – which can have critical consequences. British military conversations with France from 1905 onwards virtually tied the hands of the government over the decision for war in August 1914. Ukraine's attempt to move closer to the European Union after 2004 led eventually to a crisis with Russia.
- *How far to intervene against regimes which seem to pose a threat to international order*. Military actions, sanctions and even propaganda always entail costs and hostile reactions.
- *How to manage a military–industrial complex*, whereby parts of society in an internationally active state can become dependent on the armed services and the production of weapons, even to the point of creating a security state.
- *How to mediate new political trends – and forms of polity*. This is the case inside many regions and organizations. The Concert of Europe was in part a foreign policy mechanism for dealing with transnational political change. Members of ASEAN reacted strongly against Western human rights pressures, asserting their preference for 'Asian values'.
- *How to manage the 'memory wars' that the scars left by history make possible*. Foreign policy is in the front line of the growing cultural dimension of international relations, from demands for the return of national treasures to rows over history schoolbooks.
- *How to manage state cohesion in the face of substate foreign policies*, and/or the ability of other states to find interlocutors other than central government. If regions and cities develop the ability to conduct their own external relations then it is a significant challenge to central government.

This last development is noteworthy because, with globalization, it represents the other part of a pincer movement in which many think the nation-state is caught – between the global and the local. If a state cannot even claim a monopoly over foreign policy, then what is left to it? As John Hall (2003, p. 25) says, however, this is a 'vastly over-stated view'. In practice substate 'foreign policies' are not yet worthy of the name, despite a number of interesting developments. Quebec challenged Canadian sovereignty through asserting its relationship with France at the time of de Gaulle. But this quickly led to a reassertion of federal competence, and no sub-unit has gone so far since in its external relations. The German *Länder* have important powers within the European Communities, but no significant role in the Common Foreign and Security Policy or in Germany's bilateral political relationships. The Australian states have a profile independent of the Canberra government, including offices overseas, but their activity is almost wholly limited to trade and tourism promotion. The Chinese provinces are increasingly important points of contact for foreign consulates and business but there is no question of an independent political role (Tang and Cheng, 2001). The same is broadly true of the states of the American union, despite their long heritage. The shadow of the Civil War still hangs over them – and indeed others.

Foreign policy from below, therefore, is more an intermittent impulse than something easy to achieve. Yet to the extent that it represents a desire to be free of a metropole it actually reinforces the notion of foreign policy by showing how much it matters to be able to conduct one's own relations with third parties. If pushed to its logical extent this means full independent statehood. Thus United Kingdom has been subject to an intensely divisive debate over Scottish independence, in which two of the key reasons for the growing popularity of the Scottish National Party (SNP) have been foreign policy-related – first opposition to the nuclear deterrent, and particularly to its bases on the Clyde, and second a fear of losing EU membership because of the numerical weight of English Eurosceptic votes in a possible referendum. The latter at least has the potential to make the demands for Scottish independence irresistible.

Foreign policy is still the focal point for agency in international relations, despite the increasingly pluralist character of the system. Yet the state itself is constantly engaged in a struggle to achieve policy coherence in the face of bureaucratic politics and the increasingly parastatal role of NGOs. In this it is helped, paradoxically, by the many international organizations in which both states and NGOs participate. In developed systems like those of the EU this has produced an extra layer of foreign policy coordination superimposed on (but not replacing) that conducted spontaneously by states, substate units and transnational actors (Bulmer, Maurer and Paterson, 2001, pp. 182, 198).[2] Elsewhere, the state may be capable of maintaining more of a monopoly on foreign policy, so that IGOs like ASEAN or the Shanghai Cooperation Organisation insist on the primacy of sovereignty at the same time as acknowledging a need for coordination. They thus accept the primary role of national diplomacy, unlike the EU and NATO which are ambivalent about it.

While foreign policy is thus a contested and complex area the pressing need for action in many areas of international life, and the lack of alternatives to intergovernmentalism has restored its prominence after the interlude of 'globallusions'. States have a crucial role to play in knitting together the burgeoning activities of the international system. Of course foreign policy is a means, not a solution in itself, and even progress in multilateralism is no guarantee of major substantive achievements. What is really needed is the rebalancing of thinking in more states so as to recognize the interdependence between national goals and international society, especially over the long term. In another paradox this change is quite likely to be promoted by transnational movements.

Transnational actors, as we saw in Chapter 8, are now major factors in the environments of states and at the heart of the ways in which identities are being reframed in a fast-moving world. Whether companies, churches, diasporas or political groups their ability to dispose of resources complicates state foreign policies, and they often have strategies which are the virtual equivalent. They operate alongside states, not in place of them. Even major players like Apple which dictate taste have no desire to run society or to take on any other political functions. Yet because they act upon all levels of world politics, from national societies through governments and IGOs to the operations of world capitalism, their horizontal and functional communities are gradually weakening the barriers to international cooperation. It is true this has been said before, with hope often triumphing over experience (Mitrany, 1943). But gradually the compatibility between states and all but the most violent and nihilistic NSAs has been recognized. States take *responsibility* for actions and structures while NSAs increasingly shape both social inputs and eventual outcomes. Transnationalism works today as ideology, class or religion did in previous eras, but with greater institutionalization, reach and technological support. It helps and hinders states, according to the goals being pursued (S. Cohen, 2003, pp. 169–74).

The argument of Chapters 5 and 6 was that foreign policy necessarily involves the pursuit of many goals simultaneously, with no *a priori* way of ranking them; similarly, that there are no rules of thumb for employing the instruments of foreign policy. What is decisive is the context. On the one hand the criteria derive from classical realism, such as balance, flexibility, self-preservation, prudence and the need to keep ends and means in sync. On the other hand, they must also involve empathy and imagination, the ability to understand what can be achieved through cooperation, and the capacity to make joint ventures work, bilaterally and multilaterally. This means understanding where possessional and milieu goals fold into each other. It is at this point that debates about the ethics of foreign policy begin. We shall come to this when discussing the theme of responsibility, but it is first necessary to consider the problem of choice – what does it mean to 'choose' in the context of foreign policy?

Choice: The Margins of Manoeuvre

The making of choices is central to modern economics and to psychology (Kahneman, 2011). In political science, the theories of rational choice and public choice have come to dominate American scholarship and are steadily extending their sway elsewhere. They have not, however, made much impact on foreign policy analysis, despite the latter's focus on decision-making. It is not that formal methods might not in principle be useful. Game theory evidently helps us to understand patterns of conflict and cooperation, and the strategy required in structured, limited-participant negotiations. Where voting and coalition-building is a principal activity, as in the United Nations or the EU General Affairs Council, the problems of collective action, such as free-riding, which public choice theory addresses, must be high on the research agenda. The problem lies in the fact that such activities are only one part of foreign policy, and a relatively small one at that. The character of a policy arena, the number of parties, the roles of ideas and personalities, and the nature of the problems at stake all require a much more eclectic set of intellectual tools.

If, for example, we take the problem of preference formation so central to political science, we run straight into the question of 'whose preferences?'. The work of Neustadt, Allison and others in the 1960s laid to rest the notion that the state was a unitary and/or, 'rational actor' in international affairs. Because it covers the whole waterfront of a state's concerns foreign policy is subject to competition from differing parts of the national bureaucracy, so that even in monolithic systems like that of the Soviet Union one cannot assume that leaders will be in full control of their country's behaviour. Of course the bureaucratic politics model is itself based on a form of methodological individualism which assumes that individuals, or small groups, might follow the precepts of rational choice. But subsequent work has made it clear that understanding foreign policy requires far more than aggregating the preferences of individual units. There are too many players involved, while the values at stake, involving diffuse notions such as international stability, prestige and historical memory, are difficult to translate into pay-offs. If governments rely too heavily on the basis of conventional rationalism, meaning a limited cost–benefit analysis, as arguably Israel did in relation to Syria and the Lebanon in 1982, they risk disastrous miscalculations (R. Cohen, 2001b, p. 153).

Since the nature and sources of preferences in foreign policy cannot be taken as given it follows that choice is a complex matter – certainly too complex for the old-fashioned shorthand of the national interest. The external environment has no clear structure and is characterized by perpetual flux. States and the international fora in which they come together provide key points of reference, but since the internal affairs of states are now as much part of their environment as is diplomacy the world presents a cosmopolitan challenge. The range of differences which exists within and between societies rules out making policy on the basis of a parsimonious set of criteria.

Rationality in foreign policy means in the first instance not making *irrational* choices, as when pursuing personal obsessions or relying on stereotypes of 'people of whom we know nothing', to adapt Chamberlain's infamous phrase. It also means having the flexibility to adjust policy within the framework created by the broad strategies which are indispensable if any kind of intellectual order is to be maintained and improved. Hardly any actor believes that the international system is satisfactory as it is, and so there is a persistent pressure towards change. This movement represents risks as well as possibilities, as some believe that they possess the secret of remaking the world and may take on too much in the attempt to hasten events. Some will adopt the ostrich posture in a spasm of suspicious conservatism. It is inherently difficult to think strategically and flexibly while responding to a country's immediate needs.

Foreign policy decision-making even more than any other area needs to start from the assumptions that preferences are not the same as choices, while choices are a very different matter from outcomes. Leads and lags are exceptionally long, whether in relation to nuclear missile defence or the enlargement of the European Union. Almost every strategy needs negotiating with a wide range of other actors, many of them bewildering and intractable in their conduct. As planning ahead is particularly problematic so an acceptance that eventual outcomes may be unrecognizable to their initiators must be built in to any idea of implementation. Certainly they are unlikely to be 'final', for international relations take place as in minds and on paper as much as through physical dispositions. Some agreements achieve permanence, perhaps through physical institutions, but in general the outcomes of foreign policy are contingent and perpetually contestable. Attempts to fix matters through measures such as iron curtains or forced migration just create new tensions.

The issue of how to choose is closely tied to that of how much choice exists. The emphasis thus far on the complexity of the environment can leave the impression that the margins of manoeuvre in foreign policy are barely perceptible. But this is not the whole story. For one thing, the lack of homogeneity and ramshackle structure of the international system create air pockets in which individual players may operate relatively undisturbed. One good example is small states. An extensive literature has demonstrated that smaller states have often enjoyed a surprising latitude of choice, resisting both powerful neighbours and apparently irresistible forces (Chong and Maass, 2010; Commonwealth Secretariat,

1997; Fox, 1959; Vital, 1971). The continuity of Swiss policy in the face of the diverse challenges of war and European integration is a case in point, but North Vietnam, Cuba, Romania, Finland and Yugoslavia managed to plough their own furrows during the Cold War, and Morocco, Singapore and Taiwan provide examples today. The decision-makers in these countries have benefited from self-fulfilling prophecies. Because some degree of independence has been asserted in the past, their options seem wider in the present and they may consider themselves to have the luxury of choice. They naturally concentrate on improving their overall milieu and raising their status where it can be done without risk (de Carvalho and Neumann, 2015).

At times, states may perceive too much freedom of choice. There are many examples of decision-makers asserting themselves, often when newly entered into office, by restructuring their countries' foreign policies (Rosati, 1994; Welch, 2005). Not many are successful. Either the policy turns out to have been the product of mere hubris or the external environment is itself in the process of becoming less malleable through other dynamics. An example which combines the two is Anwar Sadat's reorientation of Egyptian foreign policy in 1977 so as to make peace with Israel. This succeeded in its immediate goal, and indeed relations between the two countries remain normalized, but it cost the president his own life in 1981 and Egypt has had to pay high maintenance costs ever since both domestically and in the wider Arab world.

This is in part a matter of the continuum between voluntarism and determinism which is central to the human experience. It is a truism that even for powerful states, foreign policy lies closer to the latter end of the continuum than the former. Yet this does not mean that choice is so restricted as to become politically or intellectually uninteresting. Foreign policy exists always on the cusp between choice and constraint. Depending on the actor, the moment and the situation, opportunities are constantly being carved out from unpromising circumstances, producing actions which then constrain both the self and others in the future. The attainment from time to time of a *decisional space*, in which choices may be considered and made with some sense of freedom, is a precondition of having a foreign *policy*, rather than a mere set of pressurized reactions to external events. Choices and constraints, exercised by the multiple exponents of foreign policy, are in a continuous process of making and remaking each other. To put it in social science terms, foreign policy is not necessarily a dependent variable; that is, it is not *always* a dependent variable, just as the domestic and external environments cannot be taken always as independent variables. While at times circumstances prevail, foreign policy may also be the site of significant initiatives with the capacity to influence both domestic and international systems.

This dialectical relationship may be seen as structurationism applied to foreign policy analysis: structures shape actors, and actors make structures. Yet such an observation should be a starting point and not an end itself. Empirical research is the only way to show how interaction takes place, and when opportunities are real or illusory. It is also the means by which we do justice to historical periods, and analyse which actors make most contribution to shaping structures, as well as their own fates – the answers are often far from obvious, as with Slovenia's critical role in the break-up of Yugoslavia. Furthermore, just because actors and structures are tied together in endless systemic loops does not mean that they dissolve into each other. Rather, they are inherently related, because actors have goals (sometimes, but not always, 'strategic') which are pursued within observable (if not necessarily concrete) templates (structures), which then evolve in response to some of these actions. This process is neatly described as the 'strategic-relational model' (Brighi, 2013, pp. 10–43).

The existence of identifiable foreign policy-making processes tells us where attempts at choosing and self-assertion are made. For example, the claims made for and by the institutions of EU foreign policy enable us to analyse the extent to which a collective diplomacy is emerging in parallel to that of the member states, and to measure its degree of independent impact on the international environment. The degree to which attempts at choice are successful is beside the point.

There is, ultimately, no need to make a choice between actors and structures in the search for explanations of foreign policy, nor to take refuge in an undifferentiated process of structuration. Robert Gilpin (1981) provided a notable version of the realist 'solution' to this problem, whereby all states have to adapt to living in a hostile, lawless world, but some have the capacity to shape the system in their own image, with the consequence that the weak do 'as they must' – in Thucydides' timeless formulation.[3] More open-ended, and allowing for the fact that international actors, in their diversity, operate in many other structures than grand strategy, is Wolfram Hanrieder's neglected schema. Hanrieder (1967) saw foreign policy as needing both consensus and compatibility: consensus in the sense of support for a policy in the domestic context, where it is generated, and compatibility in terms of it being a feasible move in the outside world, where it has to be implemented. If it failed on the first criterion then achievement on the other would be undermined, and vice versa. Ideally some sort of equilibrium would be reached between internal and external structures, even if at times one might be particularly pressing and the other relatively insignificant. Moreover leadership is critical if the balance is to be achieved. It is dangerous to conduct foreign policy as if it is primarily about either international affairs or domestic politics, as in their different ways both Richard Nixon and Slobodan Milošević discovered.

In relation to choices, the two big issues in foreign policy are the way they get framed (decision-making) and the extent to which choice is illusory (determinism). They are connected in that policy-makers always have to estimate how much room for creativity they have; that in turn will determine whose views are heard and which options are considered. At one end of the spectrum gambles do sometimes come off, while an apparently constricting situation can be loosened by dramatic initiatives (witness the use of the oil weapon in 1973). More commonly, ambitious efforts to make a mark on history are reeled in remorselessly, less by opposition from any one adversary than by the unbreakable force of circumstance. In the event of particularly dire failure, foreign policy can bring down a leader or even a regime.

Foreign policy-makers have to have some broad guidelines (which they mindlessly cast in the language of 'national interest'). On the one side are factors arising from the very existence of the state for which they are responsible, such as self-preservation, independence, security and prosperity. On the other will be the more problematical matter of domestic values, by which is meant the particular set of principles which the government asserts, as well as those which society as a whole (or the 'nation') seems to embody. Together they produce positions aiming to promote, at home and abroad, the preferred way of life. These positions automatically contain judgements about the risks of external action – will it be too costly, or draw the enmity of a powerful neighbour, or distract from other, less grandiose priorities, and so on. In that sense foreign policy choices are entangled with those at the domestic level while both are subsets of some notion, however ill thought out, of a desirable world. In this, however, they run into the difficult obstacle of how much responsibility to take, and for whom. In any country's foreign policy, therefore, the practical and the ethical inexorably converge.

Responsibility: The Ethic and the Practice

Good foreign policy analysis must find ways of doing justice to this convergence. It is a persistent challenge and there is no panacea. But the notion of responsibility does give us a useful handle on the problem. It enables us to ask who is responsible for what and for whom, thus bringing together considerations of accountability and statehood with the issue of the best approach to the international milieu. Like power, responsibility is a relational concept in that it does not make sense if applied to an actor in isolation. Foreign policy-makers have little option but to juggle multiple constituencies and competing criteria; they are no more able to suspend the practical constraints within which they work than to avoid the normative implications. But in this at least they are grappling with real political problems, in contrast to the undifferentiated pursuit of 'global responsibilities' held up as a totem by Third Way politicians and anti-globalization protesters alike. They have, and usually feel keenly, a serious responsibility to set priorities.

What does 'responsibility' mean? There are two linked parts to any definition. First are the formal duties which a person has to others by virtue of their *role*. For example a doctor has a responsibility to all those patients on his or her list. But this is only within reasonable limits. If the doctor comes across a road accident, then professional duty instinctively leads him or her to take charge. On the other hand, no one would expect doctors to accept responsibility for the healthcare of all their friends and neighbours. The relational element here is both official and personal, in terms of the trust which is naturally placed in someone who is responsible – the French word '*responsable*' also means '*digne de confiance*', or worthy of trust. Either way, someone who 'has a responsibility' for something knows that he or she must live up to their office and take into account the needs of specified others.

The second aspect of responsibility is the internalized sense of duty found in '*un responsable*'. Taking responsibility for oneself means not blaming others for one's mistakes; it is often taken to be a definition of adulthood. The captain of a sinking ship is the last to leave – the buck stops there.[4] In this sense responsibility means accepting the burden of taking decisions together with their consequences, however unjust. Conversely, behaving irresponsibly means ignoring any actual obligations one might have to others and being carefree in relation to consequences – even for oneself (Deng et al., 1996, pp. 27–33; M. Weber, 1917b, 1919b, pp. 126–8).

In the context of foreign policy these definitions alert us to the formal responsibilities which decision-makers take on by virtue of their role, not just for their own citizens but also – depending on the state and its outlook – for certain features of the international system. These could be ambitious, like 'leadership of the free world' or halting climate change, or limited such as taking in refugees or hosting an international court. Furthermore, an internalized sense of responsibility adds further ideas about international commitments according to the individual and the elite he or she belongs to. Some are all too eager to take on the weight of decision-making for a wider constituency; others will take a minimalist view. This is by no means determined only by the geopolitical situation of the state, as a realist might presume. It also depends on the interactions between individual leaders, domestic culture and world politics.

A list of the likely constituencies perceived by democratic foreign policy-makers would be extensive. It would begin with the constitutional remit to serve the sovereign people and its political equivalent, public opinion. It would include the responsibilities felt to government and to party colleagues, and would then move outside the state to the links with allies or privileged partners. The list would extend to some elements of the 'international community', given that democratic politicians acknowledge the importance of international law, of international organizations and of the views of those other states they respect. More subjectively decision-makers are likely also to attend to their own conscience, feeling some responsibility to history (in the sense both of past generations who have made sacrifices and grandchildren yet unborn) and even to humanity as a whole.

No clear guidance exists as to how these competing responsibilities may be reconciled, but at least the extent of the challenge should be apparent to modern leaders. States and TNAs have to look to their own members first, but will vary in their attitudes to the problems of third parties. Since foreign policy is precisely about juggling these various considerations, the problem needs clarifying. This can be done by reference to three key dimensions: legitimacy, identity and ethics. To the extent that a constituency is perceived as (i) having legitimate rights to ask for action on its behalf; (ii) being part, in some sense, of one's own group and (iii) having a strong moral claim, it is very likely to attract foreign policy support. Where it is perceived as lacking something on one or more of these criteria, it will struggle to do so.

Legitimacy involves the two-way relationship between those making foreign policy and those on whose behalf policy is being made. Although decision-makers get their basic legitimacy from their constitutional position, the international system also has an important say through the need for recognition. The leaders of Taiwan, for example, while clearly legitimate internally, represent problems for other governments who also wish to deal with the People's Republic of China (Alden, 2001).[5] Accordingly their foreign relations are more restricted than would otherwise be the case. Conversely, Sinn Féin republicans have long resisted the right of what they call 'the British government', their perpetual Other, to speak for them on the world stage. They attracted considerable legitimacy through sympathy in other countries including the United States, despite being a minority in Northern Ireland (and indeed the Irish Republic). In so doing they significantly complicated the UK government's ability to exercise its formal responsibilities.

The most basic legitimacy problem occurs when a regime is accused of failing to live up to its responsibilities. This is usually the argument made by the military when overthrowing a civilian government, as in Franco's uprising against the Spanish republican government in 1936. But the same argument was made by civilian opponents of the Assad dictatorship when in 2011 they tried to extend the Arab Spring to Syria. The ensuing chaos, as the stalemated civil war drew in Islamic fundamentalists, created confusion among concerned outsiders, both neighbours and major powers. No one is clear as to who has or should have responsibility for relieving the suffering of the Syrian people and restoring stability to the region. This is naturally also a matter of power politics, with the UN Security Council divided, but the loss of legitimacy by almost all parties to the conflict has undermined the capacity of any one of them to build a consensus around the notion of their primary responsibility for resolving matters. Even power does not exist in a vacuum. As Henry Kissinger has concluded after more than half a century of high-level diplomacy, to be effective power needs to be seen as legitimate and responsible (Kissinger, 2014).

Where both internal and external legitimacy exist a government can, and indeed should, act internationally to exercise its responsibilities. Where one or both are compromised an actor may enjoy a superficially attractive freedom from responsibility, but risks marginalization in the process. The Taliban regime in Afghanistan contemptuously dismissed outside opinion over many things, from women's rights to the destruction of Buddhist statues. This approach succeeds only up to the point where the regime needs cooperation from others in order to achieve its goals. When the patience of outsiders is exhausted then the weakness of a self-regarding foreign policy becomes apparent. This is increasingly true of the Netanyahu government's determination to ignore the widespread condemnation of its treatment of the Palestinians, and in particular of its colonization of the West Bank. Israeli power is unchallengeable, but the policy is leading to a gradual loss of legitimacy through the perception of irresponsible behaviour. This is likely to have costs which cannot be blithely ignored, especially given that the United States' staunch support cannot be taken for granted.

The twin faces of legitimacy reflect the structures within which foreign policy operates. In Martha Finnemore's (1996, p. 145) words, 'states are embedded in an international social fabric that extends from the local to the transnational'. The patterns of this fabric may resemble those of a kaleidoscope, but they are much more stable than those of globalization, where neither agents nor structures can be identified with any confidence, let alone any sites of legitimate political decision-making. Legitimacy fosters a sense of responsibility just as formal responsibility connotes a certain legitimacy. Furthermore if democracy is to have an international meaning beyond its development inside states, it will need to be anchored to sites of decision-making which have collective legitimacy, and which allocate specific responsibilities. Rosecrance (1999, pp. 18–19) has said that the rise of the virtual state 'portends a crisis for democratic politics … because national governments have insufficient jurisdiction to deal with global problems'. On the other hand, he also concludes that 'democracy does not exist in any other place [than the nation-state] – religious, corporate or cultural' (1999, p. 211).

At present foreign policy represents our only serious means of holding to account those who negotiate in the international arena. Over the last decade it has attracted more sustained interest from domestic publics and is now accepted as an integral part of public policy – no longer a world apart. Direct action and transnational pressure groups have an important role in placing and keeping issues on the political agenda, but they are a necessary rather than a sufficient condition of democratic participation. Multinational parliaments like the NATO Assembly are at best gatherings of specialists and at worse excuses for political tourism. 'Cosmopolitan democracy' resembles the latest version of idealist internationalism far more than a working model of popular sovereignty at the global level. However unpalatable it may be, the way the US Congress obstructs the UN is an example of democracy influencing events through the foreign policy process. Amnesty International's campaign against capital punishment worldwide is not – it represents, rather, the vital freedom *enabled* by democracy to raise the level of civilized discourse about politics, which is another matter. The familiar challenge is therefore to ensure that democracy has its voice while attempting to provide practical political leadership in an international environment in which there will always be robust differences of view.

A balancing act of this kind is most likely to succeed where both subjects and objects of foreign policy share some sense of common *identity*. Ultimately this could mean a functional balance between feelings of citizenship and common humanity for all of us, worldwide, but for the present this is not realistic. Accepting responsibility means both acknowledging the obligation on the subject (in this case, the foreign policy decision-maker) and the attachment to the object, which may include certain groups of 'foreigners' with whom there is a clear sense of community, or at least affinity, however temporary and issue-driven. The attachment to domestic constituents can be taken for granted, except that the inadequacy of mechanisms for foreign policy accountability places great weight on internalized obligations and 'notional constraints' of the kind referred to in Chapter 10 in relation to public opinion.

If there is too much attachment and identification this can be just as big a problem. Hitler and Mussolini both began by asserting the superiority of their own *Volk*, but ended with bitter contempt for the way their own peoples had 'failed' them. Their record also demonstrates how a lack of any sense of responsibility for anyone outside the state, including the principle of international order, leads to a purblind nationalism, xenophobia and ultimately a loss of touch with reality. Even a lesser form of nationalism, if strongly majoritarian, might drive some minorities to seek foreign help, thus challenging sovereignty and producing further international tensions. This has long been the story of Turkey's relations with its Kurdish population and it was the essence of the Kosovo crisis which finally blew up in the face of Serbia in 1999.

On the other side of the coin, if a government exaggerates its international responsibilities it risks both neglecting its primary constituency and inciting competitive reactions from other states. This was the case with Fidel Castro's persistent hopes for international revolution which led him to expend scarce resources on armed forces – in 1985 they ranked third in size in the Americas behind only the US and Brazil – and on entanglements in Angola, the Congo and various Latin American trouble spots. Given the existing hostility of the United States this predictably worsened the sanctions against Cuba and damaged the well-being of his own people. Only they could judge whether the sacrifice was justifiable, but were not in a position to express their views freely on the matter.

At the theoretical level, foreign policy and national identity are closely related. While 'identity is an inescapable dimension of being' it is also 'a site in which political struggles are enacted' (Campbell 1998, p. 226). Campbell distinguishes between 'foreign policy' (the representational practices of a general kind which lead us to dichotomize relationships between self and other) and 'Foreign Policy', which is the 'conventional' phenomenon associated with the state. In his view the latter is a privileged discourse which reproduces the boundaries of identity already achieved by the persistent association in any society between attitudes to outsiders and feelings of danger and enmity (1998, pp. 68–72). Either way, 'foreign' policy is a key means of ensuring that an exclusive 'us versus them' mentality is perpetuated within the sovereign states out of which it has grown.

The position here is that this goes too far, and that in fact foreign policy can enlarge our ethical and emotional range if conducted legitimately and with a self-conscious sense of responsibility. The changing politics of both the state and international relations since the dawn of the Cold War have led many foreign policy-makers to reconfigure their approaches, given that their feelings of identity, and those of their fellow citizens, are no longer uncomplicatedly confined within the paradigm of the nation-state (if, indeed, they ever were). Accordingly it is neither possible nor desirable to define just in domestic terms the particular set of concerns which constitute a country's foreign policy – any given 'solution' will invariably involve some compliance by other states and change in the international system. Any degree of identification with outsiders therefore, however partial, changes perceptions about responsibilities, which start to extend beyond the formal boundaries of the state.

Identity and foreign policy certainly are sites for 'political struggles', as with Latin American views of 'Yanqui imperialism', or the conflicts over the degree to which Russia and Turkey can be seen as part of Europe. But these struggles do not always go the way of the exclusivists and dichotomizers. Indeed foreign policy in the twenty-first century is unavoidably about how a society may come to terms with living *in* the world, rather than despite it, and about how agents must be understood as embedded within international structures, not separate and above them. The subjects and objects of foreign policy are far from sharing the same sense of identity, but to the extent that there are increasing overlaps, the ties of responsibility will be strengthened.

Although the concept of responsibility incorporates the ideas of legitimacy and identity, *ethics* is at its heart. Since the emergence of human rights concerns in the 1970s, institutionalized by the Helsinki Accords of the Conference on Security and Cooperation in Europe, there has been ever more talk about following an 'ethical foreign policy', or – in the more cautious formulation of British Foreign Secretary Robin Cook, providing an 'ethical dimension' to foreign policy. The end of the Cold War spheres of influence naturally gave a big boost to this movement, and eventually produced the R2P doctrine which has influenced official discourse, if not practice, in many countries.

The content of an ethical foreign policy is a problem which goes beyond the ambitions of this book. It has generated an extensive and sophisticated political theory literature (Bell, 2010; C. Brown, 2010; Vincent, 1986b). Certain contextual comments are, however, in order. First, foreign policy cannot avoid having an ethical dimension, even if it is only discussed overtly at certain junctures. Even the most hardened realist has views about international order which have a value content. Foreign policy always has consequences for others which have to be weighed up on criteria which are rarely so crude as to relate only to immediate self-interest. Any use of international law, even to make technical agreements, makes implicit judgements about such things as trust, obligations and principles of distribution. Second, if ethical concerns are to be acted upon in international relations there are few other sites available than foreign policy. It is a true optimist who has faith in the self-executing properties of cosmopolitan democracy.

Third, foreign policy by definition cannot be primarily cosmopolitan, let alone self-abnegatory, in its ethic. It exists, in the first instance, as the instrument of a very particular political process and set of concerns and thus reflects the values behind them – which is why, in the 1990s wave of internationalist enthusiasm, foreign policy was often seen as anti-progressive and anachronistic. Yet these 'concerns' are precisely not synonymous with narrowly drawn interests. Interests, or stakes, are an important part of the story but are conjoined with ideas about preferred ways of living in which the nation-state in question is inevitably one part of a wider whole, whether the European Union, the Islamic world, the West or the international community. They thus will sometimes lead to actions which do not reflect obvious self-interests, as with the high levels of development aid committed by most of the Scandinavian countries. Even when this kind of high-mindedness is absent, or cannot be afforded, a foreign policy will still represent a form of ethical compromise between specific values which arise from a country's distinctive experiences, those which are shared with like-minded states, and those which involve taking longer and wider perspectives to think about how to improve the overall environment in which all have to work.

Fourth, therefore, the popular discourse about a contest between interests and morals in foreign policy must be put to rest. Every community pursues some concerns which are particular and some which are general. This is the key distinction made by Arnold Wolfers between possessional and milieu goals. But we need to go further to accept that the two types cannot always be sharply distinguished, for some possessional goals will either be identical with those of some other states, or will significantly overlap with them. What may seem pure self-interest can indeed shade into a general principle. Nor is this always a matter of gradually creating a bigger unit through integration. Often the overlapping will be with states or groups beyond regional or alliance partners, or it will be partial and intermittent. If international relations contains many cross-cutting cleavages, foreign policy can be about the obverse: creating cross-binding ties. A real sense of ethical responsibility towards outsiders, if without clear boundaries or structure, is thus an inherent quality of much contemporary foreign policy, without falling back on mere moralising. The idea of 'good international citizenship', formulated by Gareth Evans (2008) when he was the Australian foreign minister, is an interesting attempt to provide guidelines for this dual approach, and from the perspective, for once, of practical policy-making (Linklater, 1992; Wheeler and Dunne, 1998, 2001, pp. 169–70).

At the highest level of generality foreign policy is a means of mediating between possessional and milieu concerns, between one community and the community of communities which is the international system. It entails a constant series of actions and choices over resources, values and partners – in short, over the nature of responsibility. It is rarely used simply as a battering ram for maximising national interests regardless of the wider impact, and when it is it produces shock waves across the system, as over Ukraine in 2014. The problem is more often the reverse, in that national diplomats often attract criticism at home precisely because they are immersed in the international environment, having to represent its needs to the domestic audience as well as vice versa. They are therefore in a double bind: of having responsibilities to a number of different constituencies but possibly the backing of none. This is a formidable ethical and practical challenge.

Expectations of Foreign Policy

Foreign policy suffers from having too little and too much expected of it. The academic subject of International Relations attracts ever more researchers, but often those with apparently little interest in *politics*. Instead they continue to head off enthusiastically towards the frontiers of meta-theory, or to import concepts from other social sciences, especially sociology and anthropology. In the powerful US profession, by contrast, the influence of economic thinking is still predominant. Where it is not, and scholars grapple with actual policy dilemmas, they tend to be preoccupied with debates inside the Washington Beltway. Either way, through scholasticism or ethnocentrism, some of the important intellectual and practical issues generated by international politics get neglected. Foreign policy studies, in particular, suffer from the preference for horizontal issues over country studies and the discussion of structure more than agency. Incredibly, in the rich and vibrant universities of Europe it is now difficult to find courses on the government and politics, let alone the foreign policies, even of France, Germany and the UK, such is the fatalism about the fate of the nation-state. This represents a failure of responsibility on the part of the IR community.

In the world of political argument, by contrast, too much is expected of foreign policy. For liberal states it is becoming ever more difficult to turn a blind eye to serious unrest anywhere in the world. Foreign policy now focuses not just on problems between states, but on their internal affairs – and well beyond the proper concern with genocide which has driven on R2P. This does not mean that effective action is taken, or indeed that it is often feasible. But the interest in human rights and good governance does raise expectations and lead to corresponding disappointments. In many ways, as seen over Syria, the worst of all outcomes is to talk loudly and carry a small stick. This draws fire and complicates events, but resolves nothing. European Union foreign policy has very often been guilty of such behaviour (Hill, 1993b, 1998).

It is true that Western states have reduced their defence expenditures in recent years, and that the quagmires in Iraq and Afghanistan have made them increasingly allergic to the idea of military intervention. This did not, however, prevent regime change in Libya, or the horribly over-optimistic assumption that the chaos of post-Saddam Iraq would not be repeated. Nor has it attenuated the persistent French assumption that it has a historic role to be the gendarme of Africa, illustrated in 2013 and 2014 by its sending of troops to Mali and to the Central African Republic. Only a negative vote in the British Parliament in 2014 prevented the bombing of Syria. Even so, after some horrific videos of the beheading of hostages by Daesh, the air forces of a number of Arab and NATO countries were committed to bombings in Iraq with a prob-able extension of operations into Syria. It may be that these operations will succeed in stabilising the region and defeating the jihadists, but it is just as likely that the states involved realize that little more can be achieved than damage limitation.

More common even than hubris in foreign policy is the desire to do *something* – to respond to the challenges of a world in which change seems often to come out of left field. The optimistic certainties of the mid-1990s are now a distant memory. Even the most assertive and powerful states are struggling to manage the intractable conflicts in the Middle East, and in more than one region of Africa. And yet the ever more numerous pressure groups, together with decision-makers them-selves, expect a great deal of the foreign policies of their own state and of others. This existential reaction against fatalism, partly fuelled by ethics, is wholly understandable. Foreign policy has an indispensable part to play in helping human beings to assert some control over their own destiny. It also represents the route by which states can coordinate common strategies and achieve a multiplier of power on difficult prob-lems.

The United Nations Organisation is the established forum for inter-national discussion, and much foreign policy is conducted there. But the UN suffers from such severe limitations that expectations have almost fallen below the organization's actual capability (Paul Taylor, 2000, pp. 304–5). The reality is that no world organization (let alone the mystical 'global governance') is capable of delivering *in and of itself* serious and specific decisions on change. It is the actors, primarily states, which do that by reaching collective agreement – sometimes in international organizations, but just as often outside them. Until the world no longer consists of self-standing, constitutionally independent communities which engage in systematic relations with each other, there will always exist something which amounts to foreign policy, however it is labelled.

The purposes of foreign policy are articulated by elites and to some extent are shaped by mass society. As usually stated, they are banal. Yet beneath the surface this is one of the most creative, demanding and exciting of human activities, worthy of serious intellectual attention. It carries heavy responsibilities for the lives of ordinary people in every country, in terms of their vulnerability not just to war and devastation, but also to environmental degradation, population pressure, economic dislocation and ideological conflict. These problems cannot be 'solved', but they have to be managed. Agreements reached through foreign policy, which entails negotiation precisely because it derives from diverse perceptions, interests and values, are the only way forward. Foreign policy and international organization (including INGOs as well as IGOs) are necessary but not sufficient conditions of international order. They are partners, not opposites.

The political strategies of international actors confront, *mutatis mutandis*, the same great challenge as politics within a single community, which has exercised political philosophers down the centuries: how to reconcile 'our' legitimate needs and preoccupations, whether as individuals or subgroups, with (i) the equivalent concerns of others; (ii) the less tangible issues of collective goods and structures; (iii) obligations to future generations (abstract), including our children and grandchildren (compelling). In its fundamentals, foreign policy is about these first order questions, which is why major theorists like Walzer and Rawls have been drawn inexorably outwards, to reflect on the nature of 'liberal foreign policy'.

Of course not all states are liberal. Many are struggling with difficult problems of economic development, some are seriously unstable and yet others seem confident that they can manage their own affairs without following the uneasy mixture of preaching, post-colonial angst and economic self-interest which tends to characterize the foreign policies of Western countries. Significant powers like Brazil, China, India, Indonesia, Nigeria, Russia and Saudi Arabia now pursue more assertive diplomacies reflecting their own distinctive histories and value systems – which currently means clinging more tenaciously to the European invention of sovereignty than do the Europeans themselves. Yet they too show signs of recognising that 'rising power' involves more than just aspiring to the place in the sun dreamed of by nineteenth-century Prussian nationalists. Crude power-grabs still happen in the international system, but for the most part its growing complexity renders them counterproductive. If they, and the older states of the West, can accept during the twenty-first century that foreign policy has the potential for many constructive uses, and does not have to be a discourse of fear and antagonism, then there is a chance that our revived, and revised, expectations of the practice will be justified.

Notes

1 Although mainly about war Walzer (1977) is extremely relevant to these issues, especially in the preface to the revised edition (2006) which discusses the problem of regime change.

2 In Germany the influence of the *Länder* is significant, if mainly felt indirectly, via consultations on EU intergovernmental conferences (IGCs) and on the implementation of trade policy. Enlargement and migration are other obvious areas where the federal government has to work with the *Länder*. They also have a constitutional role in the Bundesrat, which has committees dealing with both foreign affairs and defence. Individual *Länder* like Bavaria only have occasional foreign visibility on matters like relations with the Czech Republic, or the politics of export promotion.

3 Thucydides' comment is from the Melian Dialogue: 'the strong do what they have the power to do and the weak accept what they have to accept' (Thucydides, p. 402).

4 This is why there was such an uproar over the behaviour of Francesco Schettino, the captain who abandoned his passengers on the *Costa Concordia* after it hit rocks in 2012 off the Italian island of Giglio.

5 Nelson Mandela faced the dilemma almost as soon as he took power, being grateful to Taiwan for support to the ANC under apartheid, but also needing to have relations with Beijing.

Further Reading

Brown, Chris, 2010. *Practical Judgement in International Political Theory: Selected Essays*. Much sharp analysis can be found here from one of the few at ease in both international political theory and foreign policy analysis.

Donelan, Michael, 2007. *Honor in Foreign Policy*. Stimulating and unorthodox, this approach to the problem of motives in foreign policy uses natural law and historical debates to challenge the preoccupation with interests.

Lebow, Richard Ned, 2010. *Forbidden Fruit: Counterfactuals and International Relations*. These stimulating essays from a senior figure in both IR and political psychology consider how things might have been different, challenging the orthodox approach to causation.

Walzer, Michael, 1977. *Just and Unjust Wars: A Moral Argument with Historical Illustrations*. This is the classic text for anyone thinking about duties beyond borders.

Bibliography

Aaronovitch, David, 2009. *Voodoo Histories: The Role of the Conspiracy Theory in Shaping Modern History*. London: Jonathan Cape.

Abdelrahman, Maha, 2014. *Egypt's Long Revolution: Protest Movements and Uprisings*. Abingdon, UK: Routledge.

Abelson, Donald E., 2009. What were they thinking? Think tanks, the Bush presidency and US foreign policy. In: Inderjeet Parmar, Linda B. Miller and Mark Ledwidge, eds, 2009, *New Directions in US Foreign Policy*. Abingdon, UK: Routledge.

Abse, Leo, 1989. *Margaret, Daughter of Beatrice: A Politician's Psychobiography of Margaret Thatcher*. London: Cape.

Adamthwaite, Anthony, 1977. *France and the Coming of the Second World War*. London: Frank Cass.

Addison, Paul, 1975. *The Road to 1945: British Politics and the Second World War*. London: Cape.

Adler, Emanuel, 2002. Constructivism and International Relations. In: Walter Carlsnaes, Thomas Risse and Beth A. Simmons, eds, 2002, *Handbook of International Relations*. London: Sage.

Adorno, Theodor W., Frenkel-Brunswik, Else, Levinson, Daniel J. and Sanford, R. Nevitt, 1950. *The Authoritarian Personality*. New York: Harper & Bros.

Aggestam, Lisbeth, 2004. A European foreign policy? Role conceptions and the politics of identity in Britain, France and Germany. PhD dissertation, Stockholm University.

Alden, Chris, 2001. Solving South Africa's Chinese puzzle: Foreign policy-making and the 'two Chinas' question. In: Jim Broderick, Gary Burford and Gordon Freer, eds, 2001, *South Africa's Foreign Policy*. London: Palgrave.

——, 2007. *China in Africa*. London: Zed Books.

—— and Aran, Amnon, 2012. *Foreign Policy Analysis: New Approaches*. London: Routledge.

Aldrich, Richard J., Andrew, Christopher and Wark, Wesley K., eds, 2009. *Secret Intelligence: A Reader*. London: Routledge.

Alger, Chadwick, 1962. The external bureaucracy in United States foreign affairs. *Administrative Science Quarterly*, 7(1), pp. 50–78.

——, 1977. 'Foreign' policies of US publics. *International Studies Quarterly*, 21(2), pp. 277–318.

——, 1990. The world relations of cities – closing the gap between social science paradigms and everyday human experience. *International Studies Quarterly*, 34(4), pp. 493–518.

Allison, Graham, 1969. Conceptual models and the Cuban Missile Crisis. *American Political Science Review*, 63(3), pp. 689–718.

——, 1971. *Essence of Decision: Explaining the Cuban Missile Crisis.* Boston, MA: Little, Brown.

—— and Szanton, Peter, 1976. *Remaking Foreign Policy: The Organizational Connection.* New York: Basic Books.

—— and Zelikow, Philip, 1999. *Essence of Decision: Explaining the Cuban Missile Crisis.* Second edition. New York: Addison-Wesley.

Almond, Gabriel, 1950. *The American People and Foreign Policy.* New York: Harcourt and Brace.

Alterman, Eric, 1997. Reading foreign policy: Are those journals talking to us? *The Nation,* 27 October.

Ambrose, Stephen E., 1991–2. The presidency and foreign policy. *Foreign Affairs,* 70(5), pp. 120–37.

——, 2012. *Rise to Globalism: American Foreign Policy Since 1938.* Ninth edition. London: Penguin.

Anderson, Benedict, 1991. *Imagined Communities.* London: Verso.

Andreae, Lisette and Kaiser, Karl, 2001. The 'foreign policies' of specialized ministries. In: Wolf-Dieter Eberwein and Karl Kaiser, eds, 2001, *Germany's New Foreign Policy: Decision-Making in an Interdependent World,* pp. 38–57. London: Palgrave.

Andreatta, Filippo and Hill, Christopher, 1997. Italy. In: Jolyon Howorth and Anand Menon, eds, 1997, *The European Union and National Defence Policy.* London: Routledge.

Andrew, Christopher, 1989. Churchill and intelligence. In: Michael I. Handel, ed., 1989, *Leaders and Intelligence,* pp. 181–93. London: Cass.

——, 2009. *Defence of the Realm: The Authorized History of MI5.* London: Allen Lane.

Anholt, Simon, 2006. *Competitive Identity: The New Brand Management for Nations, Cities and Regions.* London: Palgrave.

Aran, Amnon, 2009. *Israel's Foreign Policy Towards the PLO: The Impact of Globalization.* Brighton, UK: Sussex Academic Press.

Archibugi, Daniele, Koenig-Archibugi, Mathias and Marchetti, Raffaele, eds, 2011. *Global Democracy: Normative and Empirical Perspectives.* Cambridge: Cambridge University Press.

Arendt, Hannah, 1958. *The Human Condition.* Chicago: University of Chicago Press.

Armstrong, Anne, 1989. Bridging the gap: Intelligence and policy. *Washington Quarterly,* 12(1), pp. 21–34.

Armstrong, David, 1993. *Revolution and World Order.* Oxford: Clarendon Press.

——, 1999. Law, justice and the idea of a world society. *International Affairs,* 75(3), pp. 547–61.

Aron, Raymond, 1966. *Peace and War: A Theory of International Relations.* London: Weidenfeld & Nicolson.

——, 1975. *Imperial Republic: The United States and the World.* London: Weidenfeld & Nicolson.

Ashton, Nigel, 2008. *King Hussein of Jordan: A Political Life.* New Haven, CT: Yale University Press.

Aspaturian, Vernon, 1971. *Process and Power in Soviet Foreign Policy.* Boston, MA: Little, Brown.

Auger, Vincent A., 1996. *The Dynamics of Foreign Policy Analysis: The Carter Administration and the Neutron Bomb.* Lanham, MD: Rowland and Littlefield.

Aust, Helmut Philipp and Vashakmadze, Mindia, 2008. Parliamentary consent to the use of German armed forces abroad: The 2008 decision of the Federal Constitutional Court in the AWACS/Turkey case. *German Law Journal*, 9, pp. 2223–36.

Axelrod, Robert, ed., 1976. *Structure of Decision: The Cognitive Maps of Political Elites.* Princeton, NJ: Princeton University Press.

Bacchus, William L., 1983. *Staffing for Foreign Affairs: Personnel Systems for the 1980s and 1990s.* Princeton, NJ: Princeton University Press.

Bachrach, Peter and Baratz, Morton, 1970. *Power and Poverty: Theory and Practice.* New York: Oxford University Press.

Baldwin, David, 1985. *Economic Statecraft.* Princeton, NJ: Princeton University Press.

Barber, James, 1979. Economic sanctions as a policy instrument. *International Affairs*, 55(3), pp. 367–84.

Barber, James D., 1972. *The Presidential Character: Predicting Performance in the White House.* Englewood Cliffs, NJ: Prentice-Hall.

Barkawi, Tarak, 2008. 'Small wars', big consequences and Orientalism: Korea and Iraq. *Arena*, 29/30, pp. 59–80.

—— and Laffey, Mark, eds, 2001. *Democracy, Liberalism, and War: Rethinking the Democratic Peace Debate.* Boulder, CO: Lynne Rienner.

Barston, Ronald P., 1997. *Modern Diplomacy.* Second edition. London: Longman.

——, 2013. *Modern Diplomacy.* Fourth edition. Harlow: Pearson.

Bartsch, Sebastian, 2001. Political foundations: Linking the worlds of foreign policy and transnationalism. In: Wolf-Dieter Eberwein and Karl Kaiser, eds, 2001, *Germany's New Foreign Policy: Decision-Making in an Interdependent World.* Houndmills, UK: Palgrave.

Baumann, Rainer and Hellmann, Gunther, 2013. Germany and the use of military force: 'Total war' the 'culture of restraint' and the quest for normality. In: Douglas Webber, ed., 2013, *New Europe, New Germany, Old Foreign Policy? German Foreign Policy since Unification.* Second edition, pp. 61–82. Abingdon, UK: Routledge.

—— and Stengel, Frank A., 2014. Foreign policy analysis, globalization and non-state actors: State-centric after all? *Journal of International Relations and Development*, 17(4), pp. 489–521.

Baylis, John, Smith, Steve and Owens, Patricia, eds, 2011. *The Globalization of World Politics: An Introduction to International Relations.* Fifth edition. Oxford: Oxford University Press.

Beach, Derek, 2012. *Analyzing Foreign Policy.* Houndmills, UK: Palgrave Macmillan.

Beckley, Michael, 2011. China's century? Why America's edge will endure. *International Security*, 36(3), pp. 41–78.

Beckwith Charlie A. and Knox, Donald, 1984. *Delta Force: The US Counter-Terrorist Unit and the Iranian Hostage Rescue Mission.* London: Arms and Armour Press.

Bell, Duncan, ed., 2010. *Ethics and World Politics.* Oxford: Oxford University Press.

Berkovitch, Jacob, ed., 1988. *ANZUS in Crisis: Alliance Management in International Affairs.* London: Macmillan.

Berridge, G. R., 2010. *Diplomacy: Theory and Practice.* Fourth edition. Houndmills, UK: Palgrave Macmillan.

——, 2011. *The Counter-Revolution in Diplomacy and Other Essays.* Houndmills, UK: Palgrave Macmillan.

——, 2012. *Embassies in Armed Conflict.* London: Bloomsbury.

—— and James, Alan, 2003. *A Dictionary of Diplomacy.* Second edition. Houndmills, UK: Palgrave Macmillan.

Beshoff, Pamela, 1988. Structuralist and realist perspectives in Jamaican foreign policy 1972–1980. Unpublished PhD thesis. London School of Economics and Political Science.

Bettelheim, Bruno, 1987. *A Good Enough Parent.* London: Thames & Hudson.

Betts, Richard, 1977. *Soldiers, Statesmen and Cold War Crises.* Cambridge, MA: Harvard University Press.

Bialer, Seweryn and Mandelbaum, Michael, eds, 1988. *Gorbachev's Russia and American Foreign Policy.* Boulder, CO: Westview.

Blainey, Geoffrey, 1973. *The Causes of Wars.* London: Macmillan.

Blair, Tony, 1999. Speech entitled 'Doctrine of the international community', 22 April. Chicago, IL, United States.

——, 2001. Leader's speech to the 2001 Labour Party Conference, 2 October. Brighton, UK.

Bleiker, Roland, and Hutchison, Emma, 2008. Fear no more: Emotions and world politics. *Review of International Studies*, 34(special issue), pp. 115–35.

Blondel, Jean and Müller-Rommel, Ferdinand, 1997. *Cabinets in Western Europe.* Second edition. London: Macmillan.

Boateng, Paul, 2014. Debate on 'Soft power and conflict prevention'. Hansard of the House of Lords, 5 December, col. 1533.

Booth, Ken, 2007. *Theory of World Security.* Cambridge: Cambridge University Press.

—— and Wheeler, Nicholas J., 2007. *The Security Dilemma: Fear, Cooperation and Trust in World Politics.* Houndmills, UK: Palgrave Macmillan.

Boulding, Kenneth, 1956. *The Image.* Ann Arbor, MI: University of Michigan.

——, 1989. *Three Faces of Power.* Newbury Park, CA: Sage.

Boyce, Peter J., 1977. *Foreign Affairs for New States: Some Questions of Credentials.* St Lucia: University of Queensland Press.

Braithwaite, Rodric, 2006. *Moscow 1941: A City and its People at War.* London: Profile Books.

Braybrooke, David and Lindblom, Charles E., 1963. *A Strategy of Decision: Policy Evaluation as a Social Process*. New York: Free Press.

Brecher, Michael, 1972. *The Foreign Policy System of Israel: Setting, Images, Process*. Oxford: Oxford University Press.

——, 1999. International studies in the twentieth century and beyond: Flawed dichotomies, synthesis, cumulation. *International Studies Quarterly*, 43(2), pp. 213–64.

Brenner, Philip, Haney, Patrick J. and Vanderbush, Walt, 2008. Intermestic interests and US policy toward Cuba. In: Eugene R. Wittkopf and James M. McCormick, eds, 2008, *The Domestic Sources of American Foreign Policy*. Fifth edition, pp. 65–80. Lanham, MD: Rowman & Littlefield.

Brighi, Elisabetta, 2013. *Foreign Policy, Domestic Politics and International Relations: The Case of Italy*. Abingdon, UK: Routledge.

—— and Hill, Christopher, 2012. Implementation and behaviour. In: Steve Smith, Tim Dunne and Amelia Hadfield, eds, 2012, *Foreign Policy Analysis in International Relations*. Second edition, pp. 147–67. Oxford: Oxford University Press.

Bright, John, 1858. Speech on 'foreign policy'. 29 October, Birmingham, UK. In: *Selected Speeches of the Rt. Honourable John Bright MP on Public Questions*. London: J. M. Dent & Sons, 1907.

Brown, Archie, 2014. *The Myth of the Strong Leader: Political Leadership in the Modern Age*. London: Penguin Books.

Brown, Chris, 2001. Moral agency and international society. *Ethics & International Affairs*, 15(2), pp. 87–98.

——, 2010. *Practical Judgement in International Political Theory: Selected Essays*. London: Routledge.

Brown, Michael E., Lynn-Jones, Sean M. and Miller, Steven E., eds, 1996. *Debating the Democratic Peace*. Cambridge, MA: MIT Press.

Browne, Donald R., 1982. *International Radio Broadcasting: The Limits of the Limitless Medium*. New York: Praeger.

Brownlie, Ian, 1966. *Principles of International Public Law*. Oxford: Clarendon Press.

Brzezinski, Zbigniew, 1983. *Power and Principle: Memoirs of the National Security Adviser, 1977–1981*. London: Weidenfeld & Nicolson.

Bueno de Mesquita, Bruce and McDermott, Rose, 2004. Crossing no man's land: Cooperation from the trenches. *Political Psychology*, 25(2), pp. 271–87.

Bull, Hedley, 1977. *The Anarchical Society: A Study of Order in World Politics*. London: Macmillan.

——, 2012. *The Anarchical Society: A Study of Order in World Politics*. Fourth edition, with forewords by Stanley Hoffman and Andrew Hurrell. Houndmills, UK: Palgrave Macmillan.

—— and Watson, Adam, eds, 1984. *The Expansion of International Society*. Oxford: Clarendon Press.

Bulmer, Simon, Maurer, Andreas and Paterson, William, 2001. The European policy-making machinery in the Berlin Republic: hindrance or handmaiden? In: Douglas Webber, ed., 2001, New Europe, New

Germany, Old Foreign Policy? German Foreign Policy since Unification. Special Issue of *German Politics*, 10(1), pp. 177–206.

Burke, Edmund, 1774. Speech at the Conclusion of the Poll in Bristol, 3 November 1774. In: Paul Langford, ed., 1996, *The Writings and Speeches of Edmund Burke. Vol. III: Party, Parliament, and the American War, 1774–1778.* Oxford: Clarendon Press.

Burton, John W., 1972. *World Society*. Cambridge: Cambridge University Press.

Buzan, Barry, 1995. The levels of analysis problem in International Relations reconsidered. In: Ken Booth and Steve Smith, eds, 1995, *International Relations Theory Today*. Oxford: Polity Press.

——, 2004. *From International to World Society? English School theory and the Social Structure of Globalisation*. Cambridge: Cambridge University Press.

—— and Little, Richard, 1993. *The Logic of Anarchy in International Relations: Neorealism to Structural Realism*. New York: Columbia University Press.

Byers, Michael, 1999. *Custom, Power and the Power of Rules: International Relations and Customary International Law*. Cambridge: Cambridge University Press.

——, 2008. International law. In: Christian Reus-Smit and Duncan Snidal, eds, 2008, *The Oxford Handbook of International* Relations, pp. 612–31. Oxford: Oxford University Press.

Cairncross, Frances, 1997. *The Death of Distance: How the Communications Revolution Will Change Our Lives*. London: Orion Business Books.

Calder, Angus, 1971. *The People's War*. London: Granada.

Calvert, Peter, 1986. *The Foreign Policy of New States*. Brighton, UK: Wheatsheaf.

Cameron, Fraser, 2012. *An Introduction to European Foreign Policy*. Second edition. Abingdon, UK: Routledge.

Campbell, Alistair, 2007. *The Blair Years: Extracts from the Alastair Campbell Diaries*. London: Hutchinson.

Campbell, David, 1992. *Writing Security: United States Foreign Policy and the Politics of Identity*. Minneapolis, MN: University of Minnesota Press.

——, 1998. *Writing Security: United States Foreign Policy and the Politics of Identity*. Revised edition. Manchester, UK: Manchester University Press.

Campbell, Glenn, 2013. Scottish independence: Lessons from the Czech/Slovak split. *BBC Scotland News*, 20 January.

Carbone, Maurizio, 2007. *The European Union and International Development: The Politics of Foreign Aid*. Abingdon, UK: Routledge.

Carey, Benedict, 2011. Teasing out policy insight from a character profile. *New York Times*, 28 March.

Carley, Michael, 1981. Analytic rationality. In: Anthony G. McGrew and Michael J. Wilson, eds, 1982, *Decision Making: Approaches and Analysis*, pp. 60–6. Manchester, UK: Manchester University Press.

Carlsnaes, Walter, 1992. The agency-structure problem in foreign policy analysis. *International Studies Quarterly*, 36(3), pp. 245–70.

——, 1994. In lieu of a conclusion: Compatibility and the agency-structure issue in foreign policy analysis. In: Walter Carlsnaes and Steve Smith, eds, 1994, *European Foreign Policy: The EC and Changing Perspectives in Europe*, pp. 274–87. London: Sage.

——, 2002. Foreign policy. In: Walter Carlsnaes, Thomas Risse and Beth A. Simmons, eds, 2002, *Handbook of International Relations*, pp. 298–325. London: Sage.

Carr, Edward H., 1939. *The Twenty Years' Crisis, 1919–1939: An Introduction to the Study of International Relations*. London: Macmillan.

——, 2001. *The Twenty Years' Crisis, 1919–1939: An Introduction to the Study of International Relations*. Second edition. Basingstoke: Palgrave.

Carruthers, Susan L., 2011. *The Media at War*. Second edition. Basingstoke: Palgrave Macmillan.

Carstairs, Charles and Ware, Richard, eds, 1991. *Parliament and International Relations*. Milton Keynes: Open University Press.

Cassen, Robert, 1986. *Does Aid Work?* Oxford: Clarendon Press.

Cassese, Antonio, 1993. International law. In: Joel Krieger, ed., 2001, *Oxford Companion to World Politics*. New York: Oxford University Press.

Ceadel, Martin, 1980. *Pacifism in Britain, 1914–45: The Defining of a Faith*. Oxford: Clarendon Press.

——, 1996. *Thinking about Peace and War*. Oxford: Oxford University Press.

Cerny, Philip G., 2000. Political agency in a globalizing world: Towards a structurational approach. *European Journal of International Relations*, 6(4), pp. 435–63.

Chang, Ha-Joon, ed., 2003. *Globalization, Economic Development and The Role of the State*. London: Zed Press.

——, 2010. *23 Things They Don't Tell You About Capitalism*. London: Allen Lane.

Chang, Jung and Halliday, Jon, 2005. *Mao: The Unknown Story*. London: Jonathan Cape.

Charillon, Frédéric, 1999. *La Politique Étrangère à L'épreuve du Transnational: Une Étude des Diplomaties Française et Britannique dans la Guerre du Golfe*. Paris: l'Harmattan.

——, ed., 2002. *Politique Étrangère: Nouveaux Regards*. Paris: Presses de Sciences Po.

Chase, Robert, Hill, Emily and Kennedy, Paul, eds, 1999. *The Pivotal States: A New Framework for US Policy in the Developing World*. New York: W. W. Norton.

Chong, Alan and Maass, Mathias, eds, 2010. The foreign policy power of small states. Special section of the *Cambridge Review of International Affairs*, 23(3), pp. 381–453.

Clark, Christopher, 2013. *The Sleepwalkers: How Europe went to War in 1914*. London: Penguin Books.

Clark, Ian, 1997. *Globalization and Fragmentation: International Relations in the Twentieth Century*. Oxford: Oxford University Press.

——, 1998. Beyond the great divide: Globalization and the theory of international relations. *Review of International Studies*, 24(4), pp. 479–98.

——, 1999. *Globalization and International Relations Theory*. Oxford: Oxford University Press.

Clarke, Ian M., 2013. *The Spatial Organisation of Multinational Corporations*. Second edition. London: Routledge.

Clarke, Michael, 1992. *British External Policy-Making in the 1990s*. London: Macmillan.

Cobban, Alfred, 1963. *A History of Modern France, Vol. 1: 1715–1799*. Third edition. Harmondsworth: Penguin.

Cohen, Bernard C., 1973. *The Public's Impact on Foreign Policy*. Boston, MA: Little, Brown.

Cohen, Raymond, 1987. *Theatre of Power: The Art of Diplomatic Signalling*. London: Longman.

——, 1997. *Negotiating across Cultures: International Communication in an Interdependent World*. Revised edition. Washington, DC: United States Institute of Peace Press.

——, 1998. Putting diplomatic studies on the map. Diplomatic Studies Programme Newsletter, 4 May.

——, 2001a. Resolving conflict across languages. *Negotiation Journal*, 17(1), pp. 17–34.

——, 2001b. Living and teaching across cultures. *International Studies Perspectives*, 2(2), pp. 151–60.

Cohen, Samy, 2003. *La Résistance des États: Les Démocraties Face aux Défis de la Mondialisation*. Paris: Seuil.

Cohen, Warren I., 1993. *America in the Age of Soviet Power*. Cambridge: Cambridge University Press.

Coker, Christopher, 1989. *Reflections on American Foreign Policy*. London: Pinter.

Collier, Paul, 2007. *The Bottom Billion: Why the Poorest Countries are Failing and What Can be Done About It*. New York: Oxford University Press.

——, 2010. *Wars, Guns and Votes: Democracy in Dangerous Places*. London: Vintage.

Collins, Alan, 2002. East Asia and the Pacific Rim: Japan and China. In: Mark Webber and Michael Smith, eds, 2002, *Foreign Policy in a Transformed World*. Harlow: Prentice Hall

Commonwealth Secretariat, 1997. *A Future for Small States: Overcoming Vulnerability*. London: Commonwealth Secretariat.

Cooper, Richard N., 1968. *The Economics of Interdependence*. New York: Council on Foreign Relations and McGraw-Hill.

Cooper, Robert, 1996. *The Post-Modern State and the World Order*. London: Demos.

——, 2003. *The Breaking of Nations: Order and Chaos in the Twenty-First Century*. London: Atlantic Books.

——, 2012. Hubris and false hopes. *Policy Review*, 30 March. Hoover Institution (www.hoover.org/research/hubris-and-false-hopes). 8 June 2015.

Cowper-Coles, Sherard, 2012. *Cables from Kabul: The Inside Story of the West's Afghanistan Campaign*. London: HarperPress.

Cradock, Percy, 1994. *Experience of China*. London: John Murray.

——, 1997. *In Pursuit of British Interests: Reflections on Foreign Policy under Margaret Thatcher and John Major*. London: Murray.

Crenson, Matthew A., 1971. *The Un-politics of Air Pollution: A Study of Non-Decisionmaking in the Cities*. Baltimore, MD: Johns Hopkins University Press.

Dallin, Alexander, 1985. *Black Box: KAL 007 and the Superpowers*. Berkeley, CA: University of California Press.

Danchev, Alex, 1993. *Oliver Franks*. Oxford: Oxford University Press.

Darby, Philip, 1973. *British Policy East of Suez, 1947–1968*. Oxford: Oxford University Press.

Dawisha, Adeed I., 1976. *Egypt in the Arab World: The Elements of Foreign Policy*. London: Macmillan.

——, ed., 1985. *Islam in Foreign Policy*. Cambridge: Cambridge University Press.

Dawisha, Karen, 1980. The limits of the bureaucratic politics model: Observations on the Soviet case. *Studies in Comparative Communism*, 12(4), pp. 300–26.

——, 1984. *The Kremlin and the Prague Spring*. Berkeley, CA: University of California Press.

de Carvalho, Benjamin, and Neumann, Iver B., eds, 2015. *Small State Status Seeking: Norway's Quest for International Standing*. London: Routledge.

de Courten, Franco, 2003. *Diario d'Algeria (1996–1998)*. Rome: Rubbettino.

de Gaulle, Charles, 1971. *Memoirs of Hope*. London: Weidenfeld & Nicolson.

Delahunt, Bill, 2008. The decline in America's reputation: Why? Report of the Subcommittee on International Organizations, Human Rights, and Oversight of the Committee on Foreign Affairs of the US House of Representatives, 11 June.

Deng, Francis et al., 1996. *Sovereignty as Responsibility: Conflict Management in Africa*. Washington, DC: Brookings Institution.

Denning, Brannon P. and McCall, Jack H., 2000. States' rights and foreign policy: Some things should be left to Washington. *Foreign Affairs*, 79(1), pp. 9–15.

d'Entrèves, Alexander Passerin, 1967. *The Notion of the State: An Introduction to Political Theory*. Oxford: Oxford University Press.

Department of Foreign Affairs and Trade of Australia, 1997. *In the National Interest: Australia's Foreign and Trade Policy*. Canberra: Commonwealth Government of Australia.

Department of Foreign Affairs and Trade of Ireland, 2013. A value-for-money and policy review of Ireland's bilateral diplomatic missions in European Union member states. White paper, December.

Der Derian, James, 1987. *On Diplomacy: A Genealogy of Western Estrangement*. Oxford: Basil Blackwell.

De Rivera, Joseph, 1968. *The Psychological Dimension of Foreign Policy*. Columbus, OH: Merrill.

Dessler, David, 1999. Constructivism within a positivist social science. *Review of International Studies*, 25(1), pp. 123–37.

Destler, I. M. et al., 1976. *Managing an Alliance: The Politics of US–Japanese Relations*. Washington, DC: Brookings Institution

—— and Kull, Steven, 1999. *Misreading the Public: The Myth of a New Isolationism*. Washington, DC: Brookings Institution.

Dickie, John, 1992. *Inside the Foreign Office*. London: Chapman.

Dilks, David, 1971. *The Diaries of Sir Alexander Cadogan, 1938–1945*. London: Cassell.

Dobbs, Michael, 2008. *One Minute to Midnight: Kennedy, Khrushchev, and Castro on the Brink of Nuclear War*. London: Hutchinson.

Donelan, Michael, ed., 1978. *The Reason of States: A Study in International Political Theory*. London: Allen and Unwin.

——, 2007. *Honor in Foreign Policy*. New York: Palgrave Macmillan.

Donovan, Michael, 1997. National intelligence and the Iranian revolution. In: Rhodri Jeffreys-Jones and Christopher Andrew, eds, 1997, *Eternal Vigilance: Fifty Years of the CIA*. London: Frank Cass.

Doss, Kurt, 1982. Germany: The history of the German Foreign Office. In: Zara Steiner, ed., 1982, *The Times Survey of Foreign Ministries of the World*. London: Times Books.

Doty, Roxanne L., 1996. *Imperial Encounters: The Politics of Representation in North–South Relations*. Minneapolis, MN: University of Minnesota Press.

Doxey, Margaret, 1996. *International Sanctions in Contemporary Perspective*. Second edition. London: Macmillan.

Doyle, Michael, 2012. Liberalism and foreign policy. In: Steve Smith, Amelia Hadfield and Tim Dunne, eds, 2012, *Foreign Policy: Theories, Actors, Cases*. Second edition, pp. 54–77. Oxford: Oxford University Press.

Dray, William H., 1994. Was Collingwood an historical constructionist? In: David Boucher, ed., 1994, *Collingwood Studies, The Life and Thought of R. G. Collingwood, Volume 1*. Swansea: Collingwood Society.

Drezner, Daniel and Farrell, Henry, 2004. Web of Influence. *Foreign Policy*, 145, November/December, pp. 32–40.

Dryzek, John and Dunleavy, Patrick, 2009. *Theories of the Democratic State*. Basingstoke: Palgrave.

Dumbrell, John, 2010. *Clinton's Foreign Policy: Between the Bushes, 1992–2000*. Abingdon, UK: Routledge.

Dunleavy, Patrick, 2013. *Democracy, Bureaucracy and Public Choice: Economic Explanations in Political Science*. Reprint edition. Abingdon, UK: Routledge.

Dunne, Timothy, 1998. *Inventing International Society*. London: Macmillan.

Dyson, Kenneth, 1980. *The State Tradition in Western Europe*. Oxford: Martin Robertson.

East, M. A., 1981. The organizational impact of interdependence on foreign policy-making: The case of Norway. In: C. W. Kegley, Jr. and Patrick McGowan, eds, 1981, *The Political Economy of Foreign Policy Behaviour*. London: Sage.

Easton, David, 1965. *A Systems Analysis of Political Life*. New York: Wiley.

Economist, 1988. Here be foreigners. 30 July, p. 42.

Economy, Elizabeth and Oksenberg, Michel, eds, 1999. *China Joins the World: Progress and Prospects*. New York: Council of Foreign Relations Press.

Eden, Anthony, 1960. *Memoirs: Full Circle*. London: Cassell.

Edström, Bert, 1999. *Japan's Evolving Foreign Policy Doctrine: From Yoshida to Miyazawa*. Basingstoke: Macmillan.

EIGE, 2013. Female genital mutilation in the European Union and Croatia. Report, *European Institute for Gender Equality*. Belgium: European Union.

Eisenach, Eldon, 1994. *The Lost Promise of Progressivism*. Lawrence, KS: University Press of Kansas.

Elgot, Jessica, 2013. Boris Johnson's foreign policy – not on China, but on Syria, Iran, Israel, Libya. *Huffington Post UK*, 13 October.

Elliott, Kimberly Ann, 1998. The sanctions glass: Half full or completely empty? *International Security*, 23(1), pp. 50–65.

Elman, Colin, 1996. Horses for courses: Why not neo-realist theories of foreign policy? *Security Studies*, 6(1), pp. 7–53.

—— and Elman, Miriam Fendius, eds, 2001. *Bridges and Boundaries: Historians, Political Scientists and the Study of International Relations*. Cambridge, MA: MIT Press.

Enloe, Cynthia, 1996. Margins, silences and bottom rungs: How to overcome the underestimation of power in the study of international relations. In: Steve Smith, Ken Booth and Marysia Zalewski, eds, 1996, *International Theory: Positivism and Beyond*. Cambridge: Cambridge University Press.

Erikson, Erik H., 1958. *Young Man Luther: A Study in Psychoanalysis and History*. New York: Norton.

Erskine, Toni, 2001. Assigning responsibility to institutional moral agents: The case of states and quasi-states. *Ethics & International Affairs*, 15(2), pp. 67–85.

Eteshami, Anoushiravan, 2014. Ouch! Tehran is hurting. *World Today*, 70(6) (1 December), pp. 32–3.

Etheredge, Lloyd S., 1978. Personality effects on American foreign policy, 1898–1968: A test of interpersonal generalization theory. *American Political Science Review*, 72(2), pp. 434–51.

——, 1985. *Can Governments Learn?* Elmsford: Pergamon Press.

European Commission, 2013a. EU development aid and the Millennium Development Goals. *Eurobarometer*, 79.4, results for Spain.

——, 2013b. Report on Public Opinion in the European Union. *Standard Eurobarometer*, 79, Spring.

Evangelista, Matthew, 1995. Transnational relations, domestic structures and security policy in the USSR and Russia. In: Thomas Risse-Kappen, ed., 1995, *Bringing Transnational Relations Back In: Non-State Actors, Domestic Structures and International Institutions*, pp. 146–88. Cambridge: Cambridge University Press.

Evangelopoulos, Georgios, 2013. Scientific realism in the philosophy of science and international relations. Unpublished PhD thesis. London School of Economics and Political Science.

Evans, Gareth, 2008. *The Responsibility to Protect: Ending Mass Atrocity Crimes Once and for All*. Washington, DC: Brookings Institution.

Evans, Peter B., 1993. Building an integrative approach to international and domestic politics: Reflections and projections. In: Peter B. Evans, Harold K. Jacobson and Robert D. Putnam, eds, 1993, *Double-Edged Diplomacy: International Bargaining and Domestic Politics*. Berkeley, CA: University of California Press.

Evans, Richard J., 2004. *The Coming of the Third Reich*. London: Penguin Press.

——, 2005. *The Third Reich in Power*. London: Allen Lane.

Everts, Philip and Isernia, Pierangelo, 2015. *Public Opinion, Transatlantic Relations and the Use of Force*. Houndmills, UK: Palgrave Macmillan.

Everts, Steven, 2001. Coming to terms with Germany: The slow and arduous adjustment of Dutch foreign policy after 1989. In: Robin Niblett and William Wallace, eds, 2001, *Rethinking European Order: West European Responses, 1989–97*. Houndmills, UK: Palgrave.

Farquharson, John E. and Holt, Stephen C., 1975. *Europe from Below: An Assessment of Franco-German Popular Contacts*. London: Allen & Unwin.

Ferraris, Luigi Vittorio, ed., 1996. *Manuale della Politica Estera Italiana 1947–1993 [Handbook of Italian Foreign Policy 1947–1993]*. Rome: Laterza.

Festinger, Leon, 1957. *A Theory of Cognitive Dissonance*. Stanford, CA: Stanford University Press.

Finnemore, Martha, 1996. *National Interests in International Society*. Ithaca, NY: Cornell University Press.

Foreign Policy, 2010. Failed states. *Foreign Policy*, July/August(180), pp. 74–91.

Fox, Annette Baker, 1959. *The Power of Small States: Diplomacy in World War II*. Chicago, IL: Chicago University Press.

Frankel, Joseph, 1963. *The Making of Foreign Policy*. Oxford: Oxford University Press.

Franks, Lord, 1983. Falkland Islands review: Report of a Committee of

Privy Counsellors. London: HMSO, Command Paper 8787. Also available in Danchev, 1993.

Freedman, Lawrence, 1976. Logic, politics and foreign policy processes. *International Affairs*, 52(3), pp. 434–49.

——, 2005. *The Official History of the Falklands Campaign*. Two volumes. London: Routledge.

—— and Gamba-Stonehouse, Virginia, 1990. *Signals of War: The Anglo-Argentine Conflict of 1982*. London: Faber and Faber.

Fry, Earl H., 2009. The United States of America. In: Hans J. Michelmann, ed., 2009, *Foreign Relations in Federal Countries*. Montreal: McGill-Queen's University Press.

Fukuyama, Francis, 1992. *The End of History and the Last Man*. London: Penguin.

Gallucci, Robert, 1975. *Neither Peace Nor Honour: The Politics of American Military Policy in Vietnam*. Baltimore, MD: Johns Hopkins University Press.

Galston, William A. and Makins, Christopher J., 1988. Campaign '88 and foreign policy. *Foreign Policy*, summer, pp. 3–21.

Gaubatz, Kurt Taylor, 1997. Democratic states and commitment in International Relations. In: Miles Kahler, ed., 1997, *Liberalization and Foreign Policy*, pp. 28–65. New York: Columbia University Press.

Gazit, Shlomo, 1989. Intelligence estimates and the decision-maker. In: Michael I. Handel, ed., 1989, *Leaders and Intelligence*, pp. 261–87. London: Cass.

Gelb, Leslie and Betts, Richard, 1979. *The Irony of Vietnam: The System Worked*. Washington, DC: Brookings Institution.

Geldenhuys, Deon, 1984. *The Diplomacy of Isolation: South Africa's Foreign Policy-Making*. London: Macmillan.

——, 1990. *Isolated States: A Comparative Analysis*. Cambridge: Cambridge University Press.

George, Alexander L., 1972. The case for multiple advocacy in making foreign policy. *American Political Science Review*, 66(3), pp. 751–85.

——, 1980. *Presidential Decision-making in Foreign Policy: The Effective Use of Information and Advice*. Boulder, CO: Westview Press.

——, 2006. *On Foreign Policy*. Boulder, CO: Paradigm Publishers.

—— and George, Juliet L., 1965. *Woodrow Wilson and Colonel House*. New York: John Den.

—— and Simons, William E., 1994. *The Limits of Coercive Diplomacy*. Second edition. Boulder, CO: Westview Press.

Gerth, Hans H. and Wright Mills, Charles, eds and trans., 1948. *From Max Weber: Essays in Sociology*. London: Routledge.

Giddens, Anthony, 1979. *Central Problems in Social Theory: Action, Structure and Contradiction in Social Analysis*. London: Macmillan.

——, 2011. *The Politics of Climate Change*. Second edition. Cambridge: Polity.

Gil, Jeffrey, 2009. China's Confucius Institute Project: Language and soft power in world politics. *Global Studies Journal*, 2(1), pp. 59–72.

Gilbert, Mark, 2015. *Cold War Europe: The Politics of a Contested Continent*. Lanham, MD: Rowman & Littlefield.

Giro, Mario, 1998. The Community of Saint Egidio and its peace-making activities. *International Spectator*, 33(3), pp. 85–100.

Goetz, Karl H., 1995. National governance and European integration: Inter–governmental relations in Germany. *Journal of Common Market Studies*, 33(1), pp. 91–116.

Göl, Ayla, 2013. *Turkey Facing East: Islam, Modernity and Foreign Policy*. Manchester, UK: Manchester University Press.

Gold, Ellen Reid, 1988. Politics by word power: Ronald Reagan and the art of rhetoric. *Times Higher Education Supplement*, 28 October.

Gourevitch, Peter, 1978. The second image reversed: The international sources of domestic politics. *International Organization*, 32(4), pp. 881–912.

Gowing, Nik, 1994a. Instant TV and foreign policy. *World Today*, 50(10), October.

——, 1994b. Real-time television coverage of armed conflicts and diplomatic crises: Does it pressure or distort foreign policy decisions? Joan Shorenstein Working Paper, 94(1). Cambridge, MA: Harvard University.

——, 1996. Real-time television coverage from war: Does it make or break government policy? In: James Gow, Richard Paterson and Alison Preston, eds, 1996, *Bosnia by Television*. London: British Film Institute.

Grant, Rebecca and Newland, Kathleen, eds, 1991. *Gender and International Relations*. Milton Keynes: Open University Press.

Greenstein, Fred I., 1967. The impact of personality on politics: An attempt to clear the under-brush. *American Political Science Review*, 61(3), pp. 629–41.

——, 1975. *Personality and Politics: Problems of Evidence, Inference and Conceptualization*. New York: Norton.

——, 1987. *Personality and Politics: Problems of Evidence, Inference and Conceptualization*. Third edition. Princeton, NJ: Princeton University Press.

——, 2000. *The Presidential Difference: Leadership Style from FDR to Clinton*. New York: Martin Lessler Books.

Guardiola-Rivera, Oscar, 2014. *Story of a Death Foretold: The Coup against Salvador Allende, 11 September 1973*. London: Bloomsbury.

Haas, Peter M., 1992. Introduction: Epistemic communities and international policy coordination. *International Organisation*, 46(1), pp. 1–35.

——, ed., 1997. *Knowledge, Power and International Policy Coordination*. Columbia, SC: University of South Carolina Press.

Haass, Richard N., 2013. *Foreign Policy Begins at Home: The Case for Putting America's House in Order*. New York: Basic Books.

Habermas, Jürgen, 1987. *The Philosophical Discourse of Modernity: Twelve Lectures*. Cambridge: Polity.

Hain, Peter, 2001. *The End of Foreign Policy? British Interests, Global Linkages and Natural Limits*. London: Fabian Society, Green Alliance and the Royal Institute of International Affairs.

Hale, Julian, 1975. *Radio Power*. London: Elek.

Hall, John A., 1992. *Powers and Liberties: The Causes and Consequences of the Rise of the West*. London: Penguin.

——, 2001. State. In: Joel Krieger, ed., 2001, *The Oxford Companion to Politics of the World*. Second edition. New York: Oxford University Press.

——, 2003. Conditions for national homogenizers. In: Umut Özkirimli, ed., 2003, *Nationalism and Its Futures*. London: Palgrave Macmillan.

Hall, Todd H., 2011. We will not swallow this bitter fruit: Theorizing a diplomacy of anger. *Security Studies*, 20(4), pp. 521–55.

Halliday, Fred, 1994a. Discussion on Iranian Revolution. Personal communication.

——, 1994b. *Rethinking International Relations*. London: Macmillan.

——, 1996. *Islam and the Myth of Confrontation*. London: I. B. Tauris.

——, 1997. Neither treason nor conspiracy: Reflections on media coverage of the Gulf War 1990–91. *Citizenship Studies*, 1(2), pp. 157–72.

——, 1999a. *Revolution and World Politics: The Rise and Fall of the Sixth Great Power*. Houndmills, UK: Palgrave.

——, 1999b. Soviet foreign policy-making and the Afghanistan war: From 'second Mongolia' to bleeding wound. *Review of International Studies*, 25(4), pp. 675–91.

——, 2000. *Nation and Religion in the Middle East*. London: Saqi Books.

——, 2001. *The World at 2000*. London: Palgrave.

Halper, Stefan, 2010. *The Beijing Consensus: How China's Authoritarian Model Will Dominate the Twenty-First Century*. New York: Basic Books.

Halperin, Morton, Clapp, Priscilla and Kanter, Arnold, 1974. *Bureaucratic Politics and Foreign Policy*. Washington, DC: Brookings Institution.

Hamilton, Keith and Langhorne, Richard, 1994. *The Practice of Diplomacy: Its Evolution, Theory and Administration*. London: Routledge.

Hamrin, Carol Lee, 1995. Elite politics and the development of China's foreign relations. In: Thomas W. Robinson and David Shambaugh, eds, 1995, *Chinese Foreign Policy: Theory and Practice*. Oxford: Clarendon Press.

Handel, Michael I., 1989. Leaders and intelligence. In: Michael I. Handel, ed., 1989, *Leaders and Intelligence*, pp. 3–39. London: Cass.

Hanrieder, Wolfram F., 1967. Compatibility and consensus: a proposal for the conceptual linkage of external and internal dimensions of foreign policy. *American Political Science Review*, 61(4), pp. 971–82.

Hansen, Lene, 2012. Discourse analysis, post-structuralism, and foreign policy. In: Steve Smith, Amelia Hadfield and Tim Dunne, eds, 2012, *Foreign Policy: Theories, Actors, Cases*. Second edition, pp. 94–112. Oxford: Oxford University Press.

Harding, Luke, 2014. *The Snowden Files: The Inside Story of the World's Most Wanted Man*. London: Guardian Books.

Harman, Danna, 1999. Addressing the audience back home. *Jerusalem Post*, 23 March.

Harris, Sally, 1996. *Out of Control: British Foreign Policy and the Union of Democratic Control 1914–18*. Hull, UK: University of Hull Press.

Haslam, Jonathan, 2011. *Russia's Cold War: From the October Revolution to the Fall of the Wall*. New Haven, CT: Yale University Press.

Hastings, Elizabeth Hann and Hastings, Philip K., eds, 1981. *Index to International Public Opinion, 1979–1980*. Oxford: Clio Press.

Hastings, Max and Jenkins, Simon, 1983. *The Battle for the Falklands*. London: Pan.

Hay, Colin, 1995. Structure and agency. In: David Marsh and Gerry Stoker, eds, 1995, *Theory and Methods in Political Science*, pp. 189–206. London: Macmillan.

Held, David, 1995. *Democracy and the Global Order: From the Modern State to Cosmopolitan Governance*. Cambridge: Polity Press.

——, McGrew, Anthony, Goldblatt, David and Perraton, Jonathon, eds, 1999. *Global Transformations: Politics, Economics and Culture*. Cambridge: Polity Press.

—— and McGrew, Anthony, eds, 2003. *The Global Transformations Reader*. Second edition. Cambridge: Polity Press.

Henkin, Louis, 1979. *How Nations Behave: Law and Foreign Policy*. Second edition. New York: Columbia University Press for the Council on Foreign Relations.

Hennessy, Peter, 1986. *Cabinet*. Oxford: Basil Blackwell.

——, 1989. Peter Hennessy looks at the workloads some outgoing ministers may not be sorry to leave behind. *Independent*, 25 July.

——, 2000. *The Prime Minister: The Office and Its Holders since 1945*. Harmondsworth: Penguin.

——, ed., 2007. *Cabinets and the Bomb*. Oxford: Oxford University Press.

Herman, Edward S. and Chomsky, Noam, 1994. *Manufacturing Consent: The Political Economy of the Mass Media*. London: Vintage.

Hermann, Charles F. and Peacock, Gregory, 1987. The evolution and future of theoretical research in the comparative study of foreign policy. In: Charles F. Hermann, Charles W. Kegley Jr. and James N. Rosenau, eds, 1987, *New Directions in the Study of Foreign Policy*, pp. 13–32. London: Allen & Unwin.

Hermann, Margaret G., 1980. Explaining foreign policy behavior using the personal characteristics of political leaders. *International Studies Quarterly*, 24(1), 7–46.

Herring, George C., 1987. The war in Vietnam. In: Robert A. Divine, ed., 1987, *The Johnson Years, Volume I: Foreign Policy, the Great Society and the White House*. Lawrence, KS: University Press of Kansas.

Herz, John H., 1981. Political realism revisited. With comments by Inis Claude and Herz. *International Studies Quarterly*, 25(2), pp. 182–203.

Hey, Jeanne A. K., ed., 2003. *Small States in World Politics: Explaining Foreign Policy Behavior*. London: Lynne Rienner Publishers.

Hibbert, Reginald, 1990. Intelligence and policy. *Intelligence and National Security*, 5(1), pp. 110–28.

Hill, Christopher, 1977. Theories of foreign policy-making for developing countries. In: Christopher Clapham, ed., 1977, *Foreign Policy-Making in Developing Countries*. London: Saxon House.

——, 1978. A theoretical introduction. In: William Wallace and W. E. Paterson, eds, 1978, *Foreign Policy Making in Western Europe: A Comparative Approach*, pp. 7–30. Farnborough, UK: Saxon House.

——, 1979. The decision-making process in relation to British foreign policy, 1938–1941. Unpublished DPhil thesis. University of Oxford.

——, 1989. 1939: The origins of liberal realism. *Review of International Studies*, 15(4), pp. 319–28.

——, 1991. *Cabinet Decisions in Foreign Policy: The British Experience, September 1938–June 1941*. Cambridge: Cambridge University Press.

——, 1993a. Foreign policy. In: Joel Krieger, ed., 1993, *Oxford Companion to World Politics*. New York: Oxford University Press.

——, 1993b. The capability-expectations gap, or conceptualising Europe's international role. *Journal of Common Market Studies*, 31(3), pp. 305–28.

——, 1996a. Introduction: The Falklands War and European foreign policy. In: Stelios Stavridis and Christopher Hill, eds, 1996, *Domestic Sources of Foreign Policy: Western European Reactions to the Falklands Conflict*. Oxford: Berg.

——, 1996b. World opinion and the empire of circumstance. *International Affairs*, 72(1), pp. 109–31.

——, 1998. Closing the capability-expectations gap? In: John Peterson and Helene Sjursen, eds, 1998, *A Foreign Policy for Europe?* London: Routledge.

——, 1999. 'Where are we going?' International Relations and the voice from below. *Review of International Studies*, 25(1), pp. 107–22.

——, 2000. What is left of the domestic? A reverse angle view of foreign policy. In: Michi Ebata and Beverly Neufeld, eds, 2000, *Confronting the Political in International Relations*. London: Palgrave.

——, 2001. Foreign policy. In: Joel Krieger, ed., 2001, *Oxford Companion to World Politics*. New York: Oxford University Press.

——, 2013. *The National Interest in Question: Foreign Policy in Multicultural Societies*. Oxford: Oxford University Press.

—— and Beadle, Sarah, 2014. *The Art of Attraction: Soft Power and the UK's Role in the World*. London: British Academy.

Hilsman, Roger, 1964. *To Move a Nation: The Politics of Foreign Policy in the Administration of John F. Kennedy*. New York: Doubleday.

——, 1987. *The Politics of Policy Making in Defense and Foreign Affairs: Conceptual Models and Bureaucratic Politics*. Englewood Cliffs, NJ: Prentice Hall.

Hinnebusch, Raymond and Ehteshami, Anoushiravan, eds, 2014. *The Foreign Policies of Middle East States*. Second edition. Boulder, CO: Lynne Reinner.

Hinsley, Francis H., 1967. *Power and the Pursuit of Peace: Theory and Practice in the History of Relations between States*. Cambridge: Cambridge University Press.

Hinton, Harold C., 1994. China as an Asian power. In: Thomas W. Robinson and David Shambaugh, eds, 1994, *Chinese Foreign Policy: Theory and Practice*. Oxford: Clarendon Press.

Hirano, Mutsumi, 2009. *History Education and International Relations: A Case Study of Diplomatic Disputes over Japanese Textbooks*. Folkestone, UK: Global Oriental.

Hobbs, Heidi, 1994. *City Hall Goes Abroad: The Foreign Policy of Local Politics*. Thousand Oaks, CA: Sage.

Hockenos, Paul, 2003. *Homeland Calling: Exile Patriotism & the Balkan Wars*. Ithaca, NY: Cornell University Press.

Hocking, Brian, 1993a. *Localizing Foreign Policy: Non-Central Governments and Multilayered Diplomacy*. London: Macmillan.

——, ed., 1993b. *Managing Foreign Relations in Federal States*. London: Leicester University Press.

——, 1999. Patrolling the 'frontier': Globalization, local–ization and the 'actorness' of non-central governments. *Regional and Federal Studies*, 9(1), pp. 17–39.

—— and Smith, Michael, 1997. *Beyond Foreign Economic Policy: The United States, the Single Market and the Changing World Economy*. London: Pinter.

—— and Spence, David, eds, 2005. *Foreign Ministries in the European Union: Integrating Diplomats*. Houndmills, UK: Palgrave.

Hoffmann, Stanley, 1981. *Duties beyond Borders: On the Limits and Possibilities of Ethical International Politics*. Syracuse, NY: Syracuse University Press.

Holden, Barry, ed., 2000. *Global Democracy: Key Debates*. London: Routledge.

Holden, John, 2013. *Influence and Attraction: Culture and the Race for Soft Power in the 21st Century*. London: British Council.

Hollis, Martin and Smith, Steve, 1986. Roles and reasons in foreign policy decision making. *British Journal of Political Science*, 16(3), pp. 269–86.

—— and ——, 1990. *Explaining and Understanding International Relations*. Oxford: Clarendon Press.

—— and ——, 1992. Structure and action: Further comment. *Review of International Studies*, 18(2), pp. 187–8.

Holsti, Kalevi J., 1982. *Why Nations Realign: Foreign Policy Restructuring in the Postwar World*. London: Allen & Unwin.

Hook, Glenn D., Gilson, Julie, Hughes, Christopher W. and Dobson, Hugo, 2001. *Japan's International Relations: Politics, Economics and Security*. London: Routledge.

Hopf, Ted, 2002. *Social Construction of Foreign Policy: Identities and Foreign Policies; Moscow 1955 and 1959*. Ithaca, NY: Cornell University Press.

Hosking, Geoffrey, 1992. *A History of the Soviet Union, 1917–1991*. London: Fontana.

Houtart, François and Polet, François, eds, 2001. *The Other Davos: The Globalization of Resistance to the World Economic System*. London: Zed Books.

Howard, Michael, 1991. *The Lessons of History*. Oxford: Oxford University Press.

Howe, Geoffrey, 1994. *Conflict of Loyalty*. London: Macmillan.

Howells, Jeremy and Wood, Michelle, 1993. *The Globalisation of Production and Technology, a Report Prepared for the Commission of the European Communities*. London: Belhaven.

Hudson, Valerie M., 2007. *Foreign Policy Analysis: Classic and Contemporary Theory*. Lanham, MD: Rowman & Littlefield.

Hudson, Valerie M. and Vore, Christopher S., 1995. Foreign policy analysis yesterday, today and tomorrow. *Mershon International Studies Review*, 39(10), pp. 209–38.

Hufbauer, Gary Clyde, Schott, Jeffrey J., Elliott, Kimberly Ann and Oegg, Barbara, 2008. *Economic Sanctions Reconsidered*. Third edition. Washington, DC: Peterson Institute for International Economics.

Hughes, Christopher R., 2010. Google and the great firewall. *Survival*, 52(2), pp. 19–26.

Huntington, Ellsworth, 1924. *Civilisation and Climate*. New Haven, CT: Yale University Press.

Huntington, Samuel, 1973. Transnational organisations in world politics. *World Politics*, 25(3), pp. 333–68.

——, 2004. *The Crisis of National Identity*. London: Simon & Schuster.

Hurd, Douglas, 2010. *Choose Your Weapons: The British Foreign Secretary: 200 Years of Argument, Success and Failure*. London: Weidenfeld & Nicolson.

Hurrell, Andrew, 2007. *On Global Order: Power, Values, and the Constitution of International Society*. Oxford: Oxford University Press.

Ikenberry, John and Trubowitz, Peter, 2014. *American Foreign Policy: Theoretical Essays*. Seventh edition. New York: Oxford University Press.

Irish, John, 2014. French foreign minister takes on trade, overseas growth, in expanded role. *Reuters*, 2 April.

Irving, David, 1977. *Hitler's War 1939–1942*. London: Macmillan.

Jackson, Keith and Lamare, Jim, 1988. Politics, public opinion and international crisis: The ANZUS issue in New Zealand politics. In: Jacob Bercovitch, ed., 1988, *ANZUS in Crisis: Alliance Management in International Affairs*. London: Macmillan.

Jackson, Robert, 1993. *Quasi-States: Sovereignty, International Relations and the Third World*. Cambridge: Cambridge University Press.

——, 2003. *The Global Covenant: Human Conduct in a World of States*. Oxford: Oxford University Press.

—— and Sørensen, Georg, 2003. *Introduction to International Relations: Theories and Approaches*. Oxford: Oxford University Press.

James, Alan, 1986. *Sovereign Statehood: The Basis of International Society*. London: Allen & Unwin.

Janis, Irving L., 1972. *Victims of Groupthink: A Psychological Study of Foreign Policy Decisions and Fiascoes*. Boston, MA: Houghton Mifflin.

——, 1982. *Groupthink: Psychological Studies of Foreign Policy Decisions and Fiascoes*. Boston, MA: Houghton Mifflin.

——, 1989. *Crucial Decisions: Leadership in Policy-Making and Crisis Management*. New York: Free Press.

—— and Mann, Leon, 1977. *Decision Making: A Psychological Analysis of Choice, Conflict and Commitment*. New York: Free Press.

Jean, Carlo, 1995. *Geopolitica*. Roma-Bari: Editori Laterza.

Jensen, Lloyd, 1982. *Explaining Foreign Policy*. Englewood Cliffs, NJ: Prentice-Hall.

Jervis, Robert, 1970. *The Logic of Images in International Relations*. Princeton, NJ: Princeton University Press.

——, 1976. *Perception and Misperception in International Politics*. Princeton, NJ: Princeton University Press.

——, 1997. *System Effects: Complexity in Political and Social Life*. Princeton, NJ: Princeton University Press.

——, 2001. International history and international politics: Why are they studied differently? In: Colin Elman and Miriam Fendius Elman, eds, 2001, *Bridges and Boundaries: Historians, Political Scientists and the Study of International Relations*, pp. 385–402. Cambridge, MA: MIT Press.

——, 2010. *Why Intelligence Fails: Lessons from the Iranian Revolution and the Iraq War*. Ithaca, NY: Cornell University Press.

John, Peter, 2012. *Analyzing Public Policy*. London: Routledge.

Johnson, Dominic D. P. and Tierney, Dominic, 2006. *Failing to Win: Perceptions of Victory and Defeat in International Politics*. Cambridge, MA: Harvard University Press.

Johnston, Douglas and Sampson, Cynthia, eds, 1994. *Religion, the Missing Dimension of Statecraft*. New York: Oxford University Press for the Center for Strategic and International Studies.

Joll, James, ed., 1950. *Britain and Europe: Pitt to Churchill 1793–1940*. London: Nicholas Kaye.

——, 1984. *The Origins of the First World War*. London: Longman.

Jones, Roy E., 1979. *Principles of Foreign Policy*. Oxford: Martin Robertson.

Jones, R. J. Barry, 1999. Globalization and change in the international political economy. *International Affairs*, 75(2), pp. 357–66.

Jowell, Roger and Spence, James D., 1975. *The Grudging Europeans: A Study of British Attitudes towards the EEC*. London: SCPR.

Juncos, Ana E. and Pomorska, Karolina, 2014. Manufacturing esprit de corps: The case of the European External Action Service. *Journal of Common Market Studies*, 52(2), pp. 302–19.

Kaarbo, Juliet, 2008. Coalition cabinet decision making: Institutional and psychological factors. *International Studies Review*, 10(1), pp. 57–86.

——, 2012. *Coalition Politics and Cabinet Decision Making: A Comparative Study of Foreign Policy Choices*. Ann Arbor, MI: University of Michigan Press.

Kagan, Robert, 2003. *Of Paradise and Power: America and Europe in the New World Order*. New York: Knopf.

Kahler, Miles, ed., 1997. *Liberalization and Foreign Policy*. New York: Columbia University Press.

——, 1999. Rationality in International Relations. In: Peter J. Katzenstein, Robert O. Keohane and Stephen D. Krasner, eds, 1999, *Exploration and Contestation in the Study of World Politics*. Cambridge, MA: MIT Press.

Kahneman, Daniel, 2011. *Thinking, Fast and Slow*. London: Allen Lane.

Kaldor, Mary, 2013. *New and Old Wars: Organised Violence in a Global Era*. Third edition. London: Polity Press.

Kant, Immanuel, 1795. Perpetual peace: A philosophical sketch. In: Hans Reiss, ed., 1991, *Kant: Political Writings*. Second edition. Cambridge: Cambridge University Press.

Kaplan, Morton, 1957. *System and Process in International Politics*. New York: Wiley.

Karacs, Imre, 2000. Austrian Crisis – Haider's deal lets his party join the ruling coalition. *Independent*, 2 February.

Karvonen, Lauri and Sundelius, Bengt, 1987. *Internationalization and Foreign Policy Management*. Aldershot: Gower.

Katzenstein, Peter, 1987. *Policy and Politics in West Germany: The Growth of a Semi-Sovereign State*. Philadelphia, PA: Temple University Press.

—— and Tsujinaka, Yutaka, 1995. 'Bullying', 'buying' and 'binding': US–Japanese transnational relations and domestic structures. In: Thomas Risse-Kappen, ed., 1995, *Bringing Transnational Relations Back In*. Cambridge: Cambridge University Press.

Kean, Thomas H., Hamilton, Lee H. et al., 2004. The 9/11 Commission report: Final report of the National Commission on Terrorist Attacks upon the United States. Washington, DC: National Commission on Terrorist Attacks upon the United States.

Kearns, Doris, 1976. *Lyndon Johnson and the American Dream*. London: Deutsch.

Keatinge, Patrick, 1996. Ireland and common security: Stretching the limits of commitment? In: Christopher Hill, ed., 1996, *The Actors in Europe's Foreign Policy*, pp. 208–25. London: Routledge.

Keck, Margaret E. and Sikkink, Kathryn, 1998. *Activists beyond Borders: Transnational Advocacy Networks in World Politics*. Ithaca, NY: Cornell University Press.

Kegley, Charles W. Jr. and Blanton, Shannon L., 2012. *World Politics: Trend and Transformation. 2012–2013 Edition*. Andover, UK: Wadsworth.

—— and Wittkopf, Eugene R., 2005. *American Foreign Policy: Pattern and Process*. Fifth edition. Houndmills, UK: Macmillan Education.

Kehr, Eckart, 1930. *Schlachtflottenbau und Parteipolitik 1894–1902 [Battleship Building and Party Politics 1894–1902]*. Berlin: E. Ebering.

——, 1977. *Economic Interest, Militarism and Foreign Policy: Essays on German History*. Translated from German by Grete Heinz. Berkeley, CA: University of California Press.

Kennan, George, 1997. Diplomacy without diplomats. *Foreign Affairs*, 76 (September–October), pp. 198–212.

Kennedy, Paul, 1988. *The Rise and Fall of the Great Powers: Economic Change and Military Conflict from 1500 to 2000*. London: Unwin Hyman.

Kennedy, Robert F., 1969. *Thirteen Days: The Cuban Missile Crisis.* London: Pan Books.

Keohane, Daniel, 2001. Realigning neutrality? Irish defence policy and the EU. Occasional Paper No. 24, Western European Union Institute for Security Studies, Paris, France.

Keohane, Robert O., 1984. *After Hegemony: Cooperation and Discord in the World Political Economy.* Princeton, NJ: Princeton University Press.

——, 1993. International multiple advocacy in US foreign policy. In: Dan Caldwell and Timothy J. McKeown, eds, 1993, *Diplomacy, Force and Leadership*, pp. 285–304. Boulder, CO: Westview.

—— and Nye, Joseph S. Jr., eds, 1971. *Transnational Relations and World Politics.* Cambridge, MA: Harvard University Press.

—— and Nye, Joseph S. Jr., eds, 1973. *Transnational Relations and World Politics.* Cambridge, MA: Harvard University Press.

—— and Nye, Joseph S. Jr., 1977. *Power and Interdependence.* Boston, MA: Little, Brown.

Khong, Yuen Foong, 1992. *Analogies at War: Korea, Munich, Dien Bien Phu and The Vietnam Decisions of 1965.* Princeton, NJ: Princeton University Press.

Kirkpatrick, Jean, 1982. *Dictatorships and Double Standards: Rationalism and Realism in Politics.* New York: Simon & Shuster.

Kissinger, Henry A., 1969. Domestic structure and foreign policy. In: Harold Karan Jacobson and William Zimmerman, eds, 1969, *The Shaping of Foreign Policy.* New York: Atherton Press.

——, 1994. *Diplomacy.* London: Simon & Schuster.

——, 2007. The lessons of Vietnam. *Los Angeles Times*, 31 May.

——, 2014. *World Order: Reflections on the Character of Nations and the Course of History.* London: Allen Lane.

Knox, Macgregor, 1982. *Mussolini Unleashed, 1939–1941: Politics and Strategy in Fascist Italy's Last War.* Cambridge: Cambridge University Press.

Komachi, Kyoji, 1999. Japan: Towards a more pro-active foreign ministry. In: Brian Hocking, ed., 1999, *Foreign Ministries: Change and Adaptation.* Basingstoke, UK: Macmillan.

Krasner, Stephen D., 1983. *International Regimes.* Ithaca, NY: Cornell University Press.

——, 1985. *Structural Conflict: The Third World Against Global Liberalism.* Berkeley, CA: University of California Press.

——, 1995. Power politics, institutions and transnational relations. In: Thomas Risse-Kappen, ed., 1995, *Bringing Transnational Relations Back In: Non-State Actors, Domestic Structures and International Institutions.* Cambridge: Cambridge University Press.

——, 1999. *Sovereignty: Organized Hypocrisy.* Princeton, NJ: Princeton University Press.

Kreisberg, Paul H., 1994. China's negotiating behaviour. In: Thomas W. Robinson and David Shambaugh, eds, 1994, *Chinese Foreign Policy: Theory and Practice.* Oxford: Clarendon Press.

Kubálková, Vendulka and Cruickshank, Albert, 1985. *Marxism and International Relations*. Second edition. Oxford: Clarendon Press.

Kunczik, Michael, 1997. *Images of Nations and International Public Relations*. Mahwah, NJ: Lawrence Erlbaum Associates.

Kydd, Andrew, 2010. Rationalist approaches to conflict prevention. *Annual Review of Political Science*, 13, pp. 101–21.

Lakatos, Imre and Musgrave, Alan, eds, 1970. *Criticism and the Growth of Knowledge*. Cambridge: Cambridge University Press.

Lake, David, 2001. Realism. In: Joel Krieger, ed., 2001, *Oxford Companion to World Politics*. New York: Oxford University Press.

Lamborn, Alan C. and Mummie, Stephen P., 1988. *Statecraft, Domestic Politics and Foreign Policy Making: The El Chamizal Dispute*. Boulder, CO: Westview.

Larsen, Henrik, 1997. *Foreign Policy and Discourse Analysis: France, Britain and Europe*. London: Routledge.

——, 2009. A distinct FPA for Europe? Towards a comprehensive framework for analysing the foreign policy of EU member states. *European Journal of International Relations*, 15(3), pp. 537–66.

Lauren, Paul G., ed., 1979. *Diplomacy: New Approaches in History, Theory and Policy*. New York: Free Press.

——, 1994. Coercive diplomacy and ultimata: Theory and practice in history. In: Alexander L. George and William E. Simons, eds, 1994, *The Limits of Coercive Diplomacy*. Second edition. Boulder, CO: Westview Press.

——, Craig, Gordon A. and George, Alexander L., 2007. *Force and Statecraft: Diplomatic Challenges of Our Time*. Oxford: Oxford University Press.

Lean, Geoffrey, 1998. Meet the debt-busters. *Independent*, 17 May.

Lebow, Richard Ned, 2010. *Forbidden Fruit: Counterfactuals and International Relations*. Princeton, NJ: Princeton University Press.

Leifer, Michael, 2000. *The Foreign Policy of Singapore: Coping with Vulnerability*. London: Routledge.

Leigh, David and Harding, Luke, 2013. *WikiLeaks: Inside Julian Assange's War on Secrecy*. Revised and updated edition. London: Guardian Books.

Leiken, Robert, 2012. *Europe's Angry Muslims: The Revolt of the Second Generation*. New York: Oxford University Press.

Leonardy, Uwe, 1993. Federation and Länder in German foreign relations: Power-sharing in treaty-making and European affairs. In: Brian Hocking, ed., 1993, *Foreign Relations and Federal States*, pp. 236–51. Leicester, UK: Leicester University Press.

L'Etang, Hugh, 1995. *Ailing Leaders in Power, 1914–1994*. London: Royal Society of Medicine.

Levine, Steven I., 1994. Perception and ideology in Chinese foreign policy. In: Thomas W. Robinson and David Shambaugh, eds, 1994, *Chinese Foreign Policy: Theory and Practice*. Oxford: Clarendon Press.

Light, Margot, 1994. Foreign policy analysis. In: A. J. R. Groom and Margot Light, eds, 1994, *Contemporary International Relations: A Guide to Theory*. London: Frances Pinter.

——, 2000a. Democracy, democratisation and foreign policy in post-socialist Russia. In: Hazel Smith, ed., 2000, *Democracy and International Relations: Critical Theories/Problematic Practices*, pp. 90–107. Basingstoke: Palgrave Macmillan.

——, 2000b. Information war. *World Today*, February.

Lindblom, Charles E., 1979. Still muddling, not yet through. *Public Administration Review*, 39(6), pp. 517–26.

Linklater, Andrew, 1992. What is a good international citizen? In: Paul Keal, ed., 1992, *Ethics and Foreign Policy*. St Leonards, NSW: Allen and Unwin in association with the Australian National University.

——, 1998. *The Transformation of Political Community*. Cambridge: Polity Press.

—— and Suganami, Hidemi, 2006. *The English School of International Relations: A Contemporary Reassessment*. Cambridge: Cambridge University Press.

Little, Richard, 1975. *External Intervention in Civil Wars*. London: Martin Robertson.

——, 1988. Belief systems in the social sciences. In: Richard Little and Steve Smith, eds, 1988, *Belief Systems and International Relations*. Oxford: Basil Blackwell, with the British International Studies Association.

——, 2007. *The Balance of Power in International Relations: Metaphors, Myths and Models*. Cambridge: Cambridge University Press.

Litwak, Robert S., 2000. *Rogue States and US Foreign Policy: Containment after the Cold War*. Washington, DC: Woodrow Wilson Center Press.

——, 2012. *Outlier States: American Strategies to Change, Contain or Engage Regimes*. Washington, DC: Woodrow Wilson Center Press.

Lobell, Steven E., Ripsman, Norrin M. and Taliaferro, Jeffrey W., eds, 2009. *Neoclassical Realism, the State, and Foreign Policy*. Cambridge: Cambridge University Press.

Lockhart, Charles, 1979. *Bargaining in International Conflicts*. New York: Columbia University Press.

Lorenz, Pierre-Louis, 1996. Luxembourg: New commitments, new assertiveness. In: Christopher Hill, ed., 1996, *The Actors in Europe's Foreign Policy*, pp. 226–46. London: Routledge.

Lu, Ning, 2001. The central leadership, supraministry coordinating bodies, state council ministries and party departments. In: David M. Lampton, ed., 2001, *The Making of Chinese Foreign and Security Policy, 1978–2000*. Stanford: Stanford University Press.

Lucarelli, Sonia and Manners, Ian, eds, 2006. *Values and Principles in European Union Foreign Policy*. London: Routledge.

Lukes, Steven, 1974. *Power: A Radical View*. London: Macmillan.

——, 2005. *Power: A Radical View*. Second edition. Basingstoke: Palgrave.

Luttwak, Edward, 1994. The missing dimension. In: Douglas Johnston and Cynthia Sampson, eds, 1994, *Religion, the Missing Dimension of Statecraft*. New York: Oxford University Press.

Luvaas, Jay, 1989. Napoleon's use of intelligence: The Jena Campaign of

1806. In: Michael I. Handel, ed., 1989, *Leaders and Intelligence*, pp. 40–54. London: Cass.

Luzi, Gianluca, 2001. Forze italiane a Kabul: Scontro Ruggiero-Martino. *La Repubblica*, 15 November.

Lyons, Terence and Mandaville, Peter, eds, 2012. *Politics from Afar: Transnational Diasporas and Networks*. London: Hurst.

McClanahan, Grant V., 1989. *Diplomatic Immunity: Principles, Practices, Problems*. London: Hurst.

McClory, Jonathan, 2010. *The New Persuaders: An International Ranking of Soft Power*. London: Institute for Government.

——, 2011. *The New Persuaders: A 2011 Global Ranking of Soft Power*. London: Institute for Government.

——, 2013. *The New Persuaders: A 2012 Global Ranking of Soft Power*. London: Institute for Government.

McCormick, James M., ed., 2012. *The Domestic Sources of American Foreign Policy: Insights and Evidence*. Sixth edition. Lanham, MD: Rowman & Littlefield.

McGrew, Anthony and Wilson, Michael J., 1982. *Decision Making: Approaches and Analysis*. Manchester, UK: Manchester University Press.

McGwire, Michael, 1991. *Perestroika and Soviet National Security*. Washington, DC: Brookings Institution.

Mackinder, Halford, 1919. *Democratic Ideals and Reality: A Study in the Politics of Reconstruction*. London: Constable and Company.

McLuhan, Marshall, 1964. *Understanding Media: The Extensions of Man*. London: Routledge.

——, 1989. *The Global Village: Transformations in World Life and Media in the 21st Century*. New York: Oxford University Press.

Mahan, Alfred, 1890. *The Influence of Sea Power upon History 1660–1783*. Boston, MA: Little, Brown.

Majone, Giandomenico, 2009. *Europe as a Would-Be World Power*. Cambridge: Cambridge University Press.

Mandela, Nelson, 1995. *Long Walk to Freedom*. London: Abacus.

Manfredi, Guilio, 1998. Una Farnesina a misura d'Europa. *Il Sole-24 Ore*, 24 December.

Mann, Michael, 2012a. *The Sources of Social Power, Volume 1: A History of Power from the Beginning to AD 1760*. New edition. Cambridge: Cambridge University Press.

Mann, Michael, 2012b. *The Sources of Social Power, Volume 2: The Rise of Classes and Nation-States, 1760–1914*. New edition. Cambridge: Cambridge University Press.

Mann, Michael, 2012c. *The Sources of Social Power, Volume 3, Global Empires and Revolution, 1890–1945*. Cambridge: Cambridge University Press.

Mann, Michael, 2013. *The Sources of Social Power, Volume 4: Globalizations, 1945–2011*. Cambridge: Cambridge University Press.

Mann, Robert, 2001. *A Grand Delusion: America's Descent into Vietnam*. New York: Basic Books.

Manners, Ian and Whitman, Richard G., eds, 2000. *The Foreign Policies of European Member States*. Manchester, UK: Manchester University Press.

March, James G. and Olsen, Johan P., 1998. The institutional dynamics of international political orders. *Arena* Working Paper, 5 April.

Martin, Lisa, 2000. *Democratic Commitments: Legislatures and International Cooperation*. Princeton, NJ: Princeton University Press.

Mastanduno, Michael, 1999. Economics and security in statecraft and scholarship. In: Peter J. Katzenstein, Robert O. Keohane and Stephen D. Krasner, eds, 1999, *Exploration and Contestation in the Study of World Politics*, pp. 185–214. Cambridge, MA: MIT Press.

Matthiesen, Toby, 2015. *The Other Saudis: Shiism, Dissent, and Sectarianism*. Cambridge: Cambridge University Press.

Maull, Hanns W., 1990. Germany and Japan: The new civilian powers. *Foreign Affairs*, 69(5), pp. 91–106.

May, Ernest R., 1973. *'Lessons' of the Past: The Use and Misuse of History in American Foreign Policy*. Oxford: Oxford University Press.

—— and Neustadt, Richard, 1986. *Thinking in Time: The Uses of History for Decision Makers*. New York: Free Press.

—— and Zelikow, Philip D., 1997. *The Kennedy Tapes: Inside the White House During the Cuban Missile Crisis*. Cambridge, MA: Harvard University Press.

Mayall, James, 1990. *Nationalism and International Society*. Cambridge: Cambridge University Press.

Mearsheimer, John J., 2001. *The Tragedy of Great Power Politics*. London: Norton.

—— and Walt, Stephen, 2006. The Israel Lobby. *London Review of Books*, 28(6), pp. 3–12.

—— and Walt, Stephen M., 2007. *The Israel Lobby and U.S. Foreign Policy*. New York: Farrar, Straus and Giroux.

Menesis, Emilio, 1999. The military vote. *World Today*, 55(12), December.

Mény, Yves and Knapp, Andrew, 1993. *Government and Politics in Western Europe: Britain, France, Italy, Germany*. Second edition. Oxford: Oxford University Press.

Michelmann, Hans J., ed., 2009. *Foreign Relations in Federal Countries*. Montreal: McGill-Queen's University Press.

Middlemas, Keith, 1972. *Diplomacy of Illusion: The British Government and Germany, 1937–39*. London: Weidenfeld & Nicolson.

Milbrath, Lester, 1967. Interest groups and foreign policy. In: James N. Rosenau, ed., 1967, *The Domestic Sources of Foreign Policy*. New York: Free Press.

Mintz, Alex and DeRouen, Karl, 2010. *Understanding Foreign Policy Decision Making*. Cambridge: Cambridge University Press.

Mintz, Alex, James, Patrick and Walker, Stephen G., 2007. Behavioral IR as a subfield of International Relations. *International Studies Review*, 9(1), pp. 157–72.

Mitchell, James, 1986. *International Cultural Relations*. London: Allen & Unwin.

Mitrany, David, 1943. *A Working Peace System: An Argument for the Functional Development of International Organization*. London: Royal Institute of International Affairs.

Modelski, George, 1962. *A Theory of Foreign Policy*. London: Pall Mall Press.

Mohamed, Ali Naseer, 2002. The diplomacy of micro-states. *Discussion Papers in Diplomacy*, 78, Netherlands Institute of International Relations 'Clingendael'.

Moravcsik, Andrew, 1993. Introduction: Integrating international and domestic theories of international bargaining. In: Peter B. Evans, Harold K. Jacobson and Robert D. Putnam, eds, 1993, *Double-Edged Diplomacy: International Bargaining and Domestic Politics*. Berkeley, CA: University of California Press.

——, 1998. *The Choice for Europe: Social Purpose and State Power from Messina to Maastricht*. New York: Cornell University Press.

——, 2005. The European constitutional compromise and the neofunctionalist legacy. *Journal of European Public Policy*, 12(2), pp. 349–86.

Morgenthau, Hans J., 1948. *Politics among Nations*. New York: Alfred P. Knopf.

——, 1954. *Politics among Nations: The Struggle for Power and Peace*. Second edition. New York: Knopf.

Morin, Jean-Frédéric, 2013. *La Politique Étrangère: Théories, Méthodes et Références*. Paris: Armand Colin.

Mouritzen, Hans and Wivel, Anders, 2012. *Explaining Foreign Policy: International Diplomacy and the Russo-Georgian War*. Boulder, CO: Lynne Rienner.

Mouzelis, Nicos, 2008. *Modern and Postmodern Social Theorizing: Bridging the Divide*. Cambridge: Cambridge University Press.

Muggeridge, Malcom, ed., 1947. *Ciano's Diary 1939–1943*. London: Heinemann.

Narayanswamy, Anupama, Rosiak, Luke and LaFleur, Jennifer, 2009. Adding it up: The top players in foreign agent lobbying. *ProPublica*, 18 August.

Narlikar, Amrita, 2003. *International Trade and Developing Countries: Coalitions in the GATT and WTO*. London: Routledge.

——, ed., 2010a. *Deadlocks in Multilateral Settings: Causes and Solutions*. Cambridge: Cambridge University Press.

——, 2010b. *New Powers: How to Become One and How to Manage Them*. London: Hurst Publications.

Navot, Suzie, 2014. *The Constitution of Israel: A Contextual Analysis*. London: Bloomsbury.

Neumann, Iver B., 1999. The foreign ministry of Norway. In: Brian Hocking, ed., 1999, *Foreign Ministries: Change and Adaptation*. New York: St Martin's Press.

——, 2002. Returning practice to the linguistic turn: The case of diplomacy. *Millennium: Journal of International Studies*, 31 (3), pp. 627–51.

——, 2012. *At Home with the Diplomats: Inside a European Foreign Ministry*. Ithaca, NY: Cornell University Press.

Neustadt, Richard E., 1970. *Alliance Politics*. New York: Columbia University Press.

——, 1991. *Presidential Power and the Modern Presidents: The Politics of Leadership from Roosevelt to Reagan*. Oxford New York: Free Press.

Nicolson, Harold, 1963. *Diplomacy*. Third edition. London: Oxford University Press (first edition in 1939).

Nicholson, Michael, 1996. The continued significance of positivism? In: Steve Smith, Ken Booth and Marysia Zalewski, eds, 1996, *International Theory: Positivism and Beyond*, pp. 138–40. Cambridge: Cambridge University Press.

Niebuhr, Reinhold, 1953. *Christian Realism and Political Problems*. New York: Charles Scribner's Sons.

Niemann, Arne, Garcia, Borja and Grant, Wyn, eds, 2011. *The Transformation of European Football: Towards the Europeanisation of the National Game*. Manchester, UK: Manchester University Press.

Nincic, Miroslav, 2004. Elections and US foreign policy. In: Eugene R. Wittkopf and James M. McCormick, eds, 1998, *The Domestic Sources of American Foreign Policy: Insights and Evidence*. Fourth edition, pp. 117–27. Lanham, MD: Rowman & Littlefield.

Northedge, Frederick S., 1968. The nature of foreign policy. In: Frederick S. Northedge, ed., 1968, *The Foreign Policies of the Powers*. London: Faber & Faber.

——, 1976. Transnationalism: The American illusion. *Millennium*, 5(1), pp. 21–7.

Nozick, Robert, 1993. *The Nature of Rationality*. Princeton, NJ: Princeton University Press.

Nuttall, Simon, 1997. The Commission and foreign policy-making. In: Geoffrey Edwards and David Spence, eds, 1997, *The European Commission*. Second edition. London: Cartermill.

——, 2005. Coherence and Consistency. In: Christopher Hill and Michael Smith, eds, 2005, *International Relations and the European Union*, pp. 91–112. Oxford: Oxford University Press.

Nye, Joseph S. Jr., 1990. *Bound to Lead: The Changing Nature of American Power*. New York: Basic Books.

——, 2004. *Soft Power: The Means to Success in World Politics*. New York: Public Affairs.

——, 2008. *The Powers to Lead*. Oxford: Oxford University Press.

Oppermann, Kai and Brummer, Klaus, 2014. Patterns of junior partner influence on the foreign policy of coalition governments. *British Journal of Politics and International Relations*, 16(4), pp. 555–71.

Owen, John M. IV, 2010. Domestically driven deviations: Internal regimes, leaders, and realism's power line. In: Ernest R. May, Richard Rosecrance and Zara Steiner, eds, 2010, *History and Neorealism*, pp. 29–48. Cambridge: Cambridge University Press.

Packard, Vance, 1981. *The Hidden Persuaders*. Reprint edition. Harmondsworth: Penguin.

Packer, George, 2014. The quiet German: The astonishing rise of Angela

Merkel, the most powerful woman in the world. *New Yorker*, 1 December.

Page, Edward C. and Wright, Vincent, eds, 1999. *Bureaucratic Elites in Western European States: A Comparative Analysis of Top Officials*. New York: Oxford University Press.

Pape, Robert A., 1998. Why economic sanctions still do not work. *International Security*, 23(1), pp. 66–77.

Parker, William H., 1982. *Mackinder: Geography as an aid to Statecraft*. Oxford: Clarendon Press.

Parmar, Inderjeet, 1999. 'Mobilizing America for an internationalist foreign policy': The role of the Council on Foreign Relations. *Studies in American Political Development*, 13, pp. 337–73.

——, 2000. The Carnegie Endowment for International Peace and American public opinion 1939–1945. *Review of International Studies*, 26(1), pp. 35–48.

——, 2004. *Think Tanks and Power in Foreign Policy: A Comparative Study of the Role and Influence of the Council on Foreign Relations and the Royal Institute of International Affairs, 1939–1945*. Houndmills, UK: Palgrave Macmillan.

——, 2012. *Foundations of the American Century*. New York: Columbia University Press.

Parry, Geraint, 1969. *Political Elites*. London: Allen & Unwin.

——, 2004. *John Locke*. London: Routledge.

Pearlstein, Steven, 1999. Canada's new age of diplomacy; Foreign Minister unafraid to give Americans occasional poke in the eye. *Washington Post*, 20 February.

Pedrazzi, Marco, 2000. Italy's approach to UN Security Council reform. *International Spectator*, 35(3), pp. 49–56.

Pempel, T. J., 1978. Japanese foreign economic policy: The domestic bases for international behaviour. In: Peter J. Katzenstein, ed., 1978, *Between Power and Plenty: Foreign Economic Policies of Advanced Industrial Countries*. Madison, WI: University of Wisconsin Press.

Petersen, R. Eric, Reynolds, Parker H. and Wilhelm, Amber Hope, 2010. House of Representatives and Senate Staff Levels in Member, Committee, Leadership, and Other Offices, 1977–2010. Congressional Research Service, 10 August. Washington, DC: US Congress.

Pew Research Center, 2014. From ISIS to Unemployment: What do Americans Know? *News IQ Quiz*, 2 October.

Philips, Frank, 1999. US Court overturns Burma law. *Boston Globe*, 23 June.

Pickles, Dorothy, 1962. *The Fifth Republic*. Second edition. London: Methuen.

Pilger, John, 1992. *Distant Voices*. London: Vintage.

Pinheiro, Leticia, 2013. *Foreign Policy-making under the Geisel Government: The President, the Military and the Foreign Ministry*. Brazil: Ministry of External Relations.

Poggi, Gianfranco, 1990. *The State: Its Nature, Development and Prospects.* Oxford: Polity Press.

Polk, William R., 1997. *Neighbours and Strangers: The Fundamentals of Foreign Affairs.* Chicago, IL: University of Chicago Press.

Porch, Douglas, 1996. *The French Secret Services: From the Dreyfus Affair to the Gulf War.* London: Macmillan

——, 2013. *Counterinsurgency: Exposing the Myths of the New Way of War.* Cambridge: Cambridge University Press.

Post, Jerrold M., 2008. Kim Jong-Il of North Korea: In the shadow of his father. *International Journal of Applied Psychoanalytic Studies*, 5(3), 191–210.

Power, Jonathan, 2001. *Like Water on Stone: The Story of Amnesty International.* London: Allen Lane.

Preston, Paul and Smyth, Denis, 1984. Spain, the EEC and NATO. Chatham House Papers 22. London: Royal Institute of International Affairs and Routledge & Kegan Paul.

Preston, Thomas and Hart, Paul, 2003. Understanding and evaluating the nexus between political leaders and advisory systems. *Political Psychology*, 20(1), pp. 49–98.

Pringle, Peter, 1990. Crisis in the Gulf – Congress and Bush in truce on war issue. *Independent*, 15 November.

Puchala, Donald J., 1971. *International Politics Today.* New York: Harper & Row.

Putnam, Robert D., 1988. Diplomacy and domestic politics: The logic of two-level games. *International Organization*, 42(3), pp. 427–60.

Rawls, John, 1999. *The Law of Peoples.* Cambridge, MA: Harvard University Press.

Rawnsley, Garry D., 1996. *Radio Diplomacy and Propaganda: The BBC and the VOA in International Politics, 1956–64.* London: Macmillan.

Renouvin, Pierre and Duroselle, Jean-Baptiste, 1968. *Introduction to the History of International Relations.* London: Pall Mall Press.

Reus-Smit, Christian, 2003. Politics and international legal obligation. *European Journal of International Relations*, 9(4), pp. 591–625.

Reuveny, Rafael and Prakash, Aseem, 1999. The Afghanistan war and the breakdown of the Soviet Union. *Review of International Studies*, 25(4), pp. 693–708.

Reynolds, Charles, 1973. *Theory and Explanation in International Politics.* London: Martin Robertson.

Rhodes, R. A. W., 1995. From prime ministerial power to core executive. In: R. A. W. Rhodes and Patrick Dunleavy, eds, 1995, *Prime Minister, Cabinet and Core Executive.* New York: St. Martin's Press.

Riddell, Peter, 2001. Blair as prime minister. In: Anthony Seldon, ed., 2001, *The Blair Effect: The Blair Government 1997–2001.* London: Little, Brown.

Ripley, Brian, 1993. Psychology, foreign policy and international relations. *Political Psychology*, 14(3), pp. 403–16.

Risse-Kappen, Thomas, 1991. Public opinion, domestic structure and foreign policy in liberal democracies. *World Politics*, 43(4), pp. 479–512.

——, 1994. Ideas do not float freely: Transnational coalitions, domestic structures, and the end of the Cold War. *International Organization*, 48(2), pp. 185–214.

——, ed., 1995a. *Bringing Transnational Relations Back In: Non-State Actors, Domestic Structures and International Institutions*. Cambridge: Cambridge University Press.

——, 1995b. Democratic peace – warlike democracies? A social constructivist interpretation of the liberal argument. *European Journal of International Relations*, 1(4), pp. 491–517.

Risse, Thomas, Ropp, Stephen C. and Sikkink, Kathryn, eds, 1999. *The Power of Human Rights: International Norms and Domestic Change*. Cambridge: Cambridge University Press.

Roberts, Adam, 2015. Failing states. In: Chatham House, ed., 2015, *Conference Report – The Role of the Nation-State in Addressing Global Challenges: Japan–UK Perspectives*. March, pp. 8–17. London: Royal Institute of International Affairs.

—— and Kingsbury, Benedict, eds, 1993. *United Nations, Divided World: The UN's Roles in International Relations*. Second edition. Oxford: Clarendon Press.

—— and Windsor, Philip, 1969. *Czechoslovakia 1968: Reform, Repression and Resistance*. London: Chatto & Windus for IISS.

Roberts, Dan, 2015. Obama imposes new sanctions against North Korea in response to Sony hack. *The Guardian*, 3 January.

Robertson, Justin and East, Maurice A., 2004. *Diplomacy and Developing Nations: Post–Cold War Foreign Policy-Making Structures and Processes*. Abington, UK: Routledge.

Robinson, Piers, 2002. *The CNN Effect: The Myth of News, Foreign Policy and Intervention*. London: Routledge.

——, 2012. The role of media and public opinion. In: Steve Smith, Amelia Hadfield and Tim Dunne, eds, 2012, *Foreign Policy: Theories, Actors, Cases*. Second edition, pp. 168–87. Oxford: Oxford University Press.

Roger, Simon, 2015. A Genève, semaine-clé pour les négociations sur le climat. *Le Monde*. 10 February.

Rosati, Jerel A., 1981. Developing a systematic decision-making framework: Bureaucratic politics in perspective. *World Politics*, 23(2), pp. 246–52.

Rosati, Jerel A., Hagen, Joe D, and Sampson, Martin W. III, eds, 1994. *Foreign Policy Restructuring: How Governments Respond to Global Change*. Columbia, SC: University of South Carolina Press.

Rosati, Jerel A. and Scott, James M., 2013. *The Politics of United States Foreign Policy*. Sixth edition. Boston, MA: Wadsworth International.

Rose, Gideon, 1998. Neoclassical realism and theories of foreign policy. *World Politics*, 51(1), pp. 144–72.

Rosecrance, Richard N., 1977. *Action and Reaction in World Politics: International Systems in Perspective*. Westport, CT: Greenwood Press.

——, 1999. *The Rise of the Virtual State: Wealth and Power in the Coming Century*. New York: Basic Books.

Rosenau, James N., 1967. *Domestic Sources of Foreign Policy*. New York: Free Press.

——, 1969. *Linkage Politics*. New York: Free Press.

——, 1971. The national interest. In: James N. Rosenau, ed., 1971, *The Scientific Study of Foreign Policy*, pp. 239–49. New York: The Free Press.

——, 1990. *Turbulence in World Politics: A Theory of Change and Continuity*. Princeton, NJ: Princeton University Press.

——, 1997. *Along the Domestic–Foreign Frontier: Exploring Governance in a Turbulent World*. Cambridge: Cambridge University Press.

—— and Cziempel, Ernst-Otto, eds, 1989. *Global Changes and Theoretical Challenges: Approaches to World Politics for the 1990s*. Lexington, MA: Lexington Books.

Rosenberg, Justin, 2000. *The Follies of Globalisation Theory: Polemical Essays*. London: Verso.

Rothwell, Victor, 1971. *British War Aims and Peace Diplomacy 1914–1918*. Oxford: Clarendon Press.

Rozental, Andrés, 1999. Mexico: Change and adaptation in the Ministry of Foreign Affairs. In: Brian Hocking, ed., 1999, *Foreign Ministries: Change and Adaptation*. New York: St Martin's Press.

Rubin, Barry, 1985. *Secrets of State: The State Department and the Struggle over US Foreign Policy*. New York: Oxford University Press.

——, 1994. Religion and international affairs. In: Douglas Johnston and Cynthia Sampson, eds, 1994, *Religion, the Missing Dimension of Statecraft*. New York: Oxford University Press.

Rummel, Rudolph J., 1968. The relationship between national attributes and foreign conflict behaviour. In: David Singer, ed., 1968, *Quantitative International Politics: Insights and Evidence*. New York: Free Press.

——, 1995. Democracies ARE less warlike than other regimes. *European Journal of International Relations*, 1(4), pp. 649–64.

Rusciano, Frank Louis, 2006. *Global Rage after the Cold War*. London: Palgrave.

—— and Fiske-Rusciano, Roberta, 1998. Toward a notion of 'world opinion'. In: Frank Louis Rusciano and Roberta Fiske-Rusciano, eds, 1998, *World Opinion and the Emerging International Order*, pp. 13–28. Westport, CT: Praeger.

Russett, Bruce, 1993. *Grasping the Democratic Peace: Principles for a Post-Cold War World*. Princeton, NJ: Princeton University Press.

Sagan, Scott D. and Waltz, Kenneth, 2003. *The Spread of Nuclear Weapons: A Debate Renewed*. Second edition. New York: W. W. Norton.

Santoro, Carlo M., 1991. *La Politica Estera di Una Media Potenza*. Bologna: B. Mulino.

Saunders, Frances Stonor, 1999. *Who Paid the Piper? The CIA and the Cultural Cold War*. London: Granta.

Schattschneider, Elmer E., 1975. *Semi-Sovereign People: A Realist's View of Democracy in America*. Hinsdale, NJ: The Dryden Press.

Schelling, Thomas, 1960. *The Strategy of Conflict*. Cambridge, MA: Harvard University Press.

Schimmelfennig, Frank, 2003. *The EU, NATO, and the Integration of Europe: Rules and Rhetoric*. Cambridge: Cambridge University Press.

—— and Sedelmeier, Ulrich, eds, 2005. *The Europeanization of Central and Eastern Europe*. Ithaca, NY: Cornell University Press.

Scholte, Jan Art, 2000. *Globalization: A Critical Introduction*. Basingstoke, UK: Palgrave.

Schroeder, Paul W., 2001. International history: Why historians do it differently than political scientists. In: Colin Elman and Miriam Fendius Elman, eds, 2001, *Bridges and Boundaries: Historians, Political Scientists and the Study of International Relations*, pp. 403–16. Cambridge, MA: MIT Press.

Sedelmeier, Ulrich and Wallace, Helen, 2000. Eastern enlargement: Strategy or second thoughts? In: Helen Wallace and William Wallace, eds, 2000, *Policy-Making in the European Union*. Fourth edition. Oxford: Oxford University Press.

Sen Gupta, Bhabani, 1998. Forget ideology, Give them onions! *World Today*, 54(2), February, pp. 40–1.

Serfaty, Simon, ed., 1990. *The Media and Foreign Policy*. London: Macmillan.

Shambaugh, David, 1994. Patterns of interaction in Sino–American relations. In: Thomas W. Robinson and David Shambaugh, eds, 1994, *Chinese Foreign Policy: Theory and Practice*. Oxford: Clarendon Press.

Shevchenko, Arkady, 1985. *Breaking with Moscow*. London: Cape.

Shlaim, Avi, 1982. *The United States and the Berlin Blockade 1948–1949: A Study in Crisis Decision-Making*. Berkeley, CA: University of California Press.

——, 2007. *Lion of Jordan: the Life of King Hussein in War and Peace*. London: Allen Lane.

—— and Yaniv, Avner, 1980. Domestic politics and foreign policy in Israel. *International Affairs*, 56(2), pp. 242–62.

——, Jones, Peter and Salisbury, Keith, 1977. *British Foreign Secretaries since 1945*. Newton Abbot: David & Charles.

Shuckburgh, Evelyn, 1986. *Descent to Suez: Diaries 1951–56*. London: Weidenfeld & Nicolson.

Simms, Brendan, 2001. *Unfinest Hour: How Britain Helped to Destroy Bosnia*. Harmondsworth, UK: Allen Lane.

——, 2013. *Europe: The Struggle for Supremacy from 1453 to the Present*. London: Allen Lane.

Simon, Herbert A., 1957. A behavioral model of rational choice. In: Herbert A. Simon, 1957, *Models of Man: Social and Rational Mathematical Essays on Rational Human Behavior in a Social Setting*, pp. 240–60. New York: John Wiley.

——, 1976. *Administrative Behavior*. Third edition. New York: Free Press.

——, 1982. From substantive to procedural rationality. In: Anthony G. McGrew and Michael J. Wilson, eds, 1982, *Decision Making: Approaches and Analysis*, pp. 87–96. Manchester, UK: Manchester University Press.

Singer, J. David, 1961. The level of analysis problem in International Relations. In: Klaus Knorr and Sidney Verba, eds, 1961, *The*

International System: Theoretical Essays. Princeton, NJ: Princeton University Press.

Sjursen, Helene, 2006. The EU as a 'normative' power: How can this be? *Journal of European Public Policy*, 13(2), pp. 235–51.

Sked, Alan, 1989. *The Decline and Fall of the Habsburg Empire 1815–1918*. London: Longman.

Slaughter, Anne-Marie, 2004. *A New World Order*. Oxford: Princeton University Press.

Smith, Anthony D., 1998. *Nationalism and Modernism: A Critical Survey of Recent Theories of Nations and Nationalism*. London: Routledge.

Smith, Gilbert and May, David, 1980. The artificial debate between rationalist and incrementalist models of decision making. In: Anthony G. McGrew and Michael J. Wilson, eds, 1982, *Decision Making: Approaches and Analysis*, pp. 116–24. Manchester, UK: Manchester University Press.

Smith, Karen E., 1998. The use of political conditionality in the EU's relations with the third world. *European Foreign Affairs Review*, 3(2), pp. 253–74.

——, 2010. *Genocide and the Europeans*. Cambridge: Cambridge University Press.

——, 2013. The European Union and the politics of legitimisation at the United Nations. *European Foreign Affairs Review*, 18(1), pp. 63–80.

——, 2014. *European Union Foreign Policy in a Changing World*. Third edition. London: Polity Press.

Smith, Leonard V., 2014. Empires at the Paris Peace Conference. In: Robert Gerwarth and Erez Manela, eds, 2014, *Empires at War, 1912–1923*. Oxford: Oxford University Press.

Smith, Steve and Clarke, Michael, eds, 1985. *Foreign Policy Implementation*. London: Allen & Unwin.

——, Hadfield, Amelia and Dunne, Tim, eds, 2012, *Foreign Policy: Theories, Actors, Cases*. Second edition. Oxford: Oxford University Press.

Smith, Tony, 2000. *Foreign Attachments: The Power of Ethnic Groups in the Making of American Foreign Policy*. Cambridge, MA: Harvard University Press.

Snyder, Jack, 1991. *Myths of Empire: Domestic Politics and International Ambition*. Ithaca, NY: Cornell University Press.

Snyder, Richard, Bruck, H. W. and Sapin, Burton, 1962. *Foreign Policy Decision-Making: An Approach to the Study of International Politics*. New York: Free Press.

——, —— and ——, 2002. *Foreign Policy Decision-Making (Revisited)*. Basingstoke: Palgrave.

Solingen, Etel, 2007. *Nuclear Logics: Contrasting Paths in East Asia and the Middle East*. Princeton, NJ: Princeton University Press.

Sørensen, Georg, 2001. *Changes in Statehood: The Transformation of International Relations*. Houndmills, UK: Palgrave.

Sorensen, Theodore C., 1986. A changing America. In: Andrew J. Pierre, ed.,

1986, *Domestic Change and Foreign Policy: A Widening Atlantic?* New York: Council on Foreign Relations.

Sorokin, Pitirim, 1937. *Social and Cultural Dynamics*. New York: America Book.

Sprout, Harold and Sprout, Margaret, 1962. *Foundations of International Politics*. Princeton, NJ: D. Van Nostrand Co.

—— and ——, 1965. *The Ecological Perspective on Human Affairs*. Princeton, NJ: Princeton University Press.

—— and ——, 1969. Environmental factors in the study of international politics. In: James N. Rosenau, ed., 1969, *International Politics and Foreign Policy*. New York: Free Press.

Stavridis, Stelios and Hill, Christopher, eds, 1996. *Domestic Sources of Foreign Policy: Western European Reactions to the Falklands Conflict*. Oxford: Berg.

Steans, Jill, 1998. *Gender and International Relations: An Introduction*. Cambridge: Polity Press.

Stein, Janice G., 2012. Foreign policy decision making: Rational, psychological and neurological models. In: Steve Smith, Amelia Hadfield and Tim Dunne, eds, 2012, *Foreign Policy: Theories, Actors, Cases*. Second edition, pp. 130–46. Oxford: Oxford University Press.

Steinbruner, John D., 2002. *The Cybernetic Theory of Decision: New Dimensions of Political Analysis*. Second edition. Princeton, NJ: Princeton University Press.

Steiner, Miriam, 1983. The search for order in a disorderly world: Worldviews and prescriptive decision paradigms. *International Organization*, 37(3), pp. 373–413.

Steiner, Zara, ed., 1982. *The Times Survey of Foreign Ministries of the World*. London: Times Books.

Stevens, Paul Schott, 1989. The National Security Council: Past and prologue. *Strategic Review*, 17(1), pp. 55–62.

Stevenson, David, 1988. *The First World War and International Politics*. Oxford: Clarendon Press.

Stone, Diane and Denham, Andrew, 2004. *Think Tank Traditions: Policy Research and the Politics of Ideas*. Manchester, UK: Manchester University Press.

Stopford, John, 1996. Interdependence between TNCs and governments. In: *Companies without Borders: Transnational Corporations in the 1990s*, pp. 255–79. London: International Thomson Business Press on behalf of UNCTAD.

——, Strange, Susan and Henley, John, 1991. *Rival State, Rival Firms: Competition for World Market Shares*. Cambridge: Cambridge University Press.

Strange, Susan, 1971. *Sterling and British Policy: A Study of an International Currency in Decline*. Oxford: Oxford University Press.

——, 1994. *States and Markets*. Second edition. London: Pinter.

Strong, James, 2014. Why parliament now decides on war: Tracing the growth of the parliamentary prerogative through Syria, Libya and Iraq.

British Journal of Politics & International Relations (online), pp. 1–19. (http://onlinelibrary.wiley.com/doi/10.1111/1467-856X.12055). 11 June 2014.

Stuart, Douglas T., 2008. Foreign-policy decision-making. In: Christian Reus-Smit and Duncan Snidal, eds, 2008, *The Oxford Handbook of International Relations*. Oxford: Oxford University Press.

Tang, James and Cheung, Peter, 2001. The external relations of China's provinces. In: David M. Lampton, ed., 2001, *The Making of Chinese Foreign and Security Policy in the Era of Reform*. Stanford, CA: Stanford University Press.

Tayfur, M. Fatih, 2003. *Semiperipheral Development and Foreign Policy: The Cases of Greece and Spain*. Farnham, UK: Ashgate.

Taylor, A. J. P., 1965. *English History 1914–1945*. Oxford: Oxford University Press.

——, 1993. *The Trouble Makers: Dissent over Foreign Policy, 1792–1939*. London: Pimlico.

Taylor, Paul, 1983. *The Limits of European Integration*. London: Croom Helm.

——, 2000. The institutions of the United Nations and the principle of consonance: An overview. In: A. J. R. Groom and Paul Taylor, eds, 2000, *The United Nations at the Millennium: The Principal Organs*. London: Continuum.

Taylor, Philip M., 1995. *Munitions of the Mind: A History of Propaganda from the Ancient World to the Present Day*. Manchester, UK: Manchester University Press.

Tetlock, Philip E., Lebow, Richard Ned and Parker, Geoffrey, eds, 2006. *Unmaking the West: 'What-If?' Scenarios that Rewrite World History*. Ann Arbor, MI: University of Michigan Press.

't Hart, Paul, Stern, Eric K. and Sundelius, Bengt, eds, 1997. *Beyond Groupthink: Political Group Dynamics and Foreign Policy-making*. Ann Arbor, MI: University of Michigan Press.

Thatcher, Margaret, 1993. *The Downing Street Years*. London: HarperCollins.

Thomas, Daniel C., 1999. Boomerangs and superpowers: The 'Helsinki network' and human rights in US foreign policy. EUI Working Paper, RSC 99/23. Florence: European University Institute.

Thomas, Scott, 1996. *The Diplomacy of Liberation: The Foreign Relations of the ANC since 1960*. London: I. B. Taurus.

Thucydides, 1972. *History of the Peloponnesian War*. Rex Warner, trans. Harmondsworth: Penguin.

Tilly, Charles, ed., 1975. *The Formation of National States in Europe*. Princeton, NJ: Princeton University Press.

——, 1976. *Coercion, Capital and European States, AD 990–1990*. Oxford: Blackwell.

Toje, Asle and Kunz, Barbara, eds, 2012. *Neoclassical Realism in European Politics: Bringing Power Back In*. Manchester, UK: Manchester University Press.

Tonra, Ben, 2001. *The Europeanisation of National Foreign Policy: Dutch, Danish and Irish Foreign Policy in the European Union*. Aldershot: Ashgate.

Tower, John et al., 1987. *The Tower Commission Report*. New York: Bantam Books and the New York Times.

Toynbee, Arnold, 1972. *A Study of History*. One volume edition. London: Thames & Hudson.

Twigge, Stephen, Hampshire, Edward and Macklin, Graham, 2008. *British Intelligence: Secrets, Spies and Sources*. Kew, UK: National Archives.

Tziampiris, Aristotle, 2000. *Greek Foreign Policy: EPC and the Macedonian Question*. Aldershot, UK: Ashgate.

Ulricks, Teddy J., 1982. The Tsarist and Soviet Ministry of Foreign Affairs. In: Zara Steiner, ed., 1982, *The Times Survey of Foreign Ministries of the World*. London: Times Books.

UN General Assembly, 2000. We the peoples: The role of the United Nations in the twenty-first century. Report of the Secretary-General, A/54/2000, 27 March. New York: United Nations.

US Department of State, 2014. Agency Financial Report for Fiscal Year 2014.

Vaïsse, Justin, 2010. Eurabian Follies. *Foreign Policy*, 177, January/February, pp. 86–8.

Vasquez, John A., 1983. *The Power of Power Politics: A Critique*. London: Pinter.

Vatikiotis, Panayiotis J., 1978. *Nasser and his Generation*. London: Croom Helm.

Veremis, Thanos, 1995. *Greece's Balkan Entanglement*. Athens: Hellenic Foundation for European and Foreign Policy.

Vernon, Raymond, 1971. *Sovereignty at Bay: The Multinational Spread of US Enterprises*. Harlow: Longman.

Verrier, Anthony, 1983. *Through the Looking Glass: British Foreign Policy in an Age of Illusions*. London: Cape.

Vertovec, Steven, 2009. *Transnationalism*. London: Routledge.

Vertzberger, Yaacov Y. I., 1990. *The World in their Minds: Information Processing, Cognition and Perception in Foreign Policy Decisionmaking*. Stanford, CA: Stanford University Press.

Vickers, Rhiannon, 2000. Labour's search for a third way in foreign policy. In: Richard Little and Mark Wickham-Jones, eds, 2000, *New Labour's Foreign Policy: A New Moral Crusade?* Manchester, UK: Manchester University Press.

Vincent, R. J., 1986a. *Human Rights and International Relations*. Cambridge: Cambridge University Press in association with the Royal Institute of International Affairs.

——, ed., 1986b. *Foreign Policy and Human Rights: Issues and Responses*. Cambridge: Cambridge University Press in association with the Royal Institute of International Affairs.

Vital, David, 1971. *The Survival of Small States: Studies in Small Power/Great Power Conflict*. Oxford: Oxford University Press.

Vlcek, William, 2008. *Offshore Finance and Small States: Sovereignty, Size and Money*. Basingstoke, UK: Palgrave.

Volkan, Vamik D., Itzkowitz, Norman and Dod, Andrew W., 1997. *Richard Nixon: A Psychobiography*. New York: Columbia University Press.

Waever, Ole, 1990. Thinking and rethinking in foreign policy. *Cooperation and Conflict*, 25(3), pp. 153–70.

——, 1994. Resisting the temptations of post foreign policy analysis. In: Walter Carlsnaes and Steve Smith, eds, 1994, *European Foreign Policy: The EC and Changing Perspectives in Europe*. London: Sage.

——, 1998. The sociology of a not so international discipline: American and European developments in international relations. *International Organization*, 52(4), 687–727.

——, 2002. Identity, communities and foreign policy: Discourse analysis as foreign policy theory. In: Lene Hansen and Ole Waever, eds, 2002, *European Integration and National Identity: The Challenge of the Nordic States*. London: Routledge.

——, 2004. Discursive approaches. In: Antje Wiener and Thomas Diez, eds, 2004, *European Integration Theory*. Oxford: Oxford University Press.

Waite, Robert, 1998. *Kaiser and Führer: A Comparative Study of Personality and Politics*. Toronto: University of Toronto Press.

Walker, Martin, 1997. Mission implausible. *The Guardian*, 14 April.

Walker, R. B. J., 1993. *Inside/Outside: International Relations as Political Theory*. Cambridge: Cambridge University Press.

——, 1995. The concept of the political. In: Ken Booth and Steve Smith, eds, 1995, *International Relations Theory Today*. Oxford: Polity Press.

Wallace, Helen, 2000. Analysing and explaining policies. In: Helen Wallace and William Wallace, eds, 2000, *Policy-Making in the European Union*. Fourth edition. Oxford: Oxford University Press.

Wallace, William, 1975. *The Foreign Policy Process in Britain*. London: Royal Institute of International Affairs.

——, 1978. Old states and new circumstances: The international predicament of Britain, France and Germany. In: William Wallace and W. E. Paterson, eds, 1978, *Foreign Policy Making in Western Europe: A Comparative Approach*, pp. 31–55. Farnborough, UK: Saxon House.

——, 1996. *Opening the Door: The Enlargement of NATO and the European Union*. London: Centre for European Reform.

Waller, Michael and Linklater, Andrew, 2003. *Political Loyalty and the Nation-State*. London: Routledge.

Waltz, Kenneth, 1959. *Man, the State and War*. New York: Columbia University Press.

——, 1967. *Foreign Policy and Democratic Politics: The American and British Experience*. Boston, MA: Little, Brown.

——, 1979. *Theory of International Politics*. Reading, MA: Addison-Wesley.

——, 1996. International politics is not foreign policy, *Security Studies*, 6(1), 54-57.

Walzer, Michael, 1977. *Just and Unjust Wars: A Moral Argument with Historical Illustrations*. New York: Basic Books.

——, 2006. *Just and Unjust Wars: A Moral Argument with Historical Illustrations*. Fourth edition. New York: Basic Books.

Watson, Adam, 1982. *Diplomacy: The Dialogue between States*. London: Eyre Methuen.

——, 1992. *The Evolution of International Society: A Comparative Historical Analysis*. London: Routledge.

Watt, Donald C., 1965. *Personalities and Policies: Studies in the Formulation of British Foreign Policy in the Twentieth Century*. London: Longmans.

——, 1983. What about the people? Abstraction and reality in history and the social sciences: An inaugural lecture. London: London School of Economics.

——, 2000. The proper study of propaganda. *Intelligence and National Security*, 15(4), pp. 143–63.

——, 2001. The historiography of intelligence in international review. In: Lars Christian Jenssen and Olav Riste, eds, 2001, *Intelligence in the Cold War: Organisation, Role and International Cooperation*, pp. 173–92. Oslo: Norwegian Institute for Defence Studies.

Webber, Douglas, ed., 2001. *New Europe, New Germany, Old Foreign Policy? German Foreign Policy since Unification*. London: Routledge.

Webber, Mark and Smith, Michael, 2002. *Foreign Policy in a Transformed World*. London: Routledge.

Weber, Cynthia, 1995. *Simulating Sovereignty: Intervention, the State and Symbolic Exchange*. Cambridge: Cambridge University Press.

Weber, Eugen, 1976. *Peasants into Frenchmen: The Modernization of Rural France, 1870–1914*. Stanford, CA: Stanford University Press.

Weber, Max, 1917a. Parliament and government in Germany. In: Peter Lassman and Ronald Spiers, eds, 1994, *Weber: Political Writings*. Cambridge: Cambridge University Press.

——, 1917b. Science as a vocation. In: Hans H. Gerth and Charles Wright Mills, eds and trans., 1948, *From Max Weber: Essays in Sociology*, pp. 129–58. London: Routledge.

——, 1919a. The profession and vocation of politics. In: Peter Lassman and Ronald Spiers, eds, 1994, *Weber: Political Writings*. Cambridge: Cambridge University Press.

——, 1919b. 'Politics as a vocation. In: Hans H. Gerth and Charles Wright Mills, eds and trans., 1948, *From Max Weber: Essays in Sociology*, pp. 77–128. London: Routledge.

Weede, Erich, 1984. Democracy and war involvement. *Journal of Conflict Resolution*, 28(4), pp. 649–64.

Weinberg, Gerhard L., 1994. *A World at Arms: A Global History of World War II*. Cambridge: Cambridge University Press.

Welch, David A., 2005. *Painful Choices: A Theory of Foreign Policy Change*. Princeton, NJ: Princeton University Press.

Weller, Marc, 2009. *Contested Statehood: Kosovo's Struggle for Independence*. Oxford University Press.

Wendt, Alexander, 1991. Bridging the theory/meta-theory gap in international relations. *Review of International Studies*, 17(4), pp. 383–92.

——, 1992. Anarchy is what states make of it: The social construction of power politics. *International Organization*, 46(2), pp. 391–426.

——, 1999. *Social Theory of International Politics*. Cambridge: Cambridge University Press.

Wheeler, Nicholas J., 2000. *Saving Strangers: Humanitarian Intervention in International Society*. Oxford: Oxford University Press.

—— and Dunne, Tim, 1998. Good international citizenship: A third way for British foreign policy. *International Affairs*, 74(4), pp. 847–70.

—— and ——, 2001. Blair's Britain: A force for good in the world? In: Karen E. Smith and Margot Light, eds, 2001, *Ethics and Foreign Policy*. Cambridge: Cambridge University Press.

White, Brian, 2001. *Understanding European Foreign Policy*. London: Palgrave.

Whitten, Reid and Phelps, Corey, 2011. California and Florida lead trend of new state-level Iran sanctions. *Government Contracts*, Investigations & International Trade Blog (www.governmentcontractslawblog.com). Sheppard, Mullin, Richter & Hampton LLP. 16 June 2014.

Wight, Colin, 2002. Philosophy of social science and International Relations. In: Walter Carlsnaes, Thomas Risse and Beth A. Simmons, eds, 2002, *Handbook of International Relations*, pp. 29–56. London: Sage.

——, 2006. *Agents, Structures and International Relations: Politics as Ontology*. Cambridge: Cambridge University Press.

Wight, Martin, 1946. *Power Politics*. London: Royal Institute of International Affairs.

——, 1966. The balance of power. In: Herbert Butterfield and Martin Wight, eds, 1966, *Diplomatic Investigations: Essays in the Theory of International Politics*. London: Allen & Unwin.

——, 1978. *Power Politics*. Second edition. Leicester, UK: Leicester University Press.

——, 1991. *International Theory: The Three Traditions*. Gabriele Wight and Brian Porter, eds. Leicester, UK: Leicester University Press.

Wilhelm, Andreas, 2006. *Aussenpolitik: Grundlagen, Strukturen und Prozesse*. Munich: Oldenbourg Verlag.

Willetts, Peter, ed., 1995. *The Conscience of the World: The Influence of Non-Governmental Organizations in the UN System*. London: Hurst.

Williams, Michael, 2005. *The Realist Tradition and the Limits of International Relations*. Cambridge: Cambridge University Press.

Williamson, Samuel, 1969. *The Politics of Grand Strategy: Britain and France Prepare for War 1904–1914*. Cambridge, MA: Harvard University Press.

Wivel, Anders and Oest, Kajsa Ji Noe, 2010. Security, profit or shadow of the past? Explaining the security strategies of microstates. *Cambridge Review of International Affairs*, 23(3), pp. 429–53.

Wohlstetter, Roberta, 1962. *Pearl Harbor: Warning and Decision.* Stanford, CA: Stanford University Press.

Wolfers, Arnold, 1962. *Discord and Collaboration: Essays on International Politics.* Baltimore, MD: Johns Hopkins University Press.

Wong, Reuben and Hill, Christopher, eds, 2011. *National and European Foreign Policies: Towards Europeanization.* London: Routledge.

Woodward, Ernest L., 1954. *The Age of Reform, 1815–1870.* Oxford: Oxford University Press.

Woolf, S. J., ed., 1968. *The Nature of Fascism.* London: Weidenfeld & Nicolson.

Wright, Peter, 1987. *Spycatcher: The Candid Autobiography of a Senior Intelligence Officer.* New York: Viking.

Wright, Stephen, ed., 1999. *African Foreign Policies.* Boulder, CO: Westview Press.

Yahuda, Michael, 1996. *Hong Kong: China's Challenge.* London: Routledge

Yaniv, Avner, 1979. Domestic structure and external flexibility: A systemic restatement of a neglected theme. *Millennium: Journal of International Studies,* 8(1), pp. 25–37.

Zacher, Mark, 2001. International organizations. In: Joel Krieger, ed., 2001, *The Oxford Companion to Politics of the World,* pp. 418–20. New York: Oxford University Press.

Zarakol, Ayşe, 2011. *After Defeat: How the East Learned to Live with the West.* Cambridge: Cambridge University Press.

Zelikow, Philip and Rice, Condoleezza, 1997. *Germany Unified and Europe Transformed: A Study in Statecraft.* Cambridge, MA: Harvard University Press.

Index